ECOLOGY
AND THE
POLITICS
OF
SCARCITY

This ancient symbol of the "endless knot" or "knot of eternity" shows the interconnection of all things in an evolving but eternally self-regulating and self-perpetuating universe. As such, it also symbolizes the ecological laws that will have to govern in the human microcosm of the steady state.

ECOLOGY
AND THE
POLITICS
OF
SCARCITY

PROLOGUE TO
A POLITICAL THEORY OF
THE STEADY STATE

WILLIAM OPHULS

W. H. Freeman and Company
San Francisco

Library of Congress Cataloging in Publication Data

Ophuls, William, 1934–
  Ecology and the politics of scarcity.

  Based on the author's thesis, Yale, 1973.
  Bibliography: p.
  Includes index.
  1. Environmental policy. I. Title.
HC79.E50535   301.31   76-46436
ISBN 0-7167-0482-X
ISBN 0-7167-0481-1 pbk.

Printed in the United States of America

9 8 7 6 5 4 3 2

To the posterity
that has never done anything for me

Men are qualified for civil liberty in exact proportion to their disposition to put moral chains upon their own appetites. . . . Society cannot exist unless a controlling power upon will and appetite be placed somewhere, and the less of it there is within, the more there must be without. It is ordained in the eternal constitution of things, that men of intemperate minds cannot be free. Their passions forge their fetters.

Edmund Burke

CONTENTS

PREFACE

This work is designed to show that American political values and institutions are grossly maladapted to the era of ecological scarcity that has already begun. It is thus almost entirely a critique. Of course, certain general political principles that will probably have to form the basis of our community life in this new era appear to emerge naturally from the critique, and the concluding chapter discusses these. Nevertheless, I make no systematic effort to provide institutional answers or to deal with the problem of implementing a radically different set of political values.

This has distressed many readers of this work in manuscript. Like most Americans, they appeared to find a discussion of problems that offered no definite solutions—much less ones that could be called "feasible" or "realistic," to use two of the favorite adjectives of the politics of pragmatism—rather unsettling. Although I hope eventually to be able to alleviate some of this distress in a future work devoted to the kinds of issues that the present book leaves largely untouched, I would not want to do so prematurely. As students of political philosophy have long acknowledged, the answers of the so-called great theorists of politics may all be flawed, but their *questions* are eternal. Thus the value of the present work lies in the nature and quality of the questions it raises, for I am convinced that they will be central for our era, just as the relation of church and state or the grounds of justified rebellion have been the paramount issues on the political agenda of times past. And until we have these questions clearly in mind, their answers are bound to elude us.

Moreover, the fact is that we *are* in a distressing predicament, and my purpose is to make this inescapably plain. We seem to confront an array of tragic choices: business-as-usual is becoming impossible and intolerable, yet all the immediately available political alternatives appear unworkable, unpalatable, or downright repugnant. Let me state quite clearly that I take no delight in my conclusions, and I certainly did not set out to reach them. I can now regard them with some measure of dispassion only because I confronted and dealt with my own distress as I wrote the original draft. In the process, I came to see that the import of my conclusions was not as grim as I had thought. In any change in the human condition, something is lost—but something is gained too. As Hermann Hesse put it in *Steppenwolf,*

> Every age, every culture, every custom and tradition has its own character, its own weakness and its own strength, its beauties and ugliness; accepts certain sufferings as matters of course, puts up patiently with certain evils. Human life is reduced to real suffering, to hell, only when two ages, two cultures and religions overlap. . . . Now there are times when a whole generation is caught in this way between two ages, two modes of life, with the consequence that it loses all power to understand itself and has no standard, no security, no simple acquiescence.

As I see it, the only way out of the hellish suffering of the transition is to construct the new age as rapidly as possible, so that we are no longer caught "between two ages." The first step is to acknowledge our distress and understand its roots; only then can we begin to grapple constructively with the task of transition. Thus my purpose is not to spread doom and gloom, but to promote a constructive response to the crisis.

I have tried to make the book accessible to the widest possible audience, as a contribution to a great political debate over the fate of industrial civilization and how man and nature, now on a collision course, are to be reconciled. Because this is a general work, the specialist seeking discussion of methodological issues, or more extensive documentation than could be provided here, might wish to consult the dissertation from which it is drawn— *Prologue to a Political Theory of the Steady State,* Yale University, June 1973 (available from University Microfilms, Ann Arbor). Yet I have at the same time tried to avoid oversimplifying difficult problems or glossing over problematical areas in my argument. Moreover, I have certainly not abandoned scholarly canons of fact, logic, and argument. Thus the work has a dual character—that is, both scholarly and public—of which neither side denies or negates the other.

Yet it must be admitted that the two are in some ways incompatible. The true scientist addresses only questions that are in principle answerable. The writer of a political discourse does not have this luxury. He must address the crucial issues, even if this exposes him to the risk of error. The rapidity of technological and social change alone would be enough to ensure that some of what I say today will become outmoded tomorrow, or at least overtaken by events in what is clearly destined to be a highly fluid and transitional era. For this reason, I have constructed my argument so that it does not depend on such things as the success or failure of a particular technology or on the accuracy of particular figures. Nevertheless, the risk of being wrong must be taken, for when all the facts are finally in, our ecological and political fate will have been long since sealed.

The Bibliographic Note at the end of each chapter not only acknowledges principal sources of facts and ideas, but also criticizes them and suggests avenues of further exploration. Taken collectively, these Bibliographic Notes are a kind of blueprint that could enable a reader to critically retrace my own intellectual path as I conceived and wrote this work, and therefore to replicate my analysis or perhaps even to transcend it.

Acknowledging all one's personal and intellectual debts is an impossible task. Of course, one is ultimately and justly responsible for what one becomes or creates, but the more one thinks about it, the wider a network of obligation spreads. The list of people who have given encouragement and advice or who have performed mundane but vital chores seems endless, so I shall simply thank in a general way all who in the past seven years have given sage counsel and sharp criticism either in person or through their published works. I am also grateful to the individuals and organizations who have provided the logistical support without which I should never have been able to complete this work. I trust the final product will partially requite these many debts.

William Ophuls
October 1976

ECOLOGY
AND THE
POLITICS
OF
SCARCITY

INTRODUCTION

The reality and gravity of the environmental crisis can no longer be denied. What had been a somewhat remote controversy among specialists and the committed few over the limits to growth (for example, Meadows et al. 1972 vs. Cole et al. 1973) was brought home forcefully to the common man during the energy crisis of 1973–1974. We began to understand in our bones that, whatever the causes of this particular crisis, there might not always be enough material and energy to support even current levels of consumption, much less the higher levels many aspire to. No one, for example, seriously asserts any longer that ecological concern is a mere fad, which after a brief pirouette in the media limelight will cede its place to the newest crisis. Nor are there many who would still maintain that those concerned with environmental issues are perpetrating a political hoax designed to siphon money and public support away from disadvantaged minority interests. Whatever the excesses of some who have espoused the cause of environmentalism, the crisis is real, and it does indeed challenge our institutions and values in a most profound way—more profoundly, in fact, than some of the most ardent environmentalists are willing to admit. This book is about that challenge.

Of course, both theory and common sense have always told us that infinite material and population growth on a finite planet was impossible. But somehow, at least in this country, the problem has not seemed all that pressing, and for every expert who said it was, another could be found to say that it was not. Rather, said the latter, it was a problem we could safely leave to our grandchildren—and thank God, because bringing an end to material growth would present us with agonizing economic, social, and political choices. Thus, despite its undeniable reality, the environmental crisis remains controversial.

However, nobody really disagrees about the ultimate implications. For example, leading technologists, like former Chairman of the Atomic Energy Commission Glenn Seaborg (1970), and leading environmentalists, like the eminent biologist Rene Dubos (1969), agree that eventually we must learn to live in "steady-state" or "spaceship" societies characterized by great frugality in the consumption of resources and by deliberate setting of limits to maintain the balance between man and nature. Economists of high professional standing tell us the same thing (for example, Boulding 1970). The major controversy concerns the time scale. The so-called optimists believe that *(i)* the current situation in general is not quite so bad as the doomsayers make out, *(ii)* continued scientific and technological ingenuity will keep the ecological wolf from the door indefinitely, and *(iii)* there are many negative social feedback mechanisms, such as the economic marketplace, the impact of media-propagated information on values, and the political process itself, that will promote gradual human adjustment to physical limits when and if this becomes necessary. Thus, to put it crudely, business-as-usual can continue for the foreseeable future (and to look farther than that is borrowing trouble). Of course, the so-called pessimists believe, to the contrary, that *(i)* the situation is more urgent than most are willing to admit, *(ii)* limits to our scientific and technological ingenuity or to our ability to apply it to the problems we confront are already discernible, and *(iii)* the negative feedback mechanisms on which the optimists would rely have already begun to fail. Thus, say the pessimists, time is short, and far-reaching action by the current generation is imperative to avoid overwhelming the earth's capacity to support us in dignity; failure to act soon and effectively could lead us into the apocalyptic collapse—wars, plague, and famine—predicted by the dismal theories of the early demographer and political economist Thomas Malthus, whose famous essay on the dangers of overpopulation (1798) was the first explicit statement of the environmental limits to human activity.

I count myself among the pessimists. Thus the first purpose of this book is to make clear the nature of the crisis and why it is pressing. The second and more important is to draw out in full measure the political, social, and economic implications of the crisis, for even some of the more prominent environmentalists appear not to have understood their import. At least in their public statements, they maintain that a sufficient quantity of reform— fairly radical reform, to be sure—would rescue us from our ecological predicament. To the extent that more radical changes are urged, the language used is often vague; concrete political and social arrangements are rarely discussed, and really fundamental changes in our way of life or our constitutional arrangements are, one could gather, virtually unthinkable.

This book argues, to the contrary, that the external reality of ecological scarcity has cut the ground out from under our own political system, making merely reformist policies of ecological management all but useless. At best, reforms can postpone the inevitable for a few decades at the probable cost of increasing the severity of the eventual day of reckoning. In brief, liberal democracy as we know it—that is, our theory or "paradigm" of politics (see Box I-1)—is doomed by ecological scarcity; we need a completely new political philosophy and set of political institutions. Moreover, it appears that the basic principles of modern industrial civilization are also incompatible with ecological scarcity, and that the whole ideology of modernity growing out of the Enlightenment, especially such central tenets as individualism, may no longer be viable.

This conclusion may seem extreme to many. Despite the overwhelming historical evidence for the rapid mortality of all merely political structures, we tend to think of the set of political values and institutions that we inherit, whether divine-right monarchy or liberal democracy, as eternal, immutable, and, above all, *right*. They are not. Political paradigms are, in fact, extraordinarily fragile creations. (Of course, they may persist long after the conditions that made them viable have vanished—but unhappy the people that live during the long, drawn-out period of decay or the swifter decline into revolutionary turmoil.) However, our predicament is not hopeless. We can adapt ourselves to ecological scarcity and preserve most of what is worth preserving in our current political and civilizational order. But we must not delay. Events are pressing on us, and our options are being rapidly and sharply eroded; already we confront an array of potentially tragic choices. To see clearly how and why these choices are indeed forced on us, we must commence by examining basic concepts.

Ecology

This work is an ecological critique of American political institutions and their underlying philosophy.* What is this "ecology" upon which the argument rests? *Webster's Third New International Dictionary* gives three meanings.

---

*However, Chapter 7 extends the argument to other developed countries and the international arena. This might seem to put the cart before the horse. After all, the environmental crisis is global and civilizational in character. However, there are a number of advantages— such as familiarity to the reader and availability of information—to beginning with the American case. Also, American society epitomizes the modern way of life in most respects, and if it can be shown that modernity will no longer work here, then it can be presumed to be in trouble elsewhere. Indeed, as we shall see, very little modification is needed to make the argument apply comparatively and internationally.

Box I–1. Paradigms and Political Theories

The political theories and institutions by which men govern themselves have a high degree of intellectual, emotional, moral, and practical coherence. A political society is characterized by definite institutional arrangements, both explicit and tacit standards for political behavior, and widely shared understandings on such issues as what makes political power legitimate and how constituted authority ought to treat members of society (especially how the norms of the political association are to be enforced). We can speak of this ensemble of institutions, practices, and beliefs as the political "paradigm" of the society (Wolin 1968, 1969).

Since political paradigms have the same kind of internal consistency as scientific theories, the process of political change is analogous to scientific change. Most scientific inquiry—so-called normal science—aims at routine puzzle-solving under the conceptual umbrella of a fundamental scientific theory or paradigm (Kuhn 1970), like the famous DNA or double-helix model of gene replication in molecular biology. As long as such basic (and partly metaphysical) theories are successful in solving the puzzles thrown up by nature, allowing normal science to make apparent progress, all is well. However, once the puzzles can no longer be solved and disturbing anomalies resist all efforts to incorporate them into normal theory, then the community of scientists sharing this paradigm is ripe for revolution. Scientists begin to cast around outside the framework of the old paradigm for answers to the crucial anomalies; from this episode of "extraordinary" science emerges a new paradigm that overthrows the old, just as one regime replaces another in a political revolution.

Putting this in political terms, every society undergoes stresses. New classes, new economic relationships, and new religious or racial patterns emerge. But political associations are conservative. Retooling the paradigm is "unthinkable" and is likely to be resisted to the bitter end; before it considers radical change, a political society will exhaust all possibilities for reform by normal politics—that is, reform within its basic constitutional structure. If the puzzle is more or less solved by such reform, then

---

1. A branch of science concerned with the interrelationship of organisms and their environments.

2. The totality or pattern of relations between organisms and their environment.

3. Human ecology, [that is,] a branch of sociology that studies the relationship between a human community and its environment; specifically, the study of the spatial and temporal interrelationships between men and their economic, social, and political organization.

The first definition describes the work of the professional ecologist, who uses laboratory or field observation and experimentation to understand the laws governing the interactions of organisms with their living and non-living environment. The second definition indicates a more general use of the word— for example, one can as readily speak of "the ecology of a peasant community" as "the ecology of a mountain pine." Thus one would indeed expect human ecology to concern itself with the totality of the relationship between a human community and its environment. Unfortunately, as the second part

the political paradigm carries on as before, slightly modified but not fundamentally changed. An example is the extension of suffrage to the working class in England. By contrast, the same set of political "facts," rising political consciousness and assertiveness among non-elites, could not be accommodated by the political paradigm of Czarist Russia. Reform efforts were unsuccessful, and the new political facts therefore constituted an anomaly that led to political crisis and eventually revolution as the only solution.

There are, of course, significant differences in the way the scientific and political communities respond to anomaly. First, although it is rare for the ability of the leaders of the scientific community to be impugned, this is one of the most characteristic responses of the political association to impending crisis. As part of its effort to cope with change through normal politics—provided the paradigm allows for it, whether by election or routinized coup d'etat—it will throw one set of leaders out in hopes that the next lot will solve the puzzle better. This is often successful. However, a genuine anomaly cannot be solved in this fashion, and once it is clear that changes in leadership will not produce a solution the political community can no longer avoid confronting its crisis. Second, for a great variety of reasons political communities are much more long-suffering than scientific communities. Unlike scientists, who make radical efforts to replace a suspect theory as soon as possible, members of a political community can tolerate gross anomalies—for example, the difference between the theoretical and the actual status of American blacks during the century following the Civil War—for generations. However, when the "facts" that constitute anomaly will not go away and can no longer be ignored or borne, then revolutionary (but not necessarily violent) change becomes inescapable.

The crisis of ecological scarcity constitutes just such a gross and ineluctable political anomaly.

of the third definition reveals, the purview of human ecology has in practice been rather limited, so that at present there exists no genuine science of human ecology in the full sense. It is such a science that environmentalists wish to create. Meanwhile, they are trying to broaden the meaning of the term "human ecology" to embrace the totality of man's relationships with his physical and living environment, and it is in this sense that I shall employ the word "ecology," except where the context makes clear that the reference is to the science of ecology described in the first definition.

There is etymological justification for this broad use of the term. The root of the prefix "eco" is the Greek word *oikos,* meaning "household." Thus, ecology logically is the science or study of the household of the human race in its totality. Interestingly enough, the original meaning of "economics," derived also from *oikos,* was "a science or art of managing a house or household," while economy was "the management of a group, community, or establishment with a view to insuring its maintenance or productiveness." Today, economics has become "a social science that studies the production, distribution, and consumption of commodities." Thus, from the science of management of man's household in all its dimensions, economics has narrowed itself to an exclusive focus on the problems of a particular sub-system of ecology—the money economy—treating this sub-system as though it were autonomous.

Of course, professional ecologists are often equally guilty of the narrowmindedness that comes from overspecialization. Indeed, economist and ecologist alike are victims of the almost vicious degree of specialization characteristic of the modern world. The science of human ecology now abuilding is an effort to bridge the gap between specialties and make possible the rational management of the whole human household. This effort will require us, in effect, to become specialists in the general. Its spirit is well reflected in the redefinition of ecology offered by Paul Sears, dean of American professional ecologists:

> It may clear matters somewhat to modify the usual definition of ecology as the science of interrelation between life and environment. Actually, it is a way of approaching this vast field of experience by drawing upon the *best information available* from whatever source it may come [Sears 1971].

To be human ecologists of the kind Sears envisions, it appears that we must integrate the better part of all human knowledge, clearly an impossible goal. Yet, it must be attempted. We must hope that, although any individual work in human ecology will fall well short of the ideal, there will emerge a body of works that complement each other and give us the global understanding we need to find our way out of the environmental crisis. What follows, therefore, is the work of one human ecologist who happens to be concerned principally with the political aspects of managing man's household and who therefore has drawn on ecology, other natural sciences, engineering and technology, the social sciences, and even the humanities to construct a human-ecological critique of the American political economy.

Politics

Much of the ensuing argument will appear not to be about politics at all as this is usually defined by the man in the street or the academic specialist in politics. The difficulty arises in large part from a narrow definition of politics. The word is used to mean either the winning and losing of elections and other political battles, for which a more appropriate word is politicking, or the organization and administration of units of government, thereby excluding economic and social phenomena as well as religion and many other matters that were once considered part and parcel of politics. This pinched understanding of politics reflects the impoverished, fragmented view of reality due to excessive academic specialization, which has created a gap like the one between economy and ecology, with equally evil consequences. The basic political problem is the survival of the community; two of the basic political tasks are the provision of food and other biological necessities and the establishment of conditions favorable for reproduction. Neither of these can be accomplished except in the human household provided by nature, and in this sense politics *must* rest on an ecological foundation.

The model for such a comprehensive view can be found in the political theories of the classical world. As any reader of Plato's *Republic* or Aristotle's *Politics* knows, for the ancient philosophers politics was all inclusive: religion, poetry, education, and marriage were just as much political matters as war, the regulation of property, and the distribution of administrative office. Aristotle's famous description of man as the "political animal" graphically conveys man's uniqueness in being responsible for organizing his own communal life. Aristotle said that men without politics would be either gods or beasts. Beasts are ruled by instinct and natural necessity; their government is, in all but minor respects, genetically given. Likewise, the spontaneous, infallible right action of the gods is ordained as part of Creation; free of all mortal necessities, they need no artificial government. Only man—half-beast, half-god—struggles to govern himself with no certain guide and no assurance of success. For Aristotle, as well as for Plato and other major political theorists, "politics" concerns this struggle to live in community on the earth, and it therefore extends to many things besides government narrowly defined. Aristotle asks how this political animal can design and create institutions that will assure the survival of the city of man and some measure of the good life within it. It is such a broad conception of politics that informs this work: Is the way we organize our communal life and rule ourselves compatible with ecological imperatives and other natural laws?

Ecology is about to engulf economics and politics, in that how we run our lives will be increasingly determined by ecological imperatives. For example, one definition of politics prevalent among academic specialists is "the authoritative allocation of values"; but as Woodhouse (1972) points out, what happens in the beds and on the sleeping mats of the world should therefore be considered politics, for no single thing is likely to determine the general world allocation of values in the years to come more "authoritatively" than the reproductive behavior of millions of anonymous human beings.

Thus, whether we desire it or not, the larger conception of politics characteristic of the early political theorists is becoming virtually inevitable, which is sufficient justification for carefully delineating the nature of the laws of human ecology that our politics must henceforth reflect. Moreover, practically speaking, the cogency of many of the arguments in the second half of this book depends for the most part on the existence of the kinds of ecological imperatives documented in the first half. Thus, expanding our conception of politics to include these ecological imperatives is an important first step toward coming to terms with ecological scarcity.

Scarcity

The habitual condition of civilized man is one of scarcity. Goods have never been available in such abundance as to exhaust men's wants; more often than not, even their basic needs have gone unfulfilled. The existence of scarcity has momentous consequences, of which one of the most important is the utter inevitability of politics. The philosopher David Hume pointed out that if all goods were free, like air and water, any man could get as much as he wanted without harming others. Men would thus willingly share the earth's goods in common "as man and wife." However, without a common abundance of goods "selfishness and the confined generosity of man, along with the scanty provision nature has made for his wants," inevitably produce conflict; thus a system of justice that will restrain and regulate the human passions is a universal necessity (Hume 1739, III-2-11). The institution of government, whether it takes the form of primitive tabu or parliamentary democracy, therefore has its origins in the necessity to distribute scarce resources in an orderly fashion. It follows that assumptions about scarcity are absolutely central to any economic and political doctrine and that the relative scarcity or abundance of goods has a substantial and direct impact on the character of political, social, and economic institutions.

Unfortunately, the past three centuries have been an era of abnormal abundance, which has shaped all our attitudes and institutions. The *philosophes* of the Enlightenment, dazzled by the rapid progress of science and technology and the beginnings of the Industrial Revolution, envisioned the elevation of the common man to the economic nobility as the frontiers of scarcity were gradually pushed back. The bonanza of the New World and other founts of virgin resources, the take-off and rapid-growth stages of science and technology, the availability of "free" ecological resources such as air and water to absorb the waste products of industrial activities, and other, lesser factors allowed this process to unfold with apparent inexorability. Karl Marx, who documented and criticized the horrors and inhumanities of the Industrial Revolution, nevertheless celebrated its coming because the enormous productive forces unleashed by the bourgeois overthrow of feudalism could be used to abolish scarcity. With scarcity abolished, poverty, inequality, injustice, and all the other flowers of evil rooted in scarcity would simply wither away; not even a state would be needed, since everything would be a free good, like Hume's air and water, that humankind could share together "as man and wife."

Marx's utopian assessment of the possibilities of material growth was shared or came to be shared by almost all in the West, if in a less extreme form and with considerable difference of opinion on how the drive to utopia should be organized. For example, the works of the political philosopher John Locke and the economist Adam Smith, the two men who gave bourgeois political economy its fundamental direction, are shot through with the assumption that there is always going to be more—more land in the colonies, more wealth to be dug from the ground, and so on. Thus virtually all the philosophies, values, and institutions typical of modern society are the luxuriant fruit of an era of apparently endless abundance. The return of scarcity in any guise therefore represents a serious challenge to the modern way of life.

Worse, scarcity appears to be returning in a new and more daunting form that I call "ecological scarcity." Instead of simple Malthusian overpopulation and famine, we must now also worry about shortages of the vast array of energy and mineral resources necessary to keep the engines of industrial production running, about pollution and other limits of tolerance in natural systems, about such physical constraints as the laws of thermodynamics, about complex problems of planning and administration, and about a host of other factors Malthus never dreamed of. Ecological scarcity is thus an ensemble of separate but interacting limits and constraints on human action, and it appears to pose problems far surpassing those presented to our ancestors by scarcity in its classical form.

The nature and difficulty of the challenge we confront is apparent from the ironic fact that the very things Hume used to illustrate the state of infinite abundance—air and water—have become scarce goods that must be allocated by political decisions. The profundity of the challenge is also apparent in the economist Kenneth Boulding's use of the concept "spaceman economy" to describe the consequences of ecological scarcity. According to Boulding, since our overpopulated globe is beginning to resemble more and more a spaceship of finite dimensions, with neither mines nor sewers, our welfare depends not upon increasing the rate of consumption or the number of consumers—both of these are potentially fatal—but on the extent to which we can wring from minimum resources the maximum richness and amenity for a reasonable population. A good, perhaps even affluent, life is possible, but "it will have to be combined with a curious parsimony"; in fact, "far from scarcity disappearing, it will be the most dominant aspect of the society; every grain of sand will have to be treasured, and the waste and profligacy of our own day will seem so horrible that our descendants will hardly be able to bear to think about us" (Boulding 1966). There is, of course, no historical precedent for such a society. What is ultimately required by the crisis of ecological scarcity is the invention of a new mode of civilization, for nothing less seems likely to meet the challenge.

Political Theory

It is not the aim of this book to prescribe the form of post-industrial civilization, but to document the existence of ecological scarcity, show how it will come to dominate our political life, and then make plain the inability of our current political culture and machinery to cope with its challenges. From this analysis, a range of possible answers to the crisis will emerge. For example, if individualism is shown to be problematic in an era of ecological scarcity, then the answer must lie somewhere toward the communal end of the political spectrum. Also, certain general dilemmas that confront us—for example, the likely political price attached to continued technological growth—will be made explicit.

In brief, then, this work is a prologue to a political theory of the steady state. Yet although it stops well short of a genuine political theory of the steady state, it is directly concerned with the great issues that have dominated traditional thought about politics. My essential purpose is to show how the perennial, but dormant, questions of political philosophy have been revived by ecological scarcity. We shall see, for example, that the political problems related to the task of environmental management have to do primarily with the ends of political association, rather than with the political means needed to achieve agreed-upon goals; the questions that arise from the ensuing analysis are mostly and essentially value questions: What is the common interest? Under current conditions, is liberal democracy a suitable and desirable vehicle for achieving it? What, indeed, is the good life for man? In other words, we confront the same kinds of questions that Aristotle, in common with the other great theorists of politics, asks. We are obliged by the environmental crisis to enlarge our conception of politics to its classical dimensions. To use a famous capsule description of politics, the questions about *who* gets *what, when, how,* and *why* must be reexamined and answered anew by our generation. This book tries to set the agenda for such a philosophical reexamination of our politics.

However, I do not approach this task as a traditional political philosopher. Past theorists seeking guidance for human action have grounded their ideas on revelation or induction. Either, like Plato, they have appealed to some a priori metaphysical principle from which the shape of the desirable political order can be deduced, or, like Aristotle, they have examined man-the-political-animal's behavior over time to see if certain kinds of political institutions are more effective than others in producing a happy and virtuous people. Of course, many theorists have mixed both approaches, and some have introduced other considerations. In almost all cases, however, man's linkage to nature has counted for little. By contrast, like Malthus, I start with man's dependence on nature and the basic human problems of biological survival.

To be sure, most political and social thinkers have acknowledged man's ultimate dependence on nature, and a few have given some attention to the specific effects environmental constraints have had on man. For example, in Book One of *The Politics* Aristotle discusses scarcity and other ecological limits, implying that because of them slavery may be necessary for civilized life. Plato in Book Two of *The Republic* and Rousseau in *The Second Discourse* also display a subtle awareness of the impact the evolving process of getting one's daily bread can have on social institutions. Nevertheless, with the major exception of Malthus, political and social theorists have tended to take man's biological existence as given, and this is no longer possible.

Nor is it possible any longer to ignore man's impact on the environment. Of course, concern about this impact and the consequent damage to human welfare also has a long history (Glacken 1956). Over two thousand years ago, Plato in Greece and Mencius in China both worried about the destruction of habitat caused by overgrazing and deforestation. The early Christian writer Tertullian called wars, plagues, famines, and earthquakes blessings because they "serve to prune away the luxuriant growth of the human race" (Hardin 1969, p. 18), and Aristotle found the poverty caused by population growth to be the parent of revolution and crime: "If no restriction is imposed on the rate of reproduction . . . poverty is the inevitable result; and poverty produces, in its turn, civic dissension and wrong doing" (Barker 1952, p. 59). Thus, certain of the environmental problems we face today have been with man since the very beginning of civilization.

The character of the problems, however, has changed markedly through time. In ancient times, man's impact on the environment was local; by the eighteenth century, worldwide effects were becoming apparent; writers of the nineteenth century remarked on the extent of the impact and its cumulative effects; and observers in this century have focused on the acceleration of change. Accumulating quantitative impact has thus brought about a qualitative difference in our relation to the physical world; we are now the prime agent of change in the biosphere and are capable of destroying the environment that supports us. In sum, therefore, the radically different conditions prevailing today virtually force us to be ecological theorists, grounding our analysis on the basic problems of human survival on a finite and destroyable planet with limited resources.

A second contrast between this work and traditional political theory is that, again like Malthus, my effort throughout is to identify the critical limits to and constraints on human action. I wish to discover what is possible—or, alternatively, what we are forced to do—rather than what is desirable. In other words, values come last in my supposedly philosophical analysis. This is not because I disdain the eternal questions of value, but because a value-neutral approach is called for on very practical grounds.

First of all, philosophical, ethical, and spiritual arguments seem to appeal only to the converted. Hard-headed scientists, technologists, bureaucrats, and businessmen—that is, the men who make the basic decisions determining our futures—do not as a rule pay much attention to such arguments. If one is to argue constructively with the men who incarnate our cultural and political norms, one must argue the case in their own terms. This requires a fundamentally empirical and scientific or agnostic approach, putting aside the question of values, at least temporarily, to find instead what is possible given the natural laws that govern our planet.

However, one of the most important reasons for focusing on limits and constraints is the nature of our predicament. Although the human species has never enjoyed total freedom of choice, at some times and places there has been a relative abundance of everything needed for the maintenance of life and the construction of culture, and the latitude of choice was correspondingly large. By contrast, people cast adrift in a lifeboat with short supplies, or the trapped inhabitants of a besieged town, face many painful dilemmas; if they wish to survive, they must adopt stringent limits to their behavior. Similarly, by its very nature a spaceship imposes a certain type of social design on those embarked. As our circumstances come to resemble those of space travellers, we may expect knowledge of this social design to tell us a great deal about what we must do—in other words, the relatively narrow range within which the values and the moral requirements can lie. Nature's prejudices must become our policies if we wish to survive.

Of course, to mention the word "survival" is immediately to raise the question of values, even though survival should properly be regarded as a precondition for having any values at all rather than as a prime value itself. Nevertheless, value questions are inescapable. There being no agreed prime value—not even survival—that dominates all others, every problem of public and private morality compels complex trade-offs between desired goods. To illustrate briefly, even if ecologists could predict with absolute certainty that a continuation of current trends would produce massive death and other catastrophes by 2000 A.D., people might still decide, in a spirit of profligate fatalism, to doom posterity rather than forgo current enjoyment. Moreover, we shall not face totally forced choices. There are a number of possible solutions to the lifeboat problem and an even larger number to the spaceship problem, so that the outcome will be the result of a complex interplay between limits and constraints, our present and future capacity to evade or manipulate limits, and our values. In brief, science can only define the limits to political and social vision; it cannot prescribe the contents. Where science ends, wisdom necessarily begins, and I am hopeful that this book will lead the reader to that point.

The Steady State

Those who examine our ecological predicament tend to agree generally that we are headed toward a "steady-state" society.* Although the concept must be refined further, a steady-state society is one that has achieved a basic long-term balance between the demands of a population and the environment that supplies its wants. Implicit in this definition are the preservation of a healthy biosphere, the careful husbanding of resources, self-imposed limitations on consumption, long-term goals to guide short-term choices, and a general attitude of trusteeship toward future generations. Useful analogies are living off annual income instead of eating up capital, and managing the earth as we would a perpetual-yield forest, so that it continues to provide a good income "for as long as the grass shall grow and the sun shall shine." The rest of the book will help make these abstractions somewhat more concrete. For one thing, from an analysis of our current errors we can infer at least some part of what the steady-state society would have to be like, even though a full and systematic description is beyond our present ability. However, it is important to understand from the outset that the exact nature of the balance at any time depends on technological capacities and social choice, and as choices and capacities change, organic growth can occur. For this reason, the steady state is by no means a state of stagnation; it is instead a dynamic equilibrium affording ample scope for continued artistic, intellectual, moral, scientific, and spiritual growth.

Indeed, without substantial human growth in every dimension, the steady-state society can never be realized. Devising an ecological technology or a new set of political institutions for the steady state is the lesser part of the problem, for its core is ethical, moral, and spiritual. This is expressed well by a metaphor of George Perkins Marsh, a major figure in the history of the American conservation movement and the greatest pioneer of human ecology after Malthus. Marsh's major work (1864) depicts the human race as a heedless cottager tearing down his earthly abode for kindling in order to keep a lively but evanescent fire blazing in the hearth. By inference, the men and women of a steady-state society would take excellent care to see that their earthly household was preserved intact, knowing that posterity (if not they themselves) would have use for it. Through frugality and good stewardship, they would seek ways to be warm that would nevertheless allow them to pass the cottage—improved if possible, but at all costs undamaged—down to their children. The ultimate goal, then, is as much an ethical

---

* "Stationary-state" and "equilibrium" society are alternative terms. The former is the traditional economic label for a state of zero growth. Because it tends to imply a condition of rigor mortis, it is not entirely suitable as a description of what is in store for us. Some believe that even "steady-state" is too static and prefer "equilibrium." However, rightly understood, "steady-state" is appropriate, and since it is also the most commonly used term, I shall employ it.

ideal—the good stewardship enjoined by the Biblical parable—as a concrete set of political, economic, and social arrangements.

We shall return to this point at the end of our analysis. Meanwhile, let us in Part I explore ecology and the ecological limits and constraints now beginning to press down on us, and then in Part II go on to examine the political challenges. Perhaps then we shall understand better why we need not only a new theory of political economy, but probably a new theology as well.

BIBLIOGRAPHIC NOTE

GENERAL

Since human ecology includes almost everything, the number of books and articles to be read is potentially unlimited. Moreover, the state of knowledge changes weekly as new studies of long-neglected problems are published. Thus much important material can be found only in recent periodicals, of which six are indispensable: *Science,* the official organ of the American Association for the Advancement of Science (AAAS), is published weekly and contains authoritative articles, research reports, and penetrating commentary on scientific and technological matters, including all aspects of the environmental crisis; *New Scientist,* a British weekly newsmagazine for scientists, contains useful commentary and relatively non-technical, short articles on science broadly defined (including its political and social consequences), as well as general news items and brief reports of interesting papers appearing elsewhere; *Technology Review,* published by MIT monthly during the academic year, also contains an excellent news review section and publishes many fine articles on environmental problems; *The Ecologist,* a British monthly, is the best of the environmental magazines for the social and political aspects of the crisis—it achieved a deserved world reputation for its special issue, "A Blueprint for Survival," which recommended fairly radical simplification of our lives, an indication of the editorial point of view; *Environment,* by contrast, is issued monthly by the Scientists' Institute for Public Information and stresses authoritative but comparatively non-technical reviews of environmental and scientific literature, with the aim of providing solid information, rather than political and social argument; and lastly, *Conservation Foundation Letter,* published monthly by the Conservation Foundation, a respected independent research organization, takes up the socioeconomic and political aspects of environmental problems and covers one of them in depth in each issue. Two periodicals in the second echelon of importance are *Bulletin of the Atomic Scientists* and *Not Man Apart* (the organ of the environmental group Friends of the Earth).

Bibliographies are few and become obsolete even before publication. The best general one is *Science for Society,* published by the AAAS Commission on Science Education; it is revised annually and covers all aspects of the environmental crisis that have to do with science broadly defined; it is as complete as its

124 pages permit and has brief annotations. Of the bibliographies specifically on the environment and man, all are now out of date. The best is Robert Durrenberger's *Environment and Man: A Bibliography,* which has 2225 entries and is well indexed. Some more specialized bibliographies will be noted in later chapters.

Directory of Environmental Information Sources (2d ed.; Boston: National Foundation for Environmental Control, 1972) is the major general reference work of its type on the subject; it contains information on U.S. government agencies, citizens' groups, and educational programs, as well as reviews of many books, reports, and documents. However, three more specialized directories are also available: *World Directory of Environmental Education Programs* (New York: Bowker, 1973), *World Directory of Environmental Research Centers* (2d ed.; New York: Oryx/Bowker, 1974), and *Environment U.S.A.: A Guide to Agencies, People, and Resources* (New York: Bowker, 1974).

U.S. government documents are also excellent sources of information. Reference to important documents is made in *Science for Society* and the specialized bibliographies mentioned above, as well as in many of the works to be cited in later chapters. However, most government documents are useful primarily to the specialist in a particular issue or topic; moreover, the information in government documents important to the more broadly interested human ecologist tends to get widely reported in the environmental press, so that one can readily follow this literature at second hand.

INTRODUCTION

My purpose throughout these Bibliographic Notes is to identify and criticize the major sources as well as to point out avenues for further exploration (especially, stimulating works I believe to be neglected). However, unlike the chapters to follow, the Introduction has not been based on particular sources. Thus I merely suggest here a number of works that usefully amplify the Introduction's necessarily very condensed and general statement of the book's argument. In particular, I cannot recommend too highly *The Structure of Scientific Revolutions,* by the philosopher-historian of science Thomas Kuhn. It raises profound questions about the nature of the scientific enterprise. For example, is science really as objective as we are led to believe? In addition, it throws light on such problems as social change and the nature of intellectual activity. Anyone interested in broad questions of this kind will be stimulated by Kuhn's book whether or not he ultimately agrees with its thesis. Kenneth Boulding's *The Image,* a discussion of the same general problems from a social scientist's point of view, and Frederick Polak's *The Image of the Future,* which documents the pervasiveness of paradigms and their great influence in human history, should also be read; they are indispensable to the would-be macro-historian or sociologist.

A more radical work that takes up some of the methodological and epistemological issues where Kuhn leaves off is Joseph Pearce's *The Crack in the Cosmic Egg: Challenging Constructs of Mind and Reality* (especially Chapters

1–5). Pearce synthesizes the work of many linguists, anthropologists, psychologists, and other students of human perception to make a strong case for man as a reality-creating animal, so that, in a far stronger sense than David Hume intended, reason is indeed the "slave of the passions." Neuropsychiatrist Robert Ornstein's *The Psychology of Consciousness* is another work that approaches this central issue in a new and stimulating fashion. Ornstein concludes on the basis of considerable experimental evidence (which dovetails rather neatly with traditional psychologies—for example, Buddhism) that there are in effect two almost mutually exclusive yet equally valid modes of knowing. These two books are evidence that there is in prospect a scientific revolution in psychology and epistemology of Copernican dimensions.

Just as we need the microcosmic self-awareness that flows from the study of epistemology and psychology, we also need the macrocosmic understanding that philosophical biology, which attempts to comprehend the totality of life, can give us. Take, for example, the phenomenon of involution, in which organisms become so excessively adapted in particular ways that they place their long-term general adaptiveness in jeopardy. Human cultures display a similar tendency to overdevelop certain characteristics (Dubos 1972, Chapter 11; Geertz 1966). Since involution has frequently been a one-way trip to physical or cultural extinction, the obvious question it raises is whether our total commitment to the technological way of life could be a lethal form of involution. Two works that draw such insights from a reflective reading of biology are Garrett Hardin's *Nature and Man's Fate*, written from an evolutionary perspective, and Francois Jacob's *The Logic of Life*, written from a microbiological point of view.

The study of history is also indispensable for a sense of perspective. The number of even introductory works, however, is vast. I shall simply recommend Kenneth Boulding's *The Meaning of the Twentieth Century*. This broad-brush portrait of our era covers the transformation being wrought by science, war, population, entropy, ideology, and many other factors in a stimulating fashion and provides the beginnings of a macro-historical perspective. The reader could study with profit some of the landmark works in human ecology. Malthus' 1830 essay, "A Summary View of the Principle of Population" (which is more succinct and cogent than his original essay of 1798), would be the obvious starting place. The next stop should be George Perkins Marsh's *Man and Nature*. Subtitled *Physical Geography as Modified by Human Action*, this classic work was the first to study man as a geological agent in a systematic way; it made Marsh the father of conservation and modern human ecology, whose spokesmen today do little more than repeat Marsh's basic insights, using fresher data. Inspired in large part by Marsh's work, the Wenner-Gren Foundation sponsored a major interdisciplinary symposium in 1956; the resulting massive collection of essays, *Man's Role in Changing the Face of the Earth*, edited by William L. Thomas, Jr., has become a modern classic. Some of the essays are now dated, but most are still useful. Another work published at about the same time, Harrison Brown's *The Challenge of Man's Future*, is very close in spirit to my own (albeit much less political) and has also become a classic. Although now somewhat dated and marred by excessive technological optimism and a partial blindness

to some of the side effects of technology and growth, it remains one
studies of the natural limits to man's activities and can still be recom..
an introduction to the broad issues of human ecology. Numerous other wor...
(among them Osborn 1948, Sears 1935, and Vogt 1948) testify that we have had
plenty of warning about the problems we now confront. Finally, to bring the
story up to date, *The Limits to Growth* (Donella Meadows et al. 1972), the book
that did the most to shape the current debate on ecological limits, is essential
reading, perhaps in conjunction with the more polemical "A Blueprint for Survival" (Edward Goldsmith et al. 1972). The controversy aroused by *The Limits
to Growth* was enormous. The main lines of criticism are found in *Models of
Doom* (H. S. D. Cole et al. 1973), which contains a rebuttal by Donella and
Dennis Meadows. Much of the controversy hinged on the particulars of the
computer simulation used by the Meadows team. However, computer models
reflect with great fidelity the assumptions and data fed into them, so that these
are crucial. In fact, a second Club of Rome computer study, reported in *Mankind at the Turning Point,* by Mihajlo Mesarovic and Eduard Pestel, reached
essentially similar conclusions about the impending limits to material growth,
despite its very different computer modeling technique. Part I of this book is
precisely about the validity of the assumptions that went into these two models.

I

ECOLOGICAL SCARCITY
AND THE LIMITS TO GROWTH

1

THE SCIENCE OF ECOLOGY

The Synthetic Science

Ecology's synthetic nature makes it more like a point of view or perspective than a normal scientific discipline. Ecologists try to understand the whole process of life in the context of the chemical, geological, and meteorological environment by putting together the isolated knowledge of specialists into a single, ordered system. The essential concept of ecology is the ecological system or ecosystem, by which ecologists mean the community of organisms living in a specified locale, along with the non-biological factors in the environment—air, water, rock, and so on—that support them, as well as the ensemble of interactions among all these components.

Understanding the process of life requires ecologists to see ecosystems in dynamic and historical terms. The current ecosystem has evolved from certain origins and is undergoing both short-term changes and long-term evolution. Thus, in marked contrast to other life scientists, ecologists tend to describe their own discipline by using analogies from the social sciences. Ernst Haeckel, one of the founders of ecology, defined this science as "the body of knowledge concerning the economy of nature," and Charles Elton described his ecological work as "scientific natural history [concerned with] the sociology and economics of animals" (Kormondy 1969, pp. vii–ix). In sum, ecologists try to lay bare the general principles that govern the operation of the whole system called the ecosphere or biosphere, the part of the planetary system that contains or influences life; they examine the form of nature primarily to understand the creative process we call life.

From this description, it should be obvious that, since man inhabits the biosphere, ecology must also be concerned with him. There can be no valid distinction between ecology and human ecology. Nevertheless, ecology as a scientific discipline has until very recently concerned itself with the processes governing "lower" forms of life, choosing to study the economy of nature in pristine environments relatively undefiled by human intervention. In this way ecologists have succeeded in discovering the general outline of the pure economy of nature. Using their findings, I shall give a synoptic overview of the basic principles of ecology. However, my discussion is framed in terms of human rather than scientific ecology. That is, those things that have special relevance to human action are emphasized in this description of general ecological principles and the basic structure of the natural life-support system of our planetary spaceship.

Holism and Interdependence

The primordial principle of ecology is holism; that is, just as the properties of water are not predictable from the properties of oxygen and hydrogen, so the properties of ecosystems are not predictable from the properties of the living entities and nonliving matter of which they are composed. The biosphere is a unity and can be understood only in terms of itself. This principle requires ecology to be a synthetic and process-oriented science.

Flowing immediately from this first principle is the fact of interdependence. Everything within any ecosystem one chooses to examine can be shown to be related to everything else. Moreover, there are no linear relationships; every effect is also a cause in the web of natural interdependency. Of course, not all relationships are equally important or equally sensitive, and most of them are indirect. In general, however, interdependence is total. Certain kinds of important interrelationship are intuitively obvious even to the casual observer. We all know that there are predators and prey, that microbes can cause disease, and that worms will inherit our bodies when we are buried. However, the casual observer is unaware of the numerous other interrelationships in nature, many of critical importance. The number of living components alone and the variety and complexity of their couplings are bewildering. For example, no one has ever made a complete census of even so simple an ecosystem as a pond.

The fact of interrelationship is so pervasive that ecologists find one of the classic dichotomies, that between the living and the nonliving, to be all but abolished in nature: "The living and non-living parts of ecosystems are so interwoven into the fabric of nature that it is difficult to separate them" (E. P. Odum 1971, p. 10). Evolution, for example, did not take place in an already created physical environment to which life then adapted. Rather, life created the physical environment we know today, gradually transforming an extremely inhospitable environment into one favoring the further extension of life. Both air and soil are the evolutionary products of life, and their current maintenance continues to depend on the work of minute organisms. As a result of their ordinary metabolic processes, tiny plants have respired the oxygen in our atmosphere and created soils out of rock and dead organic material. If not interfered with, they will continue to supply us with the breath of life, keep our soils in health, and purify our waters. The result is a system "so intricate and beautifully organized as to render insignificant anything so far conceived by the engineering mind of man" (E. P. Odum 1971, p. 23).

The fact of interdependence makes the community concept one of the most important in ecology. Diverse organisms live together in an orderly fashion, "not just haphazardly strewn over the earth as independent beings," and the maxim "as the community goes, so goes the organism" expresses a fundamental law of life (E. P. Odum 1971, pp. 140–141). This seems like a truism, but its implications are profound, for man is inevitably a part of the natural biospheric community and cannot exist apart from it. The principle also shows that many of our practices are misguided. For example, ecologists have found that the best way of controlling a so-called pest—that is, the way that is both most effective and safest—is not in most cases to attack the pest organism directly, but to modify the community so that the pest is naturally controlled by the network of interdependencies that constitute the community.

The catch phrases used by ecologists to convey this sense of pervasive community and interrelationship are "Everything is connected to everything else" and "You can never do just one thing." These mean little in the abstract, so let us examine specific examples to see why intervention in ecosystems produces not just so-called side effects, but effects on the whole system.

Unintended Consequences, the Price of Intervention

Since every effect is also a cause, changing one factor in a well-adapted and smoothly functioning ecosystem is likely to unleash a chain of second-, third-, and fourth-order consequences. For example, when an organism from one ecosystem is transferred to another it is likely to run amok, for the new ecosystem has no history of dealing with such an organism and therefore no mechanism of control over its spread. It becomes an "instant pathogen," like the measles that decimated Eskimos and South Sea Islanders following their first contacts with Western civilization. Some of these cases—the Japanese beetle, Dutch elm blight, and the rabbit in Australia—are so well known as to require no documentation.

Just as there are dangers in adding to ecosystems, so too there are dangers in subtraction, for the whole web of interdependencies in the ecosystem may start to unravel. Many different types of man-made cause—hunting and fishing, smog, urban encroachment, fire, and others that are less obvious, like noise—can have the effect of knocking out one component of an ecosystem, which in turn causes related components to decline or collapse. However, insecticides, especially DDT, provide the classic illustrations of what happens if we try to do "just one thing." For example, in a remote jungle village in Borneo health workers sprayed the walls of the villagers' huts with DDT in order to control the mosquitoes that spread the malaria parasite. However, the lizards that patrol the walls of the huts inevitably absorbed large quantities of DDT, both from contact with the sprayed walls and from eating poisoned prey, and they died. This had the unfortunate effect of killing the cats that ate the moribund and now poisonous lizards and leaving the straw-loving caterpillars (hitherto kept in check by the lizards) that inhabited the thatched roof free to gorge without limit. The end result was a plague of rats and destruction of the roofs of the villagers' huts (Anon. 1968).

This might be simply an entertaining story were it not, in effect, a model of what man's chemicals are doing to the global life-support system. Like DDT, many of these chemicals are poisonous to a broad spectrum of life forms. Like DDT, they are also persistent. Because they are synthetic rather than natural compounds, no organisms have evolved to metabolize them; thus the quantity present in an ecosystem can build up and become dangerous in time. In addition, as with DDT, the phenomenon of "biological magnification" concentrates poisonous substances approximately ten-fold with each step up the food chain, because each grazer or predator must eat many times its own weight in smaller organisms. The release of even modest quantities of chemicals can therefore become lethal to the "top carnivores" at the end of the food chain. Thus, many life forms are even now being driven toward extinction by man's chemicals—especially the birds that, because of their high metabolic rate, are sensitive indicators of ecological health (recall the miner's canary).

People who protest that the extinction of a few top carnivores is a small price to pay for protecting our crops against the ravages of pests are missing the point. The Bermuda petrel, say, could disappear, and the richness of the biosphere would hardly be diminished. Even if many top-carnivore species were to disappear as a result of chemical poisoning our survival would not be at stake on that ground alone. However, their disappearance is evidence of ecological sickness, just as sugar in the urine is not dangerous in itself, but because it indicates that one has diabetes.

The long-term consequences of such ecological illness are potentially grave. It has been experimentally shown, for example, that many synthetic chemicals in widespread use affect the species composition of plankton in the ocean, with possibly serious implications not only for the structure of oceanic food chains (of which plankton are the base), but also for the role of plankton in the ocean's governance of the cycles that rule the biosphere. One of the most worrisome aspects of this kind of problem is that, owing to the inherent lag in biological systems, the peak concentrations, and therefore the full impact, of chemicals already released will not be experienced until some time in the future. The possibility therefore exists that we have already done irreparable damage, but that we will find out only when it is too late.

Moreover, trying to do "just one thing" frequently turns out to be futile as well as self-destructive. Chemical insecticides again provide a model. Plant-eating insects are well adapted to chemical warfare, since the principal defense of plants against being eaten is to make their vulnerable parts unpalatable or poisonous. Thus, although an application of insecticide may kill all but a few of a given pest population, these few survive to reproduce, passing on the resistant genes to their numerous progeny. Well before the sixth generation, virtually an entire population of pests will have become resistant to the chemical being used, and the war must be escalated with vastly increased dosages or new chemical weapons.* In the long term, this is a no-win strategy, for we cannot expect to stay ahead indefinitely in chemical war with insects. Indeed, it is likely to leave us worse off, because the insecticide meanwhile destroys almost all the natural controls on the pest's population. Insect-eating birds and insectivorous or parasitic insects, which ordinarily take a great toll, are killed off. (Predators and parasites, because they have much smaller populations than plant-eating insects and are not adapted to chemical warfare in the same way, are much more likely to be wiped out or to be unable to reproduce effectively.) Thus, even if they were not ecologically destructive, single-purpose technological solutions are not likely to succeed in a natural environment characterized by an all-pervading interdependence.

The human ecological problem is that all the activities we call "development" tend to involve relatively single-purpose additions to and subtractions from natural ecosystems. Cases in which the so-called side effects equalled

---

*The same kind of problem is being encountered in our war against microbes. Bacterial resistance to the common antibiotics is increasing rapidly, to the alarm of the World Health Organization (Dixon 1974).

or outweighed the intended primary effects unfortunately abound (Farvar and Milton 1968)—like the dams and irrigation projects that have spread schistosomiasis (bilharzia, an extremely debilitating parasitic disease) or that have led to loss of productive land through salinization or erosion. In order to understand more clearly how "everything is connected to everything else" and why human action can therefore boomerang ecologically, let us examine the economy of nature more closely.

Homeostatic Stability

A major characteristic of natural systems is that they are in a state of homeostasis—that is, they are designed by evolution to be self-maintaining and self-regulating in order to achieve a stable long-term balance or dynamic equilibrium.* Even certain kinds of disruption, such as fire and flood, that one might consider destructive of natural stability have very little effect on the preservation of homeostasis. Fire and flood have been around for so long that plant and animal communities have become highly adapted to these stresses. Thus, apart from local disruption due to volcanism and earthquakes, the stability of natural ecosystems is threatened only by long-term changes of climate and other phenomena associated with geological change and by the actions of man. Ecologists conceive of the biosphere as an open system in a steady state that is driven by the fairly constant input of energy from the sun and in which a finite stock of materials is constantly recycled. What characterizes this steady state and how is it maintained?

The Basic Life Cycle

Energy from the sun enables photosynthesis to occur in plants ranging from microscopic phytoplankton to giant trees. In photosynthesis, carbon dioxide and water as well as other inorganic chemicals are combined to create the carbohydrates required by plants for their own metabolism. At the same time, they respire the oxygen needed by other organisms. Because these plants take nutrients in raw inorganic form from the environment and convert them to the organic form required to support the higher levels on the

---

*The dynamic nature of the equilibrium should be noted. Nature's homeostatic process is adaptive; that is, organisms and ecosystems make positive or change-amplifying responses to stress as well as negative or change-eliminating ones. In this way, the evolution of species and the succession from one type of ecosystem to another can occur. However, particularly when discussing the kinds of abrupt and unnatural stresses man imposes on ecosystems, we can consider primarily, without distorting our understanding, the negative responses that tend to maintain organisms and systems as they are.

food chain, whose members are incapable of producing their sustenance from scratch, the plants are called producers. The producers are consumed by organisms at the next level of the food chain, the herbivores, who are the primary consumers. They in turn are eaten by the carnivores, the secondary consumers. Except for the carbon dioxide respired by the consumers, which is available for the producers, the flow of materials so far described is unidirectional; if it continued, the cycle would not be closed. Soon producers would exhaust their supplies of chemical nutrients and cease producing; the rest of the food chain would then collapse. But there is another major group of organisms, whose role is to take all organic debris—dead producers and consumers, feces, and detritus such as fallen leaves—and break it down into its inorganic components so that it can be reused by the producers to keep the system in operation. These organisms—bacteria, fungi, and insects—are called decomposers.

In reality, of course, things are much more complex than this simple schema conveys. In nature there are usually food webs rather than simple food chains, and some plants eat insects. Nevertheless, the schema describes the essence of the major cycle of life. After eons of evolutionary development, the originally rather simple system has become highly diversified and stable. Within the limits of the homeostatic range, which are wide enough to accommodate the major recurrent environmental stresses evolution has taught the system it must be prepared to face, the system is self-repairing, self-maintaining, and self-regulating. Negative-feedback controls—that is, changes tending to restore homeostatic stability—ensure that no one element of the system gets out of hand. If the population of one species starts to grow, then the population that preys on it responds by growing also. Even top predators, who need not fear being eaten themselves, are subject to parasites and disease as well as other density-dependent causes of mortality; also, if for some reason too many predators are alive, the number of prey is soon reduced to the point that predators starve and balance is restored.

Complexity, Diversity, and Stability

Let us put aside discussion of natural cycles for the moment to examine further the relationship of complexity and diversity to the homeostasis of ecosystems. Generally speaking, simple ecosystems tend to be unstable. Because of the severe environmental stress of intense cold, tundra regions do not support a complex and diversified ecosystem; many predator-prey relationships, like the one between lynxes and rabbits, are essentially one-to-one. Typically, those lower on the food chain are prolific. This is an evolutionary adaptation to the constant cropping by predators. Thus a simple rabbit-lynx system never stays in balance. The population of rabbits grows, encouraging the increase of lynxes, but at a slower rate. Because the pressure from predators is attenuated, rabbits increase even faster. Eventually, although the lynxes still lag well behind, the population of rabbits reaches the limits of its food supply, or suffers from density-dependent diseases, and reaches a peak; but since the breeding of the lynxes lags behind the increase in the rabbit population, the population of lynxes overshoots the level that would be just right to achieve stability with the rabbits. There are now more lynxes than the population of rabbits, weakened now by environmental stress, can support over the long term. Intensified cropping by the lynxes, along with the toll of disease, causes the population of rabbits to crash, and the resulting famine causes a similar crash of the lynx population. Then the cycle starts all over again. In such an unstable system there is always the chance that the crash will be total for one of the species, and that homeostatic balance will be destroyed. However, if other species are added to the relationship the stability of the system improves markedly. If the lynxes had other food available and were not totally dependent on rabbits, then there would always be enough lynxes to control an incipient population boom among rabbits.

Complexity is thus one of the major means nature uses to achieve stability. Whenever environmental conditions permit, predator-prey relationships, as well as other interrelationships in ecosystems, are not simple linear chains but webs. A large number of species of different types, all interacting in a highly complex way, contributes to homeostasis (and to long-term adaptiveness as well); the diversity of negative-feedback controls tends to keep the population of each component of an ecosystem at the level most appropriate for the smooth functioning of the ecosystem as a whole.

It is the absence of such complexity in man's agricultural fields that is responsible for pest problems. A monoculture of corn or any other crop is a highly simplified ecosystem containing large numbers of one highly succulent species of plant. Responding to the banquet spread before them, insects multiply rapidly and become pests. When farmers attempt to kill the pests they destroy the natural controls on the pest population, thus simplifying the system still further and intensifying the problem.

Ironically, complexity can sometimes be a liability, for a simpler organism or ecosystem is more likely to survive extreme stress. For example, weeds are ineradicable, as any gardener knows, whereas tropical rain forests that are extremely stable within the limits of stress evolution has programmed them to tolerate are quite likely to collapse totally if these limits are breached. Thus, although in general complexity confers advantages, because extreme stresses are rare in nature, simplicity also has its adaptive virtues, particularly in an era dominated by technological man.

An important consequence of complexity is that it tends to produce an ecosystemic optimum. For example, the optimum population level of organisms in natural systems is observed to be well below the carrying capacity that could be attained if all energy and spatial resources were fully utilized. One obvious reason for this is that maximum numbers are antithetical to good disease resistance and a general capacity to tolerate normal environmental fluctuations and stresses. Moreover, this optimum level, which may be as little as fifty percent of the theoretical maximum, appears to promote the health of the individuals making up the population. Although the checks and balances that result from complexity may seem at first glance to hamper a particular population or to be inefficient, they ensure the stability and continuity of the whole system, and the survival of the whole ensures the survival of the parts.

The Basic Character of Cycles

In addition to the basic life cycle, there are many other cycles of critical importance to the operation of the biosphere. In the well-known water cycle, water evaporates from the oceans and other bodies of water to be transported by the atmosphere (using energy from the sun) over the land, where it precipitates to evaporate once again or run off eventually to the sea, thus closing the cycle. The nitrogen cycle, on the other hand, is a major biogeochemical cycle little appreciated by the nonspecialist. Plants need nitrogen compounds to grow, but the nitrogen gas in the atmosphere is biologically inert and cannot be used directly by the plants. Various bacteria and algae, some living free in the soil and others associated with the roots or leaves of plants, are capable of fixing the nitrogen from the atmosphere. Other microorganisms decompose fallen organic material and convert its nitrogen into a form suitable for plant nutrition. The plant may be eaten, but the nitrogen is either excreted by the animal or returned to the soil when it dies, thus closing the cycle.

All such natural cycles are of the same character: driven by the energy of the sun, the materials necessary to maintain the processes of life are created, used, and then recycled or decomposed so that they may be used again. Many of these cycles interlock in critical ways. For example, the soil is the home of the decomposers that provide terrestrial plants not only with nitrogen, but with all other necessary nutrients. Damage to the soil disrupts many different cycles. In an interdependent ecosystem, some points are more sensitive to disruption than others because their role is large or critical, and comparatively minor disruptions can be amplified into large consequences for the system as a whole. In this connection, the utter dependence of all life on the tiny creatures performing essential roles in all natural cycles cannot be overemphasized. Just as the nitrifying and denitrifying bacteria play a critical role in the nitrogen cycle, so the phytoplankton in the oceans are indispensable for the homeostatic maintenance of the oxygen and carbon cycles. The integrity of these basic cycles is therefore indispensable for long-term human welfare.

A well-functioning ecosystem reuses materials with great efficiency. Indeed, there is almost no such thing as a waste in nature, for by and large one organism's waste is another's food. Without this cycling of materials, organisms would have long ago drowned in their own wastes.

The instructive contrast with human practices should be apparent. In earlier eras, man's detritus was principally organic, and it was, like man himself, scattered thinly over the surface of the earth. In latter days, he generates large quantities of non-organic waste, and his organic wastes are highly concentrated in limited areas. Local ecosystems cannot absorb all that is asked of them. Furthermore, organic waste is no longer deposited reasonably near where the raw materials were obtained, for some regions are agricultural mines that produce food for people living far away, whose waste is not returned to the soil but dumped into the ocean. Farmers attempt to make up for this loss by applying artificial fertilizer, which not only requires a large amount of energy to manufacture, but also creates water pollution when it runs off into lakes and rivers to become another waste out of place in natural cycles.

The Limits of Ecosystems

Why are man-made wastes a problem for ecosystems? After all, if ecosystems are self-repairing, self-maintaining, and self-regulating, one could infer that they are well prepared to handle major environmental stresses. Unfortunately, this is true only within certain natural limits. As a result of evolutionary development, natural systems are adapted to conditions they have faced in the past. Thus ecosystems can cope with fire, but not with large doses of radiation, synthetic chemicals for which no corresponding decomposer exists, and other unnatural stresses. These are things that ecosystems are simply incapable of digesting. Given enough time, organisms would evolve to meet the new conditions, and ecosystems would restructure themselves to be once again in a state of homeostasis. Unfortunately, this requires time on a geological scale, and man-made stresses have come too thick and fast for the slow processes of evolution to be of any help. However, some wastes are biodegradable (for example, sewage), and some man-made stresses are natural (for example, heat) in the sense that they are not completely new to nature; yet these too can cause environmental disruption, for an ecosystem can exist only within a homeostatic range that is normal for it. Within the limits of the range, self-regulation by negative feedback tends to return a stressed ecosystem to the center point of the range. However, when certain limits are passed, when there is too large or too small a quantity of nutrients, too much heat or too little, and so on, self-regulation no longer works, and a vicious circle of positive feedback drives the sytem away from homeostatic stability toward destruction.

The process is well illustrated by the phenomenon called eutrophica-tion—overenrichment, or excess of nutrients. In a freshwater lake, algae (the producers) grow and are grazed upon by herbivorous fish (the pri-mary consumers), who in turn are eaten by carnivores (the secondary consumers). The fish release waste and die, providing food for the decom-posers, who generate the inorganic products needed as food by the algae. The system is closed and in balance. Furthermore, it is capable of han-dling normal environmental stresses. In response to the light of the sum-mer sun, the algae multiply rapidly, temporarily depleting the supply of inorganic nutrients. But the fish have been programmed by evolution to re-spond to such seasonal changes; they react by increasing their population, which creates additional organic waste for the decomposers to turn into nu-trients for the algae. A new level of seasonal stability has been attained, for the ecosystem has had to adapt to this stress annually for eons and has developed the appropriate self-regulating response.

However, when a lake is artificially enriched with inorganic phosphorus compounds (for example, detergents), the algae, ordinarily limited by the low level of phosphorus, are free to multiply very rapidly. If the additional nutrients are sufficiently abundant, the algae can become so dense that the organisms at the bottom of the algal layer no longer get enough sunlight to continue photosynthesizing their food. They die off, creating organic waste, which must be decomposed. Furthermore, with their lower metabolic rate and longer life cycle, the fish cannot respond rapidly enough to contain the algal population explosion. The amount of dead or-ganic matter to be decomposed can soon become so great that the bacteria of decay begin to deplete the oxygen content of the water. Since these bacteria need oxygen to survive, they cannot multiply fast enough to keep up with the still rapidly increasing quantity of organic waste. But the algae no longer depend on the decomposers to supply them with nutrients, so they continue to grow. And so on, in a vicious circle. Sudden enrich-ment has therefore destroyed the negative-feedback control governing algal growth, resulting in excessive production that the rest of the ecosystem cannot tolerate, given the existence of other limits like oxygen content, so that the whole system is pushed outside the homeostatic range.

Notice that two kinds of intrinsic limit operate in this case. First, there is the physical limit set by oxygen supply when the nutrients that ordinarily limit algal growth are available in excess. Second, the system is limited by the biological lag built into its self-regulating mechanisms. If fish could reproduce as rapidly as algae (and if other factors such as oxygen, needed by the fish as well as the decomposers, were not limiting), then any algal bloom could be contained; but since ecosystems are adapted to much more modest levels of stress than man is capable of inflicting, typically they find it difficult to respond to sudden or massive stress in time to prevent the system from being overwhelmed.

Because the human body is also a homeostatic organism, it responds to stress in a very similar fashion. The human body's analogue of the non-biodegradable substance in an ecosystem is a poison, which may be defined as a chemical substance the body is not readily prepared to metabolize. The intrinsic limits of the body's tolerance to stress are also well known. For example, the human body strives to maintain its internal temperature at approximately 37.0 degrees Celsius (98.6 degrees Fahrenheit). Any departure from the normal temperature calls into play self-regulating mechanisms, such as sweating and shivering, which act to push the body temperature back toward its normal value. If disease or environmental stress causes body temperature to leave its homeostatic range—that is, to exceed roughly 42 degrees or drop much below 32 degrees—death ensues more or less rapidly, as the self-regulating mechanisms break down and actually start to contribute to the body's problems (the regime of positive feedback). The limits set by biological lag are also well known. A healthy body ordinarily repulses infection without any difficulty, but a sudden invasion of bacteria from a serious wound or contaminated food can allow the invaders to outstrip the self-regulating immunity systems of the body, which require time to mobilize against invasion, so that death ensues.

On the basis of this discussion of cycles and wastes, the basic ecological axiom that "every thing must go somewhere" should be readily comprehensible. The law of the conservation of matter states that matter may be transformed but not created or destroyed. Nature has learned to accommodate the law by the development of self-maintaining cycles that circulate materials throughout the biosphere for use and reuse as long as the sun continues to provide the energy needed. Waste is essentially a man-made phenomenon; it obstructs, or destroys the natural cycles unless it is introduced into ecosystems in the proper form, in the proper amounts, and at the proper rates, which all depend upon the natural limits of the ecosystems. Merely getting rid of things does not solve our waste disposal problem in any but the most temporary fashion, for the consequence of waste is a decaying or dying ecosystem, and just as the body finds it hard to function with a damaged organ, so the biosphere's health depends intimately on the health of its constituent parts, or ecosystems. Since the biosphere is in effect our biological capital, from which we draw income in the form of food, water, and breath, to mention only the most fundamental requisites of life, the health of the biosphere is directly related to human health and survival.

The Fitness of Nature

The long evolutionary history of the biosphere has made it a near-perfect superorganism, in which individual species are fit to survive, in which the populations of plants and animals are co-adapted to fit into steady-state ecosystems, in which individual ecosystems are adapted to fit into the biosphere as a whole, and in which, therefore, any random intervention is likely to be detrimental to the general fitness of the total system. Nature now has a complex organization made up of highly compatible parts; in the absence of intervention, it runs as beautifully as a well-made watch (and never needs repairs). In fact, the rigor of natural selection, which ruthlessly weeds out harmful changes that arise naturally, suggests that nature as it exists is the best possible general arrangement for life under current climatic and geological conditions. In the course of evolution, nature, like the watchmaker, has tried many other possible designs and found them wanting. If one pokes at this arrangement carelessly, there is a strong likelihood that it will suffer damage. This is why man's intervention in nature has brought mostly trouble; by not realizing that nature is an independent whole and that it operates on the basis of cycles rather than linear events, man has tampered randomly with a delicate instrument.

The Price of Intervention

Intervention in nature is not precluded, of course. Nonintervention is not a law that man could obey even if he wanted to, except at the price of extinction. Merely by existing, all organisms intervene in nature. As long as they are confined to the evolutionary role prescribed for them, not only do they not harm the biosphere, they positively contribute to its richness. Unfortunately, man's evolutionary role in the strict biological sense is that of a hunter-gatherer without fire or other elements of even the crudest technology. Thus man transcended his purely biological role when he became technological on the most primitive level. Since then, he has had no choice but to intervene in nature to the detriment of its perfect fitness.

The issue has then become an economic one: since every intervention in nature to solve a problem or obtain a benefit simultaneously creates new problems and generates environmental costs, man must make certain that the trade-off between benefits and costs is truly in his favor. As indicated in the Introduction, environmental disruption has a very long history (even so-called primitive peoples damage the environment), but the magnitude of man's interventions has grown enormously, particularly in the modern era. In earlier days, the benefits of environmental intervention probably outweighed the costs by a large margin. Through ignorance, man damaged ecosystems more than he needed to in order to get the benefits, but his numbers and the level of technology he possessed made it impossible for him to tear asunder the fabric of nature. This is no longer true. Nature can be destroyed, at least to the point that man would find it difficult or impossible to survive except in sparse bands of hunter-gatherers, and thus the issue of trade-offs has become of central importance. What are some of the trade-offs built into the economy of nature?

The Necessity of Limits

The first thing to understand is that the trade-offs are limited. Each organism and each ecosystem has its limits; moreover, ecosystems are only as strong as the weakest link in the ecological chain. The word "limit" has a negative connotation, but the virtue of limits is that they are part of the self-regulating process that leads to community homeostasis. Organisms become programmed to use the natural periodicities governing the availability of nutrients or other requisites of life to regulate their activities for their own benefit and ultimately for the benefit of the community. It would not do, for example, for bees to begin breeding rapidly during the fall or for the seeds of desert flowers to germinate except after a heavy rainfall. Organisms thus learn to use environmental limits creatively. More important, however, *for there to be a system at all, there must be design limits.* A system without limits would not be an ordered entity, but a place where anything could and would happen. Because even the simplest system must accomplish diverse functions, some parts of the system must specialize in—that is, limit their role to—these functions. No one part can be allowed to grow indefinitely, displacing all others, for this would destroy the system and, consequently, the part itself. Thus we find the pervasiveness of negative-feedback controls, which keep each organism and sub-system performing the function for which it was naturally designed. The functions that must be performed in all ecosystems are production, consumption, and decomposition, so that each organism must be constrained to perform one of these major roles in the system. The more complex the ecosystem, the more specialized these roles or "niches" are, and organisms are correspondingly more limited in what they can do. The limitations built into the organism constrain it to fill its niche. The limitations on an individual ecosystem are those that allow it to fit harmoniously into a biosphere composed of many other ecosystems. Described this way, limitations are the complements of the positive design features of the system or organism that have allowed it to survive in a given physical environment. Thus the concomitant of natural design is limitation. To the extent that nature is intricately designed to operate in certain ways, it is also highly constrained to operate *only* in those ways.

There is another aspect of natural limitation that must concern the human ecologist—the fact that not all natural processes are perfectly cyclical. Indeed, some are irreversibly linear; that is, although in general the biosphere is characterized by closed cycling in a steady state, perfection in this process is not always achievable at particular times or places. The cycle of materials is not completely closed except over the longest spans of time. Erosion is an obvious example; also, ecosystems do not reuse chemicals with total efficiency. Thus materials eventually find their way into a sink, typically the abyss of the sea. After many years, the process of mountain building may return these materials to the active part of the biosphere to reenter the cycle, but in the short run their path is unidirectional. Similarly, fossil fuels are the residue of non-recycled organic material deposited during past geological ages; they are a stored source of solar or photosynthetic energy that we are using up and that can only be replenished, if at all, in some future geological era—a fact of some importance, whose implications will be explored later. However, one of the most important instances of irreversibility is ecological development or succession, the expression of the creative thrust of evolution within individual ecosystems. Since it sets the basic terms of most of the ecological trade-offs human beings must make in their relationship with the biosphere, succession is worth going into in some detail.

Ecological Succession

The perfect fitness of nature is not static. The biosphere is a dynamic and open steady-state system; it always contains the latent capacity to evolve if change in some element of the system should make it necessary. However, since the history of the earth consists of long periods of geological and climatological stability interspersed with much shorter episodes of relatively rapid change, at most times the major physical and chemical parameters of the biosphere have been relatively unchanging, and nature appears to have been stable, even eternal. This appearance is deceptive, for natural systems can be observed to change not only in response to natural or artificial trauma like volcanism or exploitation by man, but also in response to the inherent drive of life to multiply and become more complex.

If we could watch for a long period of time a bare boulder that had rolled down from a mountain peak to the valley below, we would see this drive in operation. Devoid of life at first, the boulder would eventually be colonized by lichen. Aided by mechanical processes like weathering, the lichen would change the chemical composition of the rock's surface until moss could grow in one or two areas. After many years, the moss would have created conditions allowing other plants to grow, and insects as well as microorganisms of various kinds would have long since found a home on the boulder. After many more years, large areas of the boulder would have been transformed by this biological activity, and one day a pine seed would be able to take root in the newly created soil. By this time, many of the early inhabitants of the boulder would have been displaced—"pioneer" species create conditions favorable for other types of organisms and thus do themselves out of a job. During the pine's growth, it would further transform the boulder, perhaps splitting it into smaller fragments and so accelerating the process of changing a large, hard piece of rock into life-supporting soil through a combination of physical and biological processes.

This brief and simple example illustrates a number of important principles. As we stated earlier, living things do not merely adjust to their environment, they create it, and lichen and mosses repeat on a much smaller scale the task performed in the primitive oceans by the microscopic creatures that created the atmosphere as we know it. From observing succession we see that nature remains a vital, creative force. The teleonomy (that is, evolution characterized by open-ended purposiveness, as opposed to evolution toward some predetermined end) of nature is also evident; nature moves from non-life to life and from simple life forms and ecosystems to more complex and diversified life forms and ecosystems, which are richer in the sense of having a higher degree of negentropy, or biophysical organization.

Since the second law of thermodynamics, one of the fundamental physical principles of the universe, tells us that entropy, or disorder, always tends to increase toward a state of uniform, random chaos, what accounts for evolution and ecological succession, for the incredible negentropic diversity and order of nature? The answer lies in the capacity of life to trap the energy of the sun and force it to do useful work to decrease entropy before the energy is degraded to dispersed, random heat in accordance with the second law of thermodynamics. Why life exists at all remains a mystery; yet the existence of life is a fact, and once it gets started, the nature of the transformations it causes in ecosystems is quite clear.

By studying the orderly succession of plant and animal communities in diverse habitats, ecologists have derived the dynamics of the process. Essentially, it recapitulates evolution on a smaller scale. An abiotic environment is colonized, and an extremely simple ecosystem characteristic of a young or pioneer stage of succession is created. Gradually the first colonizers transform the environment, until a slightly more complex pioneer ecosystem is established. This in turn creates the preconditions for more and more complex ecosystems, until the most complex ecosystem the local climate and physical environment are able to sustain comes into being. Since this is the temporary end of development, this final stage is called the climax. It will endure essentially unchanged as long as it is undisturbed by fire, human intervention, or other unusual stresses, or until major geological or climatic changes cause the process of succession to continue.

Pioneer and climax ecosystems differ sharply in almost every important attribute by which ecologists describe ecosystems. The essential differences

TABLE 1-1
The direction of ecosystem development

Pioneer state	Climax state
Few species	Many species
One or few species dominate	Relative equality of species
Quantity growth	Quality growth
Few symbioses, mostly competitive	Many symbioses, mostly cooperative
Short, simple life cycles	Long, complex life cycles
Mineral cycles relatively open and linear	Mineral cycles circular and closed
Rapid growth	Feedback control/homeostasis
Relatively inefficient use of energy	Efficient use of energy
Low degree of order (high entropy)	High degree of structured, complex order (negentropy)

After E. P. Odum 1971, p. 272.

are listed in Tables 1-1 and 1-2, first in ecological and then in everyday language. The increase in all forms of symbiosis, particularly those that are mutualistic (that is, in which both organisms derive benefits), deserves particular note. The tables can be summarized by saying that in creating a more complex and diversified ecosystem, nature replaces quantity with quality. Plants characteristic of pioneer stages grow prodigiously (like weeds, which epitomize pioneer species), and the amount of production of vegetable matter compared to the total amount of the biomass is very large. In mature stages, plants grow much more slowly and have longer lives; although total productivity (that is, photosynthesis) is actually higher in mature stages, net community production (annual "yield") is lower than in the pioneer stages because energy is invested not in a new "crop," but in the maintenance as well as the slow, organic growth of the already existing biomass. Thus, whereas energy in the pioneer stage is used in a fairly straightforward way to grow more plants, so that a relatively empty habitat can be pioneered, in the mature system much the greater part of the energy is used to enhance the quality of the existing community, which already occupies all the territory available.

Man the Breaker of Climaxes

Where does man fit into this scheme? Unfortunately, ever since he acquired technology in the form of fire, man's actions have been anti-evolutionary. He has lived as a breaker of climaxes, which contain the stored wealth of the

TABLE 1-2
The essence of evolutionary and ecological development

EVOLUTION — →	
Immaturity	Maturity
Simplicity	Complexity
Uniformity	Diversity
Fragility	Stability
Disorder*	Organization*
Poverty*	Richness*
Quantity	Quality
← — — — — — — — — — — — — — — — — — — — RETROGRESSION	

After McHarg 1971, p. 120.
   *In more technical language, immaturity is characterized by entropy, the lack of ordered information or thermodynamic content, while maturity is characterized by negentropy, a wealth of highly organized information or thermodynamic content.

ages in their plants, animals, and soil and which in their natural state do not yield rapidly enough for his civilized wants. In other words, instead of living on the income of the biological capital inherited by the species, man invaded the capital itself. One of the first and most important human interventions was the use of fire: man found that burned-over areas produced a new growth of succulent grass in abundance and that this attracted game. However, the agricultural revolution resulted in the greatest simplification of natural ecosystems, as elucidated by the cultural ecologist Roy Rappaport:

> Man's favored cultigens . . . are seldom if ever notable for hardiness and self-sufficiency. Some are ill-adapted to their surroundings, some cannot even propagate themselves without assistance and some are able to survive only if they are constantly protected from the competition of the natural pioneers that promptly invade the simplified ecosystems man has constructed. Indeed, in man's quest for higher plant yields he has devised some of the most delicate and unstable ecosystems ever to have appeared on the face of the earth. The ultimate in human-dominated associations are fields planted in one high yielding variety of a single species. It is apparent that in the ecosystems dominated by man the trend of what can be called successive anthropocentric stages is exactly the reverse of the trend in natural ecosystems. The anthropocentric trend is in the direction of simplicity rather than complexity, of fragility rather than stability [1971, p. 130].

It is not cultivation alone that simplifies ecosystems. The sheep rancher does not want bison eating the grass that could be used to feed more sheep, so the bison must go. So must the mountain lion, the wolf, the coyote, the eagle, and any other predator that might cut into production. Ecological poisons like DDT and radiation also simplify ecosystems, since they tend to kill off the organisms higher up on the food chain, leaving behind very large numbers of a few tolerant species. Overfishing and overhunting have the same effect. So does nearly every form of civilized human activity. The dilemma is clear. Man must have productive ecosystems in order to survive; but high productivity requires simple and even dangerously fragile ecosystems. Further, in a biosphere that is interconnected, other ecosystems are also simplified indirectly; if they become too simplified, natural cycles will be disrupted, materials will be lost, and the whole system of the biosphere will be rendered unstable. If every forest is cut down, what will perform their flood-retaining and oxygen-making functions? If all marshes and estuaries along our shores are developed, because that is the most "productive" use for them, what will take the place of the oxygen-producing plankton (as well as the fish dependent on them) supported by the large quantities of organic matter washed out of estuaries to the continental shelves by the tides?

In short, man does not live by food and fiber alone. However, although total maximization of production as we have traditionally defined it would totally compromise our life-support system, discreet cropping of climax ecosystems is possible only in the hunting-gathering mode of human existence. Civilized man therefore must strike a balance between production from his environment and protection of his environment. Stated another way, man must be prepared to optimize his level of production, taking into consideration the contribution of nonproductive elements of nature, like wilderness, to his well-being; maximization of productivity narrowly defined is sub-optimal and eventually fatal for the system as a whole. A fundamental principle of human ecology thus emerges: "The optimum for quality is always less than the maximum quantity that can be sustained" (E. P. Odum 1971, p. 510).

Variability of the Climax

Even in areas where climate and other general factors are the same, microclimates and habitats will differ—some areas are boggy or dry compared to the norm, some are higher than the average, some get more sunlight or are more exposed to wind, and soils are not uniform throughout a region. In accordance with these variations in microclimate and habitat, different species are advantaged or disadvantaged. We find, therefore, not one uniform climax everywhere dominant, but a general climax state that is a mosaic of the true climax association and a large number of "edaphic" climaxes, adaptations of the basic climax to special local conditions. Thus, even within the overall biogeochemical determinism of nature, there is a surprising degree of pluralism.

Sometimes an ecosystem does not attain the true climax. An area may be subjected to periodic natural stresses such as fire or inundation, which keep the area from reaching the climax state theoretically attainable. Instead, the community adapts to the stress, and produces what is known as a cyclic climax. Again, special local conditions overrule the general direction of nature.

In some cases the source of the stress is man, and the result is called an "anthropogenic subclimax." Many grasslands, for example, were produced by deliberate burning and are thus an anthropogenic subclimax. Asian paddy land, which has been cultivated for millennia, is another man-made subclimax, one that mimics a natural marsh. Anthropogenic subclimaxes are inevitably less natural than the true climax, but the best of them attain quite high levels of maturity and yet also give man quite a high yield. Even today, some productive areas of the English countryside are at this high level of ecological maturity. Unfortunately, this type is rather rare compared to the subclimaxes, like the once-fertile lands made into desert, that are the product of man's destruction of habitat. Thus natural determinism is quite strong, but never total, so that in some areas it may be possible to achieve a large measure of both production and ecological stability.

Exploiting Ecosystems for Production

How susceptible nature is to this kind of compromise is very dependent on local conditions. In temperate zones, where glaciation ceased only about 10,000 years ago, even climax ecosystems are immature compared to such ancient ecosystems as the coral reef and the tropical rain forest, which have had many more years to achieve maturity. It is a characteristic of ecosystems of rather low maturity that they support exploitation relatively well, and it is this characteristic that has made intensive agriculture of the kind we practice at all feasible. For the most part we have broken the climax and driven our fields back to the pioneer stage, where our cultigens, which are adaptations of natural weeds, flourish. In temperate areas, climate, the condition of the soil, and the nature of the broken climax all permit this to be done without immediately harmful effects, provided that it is done in the right way (that is, by not grossly simplifying ecosystems with broad-spectrum insecticides, by not mining the soil, by minimizing monocultures, and so on).

By contrast, strong exploitation of very mature tropical ecosystems can produce total collapse. For example, in a tropical forest almost all the nutrients are tied up in the biomass; very little is contained in the soil. Thus when a plot of forest is cleared for cultivation much of this biological capital is hauled away to lumber mills and is lost to the ecosystem. Most of the animals flee to still undisturbed areas, dispersing another portion of the biological capital. The slash is burned; this releases nutrients that permit a few years, typically four or five, of profitable exploitation before the action of rain and sun leaches out all the nutrients (this is why the rain-forest ecosystem puts its wealth into the biological rather than the soil bank) and the sun bakes the resulting clay into concrete (which explains why tropical forests carefully screen out the sun). As a result of ill-advised exploitation, this highly mature and stable ecosystem has been driven back to the very earliest stage of succession; it may now approximate an abiotic (lifeless) environment. Moreover, since the soil is no longer stabilized by plants, the heavy rains will cause accelerated erosion, which can effectively prevent life from making a significant comeback for many generations, if ever. Thus the seemingly most stable ecosystems—for example, the Amazon basin forests—are paradoxically the most vulnerable to man's intervention, for they can be driven by overexploitation to the point of total and irreversible collapse. And what can be lost is not merely future production, but all the invisible contributions such forests make to the general health of the biosphere. Thus, in addition to the general trade-off between production and protection, man must confront this kind of ecological paradox in an era when demands for food are rising, in the tropics above all.

Ecologists propose a basic agricultural strategy recognizing that the safest landscape is one containing all the variety of nature—crops, forests, lakes, marshes, and so forth—as well as a mixture of communities of different ecological ages. (They point out that this would also be the most pleasant landscape to inhabit.) Margalef (1968, p. 49) calls for a "balanced mosaic, or rather a honeycomb, of exploited and protected areas"—in short, compartmentalization.

Another solution is the development and utilization of compromise ecosystems; these are essentially "good" anthropogenic subclimaxes, systems that combine the virtues of production and protection. For instance, rice paddies and fish ponds, which are cultivated analogues of natural marshes and estuaries, are existing examples of compromise ecosystems based on the principle of pulse stability; although the biological and human requirements for pulse stability are exacting, such ecosystems are highly productive and more could be developed, especially in the tropics. Detritus agriculture (mushrooms) and pisciculture (carp ponds) also offer wide latitude for the invention of productive compromise systems. Yet another kind of compromise is tree cropping for food, especially in tropical areas, where it has long been practiced (but not always wisely) for cash crops, like coffee and cocoa. Also, native tropical gardening techniques are ecologically very sophisticated, and research might disclose ways to make them more productive.*

---

*As the drawbacks of modern industrial-intensive agriculture have become more and more apparent, particularly as a means of increasing food production in tropical areas, agronomists and ecologists have rediscovered some of the virtues of traditional agriculture. Unproductive in terms of the market economy they may be, but in terms of productivity per acre as a function of energy input and long-term environmental compatibility many old agricultural practices (of course, by no means all) must be adjudged superior (Armillas 1971; Rappaport 1971; Thurston 1969). Naturally, traditional techniques have their drawbacks too. One is that they are usually labor-intensive.

The basic strategy of all these compromise systems is to study the nature of the climax and then, instead of breaking it completely, to mimic it closely or to insert man into the process as a careful parasite, preserving the host while siphoning off as much food as possible. However, compromise systems will not work everywhere. Some ecosystems are too vulnerable or difficult to manage. Furthermore, the productivity of many compromise systems is not high enough to feed great masses of people living in cities. Thus for large parts of the globe we must attempt to strike a balance between production and protection by comprehensive zoning, retaining some areas as a source of biological capital from which we draw interest in the form of security and well-being, while subjecting other areas to intensive (but, one hopes, less destructive) cultivation in order to obtain the food and fiber needed for a large population. (Ecologists generally insist that the oceans must remain essentially protected areas; rational cropping of naturally occurring fish, and compromise systems of mariculture, like the growing of oysters, are all that we should expect from the oceans if we wish to avoid the risks that would be involved in exploiting this crucial regulator of natural cycles.)

In general, then, ecologists urge a move toward an overall global anthropogenic subclimax that would give the optimum trade-off between production and protection, as well as a considerable degree of amenity in the form of a varied and pleasant landscape. Ecological succession provides a model for the transformation of man's agriculture: from rapid-growth, high-production, pioneering stages to a relatively stable and mature subclimax that is optimal considering all of man's needs and that is characterized by constructive symbiosis rather than warfare between man and nature.

Life Is Energy

Whether an ecologically optimal agriculture will also serve to feed large numbers of people will depend largely on how well it adapts itself to the character of the energy flows that make the economy of nature operate. Energy is the currency of nature's economy; the biomass and stock of materials are its inventory, or capital. Natural systems are designed to trap incoming solar energy and make use of it for production; the more mature the ecosystem, the more efficiently this energy is utilized and the more is produced. Thus energy determines productivity. This seems paradoxical. If our ecologically immature agricultural systems are so inefficient in terms of energy use (see Table 1-1), why are they so productive? Part of the reason is that our cultigens are domesticated weeds, adapted by nature and then by man for rapid growth, which gives a high yield when cropped. Moreover, the total amount of radiation is so large and the total area in production is so vast that enormous quantities are produced despite the inefficiency of the process. However, to answer this question fully, it is necessary to look at the energetics of food chains and at the concept of energy subsidy in ecosystems.

An examination of food chains soon reveals that very large numbers of producers are required to maintain a much smaller number of herbivores, who in turn maintain a still smaller number of carnivores. There are several reasons for this, but the principal one is the loss of energy in food chains due to the tendency of energy to degrade into non-useful forms, as ordained by the second law of thermodynamics. Natural processes are typically of rather low thermodynamic efficiency from a mechanical engineer's point of view (but not from a biological point of view, for nature is not trying to maximize throughput). Photosynthesis, for example, is only about one percent efficient in terms of energy fixation or the amount of protoplasm created by producers in proportion to incoming solar radiation.* Also, producers have a high metabolic rate, so they tend to burn up a lot of what they produce just to stay alive; herbivores consume energy maintaining themselves and grazing the producers. Thus, at each step in the food chain, energy dribbles away in the form of waste heat. In the typical food chain, the energy available at each trophic (feeding) level declines by a factor of ten, although the ratio can vary from about seven to twenty. Thus the efficiency of agriculture in feeding people depends a great deal on where food is taken from the chain. When cereal is fed to pigs or cows raised for human consumption only about a tenth as many people can be fed as when humans themselves live as cereal and vegetable eaters. There is thus a trade-off in agriculture between the quantity and the quality of our diet. Low at best, the efficiency of agriculture in supporting human beings is even lower if they wish to eat high off the hog.

However, the crucial factor in agricultural productivity is the amount of energy subsidy provided to crops by humans. Natural energy subsidies exist, such as the tidal flushing that brings nutrients to estuaries. But energy subsidy is largely the work of man, often unintentional (and unwelcome, like the eutrophication of a lake), but more often deliberate. All agriculture, no matter how primitive, depends on an input of energy in the form of labor or materials. In traditional agricultural systems, this subsidy primarily takes the form of human labor, with some help from draft animals. The total amount of the subsidy is typically rather small compared to the yield (returns of up to fifty-to-one are possible, although fifteen-to-one is more usual). However, gross productivity is often (but not always) comparatively low. By contrast, modern technological agriculture is quite productive but

---

*This is not as inefficient as it might seem to be. Remember that enormous quantities of solar energy are used to warm the globe, evaporate water, blow clouds around, and do all the other things needed to keep natural cycles going. To use ecological language, most of the incoming energy is used for maintenance (an indicator of the biosphere's high degree of ecological maturity).

not very efficient, for it is little more than a biological machine for turning fuels into food. In fact, when all the subsidies supporting industrial agriculture are taken into account, it clearly spends more energy than it produces; in other words, the energy yield of industrial agriculture is negative.

The dependence of industrial agriculture on energy has important implications. The United States produces about three times as much food per hectare as India, but the increased production requires ten times the input of energy. (The comparison is, if anything, conservative, because the hotter the environment, the higher the metabolic rate and thus energy loss of a plant; all other factors being equal, temperate zones produce higher yields than tropical zones.) This gives some insight into the problems of raising agricultural productivity in developing areas. For them to achieve anything like the productivity enjoyed by the developed temperate zones, the energy subsidy must be increased at least ten times. In the final analysis, food, like every other aspect of life, is a matter of energy.

The Essential Message of Ecology

To recapitulate, although it is possible in principle to exploit nature rationally and reasonably for human ends, man has not done so. Because he has not been content with the portion naturally allotted him, man has invaded the biological capital built up by evolution. Moreover, due to man's ignorance of nature's workings, he has done so in a peculiarly destructive fashion. With our new ecological understanding, we can see that linear, single-purpose exploitation of nature is not in harmony with the laws of the biosphere and must be abandoned. Instead, we must learn to work with nature and to accept the basic ecological trade-offs between protection and production, optimum and maximum, quality and quantity. This will necessarily require major changes in our life, for the essential message of ecology is *limitation*: there is only so much the biosphere can take and only so much it can give, and this may be less than we desire. In the next chapter we shall explore the consequences for human action that follow inescapably from the existence of fundamental biospheric limits.

BIBLIOGRAPHIC NOTE

The indispensable work on ecology as a science is Eugene Odum's *Fundamentals of Ecology*, a complete and authoritative textbook by a scientist who has made major contributions to knowledge. Odum does more than provide a complete description of the science of ecology; the last third of the book deals with applied ecology and the issues of human ecology in a stimulating and profound way. (Chapter 20, "Ecology of Space Travel," contributed by G. Dennis Cooke, is one of the most interesting.) A 38-page bibliography and a detailed index are additional reasons why this is a valuable book. Unfortunately, despite a helpful preface that tells the reader how to use the book for his own purposes and a chapter organization that promotes selective reading, the person interested primarily in the human implications of ecology may feel a bit swamped by details. An alternative to Odum is *The Biosphere,* a reprint of a special issue of *Scientific American* devoted to that topic. The articles cover natural cycles, the nature of life, agriculture from an ecological viewpoint, and other basics of pure and applied ecology. However, since the articles use charts, diagrams, and tables in the usual *Scientific American* fashion, a modicum of scientific literacy is needed to derive full benefit from the book. Another alternative to Odum, a bit more readable than *The Biosphere* but still scientifically respectable, is Clair Kucera's *The Challenge of Ecology,* which provides general coverage of all important aspects of ecology from a human-ecological point of view. Those who prefer a less empirical or scientific treatment of ecology may still learn a great deal about ecological principles and processes from two popularizations, Marston Bates' *The Forest and the Sea* and Ian McHarg's *Design With Nature.* Bates is a biologist and a gifted writer who successfully imparts an intuitive grasp of ecosystems as he explains the economy of nature and man's place in it. McHarg is a landscape architect and planner who uses in his profession the ecological principles he writes about, and he thus demonstrates what it means to apply ecology to real human problems. Yet he also communicates the poetry of ecology, verging at times on scientific mysticism, which may be the truest mode of comprehending it. Although other worthy books abound, both texts and popular treatments, none of them is quite as useful as those mentioned above. (However, Odum is no longer virtually unchallenged as *the* ecology text; four books published in 1973—by Colinvaux, Emlen, Ricklefs, and Watt—all have their merits.) All of these books are somewhat biocentric; works written from a more geological perspective, such as H. W. Menard's *Geology, Resources, and Society,* a high-quality general geology textbook, provide a needed complement. An alternative or supplement to Menard is Peter Flawn's *Environmental Geology,* a short but complete textbook whose theme is "man as a geological agent"; Flawn discusses more specifically than Menard the interaction of the geosphere with the life process and with human affairs.

Turning finally to works dealing more with applied ecology, I suggest starting with Howard Odum's *Environment, Power, and Society.* This is more than a useful and comparatively nontechnical explanation of systems ecology; it applies the techniques and insights of systems ecology to agriculture, economics, politics, and even religion with results that will enlighten, stimulate, provoke, and occasionally baffle the reader. (This work should not be read without a basic understanding of ecology and some willingness to interpret the heuristically clear but information-dense systems diagrams.) Next, the reader should look at *The Careless Technology,* by Farvar and Milton. A conference report, the book contains case studies of about fifty ecological nightmares of all kinds resulting from development in the Third World. The conference sponsors originally hoped to explore positive examples of ecologically sound development as well but they could not find any worth discussing, so that the tenor of the book is overwhelmingly negative. Once some of the appalling consequences of anti-ecological development have been seen, *Ecological Principles for Economic Development* (Dasmann et al.), written under the auspices of the Conservation Foundation and the International Union for the Conservation of Nature and Natural Resources, will seem overwhelmingly cogent. Designed as a handbook for development planners and the decision makers who pass on their work, it is a very concise summary of ecological knowledge and experience that provides basic guidelines for making human action compatible with the biospheric processes on which the species depends. It may be especially recommended to busy, practical men of affairs.

2

POPULATION, FOOD, MINERAL RESOURCES, AND POLLUTION

Because mankind lives on a finite planet, it is certain that, like every living population and process, it must obey the law of growth depicted by the sigmoid (S-shaped) logistic curve in Figure 2-1. Moreover, numerous respected analysts have suggested—on general principle, without reference to specific ecological limits—that the phase of rapid growth is all but over (for example, McHale 1971, pp. 170–195; Salk 1973). How much faster, for example, can we send communications around the globe than we do now with television satellites? Or how much more of our available money or manpower can we possibly spend on scientific research?

Yet the Club of Rome study reported in *The Limits to Growth* (Meadows et al. 1972) provoked enormous controversy when it said essentially the same thing. In part, this was because the study appeared to show that an immediate rather than an eventual transition to the steady state was necessary and that the actions required to cope with the problems of transition violated both conventional wisdom and our current values. More important, however, was the holistic nature of the study. Past ecological warnings had tended to focus on or become identified with one particular limit to growth,

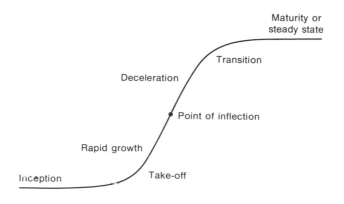

FIGURE 2-1.
The logistic or sigmoid curve and its features.

like pollution (Carson 1962) or population (Ehrlich 1968). They were therefore vulnerable to the counterargument that the problem could be solved by
using resources from other sectors. What *The Limits to Growth* purported to
show, by identifying all the important relationships between various sectors
and interlinking them in a computer model designed to reveal the resultant of
all these interactions, was that this strategy of borrowing from Peter to pay
Paul would not work much longer.

Paradoxically, however, this tended to intensify debate about particular
limits to growth, for the critics charged that it was the excessively Malthusian and pessimistic assumptions about many of these alleged limits that
largely determined the outcome of the study. Naturally, with more "reasonable" or optimistic assumptions about population dynamics, resource availability, pollution-control technology, and the like, quite different conclusions
could be reached.

What follows is a synoptic review of the various limits (primarily but not
exclusively physical) that have been identified by qualified specialists. The
general structure of the argument is that *(i)* there are indeed demonstrable
limits to the demands humanity can place on its environment; *(ii)* although
technology can help us manipulate limits to accord with human preferences,
outright repeal of the limits is impossible; *(iii)* moreover, manipulating the
limits technologically has costs (especially energy costs) that we may not be
able to bear, or wish to; and *(iv)* time is of the essence if we wish to cope
with limits effectively and humanely. In sum, an era of ecological scarcity
has dawned. The argument focuses on a few key factors, like energy, that
are truly critical for the system as a whole, and it makes as explicit as
possible the interactions among separate limits, for ecological scarcity is

not simply a series of discrete problems; it is an ensemble of problems with their interactions—a "problematique"—and can be understood in no other fashion.

FOOD AND POPULATION

No aspect of ecological scarcity has received more attention over a long period than the "population explosion." Since the primordial limit on population is food, let us consider the supply of arable land and other basic factors like water, the state of agricultural technology, and above all the costs and consequences of feeding people—especially the large numbers of additional people who will be born in the decades to come—to see how many human beings the earth can reasonably support.

The Inevitability of More People

Approximately 4 billion people now inhabit the earth. If the current rate of world population growth continues, there will be 8 billion people on the globe by 2010 and 16 billion by 2045. Of course, fertility is bound to decline from its currently high level, but even quite optimistic assumptions about the rate of decline in the years to come do little to alter this basic picture; most experts regard a world population of 12 to 15 billion as foreordained, merely postponing the arrival date to 2060 or so if they are optimistic.

The primary reason for this inevitability is the phenomenon of demographic momentum. For example, even though the United States has attained replacement-level fertility, the population is still growing. In fact, assuming that we maintain exactly this level of fertility from now on, the population will continue to grow from its current 215 million to at least 275 million in 2040 (Frejka 1968). The explanation for this is that rapid growth in decades past has bequeathed us a young population—that is, a population distribution with disproportionate numbers of young people who have yet to replace themselves. Thus the U.S. birthrate will continue to exceed the death rate for many more years. In fact, the official *low* projection for the U.S. population in 2000 is 271 million, with the 300 million mark to be reached in 2015 and stability or zero population growth not in sight for another 30 or 40 years (Commission on Population Growth 1972, pp. 19–20). Actually, for a variety of reasons the population in 2000 or 2015 could well be higher than these low projections. This would be especially true if life spans were extended, as some medical scientists hope, for then the death rate might remain below the birth rate for an additional 10 to 20 years before growth ceased.*

Of course, the U.S. population problem is of trivial dimensions compared to that of underdeveloped countries, where a replacement level of fertility is far from being achieved. Most have population growth rates of about 3 percent per annum, resulting in truly explosive growth—a doubling every 25 or 30 years. Many hope that such rapid growth is a temporary phase and that the so-called demographic transition—a drop in fertility in response to lowered death rates and economic improvement, similar to that experienced by the now rich countries in the course of their development—will begin to retard the population explosion. However, most developing countries show no signs of beginning this transition, which historically has required about 70 years. Even allowing for the somewhat more rapid transition that seems to be occurring in China, Taiwan, Korea, and a few other nations and assuming further, very optimistically, that Latin America, India, Pakistan, Indonesia, and the rest will soon begin a similarly foreshortened demographic transition, in the absence of catastrophic famine or other Malthusian checks demographic momentum in countries with extremely young populations virtually guarantees a world population of 12 to 15 billion within the period 2040–2070. Can we feed this many people?

How Many Can Be Fed?

A number of studies have tried to establish how many people the earth can support. A few conclude that we could feed a world population of 50 billion. However, to arrive at this figure a number of totally unrealistic assumptions are needed. First, all potentially arable land, regardless of fertility or suitability, must be dedicated to food production. Man could inhabit only wasteland totally unsuited to agriculture; suburbs and cities would have to be uprooted and turned into farmland; the bulk of the population would perforce be housed in Arctic regions; and so forth. Second, *all* land, even infertile land that had been pressed into production, would have to yield food at a level of production that has not been attained on our most fertile soil with the best means of which we are capable—in other words, a level plant physiologists dream about but have no real prospect of achieving outside a laboratory. Third, all the possible side effects of intensively farming every

---

*If the exceptionally low fertility rates of the last several years persist, then future population levels will be lower—for example, only 251 million in 2000 if couples were to have an average of 1.8 children instead of 2.1 (the replacement level). As the Census Bureau points out, however, such a level is unprecedented in American demographic history. Moreover, fertility trends fluctuate markedly in response to economic conditions and other factors, and many demographers believe that the trend to smaller families is too much the product of special circumstances to serve as a reliable basis for forecasting.

conceivable acre at the highest technological level must be ignored—the pollution caused by fertilizer runoff, the enormous flow of energy required for such colossal and high-technology agriculture, the climatic effects of turning all forests into farmland, the enormous demand on water resources, and so forth. Thus, 50 billion is a theoretical limit based purely on the potentiality of plant physiology, not on the realities of agriculture.

Studies that are more realistic about land supply, soil quality, water supply, the likelihood of our inhabiting the North Polar regions, and other factors reduce their estimates of the maximum number that can be supported globally to 15 billion, or roughly the level we seem foreordained to have. Unfortunately, this figure also appears to be a somewhat unrealistic and theoretical maximum. Even today, far too many suffer from sheer lack of food, and even those who have sufficient calories often do not get enough protein or other dietary essentials. The nutritional shortfall is such that even with perfectly equal distribution of the current world food production everyone would be somewhat malnourished. Thus we do not really provide for even the existing 4 billion human beings.

Recent developments in agricultural technology (the so-called Green Revolution) now being applied to underdeveloped countries show promise of staving off the catastrophic global famine predicted by many, but the Green Revolution is not immune to drought, a perennial problem in many less developed countries, and severe local famines in Sahelian Africa and India in recent years testify that the world hovers on the brink of such a disaster. Besides, as even its proponents admit, the Green Revolution is no panacea for overpopulation; it simply buys us some time to bring population growth under control. Moreover, the world already confronts severe ecological problems because of its current mode of agricultural production, and the Green Revolution intensifies these problems. (It also has a number of painful social side effects—for example, making poor farmers worse off while making rich farmers better off.) Thus the time being bought now is at the expense of the future. A more detailed examination of the difficulties, dilemmas, and contradictions in current and projected agricultural practices will show why feeding adequately even double the present number of humans will overstrain the earth's ecological and energetic resources, and therefore why feeding 15 billion is likely to be out of the question.

The Basic Agricultural Predicament: Limited Land

The fundamental fact about agriculture is that it requires land, and good agricultural land is in fixed supply. Even in the United States, virtually all good agricultural land is already in use; it is this good land that provides us with almost all our food. The best 50 percent of the land in use probably supplies 80 percent or more of the total agricultural output. The marginal lands now in use thus make only a modest contribution (although it is often critical for dietary quality).

Although there appears to be other land that could be developed, bringing into production any sizable quantity of new land would require enormous amounts of capital, energy, and above all, ecological expertise beyond any we now possess; and production gains are likely to be ephemeral. In the preceding chapter the ecological futility of trying to clear and farm tropical forest lands was explained. Yet in numerous countries the irreversible destruction of tropical forests is taking place, reaping a few years of harvest, but leaving a legacy of serious ecological problems and potential climatological consequences. Even where the soils of forest lands are capable of supporting some kind of more intensive cultivation, cutting down forests carries the risk of erosion, flooding, and desiccation of climate, the result of ignoring the ecologist's dictum that the so-called nonproductive parts of an ecosystem perform invaluable protective functions making production possible on the most suitable land. The opening up of arid and semiarid lands by irrigation and well digging has other kinds of consequences. Even when they are well conceived and confined to appropriate land, irrigation projects are capable of provoking intensified erosion, waterlogging, and salinization, serious problems that have been implicated in the collapse of numerous earlier civilizations. Likewise, the usual result of increasing the water supply to pastoralists is overgrazing and land destruction by oversized herds. Thus the hope of expanding output greatly by bringing virgin lands into production appears illusory.

In fact, much greater efforts must be made to prevent the continuing loss of currently productive land through mismanagement and abuse. Owing to ignorance and the sheer pressure on resources from overpopulation, land is almost everywhere being exploited unwisely, especially in the tropics. Loss of productive land due to erosion, desertification, salinization, laterization, waterlogging, and other problems is occurring at a rapid rate throughout the developing countries; in some areas, a ravenous scourge of peasants is virtually devouring the land. Substantial topsoil loss occurs even in the United States and other "advanced" countries. Thus even now the supply of arable land is being depleted.

Some novel kinds of ecologically sophisticated exploitation of unused land—tree culture, pisciculture, modernized versions of native gardening techniques, and so on—can provide a useful supplement (of vital protein especially) to a basic cereal diet, but except in a few favored areas they are not the answer to the present and future food needs of humankind.

. . . *And Limited Water*

The second major limitation on agricultural productivity is the availability of water, which is governed basically by climate. Thus, even apart from the issue of side effects, irrigation is only a partial answer. In many areas, such as our own Southwest, there is a clearly limited amount of water to be moved around. The lack of sufficient surface water in many areas has spurred intensive development of groundwater supplies. All over the world, fossil water from underground aquifers is already being mined faster than natural recharge takes place, in order to support the current level of irrigation. But the more intensified agriculture becomes, the more water will be needed, and the United Nations Food and Agriculture Organization has forecast a serious water shortage by the year 2000. Gigantic aqueducts to transport water very long distances already exist, requiring enormous quantities of energy to build and maintain; even more grandiose ones are being considered. However, by using natural water resources it will never be possible to irrigate more than 20 percent of arable land, no matter how grandiose our water plans become (Brown, Bonner, and Weir 1963, pp. 74–75). Even general adoption of drip irrigation and other techniques that conserve water (but boost energy costs) will not alter this picture substantially. In fact, the proliferation of waterweeds, which reduce water flow and increase evaporative loss, in many areas more than outpaces improvements in water supply.

Despite high costs, desalination is a possible answer for some local areas, but it requires such great expenditures of energy for production and transportation that its widespread use is almost ruled out. Moreover, the hot brines that are an inevitable by-product will create a pollution problem of very large dimensions. Such remote possibilities as towing icebergs from the Antarctic are occasionally advanced as solutions to this very serious limit to growth, but even the most favorable estimates relegate them to a minor, local role. It is just barely conceivable, for example, that icebergs will one day supply water to the Atacama Desert, but the ecological, economic, and practical barriers to providing North America with agricultural water from this source are immense.

Little Help from the Sea

Nor can we expect the sea to provide basic subsistence for added billions. For one thing, the oceans are for the most part biological deserts. All major fisheries depend on the few areas where large quantities of nutrients are brought to the surface by upwelling. Thus experts believe that we can count on no more than two or three times the current production. Even this may be optimistic, for the top millimeter of the ocean is critical to its productivity and general ecological health, so that we must control pollution from such sources as oil tankers and offshore oil wells if we wish to realize the potential of the seas. We must also prevent further development of the estuaries and coastal marshlands that are the principal spawning grounds and nutrient sources for many of our important fish populations. In addition, recent declines in the catches of important species imply that we are already overfishing at least some of our principal stocks. Moreover, in some cases we are trying to exploit both ends of the food chain at the same time—for example, by harvesting the zooplankton on which the Antarctic fisheries depend— and this is impossible in the long run. Yet so far efforts to curb overfishing have been half-hearted and all but fruitless. The present moribund state of the whaling industry probably foreshadows the future state of all our fisheries.

Mariculture offers some possibilities for providing protein, but it can never be a large source of calories.* Moreover, pollution and coastal development must be much more rigorously controlled for mariculture to be successful. In the United States the shellfish industry is declining because of pollution, and the very productive mariculture of Japan is experiencing similar problems in a more acute form.

Diminishing Returns from
Increased Energy Input and Intensification of Agriculture

Thus experts agree that the only possible answer to the problem of feeding double the present world population lies not in the opening up of new frontiers either on the land or in the oceans, but on the preservation and more intensive exploitation of lands that are now farmed and that are the most suitable for intensive agriculture. Even aside from its ecological consequences, intensification of production requires a vast input of energy. Modern intensive agriculture is essentially a technique for converting fossil fuels and

---

*Mariculture can be extremely productive, for it is potentially much more efficient than terrestrial agriculture at converting solar energy into animal protein. However, the requirements (of water purity, location, spacing, and so on) are extremely demanding, and the techniques of managing aquatic ecosystems are intricate. Also, many proposed forms of mariculture, such as raising pelagic organisms or constructing elaborate artificial marine environments, run thermodynamically uphill; thus resource costs would probably exceed the food benefits (Ehrenfeld 1974). Moreover, some of the more grandiose schemes for increasing oceanic productivity—for example, creating artificial upwellings or zones of deepwater illumination—could have unpleasant ecological side effects. Nevertheless, many of these ideas hold promise if they are judiciously applied, and future generations may well depend very heavily on mariculture for both nutrition and dietary variety.

minerals into grain and fiber.* As a general rule, doubling output requires increasing tenfold the energy subsidy to a crop (E. P. Odum 1971, p. 412; H. T. Odum 1971, Chapter 4). Thus to make the agriculture of India as intensive and productive as that of Japan by highly technological means would require about 100 times the present input of man-made energy. Part of the energy subsidy can be in the form of greater labor inte¬sity (one reason for the high yield of Japanese agriculture is its use of labor-intensive, essentially horticultural farming techniques). However, by far the greater portion, especially in lands that are not well endowed with the good soil and abundant natural water Japan possesses and that suffer from all the liabilitiэs of tropical agriculture, must be in the form of mechanical equipment, irrigation facilities, pesticides, and especially, unstinted application of fertilizer.

This stupendous increase in energy subsidy is the essence of the Green Revolution. The new high-yield strains have been bred to function only in combination with this kind of high energy investment. Without irrigation, heavy application of pesticides, and vast quantities of fertilizer, they give yields inferior to most native cereal strains.

Assuming for the moment that the Green Revolution were to be completely successful on its own terms, and putting aside until the next chapter the question of whether we can possibly supply such quantities of energy without provoking fearsome ecological consequences, how many people could the earth feed? Some Japanese farmers produce enough grain on 0.15 of an acre to support one person on a Japanese diet. This represents about the best that it is possible to do without a quantum jump in the level of agricultural technology. Further application of fertilizer or other energy inputs would not raise production significantly; diminishing returns per unit input have nearly reached the asymptote.† Moreover, soil and water conditions are exceptionally favorable in Japan, and potential yields in tropical

---

* For example, even though the atmospheric nitrogen for making nitrogenous fertilizer is itself free (and essentially inexhaustible), the process of converting it into chemical forms usable by plants is costly in terms of materials and energy: every ton of nitrogenous fertilizer requires one ton of steel and five tons of coal to manufacture (McHale 1970, p. 12). Some of the minerals essential to intensive agriculture may come into short supply. Phosphorus, for example, is not fixed readily (either economically or chemically) from the environment; we therefore depend for this essential constituent of fertilizer on phosphate supplies that may last only another 30 years (Laing 1974).

† The phenomenon of diminishing returns in agriculture is amply documented. For instance, Brown, Bonner, and Weir (1963, pp. 62–63) note that "Japanese productivity . . . has changed but little since 1935, despite intensive technological effort." Also, plotting U.S. farm output against energy input from 1920 to 1970 produces the familiar sigmoid curve, which suggests that ultimate limits to increased productivity by intensification are near (Steinhart and Steinhart 1974, p. 310). Moreover, in some cases intensive methods have already pushed productivity very close to an absolute biological ceiling; for example, annual egg production per chicken can hardly increase much further.

areas are inherently lower than in temperate zones. Taking these and other factors into account, most ecologists and food experts believe that we would be doing very well indeed to support one person for each acre of arable land (E. P. Odum 1971, pp. 50–55, 431; H. T. Odum 1971, pp. 136, 285–287). Since there are now at most 8 billion acres of potentially arable land, the maximum conceivable population that we could support with a world-wide, high-technology, and high-energy-subsidy mode of agricultural production appears to be 8 billion people living on a cereal diet.

Why Even Eight Billion Cannot Be Fed: Nutritional Limits

It should be obvious that even this figure, scarcely double today's rapidly expanding population, is an unrealistic, purely theoretical maximum. Arable land is not evenly or equitably distributed, and the supply of it is being depleted. Besides, as we know, such theoretical efficiencies are rarely achieved in practice. Moreover, global calculations of this nature tend to sidestep the problem of dietary quality. Men do not live by the calories in grain alone; they must also have protein as well as other dietary supplements to survive. As we explained in the last chapter, animal protein can be produced in large quantities only by diverting grain from people to animals at a considerable thermodynamic loss: one cow eats for five to ten people. Even vegetable protein of the right quality is much harder than mere calories to produce in quantity. Soybeans, for example, have so far resisted the best efforts of plant geneticists to produce "miracle" strains, and output per acre is still low. The nutrition problem is compounded by the tenacity and nutritional blindness of cultural food preferences and habits. For example, Balinese regard rice as the only food fit for humans, so as population pressure increases, marginal land that might reasonably produce something else is unreasonably forced into rice production. In addition, humans need fiber and other inedible agricultural products, so that some of the world's 8 billion acres of arable land must be withheld from food production to satisfy these needs.

. . . And Ecological Limits—
Monocultures, Crop Losses, and Pollution

Even assuming that we can find sufficient energy to surmount the nutrition problem, the ecological limits to energy-intensive agriculture will almost certainly make it impossible for us to feed 8 billion. The Green Revolution aims at universalizing the methods of temperate-zone industrial agriculture. As we saw in the last chapter, these methods are profoundly antiecological. Moreover, they are particularly unsuited to the tropics (Janzen 1973). Some aspects of this issue, such as the side effects of irrigation projects, have already been treated in sufficient detail, but the liabilities of monoculture and agricultural pollution need to be explored further.

Whatever the economic justifications, the practice of monoculture is on general principles always ecologically unsound, even though an individual farmer can usually get away with it most of the time. However, the drive toward total replacement of traditional crop varieties with genetically uniform cultigens—that is, with the so-called miracle strains of the Green Revolution—creates the specter of regional monocultures, with every farmer producing the exactly same species and variety of inbred (and therefore vulnerable) crop. This is an open invitation to pest infestation and area-wide plant disease, as the Irish potato famine and recent U.S. experiences with corn blight have shown. (Nor are crop losses confined to the fields; in the tropics, post-harvest losses of up to 30 percent of the stored crop occur, and some of the miracle strains seem to be more susceptible to storage pests than the traditional varieties.) To make matters worse, in order to combat diseases and pests or to increase yields further, plant physiologists need genetically diverse raw materials for cross-breeding. However, the natural sources of genetic diversity, the many traditional varieties typically grown by peasants, are disappearing at an alarming rate as farmers everywhere rush to take up modern methods and the new genetically uniform strains. Thus the price to be paid for higher production will be exactly what the laws of ecology predict—extreme instability.

Agricultural pollution is not confined to pesticides. Intensified use of fertilizer also has its side effects. To squeeze the last increment of possible yield from a crop, fertilizer application must be increased disproportionately. However, at more than quite moderate levels of application, much of the fertilizer runs off into the water supply, causing eutrophication in lakes and rivers and polluting the groundwater supply with nitrates. This is an emerging problem in the United States and will be much more severe in arid and semiarid lands. Moreover, intensification of industrial agriculture creates non-farm pollution. For example, animal wastes are increasingly serious pollutants now that animals are factory raised. Also, fertilizer and other inputs must be manufactured and transported; agricultural products must be transported and processed. All of this entails pollution. Finally, when food is prepared and consumed in the cities an organic-waste disposal problem is created. Just as with every industrial process, therefore, pollution is the inevitable concomitant of food production; the greater the agricultural production, the greater the agriculture-caused pollution we can anticipate (and, as we shall see later in the chapter, farm pollution is essentially uncontrollable).

Emerging Conflicts over Resources

To an increasing extent, agriculture is in ecological competition for basic resources with its suppliers in the energy, mineral-extraction, and manufacturing industries. For example, every additional mine, fuel-processing plant, power plant, factory, and city dweller necessarily reduces the amount of water available for food production. Also, as populations grow, as urbanization increases, and as industry develops, productive farm land is necessarily taken over for habitation and other nonagricultural uses. The problem is most serious in the United States, with its sprawling pattern of land use. Highways and new suburbs eat up more than a million acres of prime farmland each year; in another few decades, even the United States may no longer have much surplus agricultural capacity. Most developing countries do not consume their farmlands at such a rate, but the trend is evident there too, and the sad fact is that it may make perfect economic sense to take land out of production for so-called higher uses even in a country that suffers from a severe food shortage, just as it makes perfect economic sense for Peruvian officials and businessmen to export fishmeal despite widespread protein deprivation at home.

The Effects of Climate on Agriculture

Climate is a very important ecological constraint on agriculture. Like death and other painful realities, the vulnerability of agriculture to the vagaries of the weather is simply a brute fact of existence on our planet. Yet the actual and potential impact of climate on agricultural production is rarely taken into sufficient account by the "experts." For instance, normal climatic fluctuation alone renders absurd any global calculation of how many people the earth can support "on the average," for there is no such thing as average weather except in the statistical records. During the minor periods of drought that are climatically normal, production can easily drop 30 to 40 percent. Thus, even assuming that we can indeed feed 8 billion "on the average," the number that we could expect to keep alive over the long term, in good years and bad, might well be as low as 5 billion.

The problem goes beyond the year-to-year vagaries of rainfall, as devastating as this has been and will continue to be. For one thing, major volcanic eruptions release particulates and gases that block the sun's rays and can therefore cause declines in crop production; many man-made pollutants have a similar effect. Moreover, climate is far from fixed; basic changes in climatic regime have occurred frequently in the past, and even comparatively minor shifts have had major impacts on agricultural production. Moreover, since the mild weather to which our current agricultural practices are so finely attuned is climatically·somewhat abnormal, any change is likely to be for the worse. In sum, the assumption that our weather is a constant upon which we can rely absolutely is unwarranted; both short- and long-term fluctuations adversely affecting agricultural productivity are bound to occur.

No Technological Panaceas

Surely, many will say, technological answers to most of these problems can be found. Actually, even apart from some of the general limits to indefinite technological innovation (to be considered in the next chapter), the limits discussed above strongly suggest that we have almost exhausted the possibilities of our current form of industrial agriculture. If we push our technology to an extreme, we shall make enormous demands on our energy resources and create serious pollution problems. Only a jump to a new level of agricultural technology can possibly alter this assessment. Unfortunately, such a new technology is nowhere in prospect.

Naturally, improvements in our current technology, or at least more intelligent application of it, can be anticipated. For example, entomologists are now trying to replace broadcast insecticides with "integrated control." This means using highly specific and selective chemicals, growth hormones, sex attractants, sterilized males, insect viruses and diseases, and parasites and predators to combat pest species. However, integrated control as presently conceived is still an antiecological war on nature and will clearly be much more costly than current control methods in terms of energy, materials, money, and labor. Yet integrated control would not produce more food than current methods; it would simply preserve the present stalemate between man and insect while reducing some of the noxious side effects of the struggle.

Other proposed technological fixes with some potential for expanding production abound—brackish-water agriculture, algae ponds, the reengineering of plants to be more efficient converters of solar energy or to be self-fertilizing (like the legumes), synthetic food, and so on (Wittwer 1974 reviews many of these). Some are promising, but all are unproven. Besides, as past experience and the laws of ecology tell us, improved productivity *always* is achieved at some cost—higher energy requirements, lower ecological stability, and the like. Worse, part of the price to be paid in all these cases is that we shall become ever more dependent for our food on biological engineering, largely divorced from ecological cycles. But as ecologist Howard Odum points out, biological engineering, like all other attempts to substitute man-made systems for natural systems, is inherently problematic: "Where the natural combinations of circuits and 'biohardware' have already been selected for power and miniaturization for millions of years, probably at thermodynamic limits, it is exceedingly questionable that better utilization of energy can be arranged . . . with bulky, nonreproducing, nonself maintaining engineering" (cited in E. P. Odum 1971, p. 507). In sum, further advances in industrial agricultural technology and even synthetic food technology will certainly occur, but those now visible as speculative gleams in the eyes of scientists appear to be problematic and not nearly adequate to the dimensions of problems we face.

The Dismal Prospect

It should be evident that the intensification of industrial agriculture will almost certainly not suffice to feed 8 billion people even as well as we feed 4 billion now (surely not a standard we ought to feel proud of). If we should succeed temporarily in sustaining so many, our success would be short-lived and the ecological costs from uncontrollable pollution and other side effects severe. Above all, expanding production substantially would require many times the amount of man-made energy that we now employ—from 10 to 100 times, exclusive of what might be needed for desalination or other extraordinary measures. As we shall see in the next chapter, this would have serious consequences. Thus we have run into the inescapable ecological trade-off between quality and quantity that is built into the biosphere. All in all, we are far away—and moving farther away—from the ecologist's ideal for agriculture described in the preceding chapter, "a relatively stable and mature subclimax that is optimum considering all of man's needs and that is characterized by constructive symbiosis rather than warfare between man and nature."

Unfortunately, although there are proven alternatives to industrial agriculture and there are other concepts of sound ecological farming that could be developed (Box 2-1), at this point a switchover to a very different mode of agricultural production may be nearly impossible. Owing to more people, greater affluence in some areas, and crop failures in others, demand for food has increased. Formerly surplus-producing nations like the United States no longer have large buffer stocks of food or sizable amounts of reasonably productive land in the soil bank. As indicated by the sharp rise in agricultural commodity prices during the last few years, food is scarce, and the world now lives on a very thin margin, vulnerable to the slightest diminution

Box 2–1. Ecological Farming

A mode of agricultural production that gets only a one-to-five or, worse, a one-to-ten return on its energy input may make economic sense in the short run, but it is ecological nonsense in the long run, unless energy is superabundant and ecologically harmless, which is not the case. Moreover, despite what technologists and spokesmen for agribusiness say, there is a real possibility of breaking the vicious circle of technological addiction in agriculture and shifting back towards an agriculture based on dilute but renewable and nonpolluting solar energy, but informed by a high degree of scientific understanding and biological sophistication. With care, very high yields could be obtained for millennia from such an agricultural technology. Some of the principles and techniques of ecological farming were suggested in the preceding chapter. Ironically, many of them resemble earlier farming techniques that we have scorned as primitive and inefficient—combined forestry and grazing, controlled cropping of game animals (game ranching) instead of cattle-raising in tropical areas, fish ponds that turn wastes into protein, mixed farming instead of monocultures, crop rotation and the use of both animal manure and "green fertilizer," substitution of

of supply. Thus the changeover to an agricultural technology that may be ecologically efficient but that does not promise to yield maximum production in the short run will be unacceptable both to businessmen and to humanitarians in the developed countries. The temporary loss of production during a transition period to ecological agriculture may seem even less tolerable to developing countries, for famine would be the likely result. Furthermore, in the developed countries, whose populations have largely put the farmer's life of toil behind them, the news that ecological farming is labor- rather than energy-intensive will be unwelcome, and resistance to a changeover is therefore likely.

In sum, although the specific terms of the food-population calculus have changed since Malthus first put forward his "dismal theorem" in 1798, the prospect for a species whose fertility continues to outrun its means of sustenance is still unrelievedly dismal.

MINERAL RESOURCES

People eat food. Modern industrial civilization "eats" mineral and energy resources and would collapse if these essential items of its diet were not available in sufficient abundance. Is there enough mineral "food" to satisfy the present and anticipated requirements of our industrial "population"? As with the question of the limits to growth in general, there are two basic schools of thought on the availability of minerals.

labor for herbicides and pesticides, and so forth. Especially if they are brought up to date with modern science, these techniques are highly productive (on a per-acre basis they can outproduce industrial agriculture), *but only when human labor is carefully and patiently applied.* Thus farming that is both productive and ecologically sound seems very likely to be small-hold, horticultural, essentially peasant-style agriculture finely adapted to local conditions (especially in the tropics). It should be obvious that many of the developing countries are well poised to make the transition to this modernized version of traditional agriculture. Except for the excessive use of insecticides and chemical fertilizers in some areas, the agriculture of China, Taiwan, Korea, Ceylon, Egypt, and others is already close to this mode, and has high per acre yields to show for it. By contrast, the United States and some other developed nations (Japan is a major exception) appear to face a great deal of "dedevelopment" in order to change over to this style of agricultural production, so that the transition would be socially painful. The back-to-the-land movement notwithstanding, how many Americans would willingly return to family farming?

Mineral Availability: Ecologist versus Economist

One school believes that mineral resources are essentially finite, that we are using them up at a rapid rate, and that we shall run out of the supplies of many of the raw materials our industrial civilization needs rather abruptly in the near future. The second believes that supplies of resources are not at all finite; on the contrary, *provided energy is abundant* they can be almost indefinitely expanded by means of technological innovation and substitution; spurred by the price mechanism, these will suffice to keep supplies well ahead of increasing demand, until gradually and gently demand will level off to an eternally sustainable level. Let us employ the term "ecological" for the former, and "economic" for the latter school of thought.

A review of the debate between the two schools will show that, just as for agriculture, an answer to the question turns upon ecological scarcity, rather than resource scarcity in itself. That is, for the next four to five decades the critical question is not whether we are capable of expanding mineral resources to keep up with rapidly growing demands but whether we can bear very much longer the costs of doing so, in terms of energy use, land devastation, and pollution. Let us begin by examining the dynamics of resource use with a fixed stock of a hypothetical resource, using different kinds of assumptions about supply. After this explanation of the basis of the ecological position, we shall look at the counterarguments of the economic school.*

---

*Most of the references on resource availability in the List of Sources tend to reflect the ecological school's position. However, the economic position, based primarily on the availability of abundant cheap energy and the resilience of the market, is fairly presented in a number of them, especially Barnett and Morse (1963), Brooks and Andrews (1974), Brown, Bonner and Weir (1963), Coale (1970), and Malenbaum (1973).

The Nature of Exponential Growth

A quantity grows exponentially when its rate of increase during a period of time is a fixed percentage of the changing size of the quantity. Thus a population with access to unlimited supplies of the necessities of life grows exponentially: the increase of population with each new generation means that there will be more breeders to produce a further increase in the next generation, and so on. Similarly, money put out at compound interest grows exponentially because it yields a certain percentage of both the original amount and the accumulated interest. (By contrast, money put out at simple interest yields a return on only the original amount; there is no compounding, and growth is therefore linear.) With exponential growth, at the end of some period that depends upon the percentage rate of increase the original quantity will be doubled. Naturally, raising the percentage rate of increase shortens the doubling period. At a steady 5 percent, a quantity doubles about every 14 years; at 10 percent, there are only 7 years between doublings.* Figure 2-2 illustrates the increase with time of any quantity that grows exponentially. (Note that Figure 2-2 is simply the bottom half of the familiar sigmoid curve.) However, the significance of continued exponential growth may be conveyed more vividly by two parables.

One tells of a greedy merchant who asked the king to pay for his services with grains of wheat on the squares of a chessboard—one for the first square, two for the second, four for the third, and so on to the sixty-fourth square. Unfortunately for the merchant, the king was not mathematically naive. A quick calculation showed the king that the amount of wheat required for the final square would be about 8.5×10^{18} grains, an astronomically large amount, and he quickly put the greedy and treacherous merchant to death. This story illustrates the levels that an exponentially growing quantity, starting from insignificant amounts, can reach after comparatively few doublings. As one looks higher on the exponential curve (Figure 2-2), the absolute amount of increase at each doubling soon becomes staggering. We have already seen, for example, some of the very large demands further doublings of the world population would place on the earth. It should now be intuitively obvious why the sigmoid curve is so universally observed in nature: an exponential growth curve must eventually bend over and become a flat line, for a mere twenty or thirty doublings of almost any population or quantity suffice to produce amounts that cannot be sustained or produced on a finite earth.

The second parable, popularized during the public debate over *The Limits to Growth,* concerns a lily pad growing in a fish pond. According to the

*Dividing the percentage rate of increase into 70 gives (roughly) the doubling time in years. Of course, a quantity growing linearly doubles too, but the time between doublings gets longer and longer as the series continues.

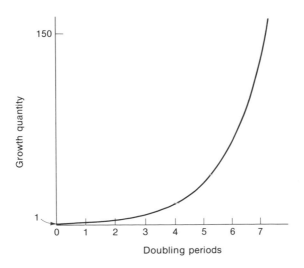

FIGURE 2-2.
The exponential curve, which describes the size of any exponentially growing quantity after a given number of doubling periods.

parable, each day the lily doubles in size, and if the lily keeps growing, in thirty days it will cover the pond, killing the fish. At first the lily is a tiny speck in the pond, and even after many doublings it remains very small relative to the pond. The farmer who owns the pond is unconcerned. He believes that he has plenty of time to cut back the lily and save his fish. Even on the morning of the twenty-eighth day, when the lily covers only one-quarter of the pond, he does not realize that by the next morning the lily pad will occupy one-half of the pond's surface and that he will then have precisely one day to cut back the now rapidly burgeoning lily. This story illustrates well the insidious nature of exponential growth when there is a finite limit. Until the very last stages of the progression, the limit appears so far away that it may seem a problem for our great-grandchildren to worry about, or at the very least, a problem that we can handle in due course once it becomes pressing. The catch is that realization of the consequences of un checked growth often comes late. Once the problem has become pressing, it may require heroic measures to check the momentum of rapid growth and prevent a crash.

Growth versus Resources: Running Out in Theory and Practice

In the light of this general understanding of the nature and power of exponential growth let us see what happens to a hypothetical mineral resource of finite dimensions as demand grows exponentially at 3.5 percent per annum, so that doubling of the absolute demand occurs every 20 years:

Doubling	Remaining stock (tons)	Current demand (tons per annum)	Static reserve (years)
Start	50,000	100	500
1st	47,000	200	235
2nd	41,000	400	103
3rd	29,000	800	36
4th	5,000	1,600	3

Thus, as demand doubles, redoubles, and doubles again, absolute demand rises from a modest 100 tons per annum to 16 times that amount by the fourth doubling, and a resource that appeared at the start to be adequate for half a millennium begins to be depleted very rapidly until, finally and abruptly, the stock is exhausted. The static reserve, the number of years of useful life at current levels of demand, is therefore a very poor indicator of how long a resource is likely to last if demand is growing. Much more important is the exponential reserve—that is, how long the reserve will last taking into account probable future demands on the resource. In this case, the exponential reserve is 83 years, less than 20 percent of the 500-year static reserve.

Suppose now that we wish to take into account new discoveries and new technologies that will expand our hypothetical resource. Let us say that instead of 50,000 tons total reserve we really have 500,000 tons, or 10 times as much. This allows usage to go on for a few more years, as continuing our tabulation under the new assumptions shows:

Doubling	Remaining stock	Current demand	Static reserve
4th	455,000	1,600	284
5th	407,000	3,200	127
6th	311,000	6,400	49
7th	119,000	12,800	9

The stock will now last for about 147 years. Thus multiplying the total available stock by 1000 percent extends the time to exhaustion by less than 80 percent.

However, a mere tenfold increase in the stock may still be too pessimistic for some, so let us assume that we start with 100 times our original stock, as an allowance for resource expansion through any conceivable combination of technological innovation and discovery of new resources. This does in fact allow growth to continue for a little longer:

Doubling	Remaining stock	Current demand	Static reserve
7th	4,619,000	12,800	361
8th	4,235,000	25,600	165
9th	3,467,000	51,200	68
10th	1,931,000	102,400	19

Alas, the impact of even such a fantastic increase in our hypothetical resource is dismayingly small. A 10,000 percent increase in the original stock gives a mere 217 years exponential reserve at a 3.5 percent growth rate. This is hardly more than double (261 percent) the original 83-year exponential reserve. Also, note how staggeringly large the absolute level of demand becomes as growth continues.

It is obvious from this hypothetical example that once absolute demand attains a substantial level, continued growth in demand begins to consume the remaining resources at an extremely rapid rate. However, the example contains a more important lesson about the insidiousness of exponential growth: to wit, even if foresight leads to adoption of a no-growth policy when about half of the stock is used up, there is very little effect on the time to exhaustion. For example, in the last tabulation, if at the time of the ninth doubling we forbid any further growth and simply continue to use up the resource at the annual rate then attained, the stock will last only an additional 68 years. In other words, assuming a 3.5 percent growth rate until then, the total life of the stock will be 248 years, only 31 years (14 percent) longer than if we simply allow the growth curve to run its course. This is so even though at the time we prudently switch to a no-growth policy *nearly 70 percent of the original stock remains*. Thus we have established three general principles:

1. Given steady exponential growth, the absolute size of the stock of any resource has very little effect on the time it takes to exhaust the resource.

2. Given already high absolute demand on a particular resource, the rate of growth in demand thereafter has almost no effect on the time it takes to exhaust the resource.

3. The time for concern about the potential exhaustion of a resource comes when no more than about 10 percent of the total has been used up.

Since demand for minerals has increased exponentially over the last two centuries and has now reached levels that are very high indeed, the concern of the ecological school appears to be amply warranted, and real-world statistics provide further support for pessimism. Table 2-1 lists identified reserves of major minerals.*

The case is clear. Almost half the static reserves are less than 100 years, the average growth rate is about 3 percent, the doubling time is 23 years, and the exponential reserve figures indicate that just over half of these major

---

*As the name implies, "identified" resources are those that are definitely known to exist, whether or not they are recoverable with current technology or under prevailing conditions. There are also resources classified (again without regard to potential economic or technological recoverability) as "hypothetical"—that is, geologically predictable from current knowledge, but not yet discovered—and "speculative"—that is, mineral deposits that may exist in unknown districts or unconventional forms. We shall see later how adding these hypothetical and speculative resources to our calculation affects reserve lifetimes.

TABLE 2-1
Identified reserves of important minerals

Mineral	Static reserve (years)	Growth rate of demand	Doubling time (years)	Exponential reserve (years)
Aluminum	110	6.4%	11	33
Chromium	730	2.6%	28	115
Cobalt	190	1.5%	48	90
Copper	52	4.6%	16	27
Gold	7	4.1%	18	6
Iron	840	1.8%	40	154
Lead	38	2.0%	36	28
Manganese	710	2.9%	25	106
Mercury	25	2.6%	28	19
Molybdenum	390	4.5%	16	65
Nickel	130	3.4%	21	50
Platinum group	100	3.8%	19	41
Silver	18	2.7%	27	15
Tin	88	1.1%	65	62
Tungsten	39	2.5%	29	27
Zinc	280	2.9%	25	76

Adapted from Meadows et al. 1974, Fig. 5-1. Their data were taken from U.S. Bureau of Mines and Geological Survey statistics and are in essential agreement with other authoritative sources (for example, NCMP 1972).

minerals will be exhausted in less than 50 years at current growth rates.* Thus the predictions of the ecological school appear to be valid, unless some combination of new discoveries and technological innovation can indeed expand mineral resources more or less indefinitely. Let us then examine the various possibilities that the economic school would rely on.

The Limits to Discovery and Substitution

Most mineral geologists and mining engineers are on the whole pessimistic about our finding substantial new supplies of ore. Sophisticated forecasting techniques have been developed to estimate the total size of any given resource under various geological and economic assumptions, and expert predictions of total potential reserves tend to agree rather substantially (that is, the highest estimate rarely exceeds three or four times the lowest). Fur-

---

*Naturally, a substantial decline in the rate of increase in demand would alter the specifics, but as with population, no foreseeable change would alter the basic shape of the forecast. Projections uniformly show large increases in world mineral consumption even with lowered growth rates.

TABLE 2-2
Maximum reserves of important minerals, assuming the growth rates listed in Table 2-1.

Mineral	Static reserve (years)	Exponential reserve (years)
Aluminum	340	49
Chromium	1300	137
Cobalt	420	132
Copper	160	46
Gold	25	17
Iron	N.A.	N.A.
Lead	490	119
Manganese	1200	123
Mercury	84	44
Molybdenum	1400	92
Nickel	350	75
Platinum group	140	49
Silver	32	23
Tin	160	92
Tungsten	N.A.	N.A.
Zinc	930	115

Adapted from Meadows et al. 1974, Figure 5-1.

thermore, geologists believe that the major metallogenic provinces, areas with a high concentration of ore deposits, are well known and for the most part well explored. Ore deposits remain to be found, but we have already skimmed off the cream, and much more sophisticated and expensive techniques must be used to ferret out the better hidden and less extensive deposits. Going deeper into the earth is no answer; the probability of ore formation decreases with depth, while the costs of extraction rise very steeply. The ocean too has been vastly overrated as a potential source of minerals. The available quantities are less than popularly imagined, and the difficulties and cost of extraction are enormous. The probability of really major discoveries has thus declined sharply and will continue to decline with each passing year. It is of course true that new developments, like the current "earth sciences revolution," may conceivably lead to some unexpected discoveries that are, unlike manganese nodules on the ocean floor, readily exploitable. However, as our hypothetical example clearly shows, given the present very high levels of absolute demand, even major discoveries will have only a modest effect on either the static or the exponential reserve; doubling the stock merely extends the time to exhaustion by one brief doubling period, and even a tenfold increase has little effect.

In fact, no amount of optimism really makes much difference, as is clearly illustrated by Table 2-2, which takes into account not only identified resources, but hypothetical and speculative resources as well (see note on p. 65). A comparison with Table 2-1 quickly shows that most static reserve figures do not improve spectacularly (only lead shows even a ten-fold increase) and exponential reserve figures differ hardly at all (resource lifetimes are extended about 25 years on the average, assuming that all hypothetical and speculative resources can be both found and mined). In sum, the optimism of the economic school about the impact of future discoveries appears to be unwarranted: there remains to be discovered very little relative to current and projected demand, and the technological difficulties and economic costs of finding and extracting hypothetical and speculative resources are far from trivial.

If discovery will at best buy us only a few decades, is substitution an answer to impending shortages? Here again there are difficulties that the economic school has not confronted. First, the resource problem is one of emerging *general* scarcity, not simply of coping with the exhaustion of one or two particular minerals. Without substantial new discoveries, we shall have to invent a new metallurgy that can do without copper, gold, tin, silver, tungsten, and mercury—and in fairly short order. Second, while it is possible, for example, to substitute aluminum for copper in most electrical uses, this transfer of demand would simply cause aluminum to be used up even more rapidly than projected. Third, even good substitutes (like aluminum for copper) are on the whole less efficient than the material they substitute for, and more energy is therefore required to perform a given function. Fourth, some metals have properties that are unique. For example, mercury is the only metal that is liquid at normal temperature and pressure; it is essentially irreplaceable in temperature- and pressure-control equipment. Other metals that would be hard to replace are cobalt for magnets, silver in many photographic uses, and the platinum group for industrial catalysts. Moreover, many metals serve the same function in metallurgy as vitamins in our diets; only small quantities are needed, but they are essential (for example, the manganese in steel). Needless to say, this will add to the difficulty of inventing new metallurgies. Fifth, plastics are often proposed as metal substitutes, but plastics are petrochemicals, and we are running out of petroleum. Also, the production of plastic involves serious pollution-control problems. Finally, many proposed technological solutions to environmental problems, such as the breeder reactor and thermonuclear fusion, require large quantities of very particular types of materials of a very high quality, and many of these major resource requirements, like helium and lithium, appear to be completely non-substitutable. It appears then that substitution will not help us much in overcoming the emerging problem of mineral scarcity. At best, it can alleviate particular shortages and buy time, but it is not a solution, either alone or in combination with new discoveries.

Limits to Extracting Minerals
from Seawater and Ever Thinner Ores

Technologists (especially those connected with the nuclear industry) and most economists usually see energy as the answer to all mineral resource problems. They say that if abundant and cheap energy is available we can, if worse comes to worst, literally burn up the rocks to obtain our minerals (and even the fuel to extract them). Resource scarcity is thus not seen as a problem, for nuclear energy will provide us with cheap, abundant, nonpolluting energy. While seductive, this argument ignores a number of crucial problems, even if the availability of energy is granted.

First, only six metals are abundant in the earth's crust (defined as present in a quantity exceeding 0.01 percent of the crust by weight)—iron, aluminum, manganese, magnesium, chromium, and titanium. All the rest of the metals are geologically scarce. It is a characteristic of the former that, as the standard for economically minable ore is lowered, the quantity of lower-grade ore increases. In other words, there is a more or less gradual continuum from the very richest ore bodies of these abundant metals to the almost infinite quantities of very low grade "ore" contained in ordinary rock. In order to keep extracting the metal, therefore, all it takes is energy and the technical ability to mine and refine ore of successively lower grades. However, the lower the grade of the ore the greater the economic cost (which rises exponentially with decline in grade), the greater the ecological cost due to pollution and increased demand for water (extractive industries are major polluters and water users), the greater the volume of rock that must be processed and disposed of per unit of useful output, and above all, the higher the energy cost per ton of metal. All of these factors are serious limitations on our ability to continue extracting the abundant metals, despite our technical ability to do so. As will be seen in the next chapter, the energy problem is particularly acute.

Second, the scarce metals are characterized by a sharp discontinuity between their concentration in currently minable ore and their average concentration in the earth's crust. Once concentrated ore deposits are mined out, lowering the grade slightly does not increase availability. Only a leap to ore which may be *leaner by 3 to 5 orders of magnitude*—that is, ordinary rock—will produce more metal. Since the economic and ecological costs, the volume of rock that must be moved, and the quantity of energy required for continued production of a scarce metal from ever thinner ores all increase exponentially with decline in ore grade, the side effects from burning the rocks to get mercury, zinc, tin, and the other scarce metals will be staggering. For example, to obtain a mere 400 tons of zinc (a tiny fraction of the over 1,300,000-ton annual U.S. demand), it would be necessary to process 5 million tons of ordinary rock with perfect efficiency, for the crustal abundance of zinc is only 0.0082 percent by weight.* Thus, in order to satisfy even a fraction of current demand for these metals under such a regime, truly astounding amounts of material would have to be obtained, processed, and disposed of; the economic, energetic, and environmental costs would be of even more astounding dimensions—current problems with stripmining would seem trivial by comparison. It thus appears extremely doubtful that we shall ever obtain zinc and the other scarce metals in any quantity from either ordinary rock or seawater—if we were to do so, these metals would cost considerably more than gold does today.

Helium: A Critical Resource

Although most nonmetallic raw materials are either abundant, easily substitutable, or readily synthesized, there are important exceptions; the most critical of these is helium. Helium is now extracted from natural gas; it can be obtained from no other source except by liquefaction from the atmosphere at very substantial cost in energy and money. Nor can substitutes be easily found for many of its unique properties. These properties have made helium a critical resource for the nuclear industry. In fact, without helium the breeder reactor, thermonuclear fusion reactors, and a number of other advanced technologies, like the transmission of electricity by superconducting power lines, will probably not work. But these are among the principal technologies that critics of the limits-to-growth thesis would rely on to provide the cheap and abundant supplies of energy they admit will be needed to cope with other environmental problems. Thus a scarcity of helium could have very important consequences. Yet such a scarcity is foreordained, at least in the sense that inordinate amounts of money and, above all, energy would be needed to obtain helium by liquefaction; experts foresee demand exceeding supply by some time between 1985 and 1992 (Metz 1974b). Moreover, the United States has unaccountably just abandoned its long-standing program of helium conservation, so that this critical resource is now literally being cast to the winds!

---

*The problem of extracting minerals from seawater, which has also been proposed, is essentially similar, but even more difficult, for the concentration of most minerals in seawater is vastly less than their concentration in the crust. Using zinc as an example again, to get the same 400 tons it would be necessary to process 9,000 billion gallons of sea water (equivalent to the combined annual flows of the Hudson and Delaware Rivers) with 100 percent efficiency (Cloud 1969, p. 140).

Reducing Demand: The Limits of Recycling and Conservation

If we cannot expect to expand supply very substantially by new discoveries, easy substitutions, or (with the possible exception of the six abundant metals) using ever lower-grade ore, can we reduce demand sufficiently to produce the same net effect? This may indeed be a more promising approach to the problem of resource scarcity, but we must still confront limits on our economies. It is often said that once the price of a metal has climbed high enough it will pay to recycle the metal scrupulously, so that we shall be able to keep reusing the same stock. Yet, first of all, by virtue of the second law of thermodynamics the recycling process can never approach 100 percent efficiency. When all the inevitable losses—in production, from friction and wear, through corrosion and other chemical processes, from outright loss and other human failure—are added up, we should be miraculously lucky to achieve the 90 percent level in recycling efficiency.* (Actual recycling efficiency for used metals is now on the order of 30 percent or less.) The only metals for which we could expect a higher ratio of recovery are the chemically non-reactive precious metals, which are hoarded rather than used. Thus, to maintain the stock in use, we shall still need raw materials. Second, many recycling processes are rather dirty, so that recycling will intensify our pollution problems. Third, recycling runs thermodynamically uphill —that is, scattered materials must be collected, transported, and transformed from a high-entropy to a low-entropy state—which requires energy, typically in rather large amounts (this is one reason why recycling is so little practiced today). Fourth, the potential efficiency of recycling and the design of products are directly related. For example, even small amounts of contamination may make a particular metal useless for many industrial purposes, and designs that make recovery impossible without cross-contamination will frustrate recycling (this is the major technical impediment to recycling the metals in junked cars) or compel us to use inordinate amounts of energy to purify scrap metal. Thus effective recycling of many major metals will require a revolutionary change in industrial processes, business practices, and design standards—and perhaps also in the nature of our cities.

A second approach to reducing demand is conservation. If we can do more with less, or even the same with less, by making more efficient and smaller machines or structures, then we can reduce levels of demand accordingly. This is often not so much a matter of technological wizardry—the

---

*Moreover, again for thermodynamic reasons, products differ radically in the theoretical efficiency with which they can be recycled. Thus metals can be recovered with high efficiency, but petrochemicals can not. For example, four old tires are needed to make the raw materials for one new tire.

savings to be made by further miniaturization and other innovations are probably rather small—as of not using materials wastefully. The typical high-rise building, for example, contains far more steel than it really needs for structural integrity. Another approach to conservation, the only one from which we can expect substantial immediate savings, is to make our products more durable. If the average car were built to last twice as long as current models do, it would reduce by nearly half the auto industry's gluttonous demand for materials. This is the kind of technically simple economy measure that would have the greatest immediate impact on the life of reserves. Paradoxically, this is also the kind of measure that is least discussed. Economic factors are probably the chief explanation: products that were more durable, easily recyclable, and fit other resource-conserving criteria would cost more, and business turnover would be less. Until the price of ordinary metals approaches that of gold, therefore, resource-conserving production will probably be at a disadvantage if matters are left to be decided purely by market forces.* In any event, conservation only buys time; if growth continues, and especially if we use some of the resource-intensive technological fixes that have been proposed, then any conceivable conservation program will have little more effect than a mere doubling of reserves.

Minerals: An Emerging Crisis

In sum, there are demonstrable limits to the expansion of mineral resources. After spending most of its history as a mineral-rich nation, the United States now finds itself increasingly dependent on imports for a very large proportion of its essential requirements. Barring a deliberate national policy of maximum autarky (which would be possible in the short run if we were willing to bear the economic and ecological costs), the dependency ratio is bound to increase rapidly in the future; as a result, we probably face major political, economic, and psychological adjustments, especially since world-wide competition for minerals appears to be increasing. The balance-of-payments problem alone—from $6 billion for mineral imports in 1971 to $20 billion in 1985 (Wade 1974c)—will present us with awkward dilemmas, particularly in view of the similar trend toward overwhelming dependence on foreign supplies of energy. There is therefore ample reason to take seriously the recent warnings of the U.S. Geological Survey and the U.S. Bureau of Mines that a U.S. and world mineral crisis impends (McKelvey 1974; Staines 1974).

---

*We shall explore these kinds of political, economic, and social impediments to ecological rationality in Part II; Metz's (1974b) brilliant reportage of how we are simply casting soon-to-be-scarce helium to the winds illustrates many of these barriers to resource conservation (and what our shortsightedness will eventually cost us).

POLLUTION

The Inevitability of Pollution

Many dangerous forms of pollution already abound; from the preceding it should be clear that the intensification of agriculture and basic-resource production will aggravate the problem. In fact, since all production and consumption entails pollution, any increase in production and consumption necessarily produces a proportionate increase in pollution. The laws of physics tell us that matter and energy can be neither created nor destroyed, only transformed. These transformation processes are never completely efficient; by-products or residuals are an inevitable result, and these are almost always noxious, or at least unwelcome, to some degree. In practice, the efficiency of industrial processes is low. For example, the most modern fossil-fuel power plant converts only about 40 percent of the energy in coal or oil into electricity; the rest of the energy escapes up the stack and into cooling water as heat, and large quantities of residuals in the form of ash and gases are produced. Thus pollution is the result of the operation of basic physical laws.

Why not simply use technological devices to control pollution? Unfortunately, for thermodynamic reasons there is no way that we can control many forms of pollution technologically. Waste heat is the prime example, but many others are also important, like fertilizer run-off or carbon dioxide from combustion. Their damage to ecosystems may be mitigated in some ways, but short of forgoing production altogether or adopting radically different technologies, there is simply no way to contain these high-entropy pollutants.*

Other forms of pollution are, of course, susceptible to technological control, *but even these pollutants cannot be controlled indefinitely,* for continued growth in industrial output must inevitably overwhelm any pollution-control technology that is less than 100 percent effective. For example, assuming output continues to grow at 5 percent (doubling period 14 years), reducing by 90 percent the quantity of pollution emitted and maintaining this level of efficiency in the future would buy only about 45 years of grace, for after that amount of time the absolute level of pollution would be the same as it is today; even a 99 percent level of control efficiency would extend this period of grace by only 46 years. Thus, with continued industrial growth, at some point pollution will reach dangerous levels under any conceivable control

---

*Uncontrollable waste heat resulting from the use of energy is probably the ultimate or limiting pollution problem, for at some point (still distant) global temperatures would rise to unbearable levels. This problem, along with the climatic effect of such pollutants as carbon dioxide and particulates, will be examined in detail in the discussion of energy in the next chapter.

regime. This point may not be very far away, for even the 90 percent level of overall control effectiveness would be difficult, if not impossible, to achieve in practice, and a considerable price in money and energy would have to be paid for it.

The Dilemmas and Costs of Technological Pollution Control

The same physical laws that make production and pollution two sides of the same coin also tell us that all technology can do is exchange one form of pollution for another. Worse, since energy must be used to "solve" the original problem there is bound to be an overall increase in both gross pollution and entropy. For instance, the catalytic converters now coming into use to control noxious automobile emissions themselves emit sulfuric acid mist and platinum particles, both of which are harmful to human health; the manufacture of the converters also occasions the production of pollution (as well as being an additional drain on our energy and mineral resources). Moreover, converter-equipped cars use more fuel. Of course, as is probably true in this case, a particular technological fix may nevertheless be desirable on economic, ecological, and esthetic grounds despite the overall thermodynamic loss, for the burden will presumably be shifted away from a sector that is harder pressed ecologically or whose degradation is more obnoxious to our senses and health. However, once the absorptive capacity of the environment has been used up, so that all sectors are about equally hard pressed, then simply converting pollution into a different form will no longer be a workable strategy. It is clear, therefore, that no matter how much money and energy are at our disposal, there must be some ultimate limit to our ability to control pollution without also controlling production.

However, we are unlikely to reach this ultimate ecological limit. Our supplies of money, energy, and other resources are not without limit, and at some point increased costs of pollution control seem likely to render further growth in production fruitless. For example, imagine a lake with a waste-absorption capacity of y units of residuals. (In fact, as we shall see later, "waste-absorption capacity" is an economist's concept that has no ecological validity.) A factory on the shore of this lake produces x units of a certain commodity and at the same time emits exactly y units of residuals. Although the factory now exercises no control over its pollution, the residuals it emits have not yet begun to degrade the quality of the lake water. However, suppose that demand for the commodity doubles, requiring either a second factory of like capacity or an equivalent addition to the old one. Without pollution control the lake would begin to die biologically because the $2y$ units of residuals resulting from $2x$ units of production would be twice what the lake can safely absorb. Thus pollution-control equipment that is 50 percent effective must be installed to reduce the residuals to a safe level. If demand doubles again, production of $4x$ units of the commodity produces $4y$ units of residuals to dispose of, and pollution control must now be 75 percent effective. It can easily be seen that if doubling of production continues, eventually 99+ percent effectiveness in pollution control becomes necessary.

Unfortunately, the energetic and monetary costs of pollution control increase exponentially rather than linearly. The cost of control that is 50 percent effective is often quite modest, but the cost of 90 percent effectiveness may be an order of magnitude higher or more. Automobile emissions are a typical example. Environmental Protection Agency estimates show that while it may take only about $25 per automobile to cut emissions 50 percent, nearly $400 per car is needed to achieve 95 percent efficiency (Kenward 1972). However, some cost curves rise steeply well before the higher levels of efficiency are attained; minor improvements even in the middle of the efficiency curve—say, from 45 to 55 percent—may double or treble the dollar costs of control. Although energetic costs tend not to rise as drastically as monetary ones, they are far from insignificant. Auto-emission controls decrease fuel economy by about one-third, but when all the other associated energy costs are considered—extraction, manufacture, maintenance, and so on—the total energetic cost of achieving the 95 percent level of control is probably double that of the 50 percent level. Thus there must clearly come a day when increasing marginal costs of production bring diminishing returns and finally no return at all.

Exactly how much pollution abatement will actually cost is a matter of some debate. In part, the different estimates reflect different assumptions about how serious the problem is and about how clean it is economically or esthetically desirable to be. If barely adequate pollution control were implemented today, the costs would probably be relatively modest, for we are roughly at the point where an overall 50 percent control level is the essential minimum. Once we had made the necessary capital expenditures, the increased operating expenses would amount to about 4 percent of the Gross National Product (GNP), and energy consumption would increase in about the same proportion (Hirst 1973). Altogether, considering both capital expenditure and operating costs, prices might have to rise 5 to 10 percent. However, this minimum level of pollution control is far less than most ecologists feel is desirable, for it would not restore the quality of already degraded ecosystems. But a genuine cleanup would be four times as expensive: according to the Organization for Economic Cooperation and Development, operating costs alone would amount to 16 percent of GNP (Anon. 1970). And these are only present costs; in time, as production grows, they will inexorably increase.

In fact, for a few critical commodities, like the automobile, the pollution-control costs have already reached staggering dimensions. According to Environmental Protection Agency figures, upgrading emission-control standards from the 83 percent level required in 1974 to the 95 percent level now required is likely to cost American consumers a total of $66 billion between 1976 and 1986 (*New York Times,* Jan. 26, 1973, p. 35). Another case in which the costs of pollution control have already begun to pinch severely is sewage treatment. Although a completely adequate technology exists, the capital costs and additional operating expenses are so high that nearly all small and medium-size communities cannot afford to install the equipment necessary to preserve water quality unless they receive massive subsidies, and even large cities probably cannot scrape up the enormous sums that they would need to upgrade their inadequate sewage and waste-water treatment facilities (Abelson 1974; Starr and Carlson 1968).

Thus the bills of past environmental neglect are beginning to come due, and the prices of some highly polluting commodities are starting to climb now. These developments foreshadow an eventual general rise in prices relative to incomes, as the necessity for pollution control begins to affect every phase of economic life from extraction to final consumption and disposal. Until now, for the most part, waste disposal and control of side effects has been provided "free" by the environment. Because pollution control makes us pay for something that used to cost us nothing and makes no contribution to productivity or product improvement, the net effect of increased commodity prices due to pollution control is a reduction of our purchasing power. Such price rises foretell the coming of the day when marginal costs of growth equal the gains and when growth will therefore cease.

A problem more serious than financial costs is that even where technological control is theoretically possible the technical problems may be extremely demanding. For example, as the above discussion suggests, despite intensive efforts we still have no really workable technological answers to smog-producing automobile emissions. Of course, future inventions may improve conditions greatly in many areas, but certain pollutants appear to be so intractable that effective technological control may never be achieved.

Radiation: The Insidious Pollutant

Radiation is the primary case in point; it is especially important to examine it in detail because so many appear to rely heavily on nuclear power generation both to circumvent the unacceptable pollution that would result from the expansion of conventional fossil-fuel power production and to compensate for the eventual disappearance of fossil fuels altogether. Moreover, radioactive compounds are only the most vicious of the wide array of dangerous chemicals we now discharge into the environment without any real knowledge of their ultimate potential for harm, so the case of radiation can serve as a model of the general long-term dangers of pollution and of the dilemmas confronting technological pollution control.

Radioactive isotopes, or radionuclides, are dangerous in extremely small doses. Exactly how small a dose is dangerous remains controversial, but numerous investigations have shown that even tiny doses have long-term adverse effects on human and ecological health. Thus experts agree that virtually any increase in radiation exposure is to be avoided.*

Why are radionuclides so dangerous? First, physical and biological concentration of radionuclides is a pervasive phenomenon. It can take the form of geographical concentration in lakes, estuaries, airsheds, or any other places where the circulation of air and water is restricted. Or it can take the form of physiological concentration in the body; for example, inhaled plutonium oxide particles tend to lodge permanently in the lung, so that they irradiate surrounding tissues intensely over a long period.†

Concentration can also take the form of biological magnification, which was described in the preceding chapter in connection with pesticides. Once a biologically active radionuclide enters a food chain, it is concentrated approximately tenfold at each higher trophic level. For example, the modest quantity of radioactive strontium 90 that falls on a pasture is concentrated in grass, in the cows that eat the grass, and lastly, in the child that drinks the cow's milk. Finally, for metabolic reasons radionuclides are concentrated selectively in particular tissues or organs. For example, strontium 90 mimics calcium in the body and is selectively concentrated in bones and bone marrow; iodine 131 is trapped by thyroid glands; cesium 137 concentrates in muscles and soft organs, like the liver and gonads. Thus radiation standards set in terms of averages or so-called whole-body doses may not be very meaningful no matter how stringently low the levels are set, for radioactive substances are certain to be concentrated in particular locations, and a dose of radiation that is well within the putative limits of tolerance on the average or over the whole body may nevertheless prove lethal.

---

*The controversy is over whether we are justified in extrapolating from tiny to miniscule doses the observed ill effects of radiation exposure. But such are the experimental difficulties of long-term, low-dose toxicology that convincing scientific answers may be unattainable (Sterling 1971; Weinberg 1972, pp. 209 211). For example, the number of mice or other experimental animals needed to support statistically valid inferences about the long-term effects of low doses of toxic materials would be astronomical; moreover, even if the mice showed no ill effects, there would still be no guarantee that humans might not suffer harm, because of the prolonged gestation and development periods that make our species especially susceptible to any form of environmental poisoning.

†Plutonium's peculiar properties and extreme toxicity make it by far the most virulent of all radioactive substances. This fact has generated a major controversy over the dangers of plutonium to public health, with the more extreme critics of the radiation standards-setting process claiming that the inhalation of as little as one particle may be sufficient to produce a significantly increased risk of contracting cancer.

In addition, there is no such thing as an "average" person for whom certain levels of radioactivity can be adjudged safe. An organism's vulnerability to damage by radioactivity (or any other pollutant for that matter) is directly related to the stage in its life cycle, as well as other accidents of personal history. The fetus is particularly vulnerable to poisonous compounds of any kind. Growing children, with their high metabolism, are also at higher risk, and the selectivity of a radioactive compound such as strontium 90, with its affinity for bone and marrow, can make it particularly devastating at certain developmental stages. Thus standards must take into account the basic ecological principle that the reproductive period is critical (E. P. Odum 1971, p. 108): what adults or the general public can tolerate may be very damaging to the young or others who are peculiarly vulnerable.

Furthermore, the effects of radiation combine synergistically with the effects of other pollutants or environmental stresses to produce disproportionate damage to bodies and ecosystems. Synergism occurs when two or more causes combine to produce a net effect that is greater than the mere addition of their separate effects. Thus, to use a well-known medical example, exposure to a modest quantity of either carbon tetrachloride or alcohol has no serious consequences, but simultaneous exposure to both causes serious illness or death. Many environmental problems are either produced by synergism (for example, photochemical smog) or aggravated by it (for example, poisoning by heavy metals). The theoretical basis for this was discussed in the last chapter: any environmental stress tends to simplify an ecosystem and therefore reduce its stability. Few studies have been done on this important problem. So many biologically active compounds have been released in such large quantities that neither the money nor the manpower is available for studying even a tiny fraction of the more important interactions. However, the deleterious effect of low-level radioactivity on the structure and functioning of ecosystems and on the human body is amply documented (Conney and Burns 1972; Wallace 1974; Woodwell 1969). In effect, radioactivity "softens up" a biological system, making it more vulnerable to disruption by other pollutants and stresses (and vice versa of course). The addition to our environment of such a potent stress as chronic radioactivity is therefore a matter for deep concern, even if no immediate effects can be observed.

It is, in fact, primarily the long-term effects of radiation exposure that are the most worrisome. Although the evidence for increased mortality or other delayed effects on the health of current generations due specifically to radionuclides already released is highly controversial, the general epidemiological evidence for increased mortality due to chronic low-level pollution over the last 50 to 100 years is incontrovertible. Epidemiologists agree that the sharp rise in death rates from emphysema, various forms of

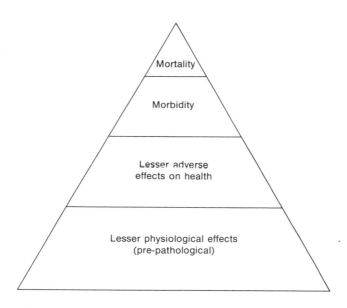

FIGURE 2-3.
Spectrum of biological responses to exposure to pollutants (after Newill 1973).

malignancy, and a number of other prominent modern ills is primarily due to pollution. Researchers estimate, for example, that between 60 and 90 percent of cancer cases (655,000 discovered each year in the U.S.) are caused by environmental factors, mostly chemicals (Maugh 1974). Moreover, mortality is only the tip of the iceberg; as Figure 2-3 illustrates, the overall damage to public health is likely to be far greater than mortality statistics alone indicate. In addition, the effect of stress on natural systems is non linear (so that doubling the dose more than doubles the resulting illness), and we can confidently expect future increments of low-level radiation (as well as other pollutants) to produce disproportionately more damage to human health than past levels of pollution. Even more important, however, is the fact that radiation is by far the most powerful mutagen known. The radionuclides released by man are therefore doubly dangerous; by exposing us to a level of radioactivity significantly higher than the so-called background radiation of the earth (which our evolutionary history has prepared us to withstand), they threaten the genetic integrity of unborn generations. It is entirely conceivable, for example, that today's adults and even today's children could escape serious harm but that our grandchildren would be grievously injured by current levels of radioactivity. In sum, despite the remaining areas of controversy, the long-term dangers from low levels of environmental radioactivity are essentially indisputable.

Finally, the threat from radionuclides is intensified by their persistence. For example, the half-lives of tritium, strontium 90, and cesium 137 are 12.4, 28, and 33 years respectively. Since the period of biological danger is roughly ten times the half-life, the tritium we release today will be a problem for 124 years and the other two will remain dangerous for about three centuries. A few other radionuclides have such long half-lives that they will be with us in virtual perpetuity. The most dangerous of these is plutonium 239 (half-life 24,000 years), which takes a quarter of a million years to decay to the point of harmlessness. (Plutonium is used in weapons and is part of the nuclear fuel cycle, either as a by-product or as a fuel.) Consequently, tiny amounts of radionuclides released year after year can over the not-so-very-long run build up a large inventory of dangerous radioactivity in ecosystems and human bodies. Thus, even if we and our immediate progeny escape harm, we could still saddle our more remote posterity with a lethal burden of radioactivity.

The conclusion is inescapable that the release of radioactive compounds to the environment in any but the most trivial amounts, made up preferably only of those compounds with very short half-lives and the least capacity for biological harm, carries with it some very serious risks. Anything less than virtually 100 percent control of radioactive emissions would be truly dangerous to the future biological health of the planet and its inhabitants, especially its human inhabitants.*

The Fallacies of Technological Pollution Control

The difference between radioactive pollutants and more ordinary pollutants is one of degree, not of kind. Radionuclides are particularly insidious and especially toxic, but many other pollutants behave in a similar way. In fact, the vast majority of the 20,000 or more synthetic chemical compounds released in any quantity are physically and biologically concentrated or magnified so as to attack certain body tissues selectively, have critical effects on reproduction or early development, react synergistically with other compounds or "soften up" natural systems, have potential or demonstrated delayed effects on ecosystems and human populations, are mutagenic, and are sufficiently persistent to allow long-term buildup of toxic material. Consequently, we already confront a public health and ecological dilemma of unknown but clearly rather large dimensions; adding additional quantities of pollution of whatever form can only worsen this situation.

For these reasons, ecologists and environmental health specialists find completely unacceptable the usual economist's position that we should use

---

*Whether we can in fact hold our release of radionuclides to trivial levels and still meet demands for energy is thus a critical question, to be considered in the next chapter.

the "natural assimilative capacity" of air and water, controlling pollution only when recreational or other economic "use values" will be damaged. This economic criterion can have ecological validity, if at all, only for non-synthetic pollutants like sewage and other organic materials that ecosystems are naturally adapted to handle in reasonable amounts. But it has no validity at all for synthetics like petrochemicals, to say nothing of radionuclides. Thus it may make ecological sense to speak of using the environment to dispose of natural organic compounds (providing, contrary to current fact, that they are not contaminated with synthetics), but these are the least dangerous and troublesome pollutants. By contrast, we must achieve virtually 100 percent control of the much more dangerous and troublesome synthetics; economics notwithstanding, there is little or no safe assimilative capacity for such unnatural compounds.

Furthermore, even if we were to allow that the environment could with impunity absorb a minimal quantity of these compounds, we could not determine the safe level of usage except by trial and error. Our ignorance about safe levels of toxic substances is paralleled, and in most cases exceeded, by our ignorance of what ecosystems can tolerate over the long term and of numerous other factors essential to administering an "economic" pollution-control strategy. Thus, whatever the technical means at his disposal, "the administrator [of pollution-control laws] is faced with a task that simply cannot be accomplished with our present knowledge" (Westman 1972, p. 772).

Nor are the technical means available to the administrator at all prepossessing. In fact, since so much pollution derives, like agricultural runoff, from "non-point" sources that can be controlled, if at all, only by truly heroic technological measures, even strict controls on readily accessible "point" sources of pollution may be almost fruitless. General urban runoff, for example, makes a contribution to water pollution about equal to that of sewage, yet there is no way to control it short of a massive hydrological reengineering of our cities (at astronomical cost); this makes spending $60 billion or more to meet the sewage-treatment standards of the Federal Water Pollution Control Act an "almost meaningless enterprise" (Abelson 1974).

In this light, our hypothetical pollution-control model now appears to be rather conservative. Not only are the original x units of residuals already an ecological and public-health threat (albeit probably not yet a large one), but because pollution is due as much to the general side effects of development as to the more easily controlled discharges of factory effluent, each doubling of production from the factory will more than double the incidence of pollution. Thus both the necessity for stringent pollution control and its expense will increase more rapidly than a simple proportional model would predict.

In sum, therefore, as a strategy of coping with the ever-increasing load of pollution that inevitably accompanies increased production, technological

---

Box 2–2. Ecological Pollution Control

From almost every point of view except short-term profitability, an ecological strategy of pollution control and waste recycling, involving as much as possible the planned use of natural recycling mechanisms, would be preferable to relying on expensive, energy-devouring, and failure-prone technological devices to perform these functions. Specifically, we should create waste-management parks—that is, portions of the environment deliberately set aside as natural recycling "plants" (E. P. Odum 1971, Chap. 16). In these parks, sewage and other controllable wastes capable of being naturally recycled (and not used directly as fertilizer on farms) would be sprayed on forests and grasslands, which would remove and reuse the nutrients that cause water pollution and return the purified water to aquifers. Forestry, fish ponds, grazing, and other means of exploiting the potentially productive energy contained in the recycled wastes would help pay the costs. This concept of pollution control is the most efficient and economical overall, for nature would do most of the work free, and productive use would be made of wastes. Also, because such a park would be in a quasi-natural state, it would serve ecologically as a protective zone, balancing more intensive development elsewhere.

---

pollution control has some very serious limitations. *Even granting, for the sake of argument, that engineers will come up with systems of pollution control that are, especially for radionuclides, virtually 100 percent effective, growth of production cannot continue forever.* In fact, if we try to double and redouble current levels of production in the United States, it seems very likely that we shall soon be restrained by rising costs of pollution control (at least for some commodities) and by rising levels of pollutants that we cannot control. Pollution control is therefore only a temporary tactic that will allow growth of production to continue for just a little longer; it is not a genuine solution to the problem of pollution, even under the most optimistic assumptions about our technological capacities and energy supply.

In addition, the basic problems of pollution control are at least as much political, social, and economic as technological. For example, it could well be that we shall come to accept levels of pollution and damage to public health that we would regard as intolerable today. If so, then growth could continue for somewhat longer, until mortality and morbidity grew to catastrophic proportions. Also, technological fixes are not ecologically optimal solutions to many important pollution problems. For example, attempts to dispose of urban organic wastes technologically are misdirected, for these wastes are really an unused resource that could be recycled as fertilizer. Unfortunately, recycling wastes, even though it is thermodynamically and ecologically rational and would probably save money and energy in the long run, is seriously impeded not only by the initial financial and energy costs of transition, but also by the numerous changes in our general way of doing

Unfortunately, such a strategy has limits. In the first place, the concept of the waste-management park assumes that resources are not so intensively exploited that we cannot afford to reserve large potentially productive areas for protective purposes. Moreover, as we have seen, many forms of uncontrollable pollution will remain despite any conceivable changes in pollution-control strategy. Also, materials like radionuclides and many synthetic chemicals, which are dangerous to introduce into ecosystems, will still have to be treated and controlled industrially. Thus the problems of technological pollution control discussed in the text may be insuperable. The only technological device that shows any real promise of overcoming them by making closed recycling/regeneration ecologically safe and economically feasible is the "fusion torch," in which the hot gases from a thermonuclear reactor would be used to reduce wastes to their constituent atoms for collection and reuse. However, the fusion torch has not yet been proven scientifically feasible; even if it is, it may not become practical for some time. Except possibly in the very long run, therefore, ecological pollution control can only mitigate pollution, not eliminate it; genuine control of pollution will oblige us to use fundamentally different types of technology (for example, solar energy) and to change social habits and values.

things that would be required to make this kind of ecological pollution control feasible (see Box 2-2). Finally, as we shall see later, it is rational to pollute and to avoid paying for pollution control. Thus even where control measures, technological or not, are readily available they usually cannot be implemented except within a general framework of political, social, and economic reforms.

BIBLIOGRAPHIC NOTE

The best general work on environmental limits is Paul and Anne Ehrlich's *Population, Resources, Environment,* an excellent basic text, but one that unfortunately lacks some of the textbook virtues (such as complete documentation, although the end-of-chapter bibliographies are ample and include hostile sources); in addition, there is a disproportionate emphasis on population. Nevertheless the work is authoritative, reasonably complete, and certainly the best starting point. (*Human Ecology,* by the Ehrlichs and John Holdren, is a less detailed and comprehensive version of the above.) Barry Commoner's *The Closing Circle* provides a good antidote to the Ehrlich's overemphasis on population, but Commoner goes to the extreme of making technology almost the sole villain. William Murdoch's *Environment: Resources, Pollution and Society,* a collection of original essays by leading experts, is almost on a par with the Ehrlichs' work overall and excels on a number of issues. *Resources and Man,* the National Academy of Sciences report edited by Preston Cloud, is equally authoritative but somewhat less comprehensive than Murdoch. Another collection of original essays that is even less comprehensive and well-integrated but that nevertheless contains several superb articles as well as the best discussion of the basic physical laws pertinent to environmental issues is *Patient Earth*, edited by John Harte and Robert Socolow.

There are many anthologies of articles on environmental topics. That edited by Holdren and Ehrlich, *Global Ecology*, is as good as any for its selection of reprints. However, Arthur Boughey's *Readings in Man, the Environment, and Human Ecology* is a more inclusive collection of articles that is designed to raise the philosophic as well as the practical questions of human ecology. An excellent book on the overall world "problematique" is Lester Brown's *World Without Borders*; Brown is a highly respected authority on the food and population problem, but he shows how inseparable that problem is from pollution and other issues, including politics and economics, which Brown understands better than most other writers on environmental problems. The reader seeking a good but very general introduction would find *Only One Earth*, by Barbara Ward and Rene Dubos, excellent and very readable. Written from a sweeping global perspective and meant to persuade, it was prepared as a keynote book for the U.N. Conference on the Human Environment at Stockholm in June 1972; it reflects contributions from virtually the entire world scientific community. Whichever work or works one chooses to read from the above list, *The Limits to Growth*, by Donella Meadows et al., remains essential; whatever the merits of its simulation model, the study obliges the reader to confront the environmental crisis as an ensemble of *interacting* problems, a need that does not come across strongly enough in any of the other works. Useful supplements (and a reminder that ecologists and many serious students of technology do not disagree substantially about the world problematique) are John McHale's *The Future of the Future* and *The Ecological Context*, which marshal a wide variety of evidence to convey better than any of the other works cited what it means to live in an age when the slope of the sigmoid curve is steepest (and must therefore begin to bend over). By contrast, Richard Meier's *Science and Economic Development* is much more optimistic about future technological advances that will expand the reserves of essential resources, but he assumes a degree of ecological and human flexibility that seems unrealistic, and I doubt that many would elect to live in the world of 50 billion people he depicts; nevertheless, exposure to this kind of technological optimism is a necessary prophylactic against failure of nerve and imagination. For a somewhat intemperate attack on the very idea of ecological limits that nevertheless brings up some important points, see John Maddox's *The Doomsday Syndrome*.

Readers interested in particular topics would do best to read the appropriate sections of the above works and follow up references on their own. However, I shall mention a few works that one might wish to consult directly. The National Academy of Sciences symposium published in *Rapid Population Growth* is comprehensive and probably the best place to start on this complex topic. Thomas Frejka's *The Future of Population Growth* is exceptionally valuable for the clear way in which it shows how varying assumptions about such things as fertility influence predictions of future population growth. On food, I suggest Lester Brown's *By Bread Alone*, an up-to-date and policy-oriented treatment of the whole food-population question as it relates to international politics and economics. However, Georg Borgstrom's somewhat older and more narrowly focused *The Hungry Planet* and *Too Many* are still to be recommended, for they are more detailed and useful than Brown's book in many areas. An important new work by Erik Eckholm, *Losing Ground,* covers desertification, erosion, salinization, deforestation, and other critical problems of land use and abuse that in the opinion of many qualified observers constitute the gravest long-term threat to mankind's ecological future. On mineral resources, Brian Skinner's *Earth Resources* is an excellent short introductory text that provides the basic background of geological knowledge needed to see the situation in perspective. For going deeper, Peter Flawn's *Mineral Resources* is first-rate. On pollution broadly defined, SCEP (Report of the Study of Critical Environmental Problems), *Man's Impact on the Global Environment,* is authoritative, definitive (as far as current knowledge permits), and full of hard information; in keeping with its title, it does not limit itself solely to industrial pollution, but covers the environmental impact of all human activities. The American Chemical Society's *Cleaning Our Environment* is an authoritative technical work on pollution narrowly defined. For those who prefer not to read a technical report, a readable work on man's impact on the environment that is still reasonably authoritative is Melvin Bernarde's *Our Precarious Habitat.* These works ought to be supplemented by Rene Dubos' *Man Adapting,* a superlative treatment of human biology in the context of modern civilization; it provides the background necessary for a full understanding of the insidious dangers that pollution poses to our health and genetic integrity. Naturally, on all these topics, one should not fail to search back issues of the recommended periodicals, especially *Science,* which has carried many excellent articles on food and population, and *Environment,* which has covered in depth most important aspects of pollution.

3

ENERGY, THE MANAGEMENT OF TECHNOLOGY, AND AN OVERVIEW OF ECOLOGICAL SCARCITY

ENERGY

Is Energy the Answer to Ecological Limits?

The need for ever more energy has been a constant theme in our discussion of food, minerals, and pollution. To expand production (in some cases even to maintain current levels of production) and to deal with emerging limits to growth in these sectors, we must have more energy. What are our energy resources and how rapidly are we consuming them? What new sources are under development? What are the dangers attached to current and future energy production? The last question is the crucial one. In one way or another, we can probably scrape up the energy needed to supply growing demand for a limited period of time, but the adverse consequences are likely to be serious, for due to the operation of basic physical laws, certain kinds of pollution are unavoidable and many of the other side effects of expanding our energy supply will be extremely problematic.

Rising Energy Demand and Inadequate Fossil Fuel Supplies

Demand for all forms of energy in the United States now grows at a rate of 5 percent and is projected to grow at a rate of 3.5 percent over the next three decades. Since at this latter rate demand doubles every twenty years, by the year 2000 Americans will need at least twice the energy they now use. Worldwide demand for energy is growing at a more rapid rate; most projections show quadrupled usage by the year 2000. Of course, all projections are based on certain assumptions, and it could be that conservation measures and more efficient technologies will make possible a greater output per unit of energy input or that rising energy prices will greatly constrain growth in demand. On the other hand, as we have seen, proposed solutions to our food, minerals, and pollution problems are more, not less, energy intensive; also, as we shall discuss in more detail later, all proposed solutions to the energy-supply problem themselves require large quantities of energy, so that energy production itself will become more energy intensive in the future. In fact, after declining steadily in the previous decades, the trend in the amount of energy needed to produce a given amount of Gross National Product has recently turned upwards (E. Cook 1971, p. 88). In addition, given the momentum of growth built into our economy and the apparent determination of politicians and the citizens who support them to meet the energy crisis by expanding supply rather than restricting demand, it seems safe to predict that U.S. demand will continue to increase for some time, and other countries evince a similar determination to continue their economic and energy-use growth. Thus it will take very great pressures to stop demand for energy from growing more or less as projected; doubled energy use in the United States and trebled world energy use by the year 2000 seem like fairly conservative projections.

World supplies of fossil fuels, with the exception of coal, are not adequate to meet expected levels of demand much beyond the turn of the century. Table 3-1 shows the pertinent figures for coal, petroleum, and natural gas. The figures indicate that the world is in the last decades of the fossil-fuel era. Even the relatively large supplies of coal will last only a century if demand continues to grow as projected; moreover, the exhaustion of natural gas and petroleum will force the substitution of coal for many uses, thus hastening the day when it too will be exhausted The U.S. supplies face roughly the same future as the world's. Domestic petroleum and natural gas will be effectively used up by about the year 2000 (as is common knowledge, the United States is rapidly becoming dependent on foreign supplies well in advance of this date).* However, like the world as a whole, the United States

---

*The political and economic implications of increased fossil-fuel imports by the United States and other developed countries are momentous, but they are beyond our scope here. (However, certain international implications will be dealt with in Chapter 7.)

Box 3–1.   Can We Meet Our Energy Demands with Coal?

Many believe that American energy needs can be met from our substantial reserves of coal until technological invention rescues us altogether from dependence on the stored-up energy in fossil fuels. Unfortunately, even if some of the technological improvements now on the drawing boards (for example, magnetohydrodynamic power generation) prove to be practical methods of extracting work from coal more efficiently and cleanly than we now do, burning more coal will still magnify our existing pollution and ecological problems. As we saw in the last chapter, perfect control of effluents is rarely possible (physically or economically), and in any event technological controls on the final step in production do nothing to mitigate ecological damage by all the other links in the chain from extraction to final use. The most striking and uncontrollable side effect of increased coal mining will be land devastation, for the most readily accessible and cleanest (that is, low-sulfur) coal must be strip-mined. The notoriously high human and ecological costs of strip-mining are blatantly evident in Appalachia, and now the West and Southwest are also under siege. Reclamation of strip-mined lands will always be inadequate. The well-known reluctance of mining companies to pay for it is the least of the problem. Even under the most favorable conditions the land is left sunken and maimed, and water quality as well as other environmental values are inevitably impaired. In the arid West, there is not enough water even to attempt restoration.

---

does have large quantities of exploitable coal (a static reserve of 660 to 2400 years, depending on assumptions).

Will new discoveries substantially alter this picture? Unfortunately, we confront the same problems that we observed earlier with respect to non-fuel resources. Owing to geological ignorance as well as differing assumptions about economics and the efficiency of extraction, resource estimation remains a fairly uncertain business. Nevertheless, certain theoretical limits are clear, and despite differing assumptions expert projections of how much remains to be recovered (which normally take into account the prospects for both new discoveries and greater efficiency of recovery) differ by no more than a factor of five (Gillette 1974b). It would therefore be wildly optimistic to believe that we could recover even ten times the quantities assumed in

TABLE 3-1
Expected lifetimes of important fossil-fuel resources

Fuel	Static reserve (years)*	Growth rate	Doubling time (years)	Exponential reserve (years)*
Coal	3100–5100	4.1%	18	118–132
Natural gas	30– 300	4.7%	17	19– 58
Petroleum	38– 110	3.9%	19	23– 43

Adapted from Meadows et al. 1974, Figure 5-1.
*The lower figure is for identified resources only; the higher figure includes hypothetical and speculative resources as well, and thus represents the likely upper ceiling of resource availability (see note on page 65 for definitions).

If all the coal mines, power stations, and liquefaction or gasification plants now projected were to be built, they would require for their operations, *exclusive* of reclamation, between three and four times the *total* amount of water now used throughout the entire country (McCaull 1974). But since water is generally coming into short supply, and farms and industry as well as ordinary individuals also need that water, it will clearly be impossible to operate all the projected mines and plants. Moreover, making coal the basis of our energy economy will require money, manpower, and a general logistical effort (for example, to build transportation facilities) of staggering dimensions, especially if we strive for a maximum of "energy independence" in the near future (A. L. Hammond 1974a). In addition, maximum coal development would also necessitate the destruction of good arable and forested land, sacrificing long-term agricultural productivity for short-term energy production.

In sum, the amount of coal we can reasonably expect to obtain and use is far less than the amount theoretically available in the ground. At best, coal offers only a temporary, stopgap satisfaction of our short-term energy requirements, and we shall very soon have to conceive and construct alternative technologies of energy supply that do not depend on such non-renewable and environmentally damaging fuels.

Table 3-1. As we have seen, given exponential growth (or even zero growth but continued high demand), such modest differences do not have much of an impact on the time to exhaustion. For example, the Alaskan North Slope field is a rather large discovery in historical terms, but even during its period of maximum production, it will supply less than 10 percent of U.S. demand for 10 to 15 years. Thus, just as with non-fuel resources, we cannot count on new discoveries to alter the basic supply picture. Moreover, here too we have skimmed the cream, and much of what we can reasonably anticipate finding will be ecologically perilous to exploit, as evidenced by the controversies over the Trans-Alaska Pipeline and offshore drilling in the Santa Barbara Channel. The exploitation of the remaining coal also presents problems. Since we have taken the easiest, cleanest, and best, we are left with coal reserves that are on the whole lower in energy content per unit volume, that are often "dirtier" (that is, higher in sulphur content, among other things), or that will require ecologically destructive techniques of extraction, like strip-mining (see Box 3-1 for a fuller discussion of coal).

The imminent exhaustion of petroleum presents a particular challenge to the current form of industrial civilization. Of course, coal can be turned into gas or liquid fuel. However, this merely transforms energy from one form to another (at a cost in pollution, energy, and money) and increases the rate at which coal supplies are used up. Oil shale and tar sand deposits are alternative sources of liquid hydrocarbons. The United States has substantial reserves of the former, Canada of the latter. However, obtaining liquid fuel from these resources will provoke the same kinds of problems that are involved in "burning the rocks" to get minerals: enormous quantities of rock must be mined, processed, and disposed of at high monetary, energetic, and environmental cost. In addition, water supply is a critical limitation on the production of oil from shale; the National Academy of Sciences has concluded that there will not be enough water to allow the hoped-for full-scale development of either Western coal or oil shale, much less both at the same time (Gillette 1973b). Furthermore, *high-grade* deposits of oil shale and tar sand are modest in extent, so that even without the limiting factors mentioned above, these unconventional sources of liquid hydrocarbons will never be able to take up the slack from falling petroleum production.*

The Potential and Peril of Nuclear Energy

Many regard the impending end of the fossil-fuel era with complacency, for they believe that, just as coal replaced wood when the latter became scarce and expensive, new technologies will take over the burden of energy production, allowing material growth to continue. In the relatively short term, say these optimists, we can turn to nuclear power. But is this the panacea many of its proponents claim? Indeed, is it even a safe and sensible stopgap source of energy until we develop thermonuclear fusion and other long-range possibilities? This is an exceedingly complicated and controversial issue. Leaving aside some of the more esoteric technical problems, let us examine the issues of uranium supply, heat, and safety, for these seem to be the main points of controversy.

Current reactor technology is extraordinarily inefficient. Although alternative technologies exist (for example, Canada's CANDU reactors), the so-called light-water reactors now predominantly used to generate power burn only naturally fissionable uranium 235, which constitutes only a tiny fraction of naturally occurring uranium (composed largely of uranium 238). The uranium 235 must be concentrated by laborious and highly energy-intensive techniques before it can be used for reactor fuel. Although minable uranium ore has not yet run out, proven reserves (especially of domestic uranium) will hardly last until 1985 if nuclear power generation grows as rapidly as projected.† Thus to keep pace with growing demand for energy a much more

---

* Very large quantities of marginal and submarginal oil shale exist in the United States and the rest of the world, but the quantity of fuel in these low-grade resources may be as little as ten gallons a ton, so that the monetary, energetic, and environmental costs of production would probably be prohibitive.

† Actual construction is lagging somewhat behind projections at present. Also, the old Atomic Energy Commission (AEC) estimate of 1000 multi-megawatt reactors by the year 2000 now seems dubious, because demand seems unlikely to grow as much as assumed. (On the other hand, nuclear plants, especially the larger ones, have yet to deliver power at their designed capacity; this shortfall will tend to raise the number of plants needed.) Nevertheless, if the demand for energy continues to grow, even if more slowly than in the past, and nuclear power is used to meet it, then a very large number of nuclear installations is implied.

intensive exploration and development effort will be necessary. Moreover, enrichment and other processing facilities, which are expensive and require a long time to construct, must also be rapidly enlarged to meet projected demand. Even if these short-term problems are surmounted, high-grade uranium ores are likely to last only about 30 years at projected rates of growth, so that if we were to continue to use light-water reactors beyond then, we should soon be forced to "burn the rocks" to obtain sufficient uranium. This may be feasible in terms of monetary cost, for the price of uranium ore has very little effect on the price of the electricity produced; however, such a uranium-mining regime would be exceedingly undesirable on health grounds, for the toxic radioactive mining wastes would be virtually impossible to control, and even large-scale coal mining would probably be preferable by comparison. In sum, it appears that fuel supplies for a vastly expanded conventional nuclear-power economy are problematic.*

Current light-water reactors are also relatively inefficient energy converters, transforming only about 30 percent of their fuel into electricity (as against the 40 percent achieved by the most efficient fossil-fuel plants). The rest of the potential energy in the uranium 235 is turned into waste heat. Because of this lower efficiency, as well as the absence of stack gases to carry off part of the heat, roughly twice as much waste heat must be disposed of in coolant water as with fossil-fuel plants. Since nuclear power plants are typically rather large, heat pollution has already become a problem at some sites; in a number of locations, plants have been required to build expensive cooling towers. If nuclear power generation in the United States grows as projected, by 1980 power generation by all methods will require cooling water equal to one-sixth the annual fresh-water runoff. However, seasonal variability would make demand during low-water seasons much higher in proportion to the water resources. If one-sixth of annual runoff is needed in 1980, one-half the runoff will be needed for three-quarters of the year. Looking further into the future, projections show that one-third to one-half of the annual fresh-water runoff may be needed by the year 2000 (Anthrop 1970, p. 40). With so many other demands being made on our water supply, it seems unlikely that we can continue to use rivers, lakes, and bays for cooling. Although cooling towers do preserve the biological resources of a river, lake, or bay from destruction, they are no real answer. The most efficient and least expensive require large amounts of water for evaporation, which can have marked effects on local climate. Closed-circuit air-cooled towers and the air-cooled gas-turbine reactors now being developed are less efficient and more costly; in addition, they too affect the microclimate (and the gas turbine requires soon-to-be-scarce helium for coolant). It is for these reasons (but also because of other siting difficulties

---

*The potential and peril of the so-called breeder reactor, which can burn the relatively abundant uranium 238, are discussed in Box 3-3.

being encountered by the nuclear industry) that many power companies are planning to build future plants offshore on the continental shelves, where a very large supply of cooling water is assured; however, given the number of plants that will have to be built—one every ten miles or so along the U.S. coast by the year 2000—the ecological consequences of the emitted heat alone may not be trivial (Carter 1974).*

However, safety is the most critical and controversial issue, making all the other problems connected with nuclear power pale into virtual insignificance by comparison. As we saw in Chapter 2, very small amounts of radiation can cause severe harm to ecosystems and people, particularly if the release of radioactive compounds continues for a number of years. Thus virtually perfect radionuclide-emission control is required. The boosters of nuclear power believe that we have the engineering and management capacity to achieve this level of control for large-scale nuclear power generation. The critics seriously question this. What are the chief points at issue?

Proponents of nuclear power reiterate tirelessly that nuclear generating plants are designed to keep emission during normal reactor operation low enough that any threat to public health is negligible. Even if one grants the validity of this position,† it is hardly decisive, for the very assumption of normalcy begs most of the important questions. Nuclear power generation can be safe *only* if the design and construction of the reactor are flawless; there are no accidents or operating errors; reactors, fuels, and other nuclear installations can be perfectly protected from acts of God, terrorism and sabotage, criminal acts, and acts of war, civil or foreign; and the release of radionuclides during all other phases of the fuel cycle (mining, processing, transportation, reprocessing, disposal) can be rigidly controlled. As critics point out, this is a rather alarming list of "ifs." In fact, the infant nuclear industry has run into trouble in almost every one of the areas mentioned.

Design has been far from perfect, and as plants are scaled up in size, design flaws become more apparent. For example, newer and larger reactors suffer from fuel densification; to cope with this problem the fuel-element cladding, which has given no trouble in smaller-capacity plants, may have to be completely redesigned to allow safe operation of the multi-megawatt plants that power companies now have on the drawing boards. Also, critics contend that the emergency core-cooling systems of current and projected light-water reactors are unproven and unsafe, so that if the primary cooling

---

*There is no escaping the waste-heat problem. The second law of thermodynamics says that the conversion of energy into work is inherently inefficient, so that waste heat will inevitably be generated (although some processes are more efficient than others). It is a corollary of the law that the efficiency of the conversion process depends directly on the availability of adequate cooling capacity.

†Many critics do not grant it, contending either that even the low-level, "normal" emissions from the few (approximately 56) and scattered plants now operating constitute a health threat or that they will once the number of plants increases substantially.

system should fail for any reason, the reactor core could melt down and burst the containment shell designed to prevent radioactivity from escaping into the environment. In addition, despite unusual attention to quality control, construction has not been flawless. Simple construction blunders are relatively common and in a few cases have caused significant releases of radioactivity. Moreover, numerous operating errors and accidents have occurred. Fortunately, none of these resulted in the release of dangerous amounts of radioactivity, but this seems to have been more a matter of luck than of skill. Indeed, considering the inevitable fallibility of the people who must design, build, and operate nuclear plants, along with the potential consequences if something should go wrong, as well as the large numbers of installations projected, one must seriously question how safe a nuclear-power economy can be expected to be. In fact, the probability of an incident involving significant release of radioactivity due to accident or error may become uncomfortably large by the end of the century (see Box 3-2 for detailed discussion). To this kind of partially calculable form of risk we must add the almost incalculable but nevertheless manifestly far from negligible hazards of earthquakes or other acts of God and deliberate sabotage or destruction of nuclear plants by madmen, criminals, terrorists, revolutionaries, or representatives of hostile powers. Thus, even if perfection in design, construction, and operation were to be achieved, there would still be no way to guarantee containment of radioactivity in nuclear power plants.

Less spectacular but more insidious (and in the long run probably more serious) is the cumulation of minor releases of radionuclides from all the other phases of the fuel cycle. Such releases are in fact rather common today. For example, so-called planned release of long-lived radionuclides during fuel reprocessing now occurs in amounts that would be intolerable if larger quantities of fuel were to be handled (Lindop and Rotblat 1971; Micklin 1974). In addition, radioactivity from uranium mine tailings is already a problem in some localities; since the tailings are easily carried away by wind and water, the more uranium production is expanded the greater and more widespread the environmental menace. As pointed out above, this will be especially true if very low-grade ores are mined.

Disposal of other nuclear wastes is an even more challenging problem. The spent fuels and other radioactive residuals of the fuel cycle must be perfectly contained and guarded for the millennia it will take for their radioactivity to decay into harmlessness. (Nuclear power plants that have reached the end of their thirty- to forty-year useful life will also present such nasty decommissioning problems that they too will probably have to become perpetually guarded monuments to the age of nuclear power generation.) Nuclear authorities are now casting around for a viable long-term solution to this problem. Until now, as a temporary measure, wastes have been stored in holding tanks. However, continual leakage has occurred, and it is clearly

Box 3–2. Nuclear Safety: The Big Gamble

Despite far greater than average attention to operating safety and fail-safe design, the nuclear industry has been plagued by a series of serious failures and accidents. For example, there were approximately 850 "abnormal occurrences," great and small, reported to the AEC between January 1972 and June 1973 (Nash 1974); in late 1973, there were two major accidents at the AEC's own facilities—the explosion of an experimental gas centrifuge at the Oak Ridge National Laboratory and serious leakage from waste-storage tanks at the Hanford Reservation; and in March 1975, a fire at the TVA's Browns Ferry plant almost led to a meltdown. Thus, there is considerable room for improvement in practice, if not in design. Also, critics find much to argue with in official studies of nuclear reactor safety. The recent Rasmussen Report, apparently designed to lay public fears to rest once and for all, claims that the probability of a "less serious" accident—defined as one involving "somewhat in the neighborhood of 200 fatalities" (as well as major releases of radionuclides to the environment)—is only one in a million per reactor year (that is, one chance in a thousand of such an accident each year if 1000 reactors are in operation). However, the Environmental Protection Agency and even some friends of nuclear power (for example, Rose 1974b) believe that such an accident may be ten times more likely than the report, which is based on a controversial method of estimation, makes out. In that case, the chances of such a serious accident would be one in a hundred per year if 1000 reactors were in operation.

However, all numerical estimates are seriously questionable, for there is simply *no* valid scientific or statistical basis for making assurances about the future safety of nuclear reactors. Reactor systems are so complex and the number of possible interactions—human, mechanical, chemical, and biological—is so large that all the estimates are only more or less informed guesses. A meaningful estimate of probabilities would have to be based on actual operating experience. Although experience so far is too brief to provide a statistically significant data base for estimating the probability of future accidents, the high incidence of failure in the past does not inspire confidence, even though no single incident has been really serious in terms of environmental contamination or loss of life. In addition, there is almost no operating experience with the large, high-power plants now being constructed, but what little there is suggests that they will pose more problems than smaller, less powerful reactors. Moreover, in order to meet future demand, reactors can no longer be produced with the painstaking craftsmanship that has prevailed until now; they must be virtually

much too expensive and risky a method for dealing with the large quantities of nuclear waste anticipated for the future. Unfortunately, all the alternatives explored so far seem to have serious drawbacks. One of the most attractive schemes—solidifying the wastes and placing them in unworked salt mines in Kansas—had to be abandoned when the dangers of water percolation became apparent. Some of the other proposals have an air of desperation about them—for example, using Antarctic glaciers as repositories (extreme transportation hazards; serious risk of upsetting the delicate heat balance of the glaciers, with potentially momentous climatological consequences) or rocketing the wastes into space (staggering expense; potentially grave consequences of rocket failure). Yet large amounts of waste are inevitable if nuclear power is used to supply the expected demand for elec-

mass produced, and it seems questionable whether even past standards of quality control can be maintained under these conditions, as any buyer of mass-produced goods will surely understand. Finally, bald statements of probability obscure the unique social risks attached to nuclear accidents. It may be true, as boosters like to assert, that a given individual is more likely to be struck by lightning than to die as a direct result of a nuclear accident, but this comparison of merely personal risks ignores almost all the special ecological and societal perils of radioactivity—like chronic, long-term ecosystem damage and adverse genetic effects.

All things considered, nuclear power appears to be a big gamble. That it may well be a bad one is indicated by the refusal of commercial insurance companies, bastions of prudence and the careful calculation of risks, to cover the nuclear industry until they were assured of drastically limited liability and government reinsurance through the Price-Anderson Act. This act limits payment for nuclear accidents to $560 million, even though the AEC's own 1965 update of a study conducted in 1957 showed that a catastrophic accident involving a medium-size 800-megawatt reactor (1300-megawatt ones are planned) might cause up to $17 billion in property damage as well as 45,000 deaths and 74,000 injuries.

Fortunately, at least one past problem seems to be on the way to solution. Although the AEC was charged with protecting the public from nuclear risks, it chose instead to concentrate on nuclear power development. In the process, it deliberately bypassed tough safety questions and, in combination with its military, congressional, and industrial allies, tried to discourage effective public participation and debate on safety issues, suppress relevant public information, and propagate misinformation about nuclear safety (Lewis 1972; Metzger 1972). However, relentless exposure of its failings and the shock of the 1973-74 energy crisis combined to inspire the Energy Reorganization Act of 1974, which split the AEC into two new agencies—an Energy Research and Development Agency (ERDA), with broader responsibilities for energy development than the old AEC, and a Nuclear Regulatory Commission (NRC), which will be responsible solely for nuclear safety and should therefore not suffer the same conflicts of interest as the old AEC. The NRC has proven more cautious and evenhanded than the AEC, and ERDA has given new emphasis to alternatives to nuclear power. Thus, although the power of the old nuclear establishment is far from broken, it appears that the issue of radiation safety will no longer be the political and bureaucratic stepchild it has been for the last three decades.

tricity, and these wastes must go somewhere that is biologically and ecologically safe. To date, despite 30 years of research, no acceptable solution has been found.

In sum, there are many difficult and for the most part unsolved safety, security, health, and pollution problems connected with the use of nuclear technology, present and planned (see Box 3-3 for a discussion of the so-called breeder reactor).* The resolution of these problems is not assured, no matter how much money and effort is expended. Indeed, some of them, like

---

*Let us not overlook the extent to which the diffusion of "peaceful" nuclear technology has tended to promote the proliferation of nuclear weapons, and therefore the likelihood of atomic warfare, the ultimate nuclear threat to humankind.

Box 3–3. The Special Problems of the Breeder Reactor

The extreme inefficiency of conventional nuclear reactors and the prospect of using up relatively high-grade uranium deposits in a few short decades has spurred the development of the breeder reactor. Whatever its particular features, a breeder reactor uses plutonium (instead of relatively scarce uranium 235) for fuel; because it simultaneously converts a surrounding blanket of comparatively abundant uranium 238 or thorium into more plutonium, it in effect creates more fuel than it burns. Obviously, this essentially eliminates any concern that uranium supplies might run out, except in the very long term, and markedly diminishes the possible side effects of uranium mining. Unfortunately, intensified pollution and safety vices go along with these virtues.

First, the technical design problems are much more formidable: liquid sodium instead of water must be used for coolant, greater heat and neutron flux impose much greater stress on materials, and so forth. In fact, although Britain, France, and the U.S.S.R. appear to be further advanced, the U.S. breeder-reactor program has encountered severe technical setbacks. The only plant yet built and operated in the United States outside of a research laboratory was plagued by a series of accidents and problems; it never generated more than a token amount of electricity and was closed down permanently after an investment of over $135 million. Second, the extreme toxicity of plutonium means that the health hazards of a reactor accident or a

---

heat pollution, must eventually become insurmountable barriers to further expansion. Also, as the size of the nuclear plant grows, the overall problem will become much more complex and demanding, so that the change in quantity will produce a qualitative change in the nature of the problem. The solution of this overall nuclear problem will impose very heavy management burdens and other social costs, important matters that will be explored later in this chapter and in Part II. All in all, nuclear power does not appear to be the panacea that some of its proponents claim. Indeed, it does not even seem very attractive as a short-term stopgap. It is not at all clear that the overall balance of risks favors nuclear power over coal power, especially if the same amount of research money and effort were to be applied to the latter as to the former. How, for example, should we trade off between chronically dirty and destructive but only mildly poisonous coal and a source of energy that may be "normally" much cleaner but is extremely toxic and devilishly unforgiving of the slightest human failure? It is at best a Hobson's choice, one of many similar dilemmas that material growth has thrust us up against.

Fusion Power: Infinite Potential versus Problems and Limitations

In theory, controlled thermonuclear fusion constitutes a potentially infinite source of energy. Many therefore regard it as *the* long-range answer to all problems of energy supply. However, although fusion is undeniably attractive on many grounds, it is by no means free of problems and limitations.

release of radioactive materials at other stages in the fuel cycle are greatly magnified. Third, unlike currently used nuclear fuels, plutonium is potential weapon material; thus many exceedingly thorny security issues are raised by the plutonium fuel cycle.

In sum, although more sparing of fuel, the breeder is even more problematic and dangerous than the conventional light-water reactor. In addition, costs are escalating rapidly and the economics of the breeder are beginning to look questionable (Cochran 1974). Thus the breeder program has come under increasingly sharp attack, not just by environmental organizations and the Environmental Protection Agency, but also by some of those who are generally friendly to nuclear power (for example, Rose 1974b). Since the earliest date for commercial acceptance of the breeder by power companies has slipped to 1987, it will be several decades thereafter before it can produce a significant proportion of our projected power requirements (by which time less problematic and dangerous alternatives like geothermal and solar power could be developed, say the critics); and since uranium supplies will be adequate for conventional nuclear power for some time, the future of this unproven and hazardous technology looks more and more clouded. In fact, as one of its first major acts, the Energy Research and Development Agency announced in mid-1975 that it would no longer push for commercial power from the breeder in this century and that it would henceforth give at least as much priority to the development of solar energy and fusion.

Above all, no one has yet demonstrated its practical feasibility, even in the laboratory, despite over twenty years of sustained international effort. Thermonuclear reactions take place in plasmas of ionized gases at temperatures and pressures comparable to those found in the sun and other stars. These plasmas cannot be physically contained, so confinement by magnetic field and other difficult and esoteric techniques have been employed in an effort to attain the levels of temperature and pressure necessary for a continuous reaction. Progress toward this objective has been made, especially in the last few years, but the best achievements still fall considerably short of what is needed. Most scientists working in this field are confident that in some fashion the laboratory breakthrough will eventually come, but the history of research in the field is that the solution to each particular problem either reveals a worse one behind it or proves to be incompatible with the solutions to other particular problems. Even optimists concede that breakthrough is unlikely before 1980, at the earliest (Rhodes 1974). In any event, laboratory feasibility is only the first of a very long and expensive series of steps in research and development that will be required to make fusion a practical achievement. The engineering problems to be solved are enormous; temperatures and pressures of stellar intensity are far beyond anything technologists and engineers have hitherto tried to tame. Therefore, even if laboratory feasibility were to be demonstrated tomorrow, it would likely be very close to the end of the century, at the earliest, before the first regular fusion power plant went into operation and an additional twenty years before fusion generated any sizable percentage of total energy needs. Thus the promise of fusion power—and it is so far just a promise—will be realized, if at all, only well into the next century.

Even if fusion power becomes practical, however, it will not be without problems. Although a virtually infinite supply of fuel is claimed by fusion enthusiasts, in fact the reactors now being invented will fuse deuterium and tritium, which must be produced from lithium.* Although deuterium is so abundant in seawater that it will be for all practical purposes infinitely available, the lithium is relatively scarce, and lithium 6, the isotope needed for the fusion reaction, is scarcer still. Thus, once readily exploitable lithium ores have been used up, it will have to be obtained by "burning the rocks." In sum, therefore, the problem of fuel supply will not necessarily be abolished by fusion power generation.

Moreover, the consequences for the environment and public safety are still very much in question. The absence of fission products makes fusion inherently much cleaner and safer than fission, but some tritium releases are inevitable; if total power generation capacity is large, this would have serious consequences.† Also, each power plant will itself contain a substantial inventory of radioactive materials. In addition, if one of the many complex engineering devices should catch on fire or otherwise fail, explosive releases of energy could occur. Finally, fusion reactors will still generate large quantities of waste heat. Thus, the proponents' claim that fusion will be pollution-free is doubtful.

An additional question concerns the potential net energy yield of a fusion reactor economy. First—just as with ordinary nuclear technology, only more so—starting up a fusion power system will require an enormous expenditure of energy. Containment and heating of the plasma require great quantities of energy; especially if the efficiency of the fusion reactors proves to be less than the hoped-for 60 percent, a very large proportion of the power output of each reactor will have to be used just to keep the reactor in operation. Producing deuterium fuel from seawater will also require expenditure of energy. Finally, any conceivable form of thermonuclear-reactor technology will demand in addition to lithium large quantities of scarce minerals such as helium, vanadium, and niobium, many of which are not produced domestically; eventually these too would have to be extracted from rock at high

---

*Fusion reactions which are not dependent on lithium are theoretically possible, but since they are up to 100 times more difficult to sustain, they are likely to remain impractical for many more years.

†Although tritium, one of the radioactive isotopes of hydrogen, is less hazardous than some radionuclides, it is still extremely dangerous both because it cannot be fully contained—at least .03 percent of the total inventory in reactors would escape each year (Metz 1972)—and because it is especially apt to be taken up and concentrated in living systems (where its half-life of 12 years makes it dangerous for over a century).

cost in energy. Thus the net yield of energy after all costs are counted may be very low.

In sum, the Promethean attempt to provide mankind· with inexhaustible stellar fire is a bold enterprise that may bring great benefits if it succeeds. But given the extraordinary challenges, the development of fusion power may take several generations, if indeed it proves possible at all. And the undeniable promise of thermonuclear fusion should not be allowed to obscure the many problems and limitations that are evident even today.

Geothermal Power: Tapping the Heat of the Earth

By contrast with fusion and the breeder, the technology for large-scale generation of electricity from geothermal resources is essentially in hand. Moreover, given due care, the environmental consequences of exploitation are comparatively benign. However, it is still very uncertain how much of the theoretically available heat in the earth can be tapped in practice (efficiencies are low) and how soon significant amounts of power can be obtained. Estimates for the United States differ by several orders of magnitude, but assuming appropriate effort, as much as 10 percent of the total energy supply in the year 2000 could come from geothermal power. What are some of the uncertainties?

Natural steam and hot-water fields have been exploited for power production for some time in a number of countries. However, such natural geothermal reservoirs are both geographically restricted and too limited in capacity to affect the overall energy-supply picture in any major way, either domestically or internationally. Thus, to produce substantial amounts of power, artificial geothermal reservoirs must be created by drilling down to areas of high heat flux in basal rocks, fracturing the rocks, pumping in water to be heated, and then extracting the heat from the resulting steam. The technology for this is becoming available, and early experiments with the technique are promising, but much more research, development, and exploration must be done before a clear picture of the extent of geothermal resources emerges.

The exploitation of geothermal power is far from pollution-free. The steam or hot water used to produce power almost always contains noxious gases and corrosive compounds; many wells emit significant quantities of radionuclides. Thus environmentally compatible ways of disposing of used steam and water will have to be found. In theory this seems feasible (for example, by reinjecting the wastes into the earth), but more practical experience is needed. Also, since even artificial geothermal reservoirs must be located in geologically suitable areas, power will be produced at some distance from markets; in the United States, for example, the most promising areas are in the relatively unpopulated West, so that the monetary and environmental costs of power transmission (as well as the attendant energy losses) may be considerable.

In sum, geothermal power has a significant potential, but only extreme optimists foresee this form of energy constituting more than 20 percent of supply. In any event, more effort and money than is currently being invested will be required for geothermal power to contribute significantly in the short and medium terms, which is when the problem of inadequate fossil-fuel supplies must be confronted.

Solar Power: The Ultimate "Fuel"

In the final analysis, almost all the energy available to man is solar: fossil fuels are simply the stored legacy of past photosynthesis; the fissionable elements were formed in a solar furnace; and a thermonuclear fusion reactor is essentially a miniature sun. However, "solar power" ordinarily refers to the use of the direct energy of the sun's rays by solar heat collectors or photovoltaic conversion cells and to the exploitation of the indirect results of solar heating—falling or moving water, wind, natural heat traps, and current photosynthetic production.

Directly or indirectly, solar energy powered all the achievements of human civilization preceding the Industrial Revolution, and it would appear to be an almost perfect source of energy for mankind's long-term future. However, solar energy is diffuse, unavailable at night, unequally distributed around the globe, variable with season and weather, and available only in limited quantities during any given period. Moreover, economies of scale are extremely small, so that the capital costs of direct collection for more than local use are likely to be quite high relative to other sources of power. Thus solar energy does not seem to recommend itself as a source of power for a highly centralized technological civilization, regardless of its level of technical sophistication, as readily as the other forms of energy supply considered above.

The diffuseness of solar energy means that it must be collected over wide areas if large amounts are required; assuming a low but reasonable 10 percent efficiency, producing 1000 megawatts of electric power (enough for a U.S. city of about 750,000) would require 42 square kilometers of collection area, an area about 4 miles square (Hubbert 1969, p. 207). Nevertheless, the absolute amounts of energy available are quite large—the energy in all of earth's stock of fossil fuels is equivalent to the sunlight that falls on the earth in about four days (Ayres 1950, p. 16)—and according to some optimistic calculations, we could expect to supply almost all of our needs in the year

2000 by turning only 5 to 10 percent of unused desert land into collection areas.* Until recently, it was thought that there was no way to gather solar energy on such a large scale that was practical but not also hopelessly expensive. However, as other sources of energy have come to be increasingly problematic, a number of ingenious (but still unproven) methods of collecting solar energy at a 10 to 30 percent level of efficiency with either relatively inexpensive, low-technology components or relatively costly and high-technology components (still uninvented for the most part) have been devised. Nevertheless, it is clear that any large-scale substitution of solar for fossil or nuclear energy would require enormous capital outlays, and that solar power's forte is small-scale local usage.

The variability of solar energy means that engineers will have difficult storage and transmission problems to solve. In addition, there is the problem of converting heat or electrical energy into gaseous or liquid fuels.† Again, tentative answers to some of these problems are emerging. For example, advances in various unconventional methods of energy storage and transmission like superconducting magnetic fields, thermal salts, and flywheels, as well as further developments in more conventional methods like battery storage, are confidently anticipated. However, the most likely avenue of future development is toward the "hydrogen economy," in which solar energy would be used to dissociate the oxygen and hydrogen atoms in water. These gases could then be burned immediately to produce heat for power generation, stored for use during periods when direct use of solar heat was impossible, or transmitted to central power stations in less sunny areas. (Another possibility, for which hydrogen is in many ways more appropriate, is home or neighborhood electric power generation with fuel cells, a promising technology now being developed.) At the same time, the hydrogen would also serve as an all-purpose fuel for non-electric needs.

Some thus foresee a solar/fuel-cell/hydrogen economy in the future. Such use of hydrogen would be relatively non-polluting, for when the hydrogen recombines with oxygen at the time of combustion, the by-product should be mostly water vapor (but hydrogen peroxide pollution is a danger). However, this vision remains speculative, and many difficult problems will have to be solved. For example, as the Hindenburg disaster showed, hydrogen is exceedingly and explosively flammable. In addition, it is very troublesome to

---

*The amount of solar energy *theoretically* available is staggering: each year the earth receives about 5000 Q (5 × 10^{18} BTU) from the sun; by contrast, man until now has consumed only about 15 Q of fossil fuel. However, most of this solar energy is not directly available to man, for it is used to keep the biosphere operating. In addition, conversion efficiency and other technological issues remain nebulous. Thus there is considerable controversy over exactly how much usable solar power can be made available, either ultimately or by certain target dates.

†This will also be necessary with nuclear power generation once fossil fuels run out, for only about 25 percent of our current energy needs are supplied in the form of electricity.

handle or store, and it causes metal to become brittle.* Moreover, although fuel cells are perhaps the most attractive way to use hydrogen, they are an unproven technology and in their current form require expensive and increasingly scarce platinum or other rare metals for catalysts. Nevertheless, none of these problems appear insuperable, so that some form of the hydrogen economy should be realizable. As suggested by the possibility of local power generation from fuel cells, what is not yet clear is how readily this kind of solar power lends itself to the current mode of industrial civilization.

The indirect uses of solar energy raise this problem in a more acute form. This is even true of water power, which was one of the earliest methods of large-scale production of electricity. Unfortunately, potential sites for large-scale hydroelectric power generation are limited, and water power now supplies only about 5 percent of U.S. demand for electricity. Output could probably be doubled at great capital expense, but only if Americans were willing to exploit every substantial source of hydroelectric potential (for example, by damming the Grand Canyon).† Furthermore, although hydroelectric power is comparatively non-polluting and in theory eternally renewable as long as the sun continues to drive the evaporation cycle, large dams do cause significant ecological disruption, and they also have finite and often rather short lives—from 50 to 250 years—because silt fills in the lakes they impound. Thus we can probably expect a long-term decline in large-scale hydroelectric power production. However, there is considerable potential for decentralized local and individual power production from falling and moving water with small water-turbine generators and other sophisticated modern descendants of the old water-power technology. Of course, the absolute amounts of power to be generated in this fashion are relatively small and the potential varies greatly with locality, so that small-scale power production from water is not an answer to the needs of an energy-intensive industrial civilization.

Wind power can have a substantial local impact in many areas, either from small windmills and rotors or from larger windmills operated by local utilities in favored locations. More grandiose schemes have been proposed for large-scale regional and national power production from wind. However, it seems unlikely that the Great Plains or our coastal waters will be filled with giant windmills to keep steel mills going in Pittsburgh; for one thing, the sacrifice of food production and other goods would probably be unacceptable. Nevertheless, certain large-scale uses of wind power can be expected with some certainty. For example, sail power is already so close to

---

*For these reasons, a number of technologists suggest that we use hydrogen in the safer and more stable form of methanol or ammonia.

†Unexploited hydroelectric potential in other parts of the world varies greatly. In developed countries, however, hydroelectric potential is for the most part rather fully utilized; in the less developed regions, only Africa has a very large unexploited hydroelectric potential.

being economic for carriage of bulk cargo across the North Atlantic that a West German syndicate has embarked seriously on the construction of an ultramodern clipper ship.

Natural heat traps or other natural sources of solar heat can also be exploited in some areas. For example, in the tropics hot brine ponds or lagoons can serve as natural solar collectors; oceanic thermal gradients can also be tapped for power (especially in combination with maricultural schemes) in tropical areas where the difference between surface and deep temperatures is the greatest; even the energy (which is geophysical as well as solar) in ocean currents like the Gulf Stream can in theory be exploited with underwater "windmills." However, all of these seem likely to be small or rather localized sources of power.

Finally, we can grow renewable energy supplies photosynthetically. Basically, this would mean establishing "energy plantations"—usually of trees, but ordinary hay, sugarcane, sunflower plants, and even kelp are sometimes proposed—to grow raw materials that can be burned directly to produce heat for power generation or used to produce fuels like methanol as well as most of the other products (for example, plastics) now obtained from coal and petroleum. This approach to solar power has many advantages over artificial solar collection: not only does nature do most of the work free at minimal capital expenditure, but unlike solar collector farms, forest lands can be used for recreation, waste disposal (in the waste-management parks discussed in Box 2-2), and environmental protection. Also, wood ash can be recycled as fertilizer. Even at today's prices, using wood in this fashion is not much more expensive than using fossil fuel. The obvious problems, however, are air pollution from wood burning, conflict with other uses for wood, and demand for space (leading to potential conflict with needs for food and fiber or, at least, living room). Thus an energy economy based primarily on wood would be a frugal one requiring rather careful management. A clear danger is that energy plantations will not be prudently managed and that out of hunger for energy mankind will instead fall back into the ancient pattern of reducing forested mountains to bare rock skeletons. In fact this pattern is prominently visible today in many poorer countries, where the populace ravages the land for wood fuel.

In short, there are definite limits to the use of solar energy in large quantities. At some point, collection facilities, natural or artificial, will interfere with the use of land for growing food, for human habitation, and for environmental protection (if artificial collectors are used). Artificial collection facilities will be costly not only in capital, but also in materials. In addition, although in principle solar power, unlike other forms of power generation, would not add an extra input of heat to the natural heat balance of the globe, in practice the process of taking energy from one area for use in another would create local and regional heat imbalances; moreover, with

---

Box 3-4. The Multiplex Energy Economy of the Future

It seems likely that in the future we shall make eclectic use of many different energy sources, from the age-old to the ultra-modern, in a "multiplex energy economy." The centralized power production characteristic of today's advanced industrial civilization is encountering various types of limit. Old fuels are running out or have become too noxious to burn; some new sources of energy, like nuclear fission, are ecologically dangerous and socially problematic; and other promising new forms of energy supply, such as geophysical or solar power, cannot supply enough power by themselves, much less in ways that fit readily into the current system. In short, energy from all sources (even fusion) will no longer be as cheap and abundant as it has been, and the resulting physical scarcity and rising cost of energy is likely to create strong pressures toward (1) greater decentralization and energy self-sufficiency and (2) intensive exploitation of every conceivable source of energy (combined with scrupulous conservation).

The possibilities for greatly increased energy self-sufficiency are virtually endless—roofs can hold solar water heaters and small windmills; household sewage and other organic wastes can be used to produce methane gas; small water turbines in local streams can produce electricity; local underground heat can be tapped; and so on. The do-it-yourself home techniques that are now being pioneered by "soft" technologists (see Box 3-7) thus seem to foreshadow at least one aspect of our future energy economy, even if, as will probably be the case, considerable quantities of electricity and other forms of energy will still be centrally generated to run cities, factories, mass transit, and the like.

In addition to considerable self-sufficiency in energy, we can probably expect energy sources to be much more varied and localized than they now are. For example,

---

major development of artificial solar heat collection the earth's albedo (reflectivity) would be changed, and the global heat balance would be substantially affected because solar radiation formerly immediately reflected back into space would be absorbed and added to the global heat inventory.* Finally, conversion to exclusive dependence on solar energy would clearly require major changes in our technology and economy in the direction of greater frugality and decentralization (see Box 3-4). Thus there are indeed limits to how much solar energy we can use without upsetting biospheric processes or compromising other desiderata, especially if the attempt is made to use solar power to run an industrial economy instead of a radically decentralized one finely adapted to localized natural sources of solar energy. Nevertheless, the more closely that solar power is examined by scientists and engineers the more its long-term technical advantages over fossil fuels and, above all, nuclear fission appear to shine forth. The advantages to society in terms of ecological health and technological simplicity are even more striking.

---

*Using orbiting collector arrays to gather solar energy and beam it down to earth, as is sometimes proposed, would result in an even larger unnatural input of heat to the biosphere.

the Great Plains may depend heavily on wind; New England on water, as it did in Colonial times; California on eucalyptus-tree energy plantations and offshore kelp beds; Florida on ocean currents or thermal gradients; and so on. No safe source of energy will be allowed to go unexploited. Even tidal power could be of some importance in certain geographically and ecologically favorable areas. It is also clear that wastes of all kinds—industrial, commercial, residential, agricultural, silvacultural—will be much more widely burned to produce heat or distilled to produce gaseous and liquid fuels, making a modest but locally significant contribution to the energy supply. Also, draft animals seem likely to make a comeback, even though their upkeep often requires heavy energy expenditure, for in many cases the alternative to draft animals is human labor.

In sum, we seem headed for a kind of multiplex, two-tier energy economy in which centralized, industrial power production will support certain key sectors but in which individuals and localities, employing a curious combination of pre-modern and post-industrial means, will be more or less self-sufficient in the energy needed for basic subsistence. Also, because no one source of energy will be able to satisfy all needs, we also seem headed toward a much more heterogenous, diversified energy economy characterized by local specialization and a high degree of opportunism in our approach to the problem of energy supply. As with agriculture (see Box 2-1), the tendency of the future appears to be in the direction of decentralization, lessening dependence on centralized systems for basic necessities, and a redressing of the extreme urban/rural imbalance created and perpetuated by cheap and superabundant energy.

Unfortunately, despite a recent upsurge of interest solar energy is still not receiving the social attention and the research funding that its demonstrable potential seems to call for. For example, federal energy research and development expenditures on solar power in fiscal year 1975 were only one-third those allotted to fusion and a mere one-fifteenth those spent on all forms of nuclear-fission research and development (Gillette 1974a); although statistics are not available, it is clear that research by the private sector is even more grossly biased in favor of fossil fuels and the nuclear option. Other than sheer inertia, this probably reflects the fact that solar energy, unlike fossil fuels or uranium, is not a resource that can be owned; nor does it appear to lend itself to exploitation by gigantic regionally-oriented utilities. Rather, it seems most adaptable to local and perhaps even individual exploitation, so it is not surprising that institutions and enterprises committed to a very different sort of energy economy are less than enthusiastic about solar power. Again, to reiterate one of the major themes of our discussion of ecological limits, the technological problems that inspire so much debate are almost superficial, for they are inescapably underlain by much larger social, economic, and political concerns.

Conflicts over Space and Other Resources

Indeed, one of the most critical limitations on many forms of energy production is that continued physical expansion will provoke essentially political conflicts with other sectors for scarce resources. We have seen, for example, that neither Western coal nor oil shale can be developed without massive supplies of water, that water supplies in the arid West are quite limited, and that therefore even partial development of these resources is likely to precipitate a conflict between energy producers and agriculturalists or other claimants to the water (many of whom have well-established, traditional usage rights). Much of the coal underlies millions of acres of good agricultural land or national-forest land now used to grow corn, graze cattle, produce wood, or provide recreational space and open-space reservoirs for environmental protection. These examples indicate that the increased cost of energy production can not be measured simply in dollars per unit supplied. Rather, we shall have to confront difficult social decisions about how much of other desired goods we are willing to sacrifice for the sake of power production.

At some point, increasing power production and population must come into conflict over space, if over no other resource; the prospect of doubled or perhaps trebled power production in the next few decades has already begun to provoke this conflict in an acute form. For instance, if nuclear plants are to be located in the ocean Ralph Lapp (1972, p. 90) foresees by the year 2000 "a fringe of artificial islands along both American coasts almost border to border." If they are to be located on shore, then demand for valuable coastal land will soar: a 3000-megawatt plant requires about 1000 acres exclusive of land for the associated facilities needed to mine, process, store, and transport fuel and waste. These auxiliary uses require a lot of land. For example, 200,000 miles of new transmission lines will be needed in the United States by 1990, requiring 3.1 million acres of land (or more than twice the area of Delaware) in addition to the 4 million already devoted to this purpose. Much effort is being expended by industry on finding technological answers to this transmission problem—like making power corridors more efficient and putting lines underground—but unless there are breakthroughs that are not now discernible these answers appear both difficult and costly, up to five times more expensive than current technology. In sum, trying to double or treble the size of an industry that is already of enormous dimensions will require an investment of about $100 billion for thousands of plants, transmission lines, substations, supply depots, and so on, which is going to make extraordinary demands on space alone, not to mention related side effects. Indeed, a considerable increase in public reluctance to concede the necessary space for energy production has become evident in recent years, and political battles over the sites of new dams, supertanker ports, oil refineries and, above all, nuclear reactors as well as over general land-use issues of every description have become staple front-page news items.

Energy, Heat, and Climate

The impact on climate is the ultimate limit on human energy use, a limit which no amount of technological ingenuity can remove. Ever since man became a technological being by inventing fire, he has significantly altered the climate of the earth, creating semiarid savannahs where once there were grasslands. Nevertheless, the impact of industrial man on global climate is potentially far greater, for the continuation of certain current trends could render the earth quite literally uninhabitable by the human race and most other species as well. But we do not really know what we are doing to climatic mechanisms. In effect, with only minimal theoretical knowledge we are running an enormous experiment with the global climate. Nevertheless, climatologists do know enough to be able to predict that crossing certain climatic thresholds would be disastrous, and they also have clear evidence that minor changes in some parameters, like temperature or albedo, can have major impacts on the processes governing climate. To greatly simplify a complex issue, the problems can be divided into those stemming from (1) industrial pollutants or by-products and (2) release of heat.

Many industrial pollutants or by-products have an impact on climate. For example, when fossil fuels are burned, carbon dioxide (CO_2) is released as a by-product; all other things being equal, the excess CO_2 in the atmosphere causes a warming or so-called greenhouse effect by inhibiting the radiation of heat into space. Since at least some of the excess CO_2 is absorbed by the oceans, it is not clear how much of an impact on climate the greenhouse effect will have, but one eminent climatologist foresees increased atmospheric CO_2 reinforcing a natural warming trend to produce "global temperatures warmer than any in the last 1000 years" by the first decade of the next century (Broecker 1975).

On the other hand, the fine particulate matter that human activities release into the atmosphere appears to have an opposite effect. Indeed, the massive amounts of particulates spewed out by major volcanic eruptions in the past (for example, Tambora in 1815) have caused abnormally cold years and crop failures in temperate areas. By 2030 or 2040, the projected atmospheric load of particulates will attain a similar level (Watt 1974, pp. 48–52, 63–64); even if the cooling effect is not quite so severe (volcanic eruptions also release massive quantities of gases that aid the cooling effect), nevertheless it is clear that the net effect of this increased particulate load will be to reduce photosynthesis and change wind and rainfall patterns.

Even more disturbing is some of the evidence coming to light about the many ways in which human activities threaten to disrupt the critical protective layer of ozone in the stratosphere. Without this layer, all life on earth would suffer harm from intense ultraviolet radiation, and many sensitive organisms crucial to global ecology would probably succumb. Three major problem areas have been identified. First, the explosion of numerous large nuclear weapons, as in a nuclear war, would almost certainly destroy the ozone layer; even single nuclear explosions cause perturbations. Second, extensive use of supersonic transport aircraft (added to already widespread military supersonic flight) would disrupt the layer significantly. Third, chlorofluoromethane gases, used in great and increasing amounts as aerosol propellants and refrigerants (for example, Freon), as well as many other chlorine (and some nitrogen) compounds released to the atmosphere can apparently catalyze the destruction of ozone beyond its natural replacement rate.*

Another potentially worrisome problem is oil pollution of the North polar ice. The Arctic ice pack is known to be one of the key regulators of the current climatic regime, and it is in sufficiently delicate balance that any substantial amount of oil pollution could well cause it to melt permanently, with potentially profound and dangerous consequences for the global weather system (Martin and Campbell 1973; Ramseier 1974).† Yet considerable exploitation of oil right on the fringes of the Arctic ice pack is already proceeding and much more is planned; major oil spills during production and transportation of the oil are almost inevitable in such a difficult working environment.

In sum, industrial man is polluting the biosphere in ways that have some potential for altering local or global climate for the worse in a scientifically unpredictable but nevertheless *reasonably foreseeable* fashion. Indeed, some climatologists (for example, Bryson 1973) profess to see major adverse effects already, and all are deeply concerned about the possibility of man-made effects combining with natural fluctuations or trends to produce rapid and irreversible climatic changes disastrous to agriculture in the comparatively near future. In short, we are tampering with the watch-like perfection of the global climatic system, not understanding clearly how it works or

---

*The worst aspect of this problem is the long time lag between atmospheric dispersal of the gas and the ultimate impact on the ozone layer; even if all use of chlorofluoromethanes ceased today, it would take several decades for all the gas already dispersed to reach the stratosphere, so that the longer we continue to use these gases in large quantities, the longer it will take before the maximum impact hits us (and the greater it will be).

† It is not clear what these consequences would be. Ramseier (1974) implies that the melting of the pack ice would lead to melting of land ice and a consequent rise in sea level, menacing coastal cities. On the other hand, Ewing and Donn (1956) hypothesize that an ice-free Arctic Ocean would provide a source of moisture making increased glaciation of the Northern Hemisphere likely.

what the consequences of our actions will be. This is a formula for ecological catastrophe.*

Naturally, the release of man-made heat also disturbs the mechanisms of climatic balance. However, by far the most worrisome long-term problem connected with heat release is sheer overheating of the globe. Man-made heat consists of more than the waste heat discussed previously, for the second law of thermodynamics ordains that *all* forms of energy must inevitably decay into low-grade heat, so that energy use and heat release are ultimately synonymous. For example, when coal is burned in a power plant the 30 to 40 percent of its original potential energy that does not become waste heat is turned into electricity. But when this electricity is transmitted some of it turns into heat and is lost to the environment. The remainder goes to electric motors, light bulbs, and other devices designed to perform useful work. Unfortunately, many of these devices are of such low efficiency that they produce mostly heat. A light bulb, for instance, turns about 5 percent of the electricity into light and rejects the rest as heat, as anybody who tries to unscrew a burning light bulb quickly finds out. But eventually, physical processes like friction and air resistance convert *all* the useful work (even the light from the light bulb) into heat as well. Thus, sooner or later, 100 percent of the coal's original energy becomes heat, no matter how efficiently it is exploited to do useful work.† In fact, the end product of all industrial processes is heat; the work obtained is a minor and transient by-product of the overall thermodynamic process of turning low-entropy (that is, useful for the performance of work) sources of energy into high-entropy (that is, unusable) low-grade heat.

If the energy for agriculture and industry came solely from natural solar sources, like wind and falling water, we would simply be making parasitic use of processes that are part of the earth's natural heat-balance system, and no disturbance would result. However, all other sources of energy—fossil fuel, fission, fusion, and even artificial solar energy (especially if gathered in space)—do produce a disturbance in the heat balance, for they inject into the biosphere additional heat that cannot be reradiated into space or even redistributed around the globe fast enough to prevent both global and local heat buildups.

It is known that very small changes in ambient global temperature (as little as 1 or 2 degrees Celsius) have been associated with comparatively

---

*In view of the above, it should hardly be necessary to remark that all the many proposed schemes for major modification of climate (for example, damming the Bering Strait) are ecologically irresponsible.

†However, making more efficient use of large sources of waste heat to warm buildings, for example, would economize on fuel used, and the overall level of heat released would presumably be less.

large changes in climate, such as the beginning or ending of ice ages. There is thus almost universal agreement that a change of this magnitude would have major effects on the climate: a rise would promote glacial melting and a higher sea level (drowning coastal cities) and a fall would foster increased glaciation. How close are we to this critical threshold?

Although the extra heat due to human use of energy now appears to be pitifully small compared to the total energy flow involved in the global heat balance (the flow of man-made heat is only about 1/15,000 or 1/20,000 the absorbed solar flux), at a 5 percent growth rate it would take only about 200 years to reach a level of artificial heat generation equivalent to 1 percent of the absorbed solar flux; this would be sufficient, say the experts, to increase global temperature past the dangerous 1°C threshold. Of course, global effects would almost certainly begin to be felt in advance of our approach to this threshold, because well before then human use of energy would equal or exceed many of the natural energy transfers, such as the kinetic energy of winds and currents or even the poleward heat fluxes, that play major roles in determining regional and continental climate. Even optimists (for example, Weinberg 1974) therefore concede that continued growth in energy use must inevitably cause a significant alteration of current climatic patterns (leading to altered capacity to grow food, shifts in areas of endemic disease, and similar ecological dangers) *within a matter of decades.*

However, human use of energy is geographically very unevenly distributed, and it seems likely that long before we experienced significant perturbation of the global climatic regime the local and regional effects of heat release on climate (or habitability) would be of major proportions. Indeed, such effects are already evident. Because of the heat released by automobiles, air conditioners, and other energy-using appurtenances of modern life, major cities, like New York and Los Angeles, are already "heat islands" averaging 3 to 6 degrees Celsius hotter than their surrounding countrysides, and projections indicate that heat release in these areas may become six times greater in a few decades. Even current levels of heat release are altering wind, convection, rainfall, and other observable meteorological phenomena; as the levels of heat release rise, the effects will become more pronounced. Moreover, the ability of many areas to tolerate additional power-plant cooling is nearly exhausted, so that ocean siting for the next generation of nuclear plants is almost inevitable. Thus, well before critical levels for the globe as a whole are reached, local and regional heat problems are likely to become sufficiently intense to bring growth in energy use to a virtual halt.

It is important to reiterate that *there is no possible technological appeal from this heat limit,* for it is a consequence of fundamental laws of the universe. This has not prevented people from trying, but all such efforts are doomed to thermodynamic futility. For example, some propose to divert sunlight from the earth with satellite mirror arrays or bands of particulates in the upper atmosphere, but this would significantly reduce photosynthesis (and thus crop production) and grossly alter the climate. Others propose to gather up the heat and pump it into space, but even assuming we had a technology capable of performing such a thermodynamic miracle, so much energy would be expended in the process that we should be worse off than when we started. It therefore appears that the maximum period of continued energy growth at current rates before unacceptable climatic consequences are unleashed is on the order of half a century.

Diminishing Returns from Conservation and Improved Efficiency

All things considered, future energy supply is problematic in both the short and the long terms. But what are the prospects for using energy with greater efficiency and therefore reducing demand significantly?

In fact, very large savings, possibly as much as 25 or 35 percent of consumption, could be made without major technological breakthroughs or drastic changes in life-style. Already, for example, the increased cost of energy has led businesses to engage in energy-cost accounting, and substantial economies (15 to 30 percent) have been made by some plants. However, once the easy targets, like sheer waste, have been dealt with, it will become progressively harder to make further economies without either technological breakthroughs or major social changes. For example, without changing the entire transportation system based on the private car, only economies that are modest relative to total demand are achievable in a sector that now accounts for 40 percent of all U.S. energy consumption (this is not to say that small savings are not worthwhile). Moreover, it will take many years before the potential economies in certain areas become effective—for example, through changes in transportation systems or in building design and operation. In addition, there is palpable public resistance to many of the measures that might substantially reduce energy consumption. For example, almost all methods of making durable goods less wasteful of energy require higher *initial* costs, and neither producers nor consumers seem to find this palatable (even though the latter would save money in the long run). What is even more important, the likelihood of an immediate, substantial shift from the private car toward mass transit for longer trips, and bicycles plus shanks' mare for short trips, is slight because it would be physically inconvenient and psychologically distressing for the average American; indeed, even relatively mild conservation measures, like slightly increased gasoline taxes, seem not to be politically feasible.

In brief, there are many institutional impediments to energy conservation, and the higher the level of conservation desired the higher the barriers

---

Box 3–5. The Thermodynamic Economy

Although the currency of nature's economy is energy, the current human economy takes energy into account only indirectly, via the monetary cost of energy production and use. It is therefore in conflict with basic laws governing our physical existence. The laws of thermodynamics tell us that we cannot get something for nothing. The matter and energy (which are thermodynamically interchangeable) from which we derive economic benefit have to come from somewhere, and the inevitable residuals remaining after we have obtained the benefits have to go somewhere. Unless the thermodynamic cost of obtaining the energy and disposing of the residuals is less than the benefits of the use to which the energy is put, the system as a whole loses. Thus a "thermodynamic economy" based directly on an accounting of energy or entropy* has become essential, for otherwise social decisions based on traditional economic criteria will continue to compromise the system through so-called externalities or side effects that create more entropy—that is, increased disorder or reduced energetic potential—in the system as a whole.

The basic insight of thermodynamic economics is that entropy is the real basis of economic scarcity. There is a fundamental difference between classical scarcity and thermodynamic scarcity—that is, between a scarcity of land and other reusable or flow resources like solar radiation and a scarcity of coal or other nonrenewable resources that, once used, are gone forever (or can only be recycled with limited efficiency and at a high cost in energy). Thus, says the thermodynamic economist, our non-renewable resources are exceedingly precious capital stocks that can never be recreated, so that to waste them or even to expend them primarily on current con-

---

become. The Ford Foundation's careful study (whose conclusions were disputed by industrial spokesmen) showed that, although a 35 percent saving in annual energy consumption by the year 2000 might be made solely by wholesale application of the best possible energy-saving devices (this would, of course, be a major institutional feat), boosting the level of energy conserved to 45 percent would require substantial (but by no means unacceptable) life-style changes and sweeping redesign of socioeconomic systems, as well as some technological breakthroughs (A. L. Hammond 1974b). Although such major social and institutional changes are inevitable, leading to a situation in which energy costs weigh as heavily as dollars in our social decisions (see Box 3-5), they will come slowly and uncertainly, perhaps accompanied by a measure of political turmoil. Again, the technical issues are really inseparable from the political, social, and economic issues, to be explored in Part II.

Unfortunately, even if all the institutional and technical barriers enumerated above can be surmounted, the long-term impact of energy conservation will be almost insignificant. For example, cutting energy consumption in

---

*Entropy is simply an index of energetic usefulness. Low-entropy energy or matter, like petroleum, is highly available or usable; high-entropy energy and matter, like the chemicals dispersed in seawater, are relatively useless or unavailable (that is, it would take added work to make them available).

sumption is absurd, no matter how rational it may be in terms of dollars and cents.

Exactly how this basic insight is to be translated into economic institutions is being debated: depletion quotas, individual energy rations, and dual price systems in which goods would have to be paid for with both monetary and energy currencies have been proposed (Daly 1973; Slesser 1974; Westman and Gifford 1973). However, certain preliminary conclusions have already emerged. First, it will never pay mankind to run a completely technological world, as some extreme technological visionaries urge, for life support is cheap if we let nature do it and fantastically expensive if we take on this burden ourselves. Second, even though collection and conversion percentages may be quite low compared to some of man's engineering creations, and despite the apparently greater economic costs, when pollution and all the other thermodynamic costs are considered solar energy and other forms of decentralized energy production are actually more efficient than methods based on using up nonrenewable resources and are therefore a thermodynamic bargain. Third, human labor may become thermodynamically cheaper than capital or other factors of production; industry will therefore become increasingly labor-intensive. Similarly, less energy-intensive materials like wood and steel will displace materials like aluminum, which are highly energy- and capital-intensive. In short, a thermodynamic (or, to put this concept in its proper context, steady-state) economy would aim at careful husbandry of resources, dependence on natural flows and processes, decentralization, more labor-intensive production, and a combination of ultrasophisticated technology with some of the energy-saving methods that sustained our forefathers.

half merely has the same effect as doubling the supply. Thus energy conservation can never be more than a short-term palliative. This is not to say that it will not be extremely useful over the next few decades in helping to alleviate the impact of fuel shortages and reducing dependence on foreign suppliers (highly desirable objectives that alone make a major conservation effort well worthwhile). But conservation can buy no more than a decade or two of time to adjust to radically altered conditions of energy supply.

The only hope of avoiding this conclusion would be if continued technological breakthroughs were to allow us to use energy with ever greater efficiency. Unfortunately, *continual* technological advance in energy conversion is not possible. For example, the most advanced steam-turbine fossil-fuel power plants are 40 percent efficient. Very little further improvement in this technology is possible (at any reasonable cost); to make any substantial gain in efficiency, a new technology must be substituted. A promising but still unproven candidate is magnetohydrodynamic power generation, which is in theory capable of 60 percent efficiency. This seems like a substantial improvement, but it is unimpressive relative both to past progress (a fortyfold gain in efficiency since the time of the first steam engines) and to prospective future demand for energy. Moreover, the 60 percent level appears to be the ultimate ceiling on efficiency of conversion of fossil fuel into electricity. Even if this were not true, it would make little difference: doubling efficiency from the current 40 percent to the 80 percent level would still buy only one doubling period of respite (a mere 14 years at current rates of growth in energy use) before demand caught up again. In fact, even attaining the thermodynamically impossible level of 100 percent efficiency would not make coal reserves, for example, last significantly longer than they would without any improvement in conversion efficiency whatsoever! Indeed, virtually all modern industrial processes offer little thermodynamic scope for improvement. In short, diminishing returns in the rate of gain of efficiency in energy production and use are all-pervasive; in the future it will be ever more difficult (and costly) to bring about even marginal improvements.

In fact, any gains in efficiency are likely to be more than counterbalanced by another form of diminishing returns—declining net energy yields. Energy is always needed to produce energy. For example, about half of the petroleum produced in Texas is also consumed there for refining, drilling, transportation, and other production-related activities, so that the net energy yield, or the ratio of usable to total energy production, is only 50 percent. Net energy yield is high (and energy is therefore likely to be cheap and abundant) when it is easy and relatively inexpensive to create energy supplies—as in the Persian Gulf, where large pressurized pools of oil lie close to the surface and provide copious flows of high-quality crude without pumping. Net energy yield is low (and energy is correspondingly scarce and costly) when energy production itself is difficult and expensive.

A prime example is nuclear power, which requires heavy investment before useful energy can be obtained. Some energy analysts estimate that when all costs are counted nuclear power plants pay back their original energy investment only after a decade or more of service and provide only a modest net energy yield over their expected lifetime (Lovins 1975); others are much more optimistic (for example, Wright and Syrett 1975). So far the only clear conclusion to be drawn from the debate is that the energy economics of nuclear power are questionable enough to warrant a careful non-partisan investigation.*

The question of low net energy yield also hangs very heavily over production from both oil shale and tar sands; except for a few favored deposits, the BTU's produced would in most cases only slightly exceed the BTU's invested, so that the nominally substantial reserves of these unconventional fossil fuels are illusory. The costs of petroleum production are also rising steeply, so that ever more money and energy must be spent per barrel delivered to the refinery; offshore and Arctic oil wells, for example, are an

---

*In large part, the controversy reflects the methodological infancy of energy analysis, which is theoretically simple but quite complex in practice and has no agreed ground rules for such key issues as what costs are to be included. There is thus ample scope for biased analysis.

order of magnitude more expensive than onshore wells in temperate zones (even many of these are now being drilled to enormous depths at costs equivalent to offshore or Arctic wells). Although coal does not seem to be experiencing the same kind of rise in cost, energy must be spent to upgrade its quality. Industrial society has only limited use for low-grade heat; it must have high-quality forms of energy, like gas and electricity, to run its complex machinery. But to make 1 BTU of gas or electricity requires 1.5 and 3 BTU's, respectively, of coal, so that increased dependence on coal instead of petroleum will also reduce net energy yield.

The trend toward declining net energy yield is therefore already in evidence, and it is certain to become more pronounced in the decades to come. Only fusion power seems potentially exempt from ecologist Howard Odum's warning (1971; 1973) that the day of zero net energy yield must come, reducing us once again to almost total dependence on solar power. Even if this day is still a long way off, there can be little doubt that the process of energy production must become much more energy (and capital*) intensive and that most calculations of reserves, because they do not take into account the increasing amounts of energy needed to turn the reserves into useful forms of supply, grossly overstate the actual quantity of net energy available to us in the future.

In sum, the prospects for modest short-term improvements through increased conservation and greater efficiency are more than counterbalanced by the inexorable long-term trend toward diminishing returns from all forms of energy production and use.

A Summary View of Energy

The era of cheap and abundant energy is decisively over. But energy is the linchpin of industrial civilization; as it becomes scarcer and more expensive, so must everything else. We have therefore come almost to the end of the industrial road characterized by ever grander high-energy solutions to the problems created by previous growth. Without the energy to back them up, such "solutions" have become merely fantastic. The only genuine solution is to begin a transition to a low-energy (yet high-technology) post-industrial civilization that depends primarily on flow resources like solar energy for the routine maintenance of life within the overall limitations on energy use that are built into the biosphere. This conclusion will be reinforced by a consideration of the limits to technological growth.

---

*Generally speaking, the two go together. However, capital costs, which will be discussed below, appear to rise more rapidly than energy costs, so that the net-profit barrier will probably be reached before zero net energy yield.

Box 3–6. Bulldozer Technology

Unless he returns to a life of hunting and gathering without either tools or fire, man is incurably technological in the sense that he will always have to transform nature for utilitarian ends by some kind of applied science. However, radically different modes of technological existence are possible. What we are here concerned with is the peculiar kind of technology that grew out of Baconian experimental science, that first had a social impact during the Industrial Revolution in England, and that has as its explicit purpose giving man power over nature in order to promote "the effecting of all things possible," to use Francis Bacon's arresting slogan (Medawar 1969).

For our purposes the most important characteristics of this kind of technology are its dependence on fossil fuel and other nonrenewable or man-made resources, its linearity and lack of integration with natural processes, its dominating scale, and its

---

TECHNOLOGY AND ITS MANAGEMENT

Is There a Limit to Technological Growth?

One of the main components of the argument against the limits-to-growth thesis is technological optimism (see Box 3-6 for a description of the type of technology at issue). The optimists believe that exponential technological growth will allow us to expand resources ahead of exponentially increasing demands. The eminent British elder statesman of science Lord Zuckerman (quoted in Anon. 1972a) complains about *The Limits to Growth* that "the only kind of exponential growth with which the book does not deal, and which I for one believe to be a fact, is that of the growth of human knowledge"; Zuckerman goes on to assert categorically that "the tree of knowledge will go on growing endlessly."

Zuckerman's extravagant claim is not merely a personal opinion, but a widely held article of modern faith. Since the age of the Enlightenment *philosophes,* the ideology of progress through science and technology has been our social religion; indeed, according to its more utopian proponents, like Karl Marx, eventually scarcity itself (and therefore age-old evils like poverty and injustice that are rooted in it) will be abolished. Thus, to challenge endless scientific and technological progress amounts to a kind of secular heresy.

Yet, as we have seen in the preceding discussions of the particular technological solutions proposed to deal with the problems of growth in the production of food, minerals, and energy, there are demonstrable limits to the technological manipulation of ecological limits. The time has come to generalize about some of these limits and to discuss some practical problems of technological management that are only partly connected with the physical limitations of the earth. It will be seen that neither in theory nor in

narrow concept of rationality or efficiency. Since all attempts at an exact yet reasonably succinct definition fall short, it might be best to resort to symbolism and call it "bulldozer" technology. The bulldozer and other earth-moving machinery make possible the airports, dams, highways, skyscrapers, and most of the other vaunted achievements of modern technological civilization. Moreover, its violent power, the single-minded way in which it reshapes nature to man's design, and its dependence on man-made energy and a complex industrial infrastructure make the bulldozer a paradigm of modern technology. It is on such a technology, rather than on some of its conceivable alternatives (Box 3-7), that proponents of exponential technological growth appear to rely.

practice can technological growth be as endless as Lord Zuckerman asserts. Already, in fact, limits to knowledge and to the human capacity to plan for and manage technological solutions to environmental problems have begun to emerge.

Limits to Knowledge and Its Application

Most scientists and technologists believe, with Zuckerman, that necessity unfailingly brings forth invention. However, although we cannot specify the exact limits and must always be aware of potential "failures of imagination and nerve" that would tend to make us overly pessimistic about future possibilities (Clarke 1962), there is at least reasonable doubt that "the tree of knowledge will go on growing endlessly." Indeed, respected research scientists (for example Stent 1969) have begun to suggest that we are close to important limits and that the golden age of scientific discovery is therefore essentially over. Of course, similar predictions have been made before, and it does seem doubtful that the enterprise of science can ever end. Moreover, such an assertion is clearly less true of some fields than others. Nevertheless, it appears that the process of *relevant* scientific discovery must eventually cease. That is, just as we have turned mechanics and classical optics into engineers' tools and therefore into played-out fields of scientific investigation, so too shall we come to the end of scientific discovery in other fields *relevant to the problem of surmounting the limits to growth.*

Indeed, diminishing returns are clearly seen from the history of science, for the more scientific work that is done, the more likely it is that new theories will be corrections or refinements of previous ones, necessarily leaving most of the old structure of knowledge intact. Thus new knowledge may not be translatable into new technology. In physics the clockwork celestial-mechanical theories of Isaac Newton have been superseded by the relativistic and quantum-mechanical theories associated with the names of Albert Einstein and Werner Heisenberg, but neither relativity nor the uncertainty principle have a significant practical impact on the ordinary physical reality of man's biological and social existence. Thus even very great future discoveries, ones that totally change our scientific world view or our view of man, may contribute little to removing the ecological limits now confronting the human species.*

Moreover, a greater scientific and technological research effort does not seem possible, for the scientific enterprise itself is now struggling with numerous limits to its own growth. For example, the costs of basic research in many areas have risen inordinately in recent years, a clear symptom of diminishing returns.

In addition, even when theory clearly favors real-world technological advance, acceptable engineering solutions may not be achievable because the technical difficulties are too great. As previously suggested, fusion could be just such an area. Even fission raises questions in the minds of a substantial minority; the Swedish physicist and Nobelist Hannes Alfvén (1972) believes that nuclear safety is a problem beyond solution no matter how much time, effort, and money is put into research and development.

Finally, as we have had occasion to note in connection with pollution control and energy production, a technology cannot be indefinitely improved without encountering either thermodynamic limits or limits of scale beyond which further improvement is of no practical interest. Many technologies are already near this point, and the rest soon will be, for the substitution of one ever more efficient form of technology for another simply cannot continue forever. In effect, the better our current technology, the harder it is likely to be to improve on it. (In the real world, moreover, there is frequently a trade-off between efficiency and reliability, so that maximizing efficiency can be self-defeating.)

In sum, there may be limits to relevant scientific and technological knowledge or to the human capacity to discover such knowledge. If so, basing our strategy of response to ecological limits on the assumption that scientific and technological knowledge will grow endlessly or even at the rate typical of the recent past appears to be imprudent.

---

*It is, of course, possible that future discoveries, like fusion power, indebted to the work of Einstein and Heisenberg will indeed alleviate some of the limits we have discussed. However, better technological mousetraps can make only a limited contribution to removing such fundamental ecological constraints as the laws of thermodynamics or the delicacy of the global heat balance. Moreover, although fusion does appear to be close to some degree of realization, it must be clearly understood that reliance on future discovery rests on faith in the power of the technological wand, not on demonstrable scientific fact.

The Overwhelming Burden of Planning and Management

Even if lack of scientific and technological knowledge proves not to be an obstacle, implementation of technological solutions to the full array of problems discussed above will place a staggering burden of planning and management on our decisionmakers and institutional machinery.

For one thing, the rates of growth now prevailing require us to double our capital stock, our use of materials, our capacity to control pollution, our agricultural productivity, and so on, every 15 to 30 years. Since we start from a very high base level, especially in the developed nations, the increment of new construction and new invention required will be gigantic. To take a specific example, if the projections are to be believed, in the United States alone we must install approximately 900 nuclear power plants (about 15 times current nuclear capacity) in the next 25 years, but innumerable bottlenecks and structural obstacles to such rapid expansion are already evident (Page 1974).*

Furthermore, the environmental crisis is not a series of discrete problems; it is an ensemble of interacting problems that exacerbate each other through various kinds of threshold, multiplicative, and synergistic effects.† Thus the difficulty and complexity of managing the ensemble of problems grow faster than any particular problem. Moreover, all the work of innovation, construction, and environmental management needed to cope with this ensemble must be orchestrated to form a reasonably integrated, harmonious whole, for otherwise the accumulation of the side effects of piecemeal solutions would almost certainly be intolerable. Since delays, planning failures, and general incapacity to deal effectively with even the current range of problems are all too visible today, we must further assume that our ability to cope with large-scale complexity will improve substantially in the next few decades. In brief, technology cannot be implemented in an organizational vacuum. Something like the ecological "law of the minimum,"

---

*Beyond the year 2000, the nuclear construction problem begins to reach absurd dimensions. Using conservative assumptions, the authors of the second Club of Rome study point out that "in order to produce the world's energy in 100 years, then, we will merely have to build, in each and every year between now and then, *four reactors per week*" as well as "about *two reactors per day* simply to replace those that have worn out" (Mesarovic and Pestel 1974, p. 132).

†Some examples: (i) even if per capita consumption and waste remain constant, a small increase in population can change a healthy river into a sewer once the river's capacity to digest wastes and pollution has been exceeded (the threshold effect); (ii) even if population and per capita consumption grow separately at quite modest rates, the total environmental demand multiplies more rapidly, so that a doubled population that uses twice as much has four times the impact on the environment (the multiplicative effect); and (iii) various forms of pollution, from noise to radiation, interact to produce more ill health than would occur simply from the addition of the particular effects (the synergistic effect).

which states that the factor in least supply governs the rate of growth of a system as a whole, applies to social systems as well as ecosystems, so that technological fixes cannot run ahead of the human capacity to plan, construct, fund, and man them—a fact that many technological optimists (for example, Starr and Rudman 1973) either overlook or assume away.

Foresight, Time, and Money as Factors in Least Supply

Our ability to achieve the requisite level of effectiveness in planning is especially doubtful. Already the complex systems that sustain industrial civilization are seen by some as perpetually hovering on the brink of breakdown; the computer and other panaceas for coping with complexity appear to have been vastly oversold; and current management styles—linear, hierarchical, economic—appear to be grossly ill adapted to the nature of the problems.

One very troublesome problem for social planners is that the consequences of our technological acts cannot be foreseen with certainty. There exist no scientific answers to such "trans-scientific" questions as what risks are attached to nuclear energy or to the use of certain chemicals (Weinberg 1972); the only way to determine these risks empirically is to run a real-life experiment on the population at large. The potential social consequences of technological innovation are even more obscure. Thus there are no technical solutions to the dilemmas of environmental management, and policy decisions about environmental problems must be made politically by prudent men, not by scientific administrators. This being the case, technology assessment, the remedy proposed for the general political problem of technological side effects, can never be the purely technical exercise many of its proponents seem to envision; instead, the planning process will come to resemble a power struggle between partisans of differing economic, social, and political values. The difficulties and delays entailed by such an adversary planning process are foreshadowed by current conflicts over nuclear power-plant siting and safety and over other environmental issues.

Of course, such drawn-out political battles may well be essential for the creation of social consensus and commitment on these difficult issues. Yet it is becoming increasingly apparent that we can ill afford the associated delays, for time will be one of our scarcest resources. Difficult as it seems, dealing with very large increments of growth is really the lesser part of the problem. Exponential growth is dangerous primarily because it is so insidious: as the example of the lily pad and pond illustrates, until a limit is very close in time it seems very far away physically and psychologically. Thus, the all too human tendency to let things slide until they are pressing is potentially fatal, for by then even heroic action may be too little and too late.

For example, we Americans have allowed the private automobile to become so central to our economy and our private lives that we cannot live without it in the short term. Yet, because of air pollution, we can no longer live with it in its current form, so we are forced to alleviate the worst of its side effects with stopgap technological responses (which may intensify or create other side effects and contribute to the difficulty of solving other problems, like the energy crisis); but this strategy will not even enable us to meet the clean-air standards mandated by Congress, without additional social and institutional changes. However, at this point we are almost helpless to do better, for we ignored the problem until it became too big to handle by any means that are politically, economically, and technically feasible now or in the immediate future. Similarly, warnings of an impending energy crisis were ignored and Americans therefore found themselves in a predicament in which, as energy officials in Washington later admitted, the actions necessary to meet the crisis would have had to be initiated *at least six years earlier* (*New York Times,* April 17, 1973, p. 1).

Nor is it enough merely to foresee an emerging problem. Planners must also anticipate the lead time necessary to take delivery of even readily available technological solutions, like strip-mining draglines (7 years) and nuclear power plants (10 years), or to replace one technology with another (10 to 20 years), as is apparently going to be necessary to bring sulphur dioxide emission from coal-fueled power plants under control. Often, however, the replacement technology does not even exist, so that more lead time must be allotted for its invention; for example, it will be at least a decade before practical technological solutions in such key areas of concern as contraception and integrated pesticide management can possibly emerge from scientific laboratories, and enormous effort and funding will be needed to keep the lag this short (Djerassi et al. 1974). Worse, it may take a very long time for any significant results to appear once a technological fix has actually been applied in the real world. For example, the absolute size of energy production is now so overwhelming that effecting rapid changes in the pattern of supply has become all but impossible. In particular, there is no way that fusion could supply 10 percent of U.S. power requirements in less than 30 years, even with an immediate scientific breakthrough and a crash program of development; in fact, historical experience with nuclear power and other forms of energy production suggests that it would be more like 40 to 60 years before fusion could make even this minimal contribution. In sum, coping with exponential growth at our advanced stage of development requires the exercise of very great foresight, and a planning horizon of 30 to 50 years is the minimum consistent with the existence of innumerable natural and social lags; but our past failure to exercise foresight means that we have already fallen far behind.

Money is also a significant practical limitation on technological growth.

For one thing, the cost of taking over the operation of natural systems ourselves, as technological visionaries like Buckminster Fuller urge, would bankrupt us. For example, the world's annual oil production would provide only enough energy to operate the global rainfall system for about 35 hours; to duplicate just one small trout stream would require a capital investment of $245 million, without the trout or other forms of life that we cannot engineer (Anon. 1972b). Thus, even assuming that we knew enough to make it possible, mastering nature technologically instead of finding ways of living in harmony with it appears to be out of the question; on financial grounds alone, we shall be obliged to let nature do as much of the work as possible.

Most technologists would deny any pretension to replacing nature. Yet there are abundant examples of failure to count the financial cost of technological schemes. One is found in the assertion, which has unfortunately begun to achieve some currency, that the way out of man's ecological bind here on earth lies in space (Chedd 1974). It is abundantly clear that, whatever the ultimate potential for founding extraterrestrial colonies or whatever the ultimate cosmic destiny of the human race, space offers no escape from the limits to growth *on this planet*. To rocket into space just one day's world population growth (approximately 200,000 people) would be a major undertaking (assuming 100 persons per shuttle flight, 2000 flights would be necessary). This alone would generate colossal environmental problems—enormous quantities of energy for fuel, pollution of the atmosphere (especially the vulnerable stratosphere) by toxic exhaust gases, and so on—and trying to keep pace with population growth would be totally out of the question. Moreover, the expense would be staggering. According to the latest NASA estimates, it will require $160 to lift each pound of payload into orbit with the space shuttle now being developed; it would therefore cost $20,000 per 125-pound person, or about $4 billion for those 200,000 persons (exclusive of space-colonization or other life-support costs, which would be substantial). Thus keeping pace with the world's population growth for just one year would require a sum exceeding the U.S. gross national product. It is apparent that even highly developed and routinized space travel is not likely to involve large-scale movement of people and materials to and from the earth, at least not in any foreseeable future.

Even less grandiose technological schemes may cost too much. Agro-industrial nuclear complexes, for example, would be quite expensive in relation to the number of people benefited, even apart from environmental drawbacks like prodigious heat release. One of the major reasons why there is no American supersonic transport (SST) program (and why the Anglo-French Concorde SST project is continually embroiled in political controversy as well as red ink) is that neither government nor private industry was willing to undertake the financial burdens.

Indeed, the mere expansion of currently feasible technology will strain our capital resources in the coming decades. In the next twenty-five years more than one trillion dollars will be needed for nuclear power plants and related backup industry, so that this one industry alone will demand approximately 20 percent of projected capital accumulation during this period (Rose 1974b). In fact, since nuclear power plants have until now operated below their planned lifetime load factor, the utility industry may be required to build more than the currently projected number of plants to attain the needed operating capacity, making capital costs even larger than expected (Comey 1974). No matter what assumptions are made, the provision of investment capital for nuclear expansion seems likely to strain the capacity of the money market (Watt 1974, pp. 23–29), especially because huge increases in investment are going to be necessary in every other sector of the energy industry. For example, development of oil shale, coal gasification, and other "synthetic" fuel industries as well as other unconventional forms of energy production like geothermal power will cost up to half a trillion dollars in the United States alone (Gillette 1973a, 1974c). (For the sake of comparison, the Manhattan Project to develop an atomic bomb cost $3 billion and the Apollo moon-landing program about $30 billion).

Increasing supply in another key sector, the production of fertilizer for the developing countries, will also demand an inordinate amount of investment capital—$165 billion between 1975 and 1990—which raises serious doubts that this essential requirement for feeding more people can be met (Ewell 1975).

Moreover, given the general capital shortage, every dollar spent on energy or fertilizer will mean investment forgone in other kinds of new plant and equipment (needed for pollution control if for nothing else), housing, social welfare and amenity, and so forth. Insufficient investment capital is therefore likely to be a very serious limitation on continued technological expansion.

Vulnerability to Accident and Error

Because major and irrevocable commitments of money, materials, and effort are required to stay ahead of exponential growth and because major risks are inherent in certain technological choices if all does not go well, it has become supremely important to make the right decisions the first time, for there may be no second chance at the problems being thrust upon us so rapidly. Yet, even supremely foresighted, intelligent, and timely decision making may do little to lessen the growing vulnerability of a highly technological society to accident and error.

The main cause for concern is that some especially dangerous technologies are beginning to be deployed. We have seen, for example, that there are inherent in nuclear power production (especially with the plutonium-fueled breeder reactor) certain risks making virtually perfect containment mandatory, and the evidence does not suggest that such perfection is achievable (Boxes 3-2 and 3-3). In addition, many other modern technologies—for example, the chemical industry, transport and storage of natural gas, and the supertanker—are capable of inflicting catastrophic ecological or human damage; experience with these technologies also shows clearly the near impossibility of preventing all accidents. Especially in the developed world, man depends on a basic technological infrastructure to such a degree that even less intrinsically dangerous accidents—for example, a sustained electric-power failure—can have devastating consequences.

Yet, as population grows and civilization becomes more complex, much more effort and skill will be needed to cope with the increasing vulnerability to disorder (entropy) and failure. But to count on perfect design, skill, efficiency, or reliability in any human enterprise is folly.* In addition, all man's works, no matter how perfect as self-contained engineering creations, are vulnerable not only to such natural disasters as earthquakes, storms, droughts, and other acts of God,† but also to deliberate disruption by madmen, criminals, terrorists, and military enemies. Nevertheless, despite the patent impossibility of achieving any such thing, modern society seems to be approaching a condition in which nothing less than perfect planning and management will do. Some will object to such a strong statement of the problem, so let us examine some of the arguments that purport to dismiss this concern.

It is sometimes said that the probability of any one of these disastrous events happening is so low as to be not worth worrying about. Of course, some risk must be run in order to reap the fruits of technology, but dismissing the problem in this fashion shows a potentially fatal misunderstanding of the laws of probability, for an apparently low probability of accident may be illusory. First, as explained in the discussion of reactor safety in Box 3-2, whether a risk is large or small depends greatly on how many sources of risk there are. That is, if the chances of some kind of reactor accident are one in a thousand per reactor year, then one accident a year is a certainty (on an average) if there are a thousand reactors in operation. Since we already do so many things that have some potential, however small, of altering the climate or unleashing other disasters, we should not be complacent about the apparently highly improbable. Second, some risks are essentially incalculable. There is no way, for example, to estimate the degree of danger to nuclear installations from fanatical political terrorists with sufficient cunning to outwit all the safety devices and security procedures. Third, even when the

---

Science reporter Robert Gillette's (1973c) analysis of an accidental radiation spill at an AEC facility is one of the best case studies of how the most elaborate safety precautions may avail little in face of the human propensity to err.

†This fact alone makes it unlikely that the requisite degree of nuclear safety can ever be achieved, especially given the human propensity to build extensively in natural flood plains, known earthquake zones, or other spots liable to natural disasters.

probabilities are truly small we cannot afford to relax, for the million-to-one shot may occur at the first event, at the millionth, or well beyond the millionth with equal probability; if the result of failure is potentially catastrophic, then we are simply engaged in playing a highly recondite version of Russian roulette. As game theorists have shown, a course of action that risks very serious loss is unlikely to be sound, no matter how attractive the potential gain; a prudent strategist limits his risks even if this also limits his gains.

Some believe that we shall soon achieve a level of material and systems reliability far above what we are now capable of; the space program is often cited in support of this belief. However, although the space program is certainly a triumph of technical engineering, most of the problems we are called upon to solve are not pure engineering problems; they contain a host of social and other "soft" factors that make them conceptually and practically several orders of magnitude more difficult than the space program. Moreover, this claim conveniently overlooks the fiery death of three astronauts and the near disaster of Apollo Thirteen, to mention only the American space program. In addition, we have neither the money nor the manpower to turn all our technological acts into a simulacrum of a moon shot. The nuclear industry is a much more realistic model of what we can expect, but as we have seen, despite far greater than average attention to safety and fail-safe design strategies, its safety record is far from perfect and there are many reasons to think that this record will worsen rather than improve once the industry moves from the elite, special-technology stage to the stage of mass production and routine operation by ordinary workers and managers.

In sum, even massive amounts of money, enormous effort, and supreme technological cleverness can never guarantee accident-free operation of technological devices, and it is indeed strange that technologists—discoverers of the infamous Murphy's Law, which sardonically states that "If something can possibly go wrong, it will"—should so often assume, to the contrary, that they can make their creations invulnerable to acts of God or fool-proof in normal operations. Indeed, the array of potential ecological and societal disasters confronting a civilization that increasingly depends on the smooth and errorless operation of technological systems should give any prudent man pause. It is not just that incredible accidents can still happen, as is well illustrated by the fate of the Titanic, whose designers believed it to be unsinkable. Rather, we are deliberately adopting new technologies in full awareness that they are by no means "unsinkable."

In fact, the supertanker may be an even better metaphor for modern technological society than the bulldozer (see Box 3-6). These massive oil barges are maritime disasters looking for a place to happen. The ecodisaster caused by the wreck of the Torrey Canyon, not a particularly large supertanker by current or projected standards, was surely a taste of things to come. Supertankers are cheaply and fragilely built to minimum standards and in such a fashion as to flout scandalously nearly all the canons of good seamanship acquired from centuries of experience (Mostert 1974). Their thin and over-stressed hulls are not equal to all the challenges of the sea; they lack an ability to maneuver or stop within any reasonable distance; and they have only a single boiler and a single screw, so that even routine failures leave them helplessly adrift with as much thermal energy in their tanks as in a fair-sized hydrogen bomb. Like the monstrous supertanker, a highly technological society appears fated to exist on the thinnest of safety margins, and there is abundant evidence from the past to indicate that such a small margin will eventually prove insufficient. To proceed on the assumption that we can achieve standards of perfection hitherto unattained would be an act of technological hubris exceeding all bounds of prudence.

The End of "Endless" Technological Growth

The important question is not "Can we do it?" in the narrow technological sense. Rather, we must ask: Can we do all the things we have to do at once, given shortages of money, manpower, and other factors potentially in least supply? At what cost and at what risk? Will we do it? Will we do it in time, given lack of foresight and the very human tendency to wait for a crisis?

What this array of questions suggests is that, even if the problems of exponential growth seemingly yield to abstract analysis and technological solution, it is possible that they will not be solved simply because we are too human and fallible to deal with them in the real world. In short, exponential technological growth is a false hope, for it can never be the endless process optimists seem to believe; even in the shorter term, technological solutions pose problems of management that can be surmounted only with great difficulty, if at all.

This judgment certainly does not mean that all technological solutions are anathema. Indeed, to counter single-minded technological optimism with an equally single-minded neo-Luddite hostility to technology in all its forms is absurd, for a non-technological existence is impossible. The question at issue is what kind of technology is to be adopted, and to what social ends it is to be applied. The whole subject of technology needs to be demythologized, so that we have a realistic view of what technology can and cannot do and of what its costs are.

The basic features of a valid alternative technology have already been identified (Box 3-7). Unlike current bulldozer-supertanker technology, it would be based on ecological and thermodynamic premises that are compatible with the coexistence of man and nature over the long term; as a consequence, it would necessarily eschew merely quantitative progress, striving instead to maximize amenity and general human welfare at minimum material cost. Such an alternative (or "soft," "appropriate," "low-impact," "intermediate") technology is certainly possible; that it would also be desirable is a theme we shall return to in Chapter 8.

Even under the most optimistic assumptions, the kinds of alternative technology under discussion probably cannot support affluence as we in the richest countries have come to define it, so a certain lowering of social sights is called for. In fact, extensive social changes are inevitable. One of the major attractions of the technological fix as a response to the problems of exponential growth is that it appears to avoid the need for awkward social change. In other words, reliance on technological growth allows the continuation of business as usual. But as we have seen throughout our discussion of ecological limits, business as usual cannot continue under any circumstances, no matter what one assumes about our civilization's technological response, for a multitude of political, social, and economic issues lie concealed within nearly all aspects of the environmental crisis. The limits to technological growth we have identified make it even clearer that the essence of the solution to the environmental crisis must be political in the sense specified in the Introduction. We shall explore these thorny issues (particularly the political side effects of continued technological growth) in depth in Part II.

AN OVERVIEW OF ECOLOGICAL SCARCITY

What Is Ecological Scarcity?

Ecological scarcity is an all-embracing concept that encompasses all the various limits to growth or costs attached to continued growth that have been mentioned above. As we have seen, it includes not only Malthusian scarcity of food, but also impending shortages of mineral and energy resources, biospheric or ecosystemic limitations on human activity, and limits to the human capacity to use technology to expand resource supplies ahead of exponentially increasing demands (or to bear the costs of doing so).*

We have seen, in particular, how critical energy is. Industrial civilization has used cheap and abundant energy not only to subsidize agriculture, mining, and other forms of production, but also to substitute for (that is, reduce the scarcity of) the basic economic factors of land, labor, and capital.

---

*A complete definition of ecological scarcity ought properly to include the social costs attached to continued technological and industrial growth, the economic problems of coping with the physical aspects of scarcity, and certain other sociopolitical factors that will be dealt with in Part II.

Box 3–7. Alternative Technology

All forms of alternative, or "soft," technology share certain characteristics. First and foremost, they are closely adapted to natural cycles and processes, so that pollution is minimized and as much of the work as possible is done by nature. Second, they are based primarily on renewable, "income" flows of matter and energy like trees and solar radiation rather than on nonrenewable, "capital" stocks like rare ores and fossil fuels. Third, the first two characteristics encourage the revival of predominantly labor-intensive modes of production. Fourth, these three together imply the creation of a "low-throughput" economy, in which the per-capita use of resources is minimized and long-term thermodynamic and social costs are not ignored for the sake of short-term benefits. Fifth, all of these seem to point to technologies that are smaller, simpler, less dependent on a specialized technical elite, and therefore more decentralized with respect both to location and to control of the means of production. Finally, among the possible social side effects of such alternative technologies are greater cultural diversity, reduced liability to misuse of technology by individuals and nations, and less overall anomie and alienation once individuals have greater control over their own lives than they do under the current technological dispensation.

Naturally, one way to achieve these goals would be to renounce modern science and technology entirely and revert to a low-technology, pre-modern agrarian society, but the proponents of alternative technology are not urging a return to some fantasied paradise of pristine closeness to nature. They propose instead a creative blend of the most advanced modern science and technology with the best of the old, pre–Industrial Revolution "polytechnics" (Mumford 1970). Yet at the same time alternative technology is indeed profoundly anti-technological, for it is diametrically opposed to *autonomous* technological growth of the kind that has produced an ecological crisis. Perhaps technology has not exerted a determining influence on modern society, as some of its more extreme critics maintain, but it is quite evident that during the last 300 years society has adapted to technology rather than vice versa. In seeking to

---

Energy has thus been the modern industrial world's all-purpose antidote to the poison of scarcity. But energy is itself becoming ecologically scarce and, if for no other reason than its potential long-term effects on the global heat balance, this antidote must eventually lose all its efficacy.* Without cheap, safe, and abundant energy, most of the proposed technological solutions to the problems of growth simply evaporate.

Another persistent theme of our discussion has been diminishing returns, which have overtaken not only agricultural production but every other economic activity—the limits to the efficiency of pollution control and of energy conversion, the need to mine ever thinner ores to get the same useful quantity of metals, the need to pour ever more money and energy into the maintenance of the basic technological infrastructure, and so on. Instead of being able to do ever more with ever less or to substitute one resource for another indefinitely, as is often claimed by economists, we shall have to

---

*Of course, there will be temporary surpluses on the way to scarcity. For example, there may be an oil glut in the 1980's as all the current efforts to expand supply bear fruit. But such temporary fluctuations of supply and demand, typical of commodity markets, will have little or no effect on the overall trend toward scarcity.

reverse this situation and bring the technological process under full social control, alternative technology poses a challenge to the current order that is in the broadest sense primarily political, not scientific or technical. (Indeed, most of the essential components of a viable alternative technology, such as solar power, are already known or invented and merely require development; the process of changeover could therefore be quite fast, unlike the Industrial Revolution, which had to wait on the slow pace of invention.) Thus, although alternative technology is technically feasible and could be installed without unacceptable social costs, its adoption will require a revolutionary break with the values of the industrial era.

A major unanswered question is how high the material standard of living will be. Unfortunately, the answer depends largely on how many people there are. It is abundantly clear that "soft" technology is able to provide an ample sufficiency of material well-being (but almost certainly not affluence) to very large numbers of people, but whether this figure is enormously less than the current 4 billion people, which is obviously too many, is not yet clear. One rough estimate is that a world population of about one billion people could be supported at the current standard of living of Norway or the Netherlands (de Bell 1970, p. 154), and this seems intuitively closer to the mark than 4 billion. It therefore appears that if we wish to maintain living standards anywhere near levels we regard as adequate for a dignified life for the many, population control is imperative. However, even if population is controlled so that living standards are kept relatively high in terms of per-capita use of resources, people will have to work for their affluence instead of depending on "energy slaves" as they now do. Thus a world in ecological balance with its resources by means of alternative technology will almost certainly contain fewer people than it does today, and those people will have to be satisfied with a more frugal and hardworking existence than the affluent minority now enjoys.

spend more money, energy, and social effort to obtain the same or even a diminished quantity of useful output. Furthermore, every proposed technological solution to the problems of growth calls for more materials (often of a very particular and scarce type), creates more pollution (or demands more technological solutions to control it), requires more energy, and absorbs more human resources. Thus the costs of coping with each additional increment of growth rise inexorably and exponentially.

We have also seen that in general all sectors are interacting and interdependent, so that on the one hand, the combination of sectoral microproblems creates an almost overwhelming macro-problem, while on the other hand, the solutions to the macro-problem as well as most of the separate micro-problems depend on the questionable availability of a host of factors potentially in least supply. Thus problems exacerbate each other. Also, the solution to one micro-problem is often inconsistent with the solution to other micro-problems or is dependent on the solution of still another problem, which depends in turn on the solution to a third problem, and so on. In short, nothing less than a coordinated strategy taking into account the full ensemble of problems and their interactions can hope to succeed.

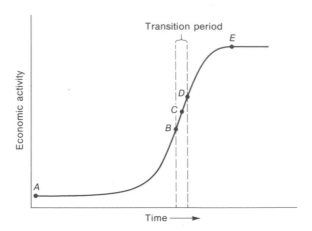

FIGURE 3-1.
Growth curve of industrial civilization: *A*, steady state (beginning of accelerating growth); *B*, end of unrestrained growth (beginning of transition period); *C*, point of inflection (beginning of deceleration); *D*, end of transition period; *E*, terminal steady state.

Thus, stating that ecological scarcity will one day bring growth to a halt is much more than asserting the truism that the earth is finite and that growth must therefore cease some day in the future. Ecological scarcity is indeed ultimately grounded on the physical scarcity inherent in the earth's finitude, but it is manifested primarily by the multitude of interacting and interdependent limits to growth that will prevent us from ever testing the finitude of the biosphere and its resources. In fact, as we shall see, ecological scarcity has already begun to restrain growth.

The overall course of industrial civilization as it responds to ecological scarcity is illustrated graphically in Figure 3-1 by the familiar sigmoid or logistic growth curve. In the period from *A* to *B,* the ecological and other resources necessary for growth are present in abundance (at least potentially) and splendid and accelerating growth ensues, as it has during the last 300 years or more. However, eventually resources are no longer abundant enough to support further growth, and technological ingenuity can no longer put off the day of reckoning. At this point of inflection *(C)* deceleration begins; in the narrow transition zone *(B* to *D)* approximately one doubling period wide about the point of inflection, considerable further growth occurs owing to momentum, but the ecological abundance that fueled accelerating growth begins to disappear, and the first warning signs of ecological scarcity are quickly succeeded by various negative feedback pressures that start to choke off further growth. Beyond the brief transition period these pressures build up quite rapidly, and deceleration continues until equilibrium *(E)* is attained. The zone of transition is therefore the most critical section of the growth curve; the entire changeover from accelerating to decelerating growth occurs in a very brief time, especially compared to the long and seemingly infinite period of growth that precedes it, during which the very idea of limits or scarcity, except as temporary challenges to ingenuity, seems ludicrous.

Thus ecological scarcity only becomes evident once the curve is within the transition zone. This being the case, the mere fact that so many aspects of ecological scarcity have been discussed and debated at great length should be ample evidence that industrial civilization is near or past the point of inflection and confronts the prospect of deceleration to a steady state. Yet, in fact, the controversy continues. As noted in the Introduction, the time factor is the crux of the debate over the limits to growth, so let us examine in greater detail the question of how far away industrial civilization is from the ultimate and proximate limits to growth.

How Far Away Is Ecological Scarcity?

The simplest impressionistic evidence ought to show convincingly that we have entered the transition zone. Rising pollution problems, not only in industrial nations but in many over-crowded and over-urbanized developing countries, were the first signs of thermodynamic bills coming due. They were sufficiently grave by the late 1960's to provoke the convening of a United Nations Conference on the Human Environment in Stockholm in 1972, leading to the establishment of the United Nations Environmental Program to monitor global pollution and coordinate international efforts to forestall further ecological degradation. Yet pollution and ecological degradation continued apace. There followed in very short order an energy crisis, which is continuing, and a food and population crisis (and famine) that in 1974 occasioned two major United Nations conferences—the World Population Conference in Bucharest and the World Food Conference in Rome; whatever their views on the long-term capacity of the earth to feed more people or provide more energy, experts agree on the short- and middle-term gravity of these interlocking crises. Even the oceans—once, along with the atmosphere, the epitome of the free good that could be used in common without let or hindrance—have become scarce resources, creating thorny political problems that a succession of United Nations conferences on the law of the sea have only partly resolved.

The rampant inflation that afflicted nearly every country in the world between 1972 and 1975 was at least in part due to ecological scarcity. Experts differ in their assignment of causes for this unprecedented global plague of inflation, but a theme common to almost all explanations is that, as production of food and other kinds of basic resources has begun to lag behind ever increasing demand (stimulated by greater affluence in some quarters and increased numbers of consumers in others), commodity prices have been bid up by individuals and nations pursuing goods that are in ever shorter supply. Thus scarcity has pushed and demand has pulled the prices of the staples of the world household higher. The four-fold increase in crude oil prices charged by the major oil exporters was only the most striking and newsworthy instance of a general trend (and it was made possible only because a real scarcity of this critical resource turned a buyer's market into a seller's market virtually overnight, although many had foreseen it). In addition, the extra costs of pollution control and of declining net energy yield, as well as diminishing returns generally, intensify this basic upward pressure on prices from genuine physical shortages. In effect, money is a symbol of the direct relationship between people and physical resources, so that when these two fall out of balance real inflation inevitably occurs, as it has many times in the past in similar circumstances (Russell 1971).*

Many find this kind of impressionistic evidence unconvincing, so let us approach the problem more quantitatively. The most authoritative study of man's impact on the environment estimated that overall environmental impact was growing at a rate of 5 to 6 percent per annum (SCEP 1970, p. 22), thus doubling approximately every 14 years. Assuming no slowdown in growth, overall environmental impact would therefore have to be four times as great as current levels in 2005 and sixteen times as great in 2033. On the basis of current evidence it is obvious that the intense stress on the world's ecosystems implied by the latter figure could not be supported, especially when it is historically clear that each increment of growth increases the environmental stress more than the previous one; even four times the current environmental stress would probably be only barely tolerable. Nor do we appear to have the resources to support the levels of demand for food, minerals, and energy implied by such figures.

Stated another way, if today the overall human demand on the environment is equivalent to a mere 5 percent of the carrying capacity of the global ecosystem, then at a 5 percent rate of growth, the environmental demand will reach the saturation point of 100 percent by about 2036. However, as pointed out in Chapter 1, saturation of the carrying capacity is a theoretical maximum, not a practical one. A substantial ecological margin is essential, and a sustainable level over the long term would have to be perhaps as little as half the maximum. Moreover, the carrying capacity is not a permanently fixed value; it *decreases* with the depletion and degradation of resources (Figure 3-2), so that this calculation of carrying capacity is doubly suspect. Above all, the assumption that 95 percent of the global carrying capacity is

---

*Naturally, this kind of cost-push and demand-pull inflation has been exacerbated in many countries by monetary inflation, which seems to be due in large part to the unwillingness of governments to permit some of the negative feedback effects tending to restrain growth to have their full impact on the national economy and the life of the citizens. This is a topic we shall explore further in Part II.

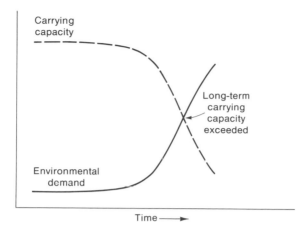

FIGURE 3-2.
Growth versus carrying capacity. If growth results in environmental degradation, the carrying capacity is progressively reduced.

presently unused simply flies in the face of all the evidence. The scale of human activities already threatens to overwhelm nature in many areas and sectors (Holdren and Ehrlich 1974, pp. 286–287; SCEP 1970, pp. 114–119). Indeed, most ecologists would argue that the carrying capacity has already been exceeded whenever one can observe dangerous levels of pollution, serious ecological degradation, or widespread disturbance of natural balances, all of which are readily observable today. Thus, although precision is not attainable, the available quantitative evidence rather strongly suggests that industrial civilization will be obliged to make an abrupt transition from full-speed-ahead growth to some kind of equilibrium or steady-state society in little more than one generation and that the process of deceleration has already begun.

The Historical Significance of Ecological Scarcity

The essential meaning of ecological scarcity is that mankind's political, economic, and social life must once again become thoroughly rooted in the physical realities of the biosphere. Scarcity and physical necessity have not been abolished; after a brief historical interlude of apparently endless abundance they have returned, stronger than ever (with political consequences, to be taken up in Part II). Because of ecological scarcity, many things that we now take as axiomatic will be inverted in the near future. For example, during the growth era capital and labor were the critical factors in the economic process; henceforth, land and resources (that is, nature) will be critical. In addition, since the United States, Europe, and Japan—the so-called "haves"—are now living to some extent beyond their ecological means, they may turn into ecological and economic "have-nots," while some current "have-nots," who are comparatively resource rich, will suddenly become the new "haves"—a transformation that is already under way. All the institutions and values of industrial societies predicated on continuous growth will be confronted with ruthless reality tests and revolutionary challenges. Above all, the sudden coming of ecological scarcity means that our generation is faced with an epochal political task. Since the transition is under way regardless of our wishes in the matter, our only proper course is to learn how to adapt humanely to the exigencies of ecological scarcity and guide the transition to equilibrium in the direction of a desirable steady-state society.

The great danger from the sudden emergence of ecological scarcity is that we will not respond to its challenges in time. We have already seen that time is probably our scarcest resource; the sheer momentum of growth, the long time constants built into the biosphere and, above all, social response rates that for various reasons lag behind events (and are in any event governed by the factor in least supply) all predispose the world system and most of its subsystems to overshoot the level that would be sustainable over the long term. But the inevitable consequence of overshoot is collapse. The trend depicted in Figure 3-2 cannot continue in the real world, for environmental demand can never long exceed the carrying capacity. Figure 3-3 represents the three basic real-world possibilities: (a) smooth convergence on the optimal equilibrium level (which is, as noted above, unlikely); (b) overshoot and collapse with eventual convergence on a relatively high equilibrium level; and (c) overshoot and collapse to a significantly lower than optimal equilibrium level, because the carrying capacity has been drastically eroded by the destructiveness associated with the overshoot.

Because the earth's carrying capacity is clearly being depleted and degraded, we are speeding rapidly toward the outcome depicted in Figure 3 c, which is highly undesirable for at least three reasons: the toll of suffering and misery created by a large overshoot of the carrying capacity will be enormous; any large overshoot seems certain to erode the carrying capacity so severely that the surviving civilization will have rather limited material possibilities; and the opportunity to build the basic technological and social infrastructure of a high-level steady-state society may be irretrievably lost— that is, unless the remaining supplies of non-renewable resources are carefully husbanded and used to make a planned transition to a high-technology steady state, only steady states comparatively poor in material terms will be achievable with the depleted resources left following overshoot and collapse.

FIGURE 3-3.
Three scenarios for the transition from growth to maturity: (a) smooth transition to equilibrium with minimal erosion of carrying capacity; (b) overshoot with substantial erosion of carrying capacity; (c) overshoot with drastic erosion of carrying capacity.

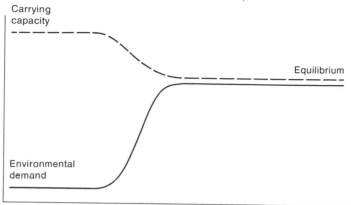

(a)

Carrying capacity

Equilibrium

Environmental demand

Time ⟶

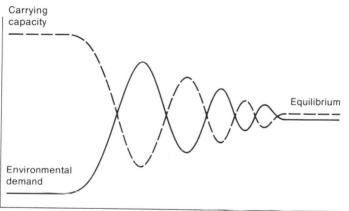

(b)

Carrying capacity

Equilibrium

Environmental demand

Time ⟶

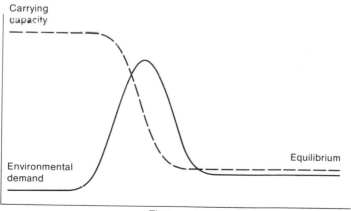

(c)

Carrying capacity

Equilibrium

Environmental demand

Time ⟶

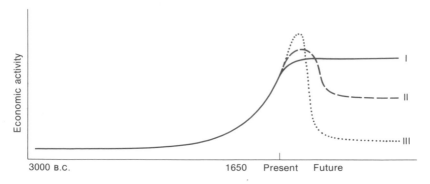

FIGURE 3-4.
The ecological history of the world—past, present, and future: I, direct transition to high-level steady state; II, belated transition to somewhat lower-level steady state; III, reversion to pre-modern agrarian way of life.

Thus, although ecological scarcity means that there is no option other than the steady-state society in which men and their demands are in balance with the environment and its resources, the current generation does have a significant say about the type and basic quality of the steady state that will be achieved. The basic policy options are presented graphically in Figure 3-4.

Throughout most of recorded history, the human race has existed in rough equilibrium with its resource base. Growth occurred, if at all, at an infinitesimal pace; even the population of relatively dynamic Europe grew at much less than 1 percent per annum between 600 and 1600 A.D. But then, very suddenly, the Industrial Revolution rocketed the scale of economic activity upward. With the arrival of ecological scarcity, the rocket cannot continue to rise. The first policy option (I in Figure 3-4) is an immediate and direct transition to a steady-state civilization relatively affluent in material terms (however frugal it might seem to many now living in the richest countries). If this option is not taken, overshoot must occasion a fall to a significantly lower steady-state level than could have been achieved by carefully planned and timely action (II), or even to a level tantamount to a reversion to the traditional pre-modern agrarian way of life (III), so that the entire Industrial Revolution from start to finish will appear as a brief and anomalous spike in humanity's otherwise flat ecological trace, a transitory epoch of a few centuries duration in which it seemed momentarily possible to abolish scarcity.*

In short, we stand at a genuine civilizational crossroads. Ecological scar-

---

*There is some risk that, in trying to make the immediate and direct transition I in Figure 3-4, we shall achieve a steady-state level somewhat lower than the maximum possible. However, the sacrifice of such a marginal gain seems small compared to the risks attached to overshoot. Moreover, it will always be possible to adjust upward if later experience or further invention make it feasible; thus the marginal gains will be forgone only temporarily.

city is not completely new in history, but the crisis we confront is largely unprecedented. That is, it is not a simple repetition of the classic Malthusian apocalypse on a larger scale, in which nothing has changed but the numbers of people, the ruthlessness of the checks, and therefore the greater potential for misery once the day of reckoning comes. The wars, plagues, and famines that have toppled previous civilizations are overshadowed by horrible checks Malthus never dreamt of, like large-scale ecological ruin or global radiation poisoning, for these checks are threats to the very existence of the species. On the other hand, we also possess technical resources that previous civilizations did not when they encountered the challenges of ecological scarcity. Thus in our case a successful response is possible: we can create a reasonably affluent post-industrial, steady-state civilization and avoid a traumatic fall into a version of pre-industrial civilization.

This imposing task devolves upon the current generation. But there is no time to lose. Already many trends, like demographic momentum, cannot be reversed within any reasonable time without Draconian measures. Moreover, as we shall see in Part II, the way ahead is strewn with painful dilemmas. Indeed, nothing can be accomplished without the frustration of many deeply ingrained expectations and the exaction of genuine sacrifices. The epoch we have already entered is a turning point in the ecological history of the human race comparable to the Neolithic Revolution; it will inevitably involve racking political turmoil and an extraordinary reconstitution of the reigning political paradigm throughout most of the modern world.

BIBLIOGRAPHIC NOTE

Most of the general works on ecological limits discussed in the preceding chapter's Bibliographic Note deal with energy. However, the book that best pursues the topic in depth is Earl Cook's recent, comprehensive, and authoritative *Man, Energy, Society*. Wilson Clark's encyclopedic *Energy for Survival* is also excellent and is especially good on alternative energy technologies. For a shorter treatment, *Energy and the Future*, by Allen Hammond, William Metz, and Thomas Maugh, is a first-rate collection of authoritative, concise, and well-written articles on energy originally published separately in *Science*. Equal both in general quality and in authority, Scientific American's *Energy and Power* neatly complements the *Science* articles (which tend to be rather narrowly topical) with general discussions of energy conversion, the role of human energy processes in the biosphere, and other broad subjects that help to put energy in its proper ecological perspective. The best of the avowedly environmentalist books on energy are Amory Lovins' *World Energy Strategies* and *Non-Nuclear Futures,* which discuss ethical as well as scientific concerns. The RAND Corporation's *California's Electric Quandary* is really a detailed case study of the energy quandary facing industrial civilization as a whole; California simply offers a microcosmic example of the enormous problems inherent in continued energy growth. Detailed figures on energy resources, projected demand, costs of alternatives, and the like for the United States as a whole are contained in two studies done for the Senate Committee on Interior and Insular Affairs: RANN's *Summary Report of the Cornell Workshop on Energy and the Environment* and RFF's *Energy Research and Development—Problems and Prospects.*

For those interested in delving further into the controversial issue of the risks and benefits of nuclear power, two books stand out from the polemical crowd by being relatively objective and fair without sacrificing trenchancy: David Inglis' textbook *Nuclear Energy—Its Physics and Social Challenge* is a comprehensive and scientifically solid (but not excessively technical) treatment of all aspects of this difficult topic (including weaponry) that serves well as a kind of all-purpose social and environmental impact statement for the nuclear age; Richard Lewis' *The Nuclear-Power Rebellion* plunges more deeply and critically into the murky and increasingly controversial politics of nuclear power and thus provides a useful complement to Inglis' more classroom-style technical discussion. The majority of the references on nuclear power in the List of Sources are frankly critical, but a number of more neutral assessments by qualified journalists (for example, the appropriate articles in Hammond, Metz, and Maugh 1973) and engineers (for example, Rose 1974b) are included, as well as some outright panegyrics to nuclear power as the cure-all for energy problems (R. P. Hammond 1974; Seaborg and Corliss 1971).

On the critical subject of climate, SMIC's *Inadvertent Climate Modification* is the most authoritative overall treatment, but it is already quite out of date, for later research (provoked in part by the impact its publication had on the scientific community) has vastly expanded the array of potentially grave climatic consequences of energy use and other human actions.

The basic work on the principles of thermodynamic economics is Nicholas Georgescu-Roegen's very difficult *The Entropy Law and the Economic Process.* Fortunately, his essential ideas are contained in two articles destined for a more general audience (1973; 1975). In addition, the List of Sources cites works by Kenneth Boulding (1964, Chap. 7; 1973), Herman Daly (1973), and Howard Odum (1971; 1973) that will aid in understanding this radically different perspective on economics.

Finally, Fred Cottrell's *Energy and Society,* a comprehensive study of the effects of energy on human life through the ages, shows how energy (much more than food) has always been the staff of civilization's life and how forms of society invariably mirror the quality and abundance of available energy. This classic work provides the essential historical background for a full and balanced appreciation of the energy quandary confronting industrial civilization today.

Unfortunately, the technological and managerial issues discussed in the second section of this chapter, like time and capital costs, have not been given the same kind of sustained and comprehensive treatment as energy and other major environmental issues. However, Victor Ferkiss' *Technological Man* and Kenneth

Watt's *The Titanic Effect* both deal with many of the issues, and the two books by John McHale mentioned in the preceding chapter's Bibliographic Note, *The Future of the Future* and *The Ecological Context,* are also useful on many points, for McHale (unlike many other technologists) gives serious consideration to the management problems inherent in super-technology. A stimulating recent book by Rufus Miles, *Awakening from the American Dream: The Social and Political Limits to Growth,* focuses on the unmanageable complexity created by a high rate of energy use. Since Miles treats in greater depth and from a more avowedly political perspective a number of the issues raised in this chapter, his book is a most valuable complement to my own analysis of the managerial limits to growth.

Again, back issues of the major periodicals mentioned in the first Bibliographic Note contain many interesting articles. *Science* is, of course, outstanding in this respect; the special issue on energy cited in the List of Sources (Abelson 1974) contains a bibliography of past articles. *Bulletin of the Atomic Scientists, New Scientist,* and *Technology Review* have covered energy extensively, and *Environment* and *The Ecologist* have given special attention to social implications and alternative technology.

II

THE DILEMMAS
OF SCARCITY

4

THE POLITICS OF SCARCITY

Having explored the general nature and meaning of ecological scarcity, we shall now delve into its political consequences. This chapter will examine the basic political dynamics of ecological scarcity; Chapters 5 and 6 will assess the specific challenge to the American market system; and Chapter 7 will extend the analysis of the preceding three chapters, showing that it applies in all important respects to the rest of the world.

The Political Evils of Scarcity

It was suggested in the Introduction that scarcity is the source of original political sin: resources that are scantier than human wants have to be allocated by governments, for otherwise, naked conflict would result. In the words of philosopher Thomas Hobbes in *Leviathan* (1651, p. 107), the life of man in an anarchic "state of nature" is "solitary, poor, nasty, brutish, and short"; to prevent the perpetual struggle for power in a war of all against all, there must be a civil authority capable of keeping the peace by regulating property and other scarce goods. Scarcity thus makes politics inescapable.

Presumably, the establishment of a truly just civil authority would completely eliminate all the political problems that arise from scarcity. With all assured of a fair share of goods, social harmony would replace strife, and men would enjoy long and happy lives of peaceful cooperation. Unfortunately, this has never happened. Although they have certainly mitigated some of the worst aspects of the anarchic state of nature (especially the total insecurity that prevails in the war of all against all), civilized polities have always institutionalized a large measure of inequality, oppression, and conflict. Thus, in addition to being the source of original political sin, scarcity is also the root of political evil.

The reason is quite simple. For most of recorded history, societies have existed at the ecological margin, or very close to it. An equal division of income and wealth, therefore, would condemn all to a life of shared poverty. Not unnaturally, the tendency has been for political institutions to further impoverish the masses by a fractional amount so as to create a surplus enabling a small elite to enjoy the fruits of civilized life. Indeed, until recently energy has been so scarce that serfdom and slavery have been the norm—justifiably so, says Aristotle in his *Politics,* for otherwise genuine civilization would be impossible. Except for a few relatively brief periods when for some reason the burden of scarcity was temporarily lifted, inequality, oppression, and conflict have been very prominent features of political life, merely waxing and waning slightly according to the character of the rulers and other ephemeral factors.

Our own era has been the longest and certainly the most important exception. During roughly the last 450 years, the carrying capacity of the globe (and especially of the highly developed nations) has been markedly expanded, and several centuries of relative abundance have completely transformed the face of the earth and made our societies and our civilization what they are today—relatively open, egalitarian, libertarian, and conflict-free.

The Great Frontier

The causes of the four-century-long economic boom we have enjoyed are readily apparent: the European discovery and exploitation of the New World, Oceania, and other founts of virgin resources (for example, Persian Gulf oil); the take-off and rapid-growth phases of science-based, energy-intensive technology; and the existence of vast reservoirs of "free" ecological goods like air and water to absorb the consequences of exploiting the new resources with the new technology. However, the first cause is clearly the most important.

Before the discovery of the New World, the population of Europe pressed hard on its means of subsistence; as a result, European societies were politically, economically, and socially closed. But with the opening up of a

"Great Frontier" in the New World, Europe suddenly faced a seemingly limitless panorama of ecological riches—the area of land available for cultivation was suddenly multiplied about five times; vast stands of high-grade timber, a scarce commodity in Europe, stretched as far as the eye could see; gold and silver were there for the taking, and rich lodes of other metals lay ready for exploitation; the introduction of the potato and other new food crops from the New World boosted European agricultural production so sharply that the population doubled between 1750 and 1850. This bonanza of found wealth lifted the yoke of ecological scarcity and, coincidentally, created all the peculiar institutions and values characteristic of modern civilization—democracy, freedom, and individualism.*

Indeed, the existence of such ecological abundance is an indispensible premise of the libertarian doctrines of John Locke and Adam Smith, the two thinkers whose works epitomize the modern bourgeois views of political economy upon which all the institutions of open societies are based. For example, Locke (1690, paras. 27–29) justifies the institution of property by saying that it derives from the mixture of a man's labor with the original commons of nature. But he continually emphasizes that for one man to make part of what is the common heritage of mankind his own property does not work to the disadvantage of other men. Why? Because "there was still enough and as good left; and more than the yet unprovided could use" (para. 33). His argument on property by appropriation is shot through with references to the wilderness of the New World, which only needed to be occupied and cultivated to be turned into property for any man who desired it. Locke's justification of original property and the natural right of a man to appropriate it from nature thus rests on cornucopian assumptions: there is always more left; society can therefore be libertarian.

The economics of Adam Smith rests on a similar vision of ecological abundance. In fact, Smith is even more optimistic than Locke, for he stresses that the opportunity to become a man of property (and therefore to enjoy the benefits of liberty) now lies more in trade and industry than in agriculture, which is potentially limited by the availability of arable land. Indeed, says Smith, under prevailing conditions, simply striking off all the mercantilist shackles on economic development and permitting a free-for-all, laissez-faire system of wealth-getting to operate instead would generate "opulence," which would in turn liberate men from the social and political restrictions of feudalism. Smith's *The Wealth of Nations* (1776) is therefore a manifesto for

---

*Of course, the idea of individualism antedated the discovery of the New World, but until then it had had little opportunity for concrete expression. However, once the boom permitted it to be expressed, individualism became the basis for almost all the most characteristic features of modernity: self-rule in democracy, self-enrichment in industrial capitalism, self-salvation in Protestantism.

the attainment of political liberty through the economic exploitation of the found wealth of the Great Frontier.

The liberal ideas of Locke and Smith have not gone unchallenged, but with very few exceptions, liberals, conservatives, socialists, communists, and other modern ideologists have taken abundance for granted and assumed the necessity of further growth. They have disagreed only about how to produce enough wealth to satisfy the demands of hedonistic, materialistic "economic" men and about what constitutes a just division of the spoils. Karl Marx was even more utopian than either Locke or Smith, for he envisioned the eventual abolition of scarcity; he merely insisted that, on grounds of social justice, the march of progress be centrally directed by the state in the interest of those whose labor actually produced the goods.

But the boom is now over. The found wealth of the Great Frontier has been all but exhausted; technology is no real substitute, for it is merely a means of manipulating *what is already there* rather than a way of creating genuinely new resources on the scale of the Great Frontier. (Moreover, as we have seen in Part I, technology is encountering limits of its own.) Thus, a scarcity at least as intense as that prevailing in the pre-modern era, however different it may be in important respects, is about to replace abundance, and this will necessarily undercut the material conditions that have created and sustained current ideas, institutions, and practices. Once relative abundance and wealth of opportunity are no longer available to mitigate the harsh political dynamics of scarcity, the pressures favoring greater inequality, oppression, and conflict will build up, so that the return of scarcity portends the revival of age-old political evils, for our descendants if not for ourselves. In short, the golden age of individualism, liberty, and democracy is all but over. In many important respects, we shall be obliged to return to something resembling the pre-modern, closed polity. This conclusion will be reinforced by a more detailed exploration of the political problem of controlling the competitive overexploitation of resources that has produced the ecological crisis.

The Tragedy of the Commons

It has been known since ancient times that resources held or used in common tend to be abused. As Aristotle said, "What is common to the greatest number gets the least amount of care" (Barker 1962, p. 44). However, the dynamic underlying such abuse was first suggested by a little-known Malthusian of the early 19th century, William Forster Lloyd (cited in Hardin 1969, p. 29), who wondered why the cattle on a common pasture were "so puny and stunted" and the common itself "bare-worn." He found that such an outcome was almost inevitable.

Men seeking gain naturally desire to increase the size of their herds. Since the commons is finite, the day must come when the total number of cattle reaches the carrying capacity; the addition of more cattle will cause the pasture to deteriorate and eventually destroy the resource on which the herdsmen depend. Yet, even knowing this to be the case, it is still in the rational self-interest of each herdsman to keep adding animals to his herd. Each reasons that his personal gain from adding animals outweighs his proportionate share of the damage done to the commons, for the damage is done to the commons as a whole and is thus partitioned among all the users. Worse, even if he is inclined to self-restraint, an individual herdsman justifiably fears that others may not be. They will increase their herds and gain thereby, while he will have to suffer equally the resulting damage. Competitive overexploitation of the commons is the inevitable result.

The same dynamic of competitive overexploitation applies to any "common-property resource," the economist's term for resources held or used in common. A classic illustration is the oil pool. Unless one person or organization controls the rights to exploit an oil pool or the owners of the rights can agree on a scheme of rational exploitation, it is in the interest of each to extract oil from the common pool as fast as he possibly can; in fact, failure to do so exposes the individual owner to the risk that others will not leave him his fair share. Thus, in the early boom days of the American oil industry, drillers competed with each other to sink as many wells as possible on their properties. The result was economic and political chaos, soon remedied by the establishment of state control boards that surveyed the pools and then allotted each owner a quota of production for each acre of oil-bearing land. Oil was thereby transformed from a common property resource to private property, and exploitation proceeded thereafter in a largely rational and conflict-free manner.

The dynamic of the commons is particularly stark in the case of oil, for one person's gains are another's losses. But even resources that could be exploited cooperatively to give a sustained yield in perpetuity are subject to the same dynamic. Fisheries are a prime example. At first, there was abundance enough for all to exploit the resource freely. Conflicts occurred, but their impact was local. Fishing a little farther away or improving techniques were alternatives to fighting over the limited resources in a particular area. However, in time even the vastness of the ocean began to be more or less fully exploited, and people responded just as they did in the early days of the oil business. Some nations attempted to privatize parts of the fishing common, so that all the benefits of the fishery would flow to their nationals. Thus fishing "wars" and other political conflicts over marine resources are now very common. Others responded by increasing the scale and technical virtuosity of their fishing operations, just as early oil drillers would sink dozens of wells on a tiny piece of land. Technological progress in the fishing industry has produced gigantic floating factories, which use ultramodern techniques to catch fish and can or freeze them on the spot, thus eliminating the time wasted by traditional methods in returning to port. The result, as one might have predicted, has been relentless competitive overexploitation and an alarming general decline in fish stocks.

Pollution also exemplifies the self-destructive logic of the commons, for it simply reverses the dynamic of competitive overexploitation without altering its nature: the cost to me of controlling my emissions is so much larger than my proportionate share of the environmental damage they cause that it will always be rational for me to pollute if I can get away with it. In short, it profits me to harm the public. (It does not pay me to benefit the public either; see Box 4-1.)

Unfortunately, virtually all ecological resources—airsheds, watersheds, the land, the oceans, the atmosphere, biological cycles, the biosphere itself—are common property resources. For example, the smoke from factories or the exhaust gases from automobiles cannot be confined so that their noxious effects harm only those who produce them. They harm all in the common airshed. Even most resources that seem to be private property are in fact part of the ecological commons. The timberman who cuts down a whole stand of trees in order to maximize his profits contributes to flooding, siltation, and the decline of water quality in his watershed; if enough timbermen cut down enough trees, even climate may be altered, as has occurred many times in the past. Now that the carrying capacity of the biosphere has been approached, if not exceeded, we are in serious danger of destroying all ecological resources by competitive overexploitation. Thus the metaphor of the commons is not merely an assertion of man's ultimate dependence on the ecological life-support systems of the planet, but an accurate description of the current human predicament.

In short, resources that once were so abundant they were freely available to all have now become ecologically scarce. Unless they are somehow regulated and protected in the common interest, the inevitable outcome will be the mutual ecological ruin that the human ecologist Garrett Hardin (1968) has called "the tragedy of the commons." We need the same kind of social rules and political controls, but much more widely applied, that have traditionally governed the use of grazing lands and other commons in the past (although these controls have not always been sufficiently strong to avert partial or even total destruction of a resource).

A Hobbesian Solution?

Beyond telling us that the answer to the tragedy is "mutual coercion, mutually agreed upon by the majority of the people affected"—by which he means social restraint, not naked force—Hardin avoids political prescrip-

Box 4-1.   The Public-Goods Problem

The public-goods problem is the obverse of the commons problem. Just as the rational individual gains by harming fellow members of the common, he loses by benefiting them with a public or collective good. At best, he gets only a small return on his investment; at worst, he is economically punished. For example, the good husbandman cannot survive in a market economy; if he maintains his soil while his neighbors mine theirs for maximum yields, sooner or later he must either abandon farming or become a subsistence farmer outside the market. He cannot afford to benefit posterity except at great personal sacrifice. Similarly, although a socially responsible plant owner might wish to control the pollution emanating from his plant, if he does it at his own expense whatever his competitors do, then he is at a competitive disadvantage. Thus the tragedy of the commons, in which the culprit gets all the benefits from transgressing the limits of the commons but succeeds in relegating most of the costs to others, is turned around. One who tries to benefit the common good soon discovers that, while he pays all the costs, the other members of the community reap virtually all of the benefits.

Of course, a producer could try to persuade consumers to pay premium prices for his products as a reward for his virtue. But he would be unlikely to find many buyers for products that, however "virtuous," were no better than the cheaper ones of his

tion. However, he does suggest that unrestrained exercise of our liberties does not bring us real freedom: "Individuals locked into the logic of the commons are free only to bring on universal ruin; once they see the necessity of mutual coercion, they become free to pursue other goals"; by recognizing the necessity to abandon many natural freedoms we now believe we possess, we avoid tragedy and "preserve and nurture other and more precious freedoms." There are obvious dangers in a regime of "mutual coercion," but without restraints on individuals, the collective selfishness and irresponsibility produced by the logic of the commons will destroy the spaceship, so that any sacrifice of freedom by the crew members is clearly the lesser evil. After all, says Hardin, "injustice is preferable to total ruin," so that "an alternative to the commons need not be perfectly just to be preferable" (Hardin 1968, pp. 1247–1248).

Hardin's implicit political theory is in all important respects identical to that of Thomas Hobbes in *Leviathan* (1651). Hardin's "logic of the commons" is simply a special version of the general political dynamic of Hobbes' "state of nature." Hobbes says that where men desire goods scarcer than their wants, they are likely to fall to fighting. They each know individually that all would be better off if they abstained from fighting and found some way of equitably sharing the desired goods. However, they also realize that they cannot alter the dynamics of the situation by their own behavior. In the absence of a civil authority to keep the peace, personal pacifism merely makes them a prey to others. Unless all can be persuaded or forced to lay down their arms simultaneously, nothing can prevent the war of all against all. The crucial problem in the state of nature is thus to make it safe for men

competitors. Another conceivable solution would be for the manufacturer who intended to control pollution to take up a collection from all those affected. After all, if his pollution is harmful to them, they should be willing to pay something to reduce or eliminate it. However, even if the considerable practical difficulties of organizing such a scheme were overcome it would almost certainly fail, for people are unlikely to contribute voluntarily to pollution reduction or the production of any other kind of public good in optimal amounts. The reason is simple: it is entirely rational for individuals to try to make others pay most or all of the costs of a public good that benefits everyone equally; thus the good is never available in optimal quantity under market conditions. For example, no government can subsist on voluntary tax payments; if external defense, internal order, rules for economic competition, public health, education, and other public goods are to be produced in quantities that are rationally desirable for the society, then taxes must be compulsory on all its members. Similarly, if ecological public goods like clean air and water or pleasant landscapes are to be provided in reasonable amounts, it will be only as a result of collective decisions. Thus, just as for the tragedy of the commons, the answer to the public-goods problem is authoritative political action.

to be reasonable, rather than merely "rational," so that they can share peacefully what the environment has to offer. Hobbes' solution was the erection by a majority of a sovereign power that would constrain all men to be reasonable and peaceful—that is, Hardin's "mutual coercion, mutually agreed upon by the majority of the people affected."*

In the tragedy of the commons, the dilemma is not as stark as it is in the state of nature—political order is not at stake—but it is in many ways much more insidious, for even without evil propensities on the part of any person or group the tragedy will occur. In the case of the village common the actors can hardly avoid noticing the causal relationship between their acts and the deterioration of the commons, but in most cases of competitive overexploitation individuals are not even aware of the damage that their acts are causing; even if they are aware their own responsibility seems infinitesimally dilute. Thus, to bring about the tragedy of the commons it is not necessary that men be bad, only that they not be actively good—that is, not altruistic enough to limit their own behavior when their fellows will not regularly perform acts of public generosity. That people are in fact not this altruistic is confirmed daily by behavior any one of us sees around him (and see Schelling 1971).

A perfect illustration of the insidiousness of the tragedy of the commons in operation is the situation of the inhabitants of Los Angeles vis-a-vis the automobile:

---

*For a fuller discussion of the virtual identity of analyses and prescriptions in Hardin and Hobbes, see Ophuls 1973.

Box 4–2. Coercion

The word "coercion" has a nasty fascist ring to it. However, politics is a means of taming and legitimating power, not dispensing with it. Any form of state power is coercive. A classic example is taxation, which is nowhere voluntary, for as the theory of public goods (see Box 4-1) tells us, the state would starve if it were. Assuming a reasonable degree of consensus and legitimacy, coercion means no more than a state-imposed structure of incentives and disincentives that is designed to achieve the common interest. Even Locke's libertarian political theory does not proscribe coercion—if the common interest is threatened, the sovereign must do whatever is necessary to protect it. Nevertheless, unlike Hobbes, Locke does try to set up inviolable spheres of private rights that the sovereign may not invade and also demands that power be continually beholden to consent of the governed. The difference between Hobbes and Locke on the matter of coercion is one of degree, with Locke demanding more formal guarantees of limits on the sovereign's power than Hobbes believes are workable. In short, coercion is not some evil specter resurrected from an odious past. It is an inextricable part of politics, and the problem is how best to tame it and bend it to the common interest.

Some aspire to do away with power politics and state coercion entirely by making men so virtuous that they will automatically do what is in the common interest. In

---

Every person who lives in this basin knows that for twenty-five years he has been living through a disaster. We have all watched it happen, have participated in it with full knowledge just as men and women once went knowingly and willingly into the "dark Satanic mills." The smog is the result of ten million individual pursuits of private gratification. But there is absolutely nothing that any individual can do to stop its spread. Each Angeleno is totally powerless to end what he hates. An individual act of renunciation is now nearly impossible, and, in any case, would be meaningless unless everyone else did the same thing. But he has no way of getting everyone else to do it. He does not even have any way to talk about such a course. He does not know how or where he would do it or what language he would use [Carney 1972, pp. 28–29].

As this example clearly shows, the essence of the tragedy of the commons is that one's own contribution to the problem (assuming that one is even aware of it) seems infinitesimally small, while the disadvantages of self-denial loom very large; self-restraint therefore appears to be both unprofitable and ultimately futile unless one can be certain of universal concurrence. Thus we are being destroyed ecologically not so much by the evil acts of selfish men as by the everyday acts of ordinary men whose behavior is dominated, usually unconsciously, by the remorseless self-destructive logic of the commons.

The tragedy of the commons also exemplifies the political problem that agitated the eighteenth-century French political philosopher Jean-Jacques Rousseau, who made a crucial distinction between the "general will" and the "will of all." The former is what reasonable men, leaving aside their

fact, this is precisely what Rousseau proposes: small, self-sufficient, frugal, intimate communities inculcating civic virtue so thoroughly that citizens become the "general will" incarnate. However, this merely changes the locus of coercion from outside to inside—the job of law enforcement is handed over to the internal police force of the superego—and many liberals (for example, Popper 1966) would argue that this kind of ideological or psychological coercion is far worse than overt controls on behavior. Nevertheless, political education cannot be done away with entirely, for without a reasonable degree of consensus and legitimacy no regime can long endure. Thus it is again a question of balance. Hobbes and Rousseau, for example, would both agree that law enforcement and political education must be combined, however much they might disagree on the fitting proportion of each.

In sum, political coercion in some form is inevitable. Failing to confront openly the issues it raises is likely to have the same effect repression has on the individual psyche—the repressed force returns in an unhealthy form. By contrast, if we face up to coercion full political awareness will dispel its seeming nastiness, and we shall be able to tame it and make it a pillar of the common interest. (Box 4-3 suggests a way of taming Leviathan, and Chapter 8 discusses the politics of a steady-state society in more general terms.)

self-interest and having the community's interests at heart, would regard as the right and proper course of action; the latter is the mere addition of the particular wills of the individuals forming the polity, based not on a conception of the common good, but only on what serves their own self-interest. The tragedy of the commons is simply a particularly vicious instance of the way in which the "will of all" falls short of the true common interest. In essence, Rousseau's answer to this crucial problem in *The Social Contract* is not much different from Hobbes': man must be "forced to be free"—that is, protected from the consequences of his own selfishness and shortsightedness by being made obedient to the common good or "general will," which represents his real self-interest. Rousseau thus wants political institutions that will make men virtuous

It therefore appears that if under conditions of ecological scarcity individuals rationally pursue their material self-interest unrestrained by a common authority that upholds the common interest, the eventual result is bound to be common environmental ruin. In that case, we must have political institutions that preserve the ecological common good from destruction by unrestrained human acts. The problem that the environmental crisis forces us to confront is, in fact, at the core of political philosophy: how to protect or advance the interests of the collectivity, when the individuals that make it up (or enough of them to create a problem) behave (or are impelled to behave) in a selfish, greedy, and quarrelsome fashion. The only solution is a sufficient measure of coercion (see Box 4-2). Following Hobbes, a certain minimum level of ecological order or peace must be established; following

Rousseau, a certain minimum level of ecological virtue must be imposed by our political institutions.

It hardly need be said that these conclusions about the tragedy of the commons radically challenge fundamental American and Western values. Under conditions of ecological scarcity the individual, possessing an inalienable right to pursue happiness as he defines it and exercising his liberty in a basically laissez-faire system, will inevitably produce the ruin of the commons. Accordingly, the individualistic basis of society, the concept of inalienable rights, the purely self-defined pursuit of happiness, liberty as maximum freedom of action, and laissez faire itself all become problematic, requiring major modification or perhaps even abandonment if we wish to avert inexorable environmental degradation and eventual extinction as a civilization. Certainly, democracy as we know it cannot conceivably survive.

This is an extreme conclusion, but it seems to follow from the extremity of the ecological predicament industrial man has created for himself. Even Hobbes' severest critics concede that he is most cogent when stark political choices are faced, for self-interest moderated by self-restraint may not be workable when extreme conditions prevail. Thus theorists have long analyzed international relations in Hobbesian terms, because the state of nature mirrors the state of armed peace existing between competing nation-states owing obedience to no higher power. Also, when social or natural disaster leads to a breakdown in the ordered patterns of society that ordinarily restrain men, even the most libertarian governments have never hesitated to impose martial law as the only alternative to anarchy. Therefore, if nuclear holocaust rather than mere war, or anarchy rather than a moderate level of disorder, or destruction of the biosphere rather than mere loss of amenity is the issue, the extremity of Hobbes' analysis fits reality, and it becomes difficult to avoid his conclusions. Similarly, although Rousseau's ultimate aim was the creation of a democratic polity, he recognized that strong sovereign power (a "Legislator" in Rousseau's language) may be necessary in certain circumstances, most especially if the bad habits of a politically "corrupt" people must be fundamentally reformed.

Altruism Is Not Enough

Some hope or assert that attitudinal change will bring about major changes in individual behavior sufficient to save a democratic, laissez-faire system from ecological ruin. However, except in very small and tightly knit social groups, education or the inculcation of rigid social norms is not sure proof against the logic of the commons. It seems to be simply not true that, once they are aware of the general gravity of the situation, men will naturally moderate their demands on the environment. A number of studies have shown that even the individuals who are presumably the most knowledgeable and concerned about population growth evince little willingness to restrain their own reproductive behavior (Attah 1973; Barnett 1971; Eisner et al. 1970). How much can we expect of the ordinary citizen? The problem is that, in order to forestall the logic of the commons, people in overwhelming numbers must be prepared to do positive good whether or not cooperation is universal; and in a political culture that conceives of the common interest as being no more than the sum of our individual interests it seems unlikely that we can prudently count on much help from unsupported altruism (this is not to say that people cannot be educated to be ecologically more responsible than they are at present).

In any event, even the most altruistic individual cannot behave responsibly without full knowledge of the consequences of his acts—and this is not available to him. If even the experts fiercely debate the pros and cons of nuclear power or the effects of a particular chemical on the ozone layer, using highly abstruse analytical techniques or complex computer programs that only the specialist can fully understand, how is the ordinary citizen to know what the facts are? An additional problem is time. High rates of change and exponential growth are accompanied by a serious lag in public understanding. For example, it seems to take two to four generations for the ideas at the frontier of science to filter down even to the informed public. We have still not completely digested Darwin, much less Einstein and quantum mechanics. How reasonable is it to expect from the public at large a sophisticated ecological understanding any time soon, especially since the academic, business, professional, and political elites who constitute the so-called attentive and informed public show little sign of having understood, much less embraced, the ecological world view?

Others pin their hopes for a solution not on individual conscience, but on the development of a collective conscience in the form of a world view or religion that would see man as the partner of nature rather than its antagonist. This will undoubtedly be essential for our survival in the long term, since without basic popular support even the most repressive regime could hardly hope to succeed in protecting the environment for long. However, mere changes in world view are not likely to be sufficient. Political and social arrangements that implement values are indispensable for turning ideals into actuality. For example, despite a basic world view that was profoundly respectful of nature, the Chinese have severely abused and degraded their environment throughout their very long history—more, ironically, than the pre-modern Europeans, who lacked a philosophy expressive of the same kind of natural harmony. Thus Chinese ideals were no proof against the urgency of human desires that drives the tragic logic of the commons. The further irony is that a reversal of this trend is now taking place under a Communist government, whose philosophy is the very antithesis of the traditional values embodied in Taoism and Buddhism, but which has a strong sense of the common interest and the will and the ability to carry it out.*

It appears therefore that individual conscience and the right kind of cultural attitudes are not by themselves sufficient to overcome the short-term calculations of utility that lead men to degrade their environment. Real altruism and genuine concern for posterity may not be entirely absent, but they are not present in sufficient strength to avert the tragedy. Only a government possessing great powers to regulate individual behavior in the ecological common interest can deal effectively with the tragedy of the commons.

To recapitulate, the tragic logic of the commons is sustained by three premises: a limited commons; cattle that need ample grazing room to prevent the commons from becoming "bare-worn"; and rational, self-seeking herdsmen. If any one of these premises is removed, the tragedy is averted. As we have already seen, the Great Frontier in fact effectively removed the first premise for nearly 400 years. It was precisely this that allowed John Locke, whose political argument is essentially the same as that of Hobbes in every particular except scarcity in the state of nature, to be basically libertarian where Hobbes is basically authoritarian. Thanks to the Great Frontier, Locke and Smith found that there was sufficient abundance in the state of nature that a Hobbesian war of all against all was unlikely; every man could take away some kind of prize, and competition would be socially constructive rather than destructive, with the "invisible hand" producing the greatest good for the society as a whole. Thus government was required only to keep the game honest—a mere referee, needing only modest powers and minimal institutional machinery—and individuals could be left alone to pursue happiness as they defined it without hindrance by society or the state. The frontier is gone now, and we have encountered the limits of the commons. However, the physical disappearance of the frontier was for a long time mitigated by technology, which allowed us to graze more cows on the same acreage of pasture. Now we have reached the limits of technology: the cows are standing almost shoulder to shoulder and the manure is piling up faster than the commons can absorb it. All that remains is to alter the rational, self-seeking behavior of the individuals and groups using the commons. This

---

*Some (for example, Reich 1971) would protest that our age is different and that a genuinely new consciousness is emerging. This view cannot simply be brushed aside, for substantial value changes are clearly occurring in some segments of American society, and out of this essentially religious ferment great things may come. For example, the "back to the land" movement has been much ridiculed, but its symbolic reaffirmation of our ties to the earth has already had a far from negligible impact on the larger society. Nevertheless, that these new values will become universal in the future appears to be essentially a matter of faith at this point. Moreover, since past hopes for the emergence of a "new man" have been rudely treated by history, it is difficult to be optimistic.

must be done by collective means, for the dynamic of the tragedy of the commons is so powerful that individuals are virtually powerless to extricate themselves unaided from its remorseless working. We must indeed be "forced to be free" by our political institutions.

Legislating Temperance

That we must give our political authorities great powers to regulate many of our daily actions is a profoundly distasteful thought. We tend to see political systems without our kind of political and economic liberties as "totalitarian," a word that brings to mind all the evil features of past dictatorships. However, even Hobbes, no matter how firm his conviction of the necessity of absolutism, certainly did not have Stalinesque tyranny in mind. Hobbes makes clear that order in the commonwealth is not the goal, but the means without which the fruits of civilization cannot be enjoyed: the sovereign power is to procure the "safety of the people. . . . But by safety here is not meant a bare preservation but also all other contentments of life which every man by lawful industry, without danger or hurt to the commonwealth, shall acquire to himself" (Hobbes 1651, p. 262). And it is part of the task of the sovereign power actively to promote these "contentments of life" among its subjects. Furthermore, Hobbes will not countenance tyranny. The sovereign power must rule lawfully, give a full explanation of its acts to its subjects, and heed their legitimate desires. Through wise laws and education, the subjects will learn moral restraint. Also, the sovereign power is not to be a dictator regulating every action of the citizen: it does not "bind the people from all voluntary actions" but only guides them with laws which Hobbes likens to "hedges . . . set not to stop travelers, but to keep them in their ways" (p. 272). Thus many different styles of rule and of life are compatible with his basic analysis.

Similarly, Hardin makes it clear that the problem is to "legislate temperance," not to institute iron discipline. He acknowledges that this may require the use of administrative law, with the consequent risk of abuse of power by the administrators. However, he believes that the application of his formula of "mutual coercion, mutually agreed upon by the majority of the people affected" would be an adequate defense against bureaucratic tyranny, for we would be *democratically coercing ourselves* to behave responsibly (Hardin 1968, p. 1247).

The question of political will is therefore crucial. Given a basic willingness to restrain individual self-seeking and legislate social temperance, social devices acceptable to reasonable men and suited to a government of laws could readily be found to serve as the "hedges" that will keep us on the path of the steady state.* For example, law professor Christopher Stone (1974) proposes giving natural objects, such as trees, mountains, rivers, and lakes, legal rights (comparable to those now enjoyed by corporations) that could be enforced in court.

However, although the socioeconomic machinery needed to enforce a steady-state political economy need not involve dictatorial control over our everyday lives, it will indeed encroach upon our freedom of action, *for any social device that is effective as a hedge will necessarily prevent us from doing things we are now free to do or make us do things we now prefer not to do.* It could hardly be otherwise: if we can safely squeeze no more cattle onto the commons, then we herdsmen must be satisfied either with the herds we now possess or, more likely, with the lesser number of cattle that the commons can tolerate ecologically over the long term. The solution to the tragedy of the commons in the present circumstances requires a willingness to accept less, perhaps much less, than we now get from the commons. No technical devices will save us. In order to be able mutually to agree on the restraints we wish to apply to ourselves, we must give up the exercise of rights we now enjoy, and bind ourselves to perform public duties in the common interest. The only alternative to this kind of self-coercion is the coercion of nature, or perhaps of an iron regime that will compel our consent to living life with less.

Technology's Faustian Bargain

Given this unpalatable conclusion, the seductive appeal of technological optimism is apparent: if adjusting human demands to the available ecological resources will entail a greater degree of political authority, then let us by all means press on with the attempt to surmount the limits to growth technologically. Thus, to the extent that the technologist concedes the necessity of a steady state, he aims at a "maximum-feasible" steady state of technological superabundance in which we will use our alleged mastery of inexhaustible energy resources to evade ecological constraints, instead of learning to live frugally on flow resources like solar energy.† As we have seen, the barriers

---

*Merely increasing the power of the state is not enough. As will be shown in Chapter 8 (and contrary to the opinion of many), mere socialism is not a real solution to the tragedy of the commons. That is, giving the state ownership of the means of production is not very useful if the state is committed to economic expansion, for the same ecologically destructive dynamic operates within a socialist economic bureaucracy as in the capitalist marketplace (see Heilbroner 1974 on this point).

†In reality, a maximum-feasible steady state is a virtual contradiction in terms, for squeezing the maximum out of nature runs contrary to basic ecological principles. Only a life lived *comfortably* within the circle of natural interdependence merits the designation "steady state." But the technological optimists customarily talk as if there were no possible model of the steady state other than the maximum-feasible one.

to success in such an enterprise are enormous, but for the sake of argument, let us put aside all questions of practicality and ask instead what would be the political consequences of implementing these kinds of technological solutions to ecological scarcity.

Alvin Weinberg, who was for many years director of the Atomic Energy Commission's Oak Ridge National Laboratory, has been a leading spokesman for the technological fix, especially nuclear power. Indeed, he has castigated environmentalists for proposing "social fixes" to ecological problems; he argues that technological solutions are "more humane" because they do not "disrupt the economy and . . . cause the human suffering that such disruption would entail" (Weinberg 1972b). Yet Weinberg himself admits that the specific technological solution he proposes comes with a truly monstrous social fix firmly attached! Because nuclear wastes will have to be kept under virtually perpetual surveillance and because nuclear technology places the most exacting demands on our engineering and management capabilities,

> We nuclear people have made a Faustian bargain with society. On the one hand, we offer . . . an inexhaustible source of energy [the breeder reactor]. . . . But the price that we demand of society for this magical energy is both a vigilance and a longevity of our social institutions that we are quite unaccustomed to [Weinberg 1972a, p. 33].

Part of this price is politically ominous:

> In a sense, what started out as a technological fix for the energy-environment impasse—clean, inexhaustible, and fairly cheap nuclear power—involves social fixes as well: the creation of a permanent cadre or priesthood of responsible technologists who will guard the reactors and the wastes so as to assure their continued safety over millennia [Weinberg 1973, p. 43].

Expanding on the "priesthood" theme, Weinberg tells us that, because "our commitment to nuclear energy is assumed to last in perpetuity," we will need "a *permanent* cadre of experts that will retain its continuity over immensely long times [but this] hardly seems feasible if the cadre is a national body," for "no government has lasted continuously for 1,000 years." What kind of organization does possess the requisite continuity?

> Only the Catholic Church has survived more or less continuously for 2,000 years or so. . . . The Catholic Church is the best example of [the International Authority] I have in mind: a *central authority* that *proclaims* and to a degree *enforces* doctrine, maintains its own long-term social stability, and has connections to every country's own Catholic Church [cited in Speth et al. 1974, emphasis added].

In proposing such a technological "priesthood," Weinberg appears to be a true heir of the French utopian social philosopher Claude Henri Saint-Simon

(1760–1825), one of the earliest prophets of technocracy, who believed that it was man's mission to transcend nature with technology. Distressed by the disruptive social effects of technology within a bourgeois, laissez-faire political economy, Saint-Simon aspired to create a stable, organic civilization like that of the Middle Ages, but with Science as its religion. To this end he proposed the creation, on the model of the Catholic Church, of a scientific priesthood that would both dispense political justice and promote the economic wealth of society. Saint-Simon stressed the necessity for authority based on scientific expertise, social planning, the subordination of the individual to the needs of society as determined by the experts, and the integration of society and technology—all themes that emerge in the writings of modern technological visionaries.

By whatever name it comes to be called, technocratic government is the likely price of Weinberg's Faustian bargain. Naturally, it will not be formally voted in, but will emerge in a series of small but fateful steps as we follow what seems to be the line of least resistance through our environmental problems. Indeed, critics are already alarmed by the civil-rights implications of the safeguards proposed by the Atomic Energy Commission in its draft environmental-impact statement on plutonium recycling; these include the establishment of a federal police force for the protection of plutonium plants and shipments, the extension of current military security-clearance procedures to include all the civilians who might have access to plutonium, and generally increased police powers to cope with the security requirements of a plutonium-based power economy (Speth et al. 1974). In sum, there may be no way to assure the social stability—indeed, the near-perfect social institutions—necessary for an era of nuclear power except with an engineered society under the direction of a technocratic priesthood.

A Pact with the Devil?

It is not nuclear technology alone that offers a pact with a devil who will in the end claim our political souls. Few technological optimists are as candid as Weinberg about the political implications of the solutions they propose, but technocracy has been looming on the horizon for some time. Harrison Brown, a scientist who foresaw most of today's ecological concerns two decades ago, predicted that the instability of industrial society would become greater as development proceeded; this and other organizational requirements would create a necessity for ever greater social control, so that "it is difficult to see how the achievement of stability and the maintenance of individual liberty can be made compatible" (Brown 1954, p. 255). Buckminster Fuller, one of the most visionary of the supertechnologists, states plainly that those who run "Spaceship Earth" cannot afford to make "concessions to the non-synergetic thinking (therefore the ignorantly conditioned reflexes) of the least well advised of the potential mass customers [that is, the average citizen]" (Fuller 1968, p. 367). Numerous other writers of varying persuasions see the same trend: more technology means greater complexity and greater need for knowledge and technical expertise; the average citizen will not be able to make a constructive contribution to decision making, so that "experts" and "authorities" will perforce rule; moreover, since accidents cannot be permitted, much less individual behavior that deviates from technological imperatives, the grip of planning and social control will of necessity become more and more complete (Bell 1973; Chamberlin 1970; Heilbroner 1974).

Thus, the question at hand is not whether technology gradually turns man into a machine. Although this may indeed become truer as technological civilization grows, it is not an essential point in the present argument.* The danger in the Faustian bargain lies rather in the mounting complexity of technology along with the staggering problems of managing the response to ecological scarcity, for these will require us to depend on a special class of experts in charge of our survival and well-being—a "priesthood of responsible technologists."

Democracy versus Elite Rule: The Issue of Competence

One of the key philosophical supports of democracy is the assumption that people do not differ greatly in competence; for if they do, effective government may require the sacrifice of political equality and majority rule. Indeed, under certain circumstances democracy *must* give way to elite rule; as the eminent political scientist and democratic theorist Robert Dahl points out, in a political association whose members "differ *crucially* in their competence, such as a hospital or a passenger ship, a reasonable man will want the most competent people to have authority over the matters on which they are most competent" (Dahl 1970, p. 58, emphasis added). In other words, the more closely one's situation resembles a perilous sea voyage, the stronger the rationale for placing power and authority in the hands of the few who know how to run the ship.

Ecological scarcity appears to have created precisely such a situation. Critical decisions must be made. Although it is true that most of them are "trans-scientific" in that they can only be made politically by prudent men, at least the basic scientific elements of the problems must be understood

---

*However, a key point in the general cultural critique of technology is germane to the current discussion: those who defend technology as socially benign do not always seem to grasp the crucial distinction made by Jacques Ellul (1967; see also Illich 1973) between "tools," which are relatively neutral instruments that can be used by individuals as they wish, and "technique," which imposes certain behavior on men (nuclear power is an egregious example).

reasonably well before an informed political decision is possible. However, the average man has neither the time to inform himself nor the requisite background for understanding such complex technical problems. Moreover, he may simply not be intelligent enough to grasp the issues, much less the important features of the problems. Indeed, it is apparent that even highly attentive and competent specialists do not always understand the problems fully. Even when they do (or claim to do), they can almost always be found on both sides of any major question of public policy. (The dispute over nuclear-reactor safety is a prime example, with Nobelists lining up both for and against nuclear power.) Thus, even assuming that the politicians and people understand the issue well enough to ask the right questions, which experts should they listen to? Can they understand what the experts are saying? If we grant that the people in their majority probably will not understand and are therefore not competent to decide such issues, is it very likely that the political leaders they select will themselves be competent enough to deal with these issues? And even if they are, how can these leaders make authoritative decisions that impose heavy present costs or that violate popular expectations for the sake of future advantages revealed to them only as special knowledge derived from complicated analysis, perhaps even as the Delphic pronouncements of a computer?

Such questions about the viability of democratic politics in a super-technological age propel us toward the political thought of Plato. In *The Republic,* the fountainhead of all Western political philosophy, Plato argued that the polity was like a ship sailing dangerous waters. It therefore needed to be commanded by the most competent pilots; to allow the crew, ignorant of the art of navigation, to participate in running the vessel would be to invite shipwreck. Thus the polity would have to be run by an elite class of guardians, who would themselves be guided by the cream of this elite—the philosopher-kings. As the quotation from Dahl suggests, to the extent that Plato's analogy of the ship of state approximates reality his political prescriptions are difficult to evade, which is precisely why, from Aristotle on, those who have favored democratic rather than oligarchic politics have concerned themselves with keeping the political community small enough and simple enough so that elite rule would not be necessary for social survival. The emerging large, highly-developed, complex technological civilization operating at or very near the ecological margin appears to fit Plato's premises more and more closely, foreshadowing the necessity of rule by a class of Platonic guardians, the "priesthood of responsible technologists" who alone know how to run the spaceship.

Such a development has always been implicit in technology, as the ideas of Saint-Simon suggest. It is simply that its necessity has become overwhelmingly manifest in a crowded world living close to the ecological limits, for only the most exquisite care will avert the collapse of the technological

Leviathan we are well on the way to creating. C. S. Lewis observed that "What we call Man's power over Nature turns out to be a power exercised by some men over other men with Nature as its instrument" (Lewis 1965, p. 69), and it appears that the greater the technological power, the more absolute the political power that must be yielded up to some men by the others. Thus we must ask ourselves if continued technological growth will not merely serve to replace the so-called tyranny of nature with a potentially even more odious tyranny of men. Why indeed should we deliver ourselves over to a "priesthood of responsible technologists" who are merely technical experts and mainly lack the excellence of character and deep philosophical understanding that Plato insists his guardians must possess in order to justify their rule? In fact, why accept the rule of even a genuinely Platonic elite possessed of both wisdom and expertise, when all history teaches us that the abilities, foresight, and goodwill of mortal men are limited and imperfect? The technological response to ecological scarcity thus raises profound political issues, in particular one of the most ancient and difficult political dilemmas—*quis custodiet ipsos custodes?* or "Who will watch the guardians themselves?"

Technology and the Path to a Brave New World

Modern man has used technology along with energy to try to transcend nature. We have seen that it cannot be done; nature is not to be transcended by a biological organism that depends on it. Worse, the attempt to do so will have momentous political and social consequences. Far from protecting us from painful and disruptive social changes, as the technological optimist is wont to claim, continued technological growth is likely to force such changes on us. We are, in fact, in the process of making the Faustian bargain without ever having consciously decided to do so. As a result, we appear to be traveling down the road to total domination by technique and the machine, to the "Brave New World" that Aldous Huxley (1932) warned was the logical end point of a hedonistic, high-technology civilization.*

Technology may not be inherently evil, but it does have side effects and it does exact a social price. Moreover, in the hands of less than perfect human beings, technology can never be neutral, as its proponents too often claim; it can only be used for good or evil. Thus technological fixes are dangerous surrogates for political decisions. There is no escape from politics. As a

---

*All the techniques of social control and biological manipulation forecast in Huxley's dystopian novel are being invented today in our laboratories (Cohen 1973; Delgado 1969; Holden 1973; Kass 1971, 1972; Skinner 1971); well before these developments, Huxley (1958) was himself appalled to discover that much of what he had imagined as taking place six or seven hundred years in the future was coming true within his own lifetime.

Box 4–3. Taming Leviathan: Macro-constraints and Micro-freedoms

The only escape from the political dilemma of ecological scarcity—authoritative rule or ecological ruin—is indicated in the Epigraph: if men exercise sufficient self-control of their passions, the fetters of external authority become unnecessary. Unfortunately, political history suggests that the level of moral restraint and altruism to be expected from the members of large, complex, mass societies is limited at best. These virtues are even less likely to be found in industrial civilization, for its citizens have been brought up to believe that satisfying their hedonistic wants is not only legitimate, but positively virtuous. Besides, in complicated and highly interdependent societies, even the most willing citizen would not know how to be ecologically virtuous without a large amount of central direction and coordination. In other words, unless we return to face-to-face, simple, decentralized, small-community living—which may be a desirable long-term goal (so Chapter 8 will argue), but hardly a short-term possibility—we are stuck with the problem of making authority palatable and protecting ourselves against those who would abuse their ecological guardianship.

Traditional political theory has proposed many answers to this problem. However, one basic principle stands out: if self-restraint is inadequate, macro-constraints are vastly to be preferred to micro-constraints, for the psychological differences between them are crucial. That is, limitations on our freedom that are indirect, remote, and impersonal are preferable to those that are direct, proximate, and personal; in the former case, the limitations become an almost invisible part of "the way things are,"

---

consequence of ecological scarcity, major ethical, political, economic and social changes are inevitable whatever we do. The choice is between change that happens to us as a "side effect" of ever more stringent technological imperatives and change that is deliberately selected to accord with our values.

Unfortunately, at this point even total renunciation of technology as dangerous to our democratic health would not avoid all the political dilemmas described above. During the transition to any form of steady state one can envisage it would be imperative to use physical resources as efficiently as possible, and this probably would mean greater centralization and expert control in the short term, even if the long-term goal is a technologically simple, decentralized society favorable to a democratic politics.

Even beyond the transition period, whether a steady-state society can be democratic (as we understand it) is at least questionable. A society cannot persist as a genuine democracy unless the people in their majority understand technology and ecology well enough to make responsible decisions; and although the technology of a frugal steady state should be more accessible to the common man's understanding than our own current brand is, the same may not be true of the ecological knowledge upon which the steady-state society will have to be based. Intuition and common sense alone are of little help in understanding the counterintuitive complexity of the human ecosystem—and nowhere else can a little knowledge be so dangerous. Thus, although not intrinsically mysterious, ecology is esoteric in the sense that only those whose talents and training have equipped them to be the "specialists in the general" discussed in the Introduction are likely to pos-

instead of obvious impositions. For example, modern man *feels* generally free despite his nearly total submission to such powerful but faceless forces as technological change and the marketplace; the feudal peasant, by contrast, was so bound up in a web of direct personal obligations that he felt much less free, even though this web of obligations may have been in important respects less tyrannical in practice than the impersonal forces to which modern man is obliged to submit. Putting the matter more abstractly, the contemporary political philosopher Isaiah Berlin (1969) has defined freedom as the number of doors open to a man, how open they are, and upon what prospects they open. All other things being equal, then, the widest number of meaningful options brings the maximum of freedom; macro-freedom is the sum of the micro-freedoms available to us. Since the destruction of the commons leaves us with few meaningful options, some of the doors now available to us must be partly or even completely closed, but if we wish to preserve a sense of freedom, then this should be done in ways that limit the micro-freedoms or close the doors of daily life as little as possible.

Thus an effective way of making authority acceptable is the application of macro-constraints encouraging the behavior necessary to maintain a steady-state society but leaving the individual with a relative abundance of micro-freedoms that, when added up, give him an overall sense of freedom. How such a steady-state society might be "designed" will be discussed further in Chapter 8.

sess the kind of competence that would satisfy Dahl's "reasonable man." The ecologically complex steady-state society may therefore require, if not a class of ecological guardians, then at least a class of ecological mandarins who possess the esoteric knowledge needed to run it well. Thus, whatever its level of material affluence, the steady-state society will not only be more authoritarian and less democratic than the industrial societies of today—the necessity to cope with the tragedy of the commons would alone ensure that—but it will also in all likelihood be much more oligarchic as well, with only those possessing the ecological and other competencies necessary to make prudent decisions allowed full participation in the political process.

Hard Political Realities and a New Paradigm

To sum up, scarcity in general erodes the material basis for the relatively benign individualistic and democratic politics characteristic of the modern industrial era; ecological scarcity in particular seems to engender overwhelming pressures toward political systems that are frankly authoritarian by current standards, for there seems to be no other way to check competitive overexploitation of resources and to assure competent direction of a complex society's affairs in accord with steady-state imperatives. Leviathan may be mitigated, but not evaded (see Box 4-3).

Ecological scarcity thus forces us to confront once again, perhaps in a particularly acute form, the hard realities and cruel dilemmas of classical

---

Box 4–4.   The Ecological Contract

The Great Frontier and the Industrial Revolution unleashed forces that eventually destroyed the medieval political synthesis, which was based generally on the Heaven-ordained hierarchy of the "great chain of being" and specifically on the "divine right of kings." Changing economic conditions gradually transferred de facto political power from monarchs, priests, and nobles to the enterprising middle classes. Although at first the bourgeois acquiesced in continued autocratic rule and aristocratic patronage, he eventually tired of supporting what he came to see as unproductive social parasites; he overthrew the ancien régime and embarked on democratic self-rule, the only form of government that could be intellectually and practically reconciled with his new sense of individualism. Such major transfers of power must be theoretically and morally legitimated, and the "social contract" theory of government was devised to fulfill this need.

In essence, the theory of the social contract says that individuals are not part of a pre-existing hierarchy to which they must unquestioningly adapt, but free to decide how they wish to be. ruled. It is thus primarily concerned with how free and equal individuals (starting from an anarchic "state of nature") can come together to erect political institutions that will preserve their individual rights to the fullest extent, yet also promote the social harmony they need to enjoy these rights in peace. Ironically, the device of the social contract was used by Hobbes to provide secular support for

---

politics, from which four centuries of abnormal abundance have shielded us. As a result, we shall have to reexamine fundamental political questions in the light of ecology and construct a new steady-state paradigm of politics based on ecological premises instead of on the individualistic, hedonistic, materialistic, and anthropocentric premises of bourgeois "social contract" theory (see Box 4-4). The alternative is to let the shape of the steady-state paradigm be decided for us by accepting the outcome of current trends toward technocracy.

Given current political values, this may not seem like much of a choice. However, the one certain thing is that current values and institutions will not be able to endure unchanged. Moreover, as we shall see in Chapter 8, the latitude of choice is wider than might be suspected; indeed, the crisis of ecological scarcity might actually be turned into a grand opportunity to build a more humane post-industrial society. The next two chapters will explore specific features of the American political economy to determine how well it is likely to cope with the challenges of ecological scarcity.

BIBLIOGRAPHIC NOTE

On the general theme of scarcity and abundance in modern history, Walter Prescott Webb's *The Great Frontier* is superlative, but scarcely balanced, for Webb means to disabuse us of the notion that progress, plenty, and democracy

monarchy, starting from the individualistic, hedonistic, and materialistic premises of the bourgeois world view. However, as it was later developed by Locke and Rousseau, the social contract became the foundation for popular sovereignty and liberal democracy (even Marxism has very deep roots in Rousseau's thought). The untrammeled individual was now king.

As a product of the Great Frontier, the theory of the social contract is fundamentally cornucopian: nature's abundance being endless and inexhaustible, one has only to solve the problem of achieving social harmony through a just division of the spoils. Nature is thus external to politics. But these cornucopian premises have become as anomalous in an age of ecological scarcity as the divine right of kings was in the era of the Great Frontier and the Industrial Revolution. Ecology and politics are now inseparable; out of prudent self-restraint, if for no other reason, a valid political theory of the steady state will be obliged to give the same weight to ecological harmony as to social harmony. Thus, just as it was the task of the seventeenth- and eighteenth-century political philosophers to create the social-contract theory of government to take account of the new socioeconomic conditions and justify the political ascent of the bourgeois class, so it will be the duty of the next generation of philosophers to create an "ecological contract" theory promoting harmony not just between men, but also between man and nature.

are our eternal and immutable birthright. Richard Wilkinson's more balanced *Poverty and Progress* provides another valuable perspective on modern economic development as merely the latest episode in a long series of historical oscillations between conditions of ecological abundance and ecological scarcity. From the point of view of the conventional wisdom and academic orthodoxy, both Webb and Wilkinson are heretics. However, the question of scarcity has lately achieved a measure of academic respectability with the American Academy of Arts and Sciences symposium on "The No-Growth Society" (cited as Olson and Landsberg 1973). The overall tone of the work is guarded optimism; nevertheless, the rapporteurs, who are impeccably "establishment" economists, believe that society must take with the utmost seriousness the issues raised by the diverse group of what they mistakenly call "no-growth" advocates (this rubric implies that to be against material growth is to be against all growth), and they acknowledge that many awkward scarcity-related problems lie ahead. Robert Heilbroner's *An Inquiry into the Human Prospect* analyzes some of these problems, arriving at much more pessimistic conclusions. (See also Odell 1975, a review of diverse opinions on the likely political impact of scarcity.)

On the tragedy of the commons, the two best academic treatments are *The Common Wealth in Ocean Fisheries,* by Francis Christy and Anthony Scott, and Mancur Olson's *The Logic of Collective Action.* These digested, one should then read Garrett Hardin's essay (1968) and the essays by Beryl Crowe (1969), myself (1973), and Peter Stillman (1975) extending the political implications of Hardin's analysis, as well as Hardin's own *Exploring New Ethics for Survival,* which expands on many points in his original essay. This should be topped off with a careful reading of Thomas Hobbes' *Leviathan.*

The spectrum of opinion on the issues raised by the "Faustian bargain" is extremely wide. At one extreme is technological visionary Buckminster Fuller, whose "Vertical Is to Live, Horizontal Is to Die" is a panegyric on the Apollo space program, which Fuller puts forward as his preferred model for the future of mankind. (See also his more theoretical "An Operating Manual for Spaceship Earth.") Charles Susskind's *Understanding Technology* is a technologist's conventional defense of his metier as socially neutral; thus he absolves technology and technologists of all blame for society's shortcomings—a position that evades many questions. Daniel Callahan's *The Tyranny of Survival* is a much more balanced assessment that blames both technology and society. Perhaps the finest modern critique is Jacques Ellul's profound and prescient *The Technological Society,* a work whose analytical subtlety (for example, the critical distinction between tool and technique referred to in the footnote on page 159) needs to be much more widely appreciated. C. S. Lewis' *The Abolition of Man,* written from a more explicitly "spiritual" perspective, is also a superb critique. In many ways all contemporary critics of technology simply repeat the arguments against machine civilization contained in Samuel Butler's anti-technological utopian novel *Erewhon,* which merits rereading in the light of our current predicament. Naturally, the technological dystopias—like those in Aldous Huxley's *Brave New World,* E. M. Forster's "The Machine Stops" (in Forster 1928), or George Orwell's *Nineteen Eighty-Four*—are also of great interest, for they indicate better than any academic analysis what some of the dire consequences of accepting technology's Faustian bargain might be. Lastly, Plato's *Republic* (cited as Cornford 1945) also deserves careful study; a spaceship earth comes uncomfortably close to fulfilling the premises of Plato's basic political metaphor, the ship of state that must be guided by a skilled pilot.

Finally, on the agonizing nature of the choices before us Karl Popper's *The Open Society and Its Enemies* (for example, Plato, Rousseau, and Hobbes) is most instructive. Popper is perhaps the most articulate and extreme exponent of the position, predominant in the theoretical polemics among political theorists in the period after World War II, that ideological political thought (that is, political thought based on values "higher" than the mere sum of individual wants) is inherently totalitarian and likely to pave the way for Hitlerian fascism. What Popper calls the "open" society has many virtues, and the loss of some of them as we move toward a more "closed" society that upholds at least some minimal common interest will be a regrettable sacrifice; but the choice is not quite as stark as Popper maintains, for an appropriate "ecological contract" could preserve both nature and basic human rights. For example, simply giving natural objects legal personality, as suggested in Christopher Stone's brilliant *Should Trees Have Standing?,* would do much to redress the current imbalance between man and nature without entailing odious political repression.

5

THE AMERICAN POLITICAL ECONOMY I:
ECOLOGY PLUS ECONOMICS
EQUALS POLITICS

Having discussed the politics of scarcity in general, we shall now turn to the particulars of the American situation. As difficult as it sometimes is to keep economics and politics separate, especially in this country, we shall discuss the economic aspects of political economy in this chapter, taking up the more political aspects in the next. However, both chapters have a common approach, one different from that taken by most critiques of the American system. We are not interested here in whether the system falls short of the democratic ideal of freedom, equality, and justice, only whether it is likely to be able to surmount without fundamental change the challenge of ecological scarcity. To this question both chapters give essentially the same answer: ecological scarcity undercuts the basic laissez-faire, individualistic premises of the American political economy, so that current institutions are incapable of meeting the challenges of scarcity; what is needed is a new paradigm of politics.

Market Failures and Social Costs

As noted in the Introduction, at least some critics of the limits-to-growth argument rely heavily on the market price mechanism to insure a smooth, gradual transition to the steady state whenever it becomes necessary. They believe that, as the costs of fuels and materials rise owing to scarcity and as the costs of pollution control increase, further growth will become uneconomic; the steady state will therefore arrive automatically by market processes. In fact, however, in its current form the competitive market system is an environmental villain—part of the problem that must be solved, rather than the solution. Let us examine how the market fails to deal appropriately with common-property resources, resource depletion and other aspects of ecological scarcity.

According to Adam Smith, self-interested participants in a competitive marketplace will be unwittingly led to promote the common good by the "invisible hand" of the market. That is, with consumers and producers acting rationally to maximize their own gain, the market will automatically allocate resources with greatest efficiency and generate a maximum of individual and social prosperity; thanks to the invisible hand, self-seeking individuals, despite the lack of any intention to do so, will benefit their fellows as they enrich themselves. Smith therefore argued for a laissez-faire, competitive market system of economics.

As we have seen, the premise of abundance necessary to support Smith's contention has vanished. Thanks to ecological scarcity, rational self-seeking individuals, despite the lack of any intention to do so, harm their fellows as they attempt to enrich themselves. As steady-state economist Herman Daly (1973, p. 17) aptly puts it, the invisible hand has turned into an "invisible foot" that threatens to destroy the common good with pollution and other "external diseconomies" or "externalities," the economist's terms for the social costs of production that are not accounted for in the price mechanism. In fact, the problem of the invisible foot is simply the economic version of the commons problem discussed in the preceding chapter. Individuals rationally seeking gain (or at least non-loss) are virtually compelled by the logic of the marketplace commons to make economic micro-decisions that are aggregated by the invisible foot into an ecological macro-decision increasingly destructive for the society as a whole—and therefore, paradoxically, for the individual as well. Thus an unregulated, competitive, laissez-faire market system, in which all have access to the economic commons and in which common-property resources are treated as free goods, has produced a tragedy of the commons—the overuse, misuse, and degradation of resources upon which we depend for ecological health and economic wealth.

Other properties of a free-for-all system of wealth-getting strongly reinforce its tendency to destroy the commons. For one thing, market decisions are inevitably short-sighted, because the economic value of the future is understated or "discounted." Future values are usually discounted at the interest rate available to a prudent investor; at a 7 percent interest/discount rate, he would just as soon have $100,000 now as $800,000 in 30 years. Why? Because if he invests the $100,000 at 7 percent, it will be worth

$800,000 in 30 years. He will have the same amount of money and will have run little or no risk to get it. Similarly, at the same interest/discount rate, a resource that 30 years from now will be worth $800,000 has a present value of no more than $100,000. In fact, for all practical purposes costs and benefits more than 20 years in the future are discounted to zero; owing in part to additional factors like the prevailing rate of return on capital, it is a rare economic decision maker whose time horizon extends more than ten years into the future. Thus, critical ecological resources essential for future well-being even 30 years from now not only have no value to a rational economic decision maker, they scarcely enter his calculations. He is therefore likely to make decisions that irreversibly deplete or destroy vital resources (especially since he realistically fears that his own self-restraint would simply hand over to another the opportunity for profit). Thus, as Karl Marx put it a century ago, the watchword of market capitalism is "Après nous le déluge," as entrepreneurs strive to maximize current benefits at the expense of the future.

An additional problem is that, although the market price mechanism handles incremental change with relative ease, it tends to break down when confronted with absolute scarcity or even marked discrepancies between supply and demand. In such situations (for example, in famines), the market collapses or degenerates into uncontrolled inflation, for the increased price is incapable of calling forth an equivalent increase in supply.* In a famine, supply and demand are eventually brought into balance by death, emigration, or the deus ex machina of relief—that is, by physical readjustments, not by the price mechanism. Thus the market is unlikely to preside over a smooth and trouble-free transition to a steady-state, for the crisis of ecological scarcity involves absolute physical scarcities, like lack of food, water, time, or human physiological tolerance for poisons, that mere money can remedy, if at all, only in part (and certainly not indefinitely or all at once). Indeed, shortages leading to rising prices may simply increase the incentives to exploit remaining resources heedlessly in a desperate attempt to meet current demand. In short, rising prices are not likely to induce timely and appropriate responses to ecological scarcity, and they will certainly not preserve resources from exhaustion and degradation. In fact, they may simply intensify the pressures producing the current mode of ecological overshoot.

There are additional reasons why the market may fail to respond smoothly and appropriately to the price signals generated by ecological scarcity. For

---

*To use the economist's terms, the market is splendid at coping with relative scarcity, shifting the burden of scarcity so that it is least uncomfortable (for example, by inducing substitution of one resource for another), but it is incapable of dealing with absolute scarcity except by raising prices in general—that is, by inflation. As noted in Chapter 3, there is reason to suspect that this is the underlying cause of the inflation now prevailing throughout the industrialized world.

one thing, scarcity tends to induce competitive bidding and preemptive buying, which leads to price fluctuations, market disruption, and the inequitable or inappropriate distribution of resources. For example, attracted by the high prices foreigners were willing to pay, American grain merchants sold too much of the stock abroad, producing a domestic grain shortage that made a major contribution to the severe inflation of 1974. Even so, Americans were better off than Indians and others in the Third World, who found themselves virtually priced out of world food markets. Similarly, despite an alleged timber shortage in the continental United States (used by logging interests as an argument against controls on ecologically destructive practices), the primeval forests of Alaska, one of the few remaining large sources of high-grade timber in the United States, are being intensively logged for export to Japan, instead of being preserved for our own future needs (Harnik 1973).

Economists also assume that consumers will respond in a reasonably elastic fashion to rising prices due to ecological scarcity. However, this is by no means obvious. For one thing, consumer decisions are based on factors other than price. For instance, very great differentials in cost are not enough to lure most drivers out of their cars into mass transit, because such factors as prestige and convenience are more important to the consumer than mere price. Thus only prohibitive increases in cost would be likely to significantly reduce private automobile ownership and use. In addition, prior investment decisions may lock consumers into using a specific resource, regardless of price. Homeowners and industries that use natural gas for space or process heat, for example, cannot easily switch to substitute forms of energy in the short term, no matter what happens to the price of natural gas. In short, even very high prices may not be sufficient to keep consumption of ecologically damaging goods and use of non-renewable resources at a level that is socially optimal.

Additional problems of a more structural nature abound. In the first place, in a market economy—where the market is *the* economic tool, not just one among others—all the incentives of producers are toward growth and the wasteful use of resources. It is in the interest of producers to have a high-throughput economy characterized by high consumption through product proliferation and promotion, rapid obsolescence, and the like. It is just not economically advantageous for a producer to make an indestructible, easily repaired, inexpensively operated car. If consumers were perfectly rational—that is, if they acted solely according to their economic advantage—they could no doubt oblige producers to turn out nothing else; but we know very well that consumers are not completely rational (about cars least of all) and that producers do everything in their power to exploit this irrationality to boost sales (for example, by advertising that plays upon consumers' social and sexual insecurities). By comparison, the incentives to satisfy needs with minimum inputs of energy and material and the lowest real or long-term cost are quite weak, as is well exemplified by the entrepreneurial flight from passenger rail transportation. In short, in their pursuit of economic advantage producers can be expected to promote higher consumption and in general to exploit every opportunity to profit by not counting the ecological costs.*

Conversely, producers lack significant market incentives to respond alertly and appropriately to many of the problems created by ecological scarcity. For example, it is simply not in the interest of oil companies or electric power companies to promote alternatives to the current fossil-fuel-based energy economy or to the centralized system of power production and distribution. In fact, for the purely "economic" man, the best of all possible worlds would be one in which people are almost literally dying for lack of what only he can supply. It is therefore entirely rational for entrepreneurs to let scarcity reach uncomfortable levels before innovating or bringing new resources to market. Thus the market price system is unlikely to favor far-sighted, much less public-spirited, investment decisions or to promote ecologically sound alternatives to current technologies, especially since some of the logical alternatives, like solar power, would reduce the dependence of consumers on producers. At the very least, producers are likely to wait until demand builds up and large profits are assured before they invest heavily in alternatives like fusion, which may require a great deal of time and money to develop to the point of commercial viability. Thus there are major structural obstacles to innovation and investment that will seriously impede response to the pressures of ecological scarcity (particularly in regulated monopoly industries, where real market competition does not exist). At best, market solutions will lag well behind the rapidly developing real-world problems of ecological scarcity.

In short, an unregulated market economy inevitably fosters accelerated ecological degradation and resource depletion through ever higher levels of production and consumption. Indeed, given the cornucopian assumptions upon which a market system of economics is based, it could hardly be otherwise; both philosophically and practically, a market economy is incompatible with ecology.†

---

*The growth orientation of the private sector is reinforced by the government, which uses its taxing, spending, and monetary powers to promote prosperity and full employment.

†As the previous discussion of a "thermodynamic" economy (Box 3-5) indicated, ecological economics is grounded on real physical flows rather than on money. An ecological theory of economics would therefore resemble the pre-modern "physiocratic" or nature-based economic theories that, subsequent to the opening up of the Great Frontier, were eclipsed by the capital- and labor-based economic theories inspired by Adam Smith. Other aspects of an ecological economics will be discussed in Chapter 8 in connection with stewardship and "right livelihood."

The New Economics Is Mostly Politics

If the market in its current form has so many serious environmental liabilities, *which is not disputed by the vast majority of economists,* why is it so heavily relied upon to save us from the consequences of ecological scarcity? The answer seems to be that, although they tend to talk as if it were already an accomplished fact, those who put forward this solution are in reality talking about a market that does not yet exist, a market whose price mechanism has been thoroughly overhauled to eliminate at least some of the liabilities discussed above. In short, those who argue for the market as an economic solution to ecological scarcity are really urging a political solution, for all of these reforms will require explicit and deliberate social decisions, as a brief review of the proposed changes will indicate.

A number of economic devices have been proposed to mitigate or eliminate the degradation of common-property resources and to promote the provision of public goods, like clean air, or the careful husbandry of nonrenewable resources—principally, administrative fiat, the creation of property rights in common-property resources, effluent or pollution taxes, the auctioning of pollution rights, severance taxes on the use of resources, and the creation of "public markets." Although their technical merits are debated by economists, there is general agreement on the main outlines of a market solution. For example, governments can simply forbid emissions above a certain level, which is the current U.S. policy with respect to automobiles, but economists tend to believe that direct administrative controls are cumbersome and inefficient (in the economic sense) in that they are not likely to provide the necessary amount of control at the least cost. Alternatively, governments can award environmental property rights to persons and corporations, thus creating a framework for bargaining, negotiation, exchange, and, if all else fails, litigation (none of which can take place effectively over property that nobody owns); according to this view, once the commons was made into private property, market forces and the legal system would work to preserve it rather than degrade it. However, economists fear that giving away common property to producers would be a tremendous windfall for them and that the dispersed citizens would not be able to organize effectively to buy amenity; on the other hand, they fear that if the public at large had individual "amenity rights" (so that a producer would have to buy pollution rights from each person affected by his effluent), the result would be economic paralysis. While recognizing that both these devices may be effective and even necessary in some cases, environmental economists generally favor restructuring the system of market prices with various taxes that would oblige producers to "internalize" (that is, incorporate) the environmental costs of production into prices.

In principle, this is a simple and just solution. Government agencies could calculate the public damage caused by the wastes of a producer and then charge him the appropriate amount as an effluent or pollution tax. Similarly, the government could levy severance taxes designed to promote more rational use of resources, especially virgin nonrenewable resources.* The producer would internalize these new costs of doing business, which would be reflected in the price he charged for his products, so that the consumer would pay the real cost of the product—that is, not only the costs of production but also the associated ecological and social costs. Those who ultimately benefited from the use or consumption would justly pay what they should and would thus be more likely to make responsible market decisions—for example, reducing consumption if the price is too high. Moreover, if the level of effluent or severance tax were carefully set, the producer would have an incentive to make his operations more efficient in an ecological and social sense—that is, cleaner and thriftier. If he did, he could pay less tax, lower his prices, and win customers away from his less efficient competitors. The theoretical outcome of well-administered internalization of environmental costs is thus a transformed market that would respond readily to the pressures of ecological scarcity.

Unfortunately, this conceptually simple and reasonably equitable approach is far from easy to implement. Some externalities can be assigned a price with relative ease—for example, extra laundry bills or house painting attributable to air pollution from a nearby factory. However, most cannot be readily quantified—for example, the health effects of air pollution, for it is almost impossible to know who suffers, to what degree, from what amount of which agents. Besides, what is the economic cost of life? A reduced life span? The risk of contracting emphysema? Being forced by smog to stay inside? Also, what criteria can be used to establish severance taxes on the use of nonrenewable resources—or even on many renewable ones, for that matter, since biologists are often uncertain about the level of exploitation that will provide a sustained yield? How do you put a price on the externalities involved in the unlikely but possible disaster, such as a serious nuclear accident? How do you decide whether irreversible development that forecloses future options, like building houses on prime farmland, should be undertaken at all, much less what price should be assigned to it? More generally, what about such social costs of industrial growth as increased commuting time or mental stress, to say nothing of the further erosion of organic community life? We have no way of knowing at present. Indeed, even with perfect information, the economists could not answer most of these questions, for they involve political, social, and ethical issues, not the

---

*Alternatively, limited pollution or exploitation rights could be auctioned off, in effect letting the market establish the tax; this would save much of the expense of information gathering and tax calculation, but, among other drawbacks, at the cost of giving advantages to those with the greatest market power.

Box 5–1. Technology Assessment

Just as laissez faire in economics generates environmental costs, so too "laissez innover," or the unrestrained freedom to innovate technologically, generates social costs. In both cases, these costs have reached unacceptable levels, and remedies are being sought. If internalization is the economists' answer to environmental costs, "technology assessment" is the technologists' cure for the social costs of laissez innover. The aim of both is the same—to make it no longer possible for individuals and groups to make micro-decisions that produce a macro-decision inimical to the common interest. As might be expected, therefore, technology assessment encounters the same kinds of problems as internalization, but in a more acute form, because the issues involved are much broader and even harder to analyze (especially in terms of quantifiable costs and benefits) than those involved in internalization. Thus decisions about the introduction of new technology are inevitably more political—or "trans-scientific," to use the technologists' term—than those confronted by environmental economists.

The heart of the difficulty is something already familiar to us from previous discussion. As Allen Kneese, a leading environmental economist and expert on cost/benefit analysis, says,

---

issue of efficient resource allocation that neo-classical, marginalist economics was designed to handle. They are "trans-economic" questions.

Thus "the new economics is mostly politics" (Wildavsky 1967). Even though economic analysis and the market itself, which is a highly effective mechanism for efficiently and automatically allocating resources and for sending signals to economic decision makers, both have a definite contribution to make, society will have to use noneconomic criteria to decide which trade-offs are to be made between production and other elements of the quality of life. (The assessment of technology poses a similar problem; see Box 5-1.) In effect, since economics itself cannot produce what economists call a "social welfare function," a means of assigning monetary values to non-market goods and bads, it will have to be invented politically. Moreover, even an overhauled price system will not eliminate all the liabilities discussed above, so that in any event an expansion of direct government intervention in the economic process will be needed—for example, to subsidize vital but risky research and development on alternative technologies. Thus, as even leading exponents of the market strategy acknowledge (for example, Freeman et al. 1973; Ridker 1972), our political system will be handed the uncomfortable and unwanted burden of making decisions hitherto left to the invisible hand; this means that open collective decision making on a scale never before attempted by our political institutions—as well as much more efficient, innovative, and timely government action in general—will be essential to the success of the market strategy of responding to ecological scarcity.

> It is my belief that benefit-cost analysis cannot answer the most important policy questions associated with the desirability of developing a large-scale, fission-based economy. To expect it to do so is to ask it to bear a burden it cannot sustain. This is so because these questions are of a deep ethical character. Benefit-cost analyses certainly cannot solve such questions and may well obscure them [Kneese 1973, p. 1].

Unfortunately, almost all discussion of technology assessment completely overlooks this point. Just like the majority of economists, who evince an almost religious faith in the tools of neoclassical economics and the technical efficacy of the market mechanism, technologists tend to look upon technology assessment as an exercise in pure cost/benefit analysis that will avoid rather than require political and ethical decisions. But if the criteria and methods of analysis are narrowly technical and economic, then there is little doubt that the Faustian bargain, for example, will be found cost effective. In its current form, therefore, technology assessment may indeed obscure rather than illuminate the most important questions connected with continued technological innovation.

The Political Costs of Internalization

Since it leans so heavily on politics, the market strategy of coping with ecological scarcity must also be evaluated in political terms. This will raise further questions about how well it can be expected to succeed in the real world of American politics, as opposed to the abstract world of economic analysis.

In the first place, letting the market adjust supply and demand can have such painful social and political consequences that governments have usually gone to considerable lengths to prevent the free play of market forces. Recession, for example, makes exceedingly bad politics. So will internalization, for to the extent that a market strategy is effective environmentally, it is bound to cause social and economic distress. The internalization of environmental costs means that people will have to pay for what they used to get free. Pollution control, for instance, will not make a production process more efficient, simply more expensive; similarly, severance and pollution taxes increase costs without increasing the quality of goods. The result will be a general rise in the level of prices, and the standard of living will be eroded by inflation—exactly what economic theory predicts must happen in the face of absolute scarcity (see note on page 169). Furthermore, as is well known, a rise in prices affects income groups selectively. The poor, those with fixed incomes, and in fact all who are not in a position to pass on the increased costs suffer disproportionately. In addition, if a policy of internalization is faithfully implemented, the price of owning certain highly desired but ecologically damaging goods, like the automobile, seems likely to rise the fastest and highest. This would cause serious disruption of the economy, which depends heavily on mass ownership of the automobile. It would also intensify the maldistributive tendency noted above, with potentially explosive political results if large numbers of people are priced out of car ownership. But in any case, ecological scarcity will have painful and disruptive effects on the economy, producing a lower standard of living as we usually conceive of it. Thus the question is whether it is desirable for the inevitable economic consequences of ecological scarcity to be distributed in a relatively laissez-faire fashion by the invisible hand, or by a planned economic contraction designed to mitigate these side effects. This will, in fact, be a prime political issue confronting the American polity as a consequence of ecological scarcity, so we shall return to it in the next chapter.

Making the Invisible Hand Visible

An additional political problem is the very openness and explicitness of the internalization process, for it will make public what has hitherto been hidden. As its name implies, one of the characteristic features of the invisible hand is that the workings of the economic process are largely concealed, and responsibility for the economic macro-decision that results from the summation and integration of many small economic micro-decisions is diffused. The outcome is due to "the market," not to any particular person or act. This greatly favors the entrepreneur, who can pursue his own private profit while ignoring the public costs this imposes on others. The result is "development." Capitalism is thus an economic system founded on hidden social costs, in which development (at least as we have experienced it) would not have occurred if all the costs had been counted in advance. For example, the gentry and the bourgeois clearly did very well by the Industrial Revolution, while the urban and rural masses suffered greatly from the disruptive side effects of development; one sees essentially the same process being repeated today in the countries of the Third World. The extreme resistance of the atomic energy establishment to a full and frank debate on the merits of nuclear power suggests just how threatening full disclosure of costs and benefits is to those who have hitherto been able to hide behind the invisible hand of dispersed, laissez-faire decision making. In brief, honesty and "progress" may not be compatible.

That openness and explicitness are not welcomed by most policy makers is evident from the brief history of the National Environmental Policy Act of 1969 (NEPA). Section 102 of that act required all Federal agencies to prepare an environmental-impact statement (EIS) on any of their activities having a significant effect on the quality of the human environment. In other words, the act requires a full public accounting of the costs and benefits of any Federal action that might have environmental consequences decision makers and the interested public should be made aware of.* The act established *no* criteria of acceptability. In theory, an agency can report that a proposed activity will cause the sky to fall by 1980 and still proceed with the project once it has satisfied the procedural requirements of the act. Nevertheless, although the courts have refused to hear arguments on the substance of the issues, in response to environmentalist suits they have forced government agencies to live up rather strictly to the requirement that a full-blown environmental-impact statement be prepared.

As a result, a number of projects have been abandoned when it appeared that an honest public accounting would be too damaging; others have been temporarily shelved for redesign to remove some of the more glaring ecological liabilities; and still others have been held up by the extensive paperwork and inter-agency consultation needed to complete an EIS. Furthermore, the statements have made splendid ammunition for environmental defenders during the regulatory proceedings that are often needed before a project can be carried out. The rapidly expanding nuclear power industry, already saddled with the heavy procedural and legal requirements involved in site location and reactor licensing, has been especially hard hit, but the Army Corps of Engineers and other development-oriented agencies have also found living up to their obligations under Section 102 to be a troublesome burden.

As the full consequences of Section 102 became apparent, an administrative and legislative backlash set in. In part, this was due to the admittedly expensive and time-consuming process of preparing a draft report, circulating it to interested agencies for criticism, and so forth. However, most of the distress was due precisely to the openness and explicitness of the process, for this gives potential opponents (usually a public-interest or environmental action group, but occasionally a rival agency) an opportunity to prevent a project from being carried out. For the sponsoring agency and its legislative and industrial constituency, especially pork-barreling congressmen, such an outcome is horrible to contemplate, for projects bring prestige, profits, political favor, and many other benefits. Predictably, since so many important interests benefit from such special-interest projects, there was an attempt to weaken NEPA legislatively. When this failed, essentially the same result was achieved by an administrative modus vivendi.

Instead of treating the process of preparing an EIS as an opportunity to improve the quality of their decision making, sponsoring agencies have turned it into pro forma, paperwork compliance with the requirements of Section 102 (Krieth 1973). Reviewing agencies have responded by giving

---

*Some states have also adopted legislation requiring similar statements for governmental (and even some private) projects likely to have a significant environmental impact.

EIS's a generally perfunctory review, thus saving themselves the money and the staff time that would have had to go into a genuine study, at the same time chalking up a political favor that can be collected when their own pet projects are passed around for criticism. Since only a few especially controversial projects are important enough to attract the attention of overworked and underfinanced public-interest groups, the vast majority of impact statements glide through with only the most cursory review. In fact, even some highly controversial projects receive pitifully inadequate reviews. For example, numerous agencies vitally concerned with important questions raised by the breeder-reactor program—including, scandalously, the Federal Energy Administration!—simply refused to comment on the Atomic Energy Commission's EIS covering the program, thus effectively sabotaging the spirit of NEPA (Abrahamson 1974a, b).

Agencies also seek to avoid the larger substantive issues as much as possible by using narrow and exclusive definitions of "project" and "environmental impact." For example, the AEC's first draft EIS covering the breeder-reactor program concerned itself solely with local ecological damage to be expected at reactor sites; it did not deal with the overall environmental impact of the breeder fuel cycle, the security costs and problems related to plutonium, whether alternative reactor types or even alternative technologies might not be preferable to the breeder, and numerous other problems. In other words, the original draft addressed almost none of the real issues, and it took a public-interest law suit to compel the AEC to prepare an EIS covering the entire breeder program. Even so, the revised draft (the one that major agencies declined to comment on) falls far short of the kind of full and explicit discussion of this dangerous technology that any prudent decision maker would wish to have (Novick 1974).

Finally, in one especially controversial case, the Trans-Alaska Pipeline, NEPA was simply set aside. When the Department of the Interior, despite intense White House pressure, could not produce an EIS favorable to the pipeline yet plausible enough to stand up in court, the Administration simply persuaded the Congress to pass legislation exempting the pipeline project from full compliance with NEPA requirements (Carter 1973; Odell 1973).

In sum, although NEPA has caused some grossly ill-conceived projects to be aborted, it has not resulted in full, open, and explicit environmental accountancy, for agencies have fulfilled the letter of the law (reluctantly) while evading the spirit, and in one important instance even the letter of the law was deliberately set aside. The reason is simple: no project sponsor or developer wants to let it be known that his gain may be the community's loss. Full disclosure of the kind of information needed to internalize the costs of production and make intelligent decisions on future development is thus deeply threatening to the industrial order and to a political and economic system that has thrived on the invisibility of the invisible hand.

One must therefore question whether the openness and explicitness needed to make internalization work can be achieved with our current institutions. At the very least, there will have to be some painful readjustments in our economic mode of life, which is based on hidden costs, and in the administrative and political process allied with it.

Into the Political Cockpit

Internalization would be resisted by important economic interests precisely to the degree that it was effective. Two leading proponents of this approach explain why:

> A system of pollution charges . . . would establish the principle that the environment is owned by the people as a whole and that the polluters must pay for the privilege of using part of the environment for waste disposal. Such massive transfers of "property rights" and the wealth they represent seldom occur without political upheaval [Freeman and Haveman 1972].

Implicit in any effective program of internalization or environmental management, therefore, is a deliberate reversal of a 200-year-old bias in favor of development and growth. Toward this end, the government will be required to take jealously guarded privileges away from and impose heavy new obligations on *some of the most important and powerful actors in the political system.* For example, companies extracting virgin materials now benefit from a substantial tax break in the form of a depletion allowance; in the new scheme of things, not only will this depletion allowance be taken away, but additional pollution and severance taxes will be imposed. It is apparent that producers have little incentive to cooperate in a program of internalization, no matter how well and fairly administered, that threatens drastically to curtail both profits and power.

The battle over the implementation of emission and safety standards for automobiles is a foretaste of the kind of long political struggle that would become pervasive as Washington tried to force producers to internalize ecological and social costs. Vital issues are at stake. Oil companies and the automobile industry rightly see a threat in higher-priced gasoline and automobiles. They realize that if the current trend is allowed to proceed to its logical conclusion, automobiles will once again be luxury items, with devastating effects on profits. Labor, too, sees the threat implicit in controls on pollution, and even consumers do not desire goods that are more expensive but no better in terms of utility. In short, internalization will inhibit if not prevent continued growth, and nobody really wants material growth to end. At the very least, everybody wants somebody else to bear the costs of restructuring the economy.

With important interests so clearly opposed, it seems doubtful that a program of internalization can be fully, fairly, and efficiently administered. At best, there will be considerable lag as time-consuming political battles are fought out in the legislature and the courts, and economists agree that substantial delay in internalizing costs will be fatal to the market strategy. At worst, internalization will be only partially (as well as belatedly) applied, and primary reliance on politically more feasible but economically less efficient measures, like direct regulation, will shackle the market with a jumble of controls that will increase the irrationality of the price mechanism without removing any of its environmental liabilities.

The market strategy thus seems likely to founder on politics, for the attempt to reform the price mechanism will transfer from the invisible hand to the highly visible political realm decisions on matters of critical importance to major interests in the society. Indeed, what is really at stake in any program of cost internalization is the abandonment of the entire market philosophy and way of life, along with the laissez-faire institutions that have supported them. If the invisible hand must be made visible and obedient to some explicit conception of the common interest, then this will inevitably bring about a basic change in the character of American government, which has relied heavily on the market mechanism. Laissez-faire economics has been, in effect, a surrogate for politics; with its demise, government seems likely to turn into a political cockpit for competing economic interests fighting desperately for survival in an age of ecological scarcity.

Farewell to Economic Man

The most fundamental concepts the system has habitually used to frame its decisions are being called into question. A laissez-faire market system of economics reflects the values of "economic man," and these values themselves, not just laissez-faire institutions, have become pernicious. For example, to a purely economic man there is no higher value than the individual wants of those living today; in pursuit of these wants it is economically optimal to keep growing until one further increment of growth will precipitate ecological catastrophe (Pearce 1973). The ultimate consequence of such a policy of ecological brinkmanship would, of course, be ruin. But who cares about ultimate consequences? In fact, any purely economic man *must* ignore the interests of posterity, for it has no agent he can bargain with in a market place and nothing of economic value to offer him. It is an economic fact that posterity never has and never will be able to do anything for us. Posterity is therefore damned if decisions are made "economically."

Thus the current paradigm of political economy, which is based on the primacy of economics, must give way to one based primarily on politics.

The market will remain an essential tool for performing vital economic tasks, but it will cease to be the dominant mode of allocating social values. Similarly, economics, instead of being the master science it has been since the beginning of the Industrial Revolution, will be reduced to the more modest but still important role of handmaiden to ecological politics, supporting the material goals of the polity and managing the human ecological household in a way that respects the laws of nature and the long-term interests of humankind.

BIBLIOGRAPHIC NOTE

An excellent way to begin thinking about ecology and economics would be to read Karl Polanyi's *The Great Transformation,* a history of the Industrial Revolution emphasizing the social devastation caused by an uncontrolled market system; the problem of social costs is hardly new. Another work useful as a prologue, showing the virtually irresistible power of narrowly economic rationality in a market society, is Samuel Hays' *Conservation and the Gospel of Efficiency,* which describes how even the conservation movement came to be dominated by naked economism.

The contemporary critique of the market economy as a generator of social costs began in 1950 with William Kapp's pioneering *The Social Costs of Private Enterprise.* (Kapp's lengthy introduction to the 1971 reprinted edition shows how later developments have only reinforced his original analysis.) In the *The Affluent Society,* John Kenneth Galbraith argued more broadly that the free play of market forces has produced private affluence but public squalor; in the *The New Industrial State,* he continued his critique by pointing out that consumer sovereignty is a myth, because producers have the ability to create markets and demands. Kenneth Boulding has been another eminent economic critic of the Gross National Product fetish of conventional macroeconomics. Unfortunately, he has scattered his criticisms among numerous essays and has never produced the major work on spaceship economics he is so well equipped to write; however, the four works by him in the List of Sources, especially his seminal essay of 1966 on "The Economics of the Coming Spaceship Earth," contain the essentials of his argument, which criticizes the market system for maximizing quantity and wastefulness instead of amenity and thrift. Economists Ezra Mishan in *Technology and Growth* and Walter Weisskopf in *Alienation and Economics* criticize the theoretical and practical defects of neoclassical economics, especially welfare economics, in a fairly technical fashion; but they both go on to raise the philosophical questions involved in social costs, concluding that we need a radical simplification of our existence and a dethronement of economics and materialism as the dominating factors in our lives. Herman Daly, in his own contributions to the collection *Toward a Steady-State Economy,* shows how and why the invisible hand has turned into an invisible foot; he argues for a steady-state economics in which macroeconomics and morality are no longer divorced. John Culbertson's

Economic Development: An Ecological Approach challenges the very concepts of "development" and "modernization" as seriously misleading and urges a "naturalistic" (that is, ecological) approach to the construction of a new general theory of economics that meets "nature's criteria for the survival of civilization." (Richard Wilkinson's *Poverty and Progress,* discussed in the Bibliographic Note of Chapter 4, approaches the same issue from a different perspective and should be read with Culbertson.) Finally, Harry Rothman's *Murderous Providence* is a Marxist critique; it is naive in its assumption that socialism will abolish all the problems connected with material growth, but it nevertheless contains telling criticisms of the way in which market economies enable a few to profit at the expense of the environment.

For a less radical but still critical discussion of environmental economics, J. H. Dales' *Pollution, Property and Prices* and Edwin Dolan's *TANSTAAFL* are both excellent. (A useful complement to the work of these two economists is Garrett Hardin's *Exploring New Ethics for Survival,* which gives an ecologist's view of so-called externalities, as well as an interesting history of the gradual internalization of external costs as the result of increased knowledge of their harmful consequences; the welfare of the labor force, for example, was treated as an external cost by early capitalists.) However, for the full flavor of the "establishment" position in environmental and resource economics, one must turn to the many works published under the auspices of Resources for the Future (RFF), a prestigious research group with long-standing interests in both areas. The three most significant works are *Scarcity and Growth,* by Harold Barnett and Chandler Morse; *Economics and Environment,* by Allen Kneese, Robert Ayres, and Ralph d'Arge; and *The Economics of Environmental Policy,* by Myrick Freeman, Robert Haveman, and Allen Kneese. In marked contrast to *Scarcity and Growth,* which fairly oozes confidence in the price mechanism and technology, *Economics and Environment* closes on a much more dismal Malthusian note (pp. 118–119). Thus, over the years, the RFF economists have moved toward the position of the radical critics; they agree totally, for example, that an unregulated market generates unacceptable environmental costs, especially the overuse and abuse of common property resources. The main remaining difference—and it is a large one— between the RFF economists and the radical critics is that the former believe the current paradigm of economics is salvageable by internalization, while the latter for the most part believe it needs to be replaced by a paradigm founded on real physical flows (or thermodynamics) and moral principles instead of prices. However, the thrust of the third RFF work mentioned above is that the economics of environmental policy has major political implications, so RFF too is beginning to move away from pure economics toward political economy.

Unfortunately, many economists would not admit that environmental problems represent a serious challenge to neoclassical economics, for they believe that everything either has its price or can be made to have one. Walter Heller's *Economic Growth and Environmental Quality,* for example, acknowledges the existence of problems but soothingly prescribes more growth so we will be rich enough to solve them, while Peter Passell and Leonard Ross in *The Retreat from Riches* simply assert their faith in the market and the technological fix. However, the most extreme and therefore the purest defense of the true neoclassical economic faith is to be found in Wilfred Beckerman's *In Defence of Economic Growth*; if one were to read only two books in favor of continued growth, Beckerman's should probably be one of them (and John Maddox's pro-technology *The Doomsday Syndrome,* discussed in the Bibliographic Note to Chapter 2, would be the other).

No full-length study on technology assessment itself has appeared. Brooks and Bowers 1971 provides the best nontechnical overview; Winner 1972 and Tribe 1971 the best sociopolitical critiques; Boguslaw 1965 and Dales 1968, Chapters 3 and 4, good discussions of the theoretical and practical drawbacks of cost/benefit analysis in general. However, Dennis Gabor's *The Mature Society* is a first-rate discussion of some of the larger issues connected with continued technological innovation.

On NEPA and the problems it has encountered, the only full-dress study is *NEPA in the Courts,* by Frederick Anderson and Robert Daniels, which is a balanced treatment.

Finally, concerning a solution, both Kapp and Culbertson explicitly urge a break with the narrow economism of the present and a return to the more philosophical and political economics of the past—as practiced, for example, even by leading market economists like Adam Smith and J. S. Mill. Perhaps, therefore, as Chapter 8 will suggest with respect to politics, we shall have to return to the classics of economics as the first step toward constructing a political economy suitable for an age of ecological scarcity.

6

THE AMERICAN POLITICAL ECONOMY II:
THE NON-POLITICS OF LAISSEZ FAIRE

The preceding chapter showed that the invisible hand is no longer to be relied upon for social decisions; we shall be obliged to make explicit political choices in order to meet the challenges of ecological scarcity. This is an embarrassing conclusion, for we Americans have never had a genuine politics—that is, something apart from economics that gives direction to our community life. Instead, American politics has been but a reflection of its laissez-faire economic system.

The Political Functions of Economic Growth

From our earliest colonial beginnings, rising expectations have been a fundamental part of the American credo, with each generation expecting to become richer than the previous one. Thanks to this expectation of growth, the class conflict and social discontent typical of early nineteenth-century Europe were all but absent in America; politics was accordingly undemanding, pragmatic, and laissez faire. Thus, said Alexis de Tocqueville in his classic study of American civilization, *Democracy in America,* we were indeed a "happy republic."

Growth is still central to American politics. In fact, it matters more than ever, for the older social restraints—the Protestant ethic, deference, isolation—have all been swept away. Growth is the secular religion of American society, providing a social goal, a basis for political solidarity, and a source of individual motivation; the pursuit of happiness has come to be defined almost exclusively in material terms, and the entire society— individuals, enterprises, the government itself—has an enormous vested interest in the continuation of growth.

The Economic Basis of Pragmatic Politics

Growth continues to be essential to the characteristic pragmatic, laissez-faire style of American politics, which has always revolved around the question of fair access to the opportunity to get on financially. Indeed, American political history is but the record of a more or less amicable squabble over the division of the spoils of a growing economy. Even social problems have been handled by substituting economic growth for political principle, transforming noneconomic issues into ones that could be solved by economic bargaining. For example, when labor pressed its class demands, the response was to legitimize its status as a bargaining unit in the division of the spoils. Once labor had to be bargained with in good businesslike fashion, compromise, in terms of wages and other costable benefits, became possible. In return for labor's abandonment of uncompromisable demands for socialism, others at the economic trough squeezed over enough for labor to get its share. Similarly, new political demands by immigrants, farmers, and so on were bought off by the opportunity to share in the fruits of economic growth. The only conflict that we failed to solve in this manner was slavery and its aftermath, and it is typical that once the legitimacy of black demands was recognized in the 1960's, the reflex response was to promote economic opportunity by job training, education, "black capitalism," and fair hiring practices—that is, the wherewithal to share the affluence of the envied whites. If blacks prosper economically, says our intuitive understanding of politics, racial problems will vanish.

As a political mode, economic reductionism has many virtues. Above all, it is a superb means of channeling and controlling social conflict. Economic bargaining is a matter of a little more or a little less. Nobody loses on issues of principle, and even failure to get what you want today is tolerable, for the bargaining session is continuous, and the outcome of the next round may be more favorable. Besides, everybody's share is growing, so that even an unfair share is a more-than-acceptable bird in hand. Most people understand that in a growth economy individuals or groups have more to gain from increases in the size of the enterprise as a whole than from any feasible change in distribution. Furthermore, people have gotten what was of primary interest to them—access to income and wealth—and with their chief aim satisfied, they could repress desires for community, social respect, political power, and other values that are not so easily divisible as money or commensurable with it.

Naturally, this characteristic style of conflict resolution presupposes agreement on the primacy of economics and a general willingness to be pragmatic and to accept the bargaining approach to political and social as well as economic issues. Unfortunately, the arrival of ecological scarcity places issues on the political agenda that are not easily compromisable or commensurable, least of all in terms of money. Trade-offs are possible, of course, but environmental imperatives are basically matters of principle that cannot be bargained away in an economic fashion. Environmental management is therefore a role for which our political institutions are miscast, because it involves deciding issues of principle in favor of one side or another rather than merely allocating shares in the spoils. Worse, a cessation or even a slowing of growth will bring opposing interests into increasingly naked conflict. Economic growth has made it possible to satisfy the demands of new claimants to the spoils without taking anything away from others. Without significant growth, therefore, we are left with a zero-sum game, in which there will be winners and losers instead of big winners and little winners. Especially in recent years, growth has become an all-purpose "political solvent" (Bell 1974, p. 43), satisfying rapidly rising expectations while allowing very large expenditures for social welfare and defense. However, without the political solvent of growth to provide quasi-automatic solutions to many of our domestic social problems, our political institutions will be called upon to make hard choices about how best to use relatively scarce resources to meet a plethora of demands. More important, long-suppressed social issues can be expected to surface—especially the issue of equality.

Ecological Scarcity versus Economic Justice

To state the problem succinctly, growth and economic opportunity have been substitutes for equality of income and wealth. We have justified large differences in income and wealth on the grounds that they promote growth and that all would receive future advantage from current inequality as the benefits of development "trickled down" to the poor. (On a more personal level, economic growth also ratifies the ethics of individual self-seeking: you can get on without concern for the fate of others, for they are presumably getting on too, even if not so well as you.) But if growth in production is no longer of overriding importance the rationale for differential rewards gets thinner, and with a cessation of growth it virtually disappears. In general, anything that diminishes growth and opportunity abridges the customary substitutes for equality. Since people's demands for economic betterment are not likely to disappear, once the pie stops growing fast enough to accommodate their demands they will begin making demands for redistribution.

Even more serious than the frustration of rising expectations is the prospect of actual deprivation as substantial numbers of people get worse off in terms of real income, owing to scarcity-induced inflation and the internalization of environmental costs. Indeed, the eventual consequence of ecological scarcity is a lower standard of living, as we currently define it, for almost all members of society. One does not need a gloomy view of human nature to realize that this will create enormous political and social tension. It is, in fact, the classic prescription for revolution. At the very least, we can expect that our politics will come to be dominated by resentment and envy—or "emulation," to use the old word—just as it has many times in the past in democratic polities.

To make the revolutionary potential of the politics of emulation more concrete, let us imagine that the current trend toward making automobile ownership and operation more expensive continues to the point where, as some fear, the car becomes once again a luxury item, available only to "the carriage trade." How will the common man, once an economic aristocrat with his own private carriage but now demoted to a scooter or a bicycle, react to his deprivation, especially since the remaining aristocrats will presumably continue to enjoy their private carriages?

Of course, such an extreme situation is probably a long way off (although many would be priced out of the market today if all the social costs attributable to the automobile were internalized). Yet it is toward such a situation that the rising costs due to ecological scarcity are pushing us. Already, in striking contrast to the last three decades, the price of a detached house in the most populous areas of the country is more than the average family can afford to pay. Also, as the cost of food and other basic necessities continues to increase, less disposable income will be left to purchase automobiles and other highly desired goods. In sum, deprivation is inevitable, even in the short term.

This point has not been lost on spokesmen for the disadvantaged, who have already protested vehemently against the regressive impact of even modest increases in the cost of energy and goods. More generally, they fear that lessened growth will tend to restrict social mobility and freeze the status quo, even turn the clock back in some areas, such as women's rights. Indeed, some of these spokesmen go so far as to say that concern for ecological scarcity is a fraudulent device being used by the already advantaged to maintain and solidify their privileged status (for example, Bruce-Briggs 1974 and Horowitz 1972).

The political stage is therefore set for a showdown between the claims of ecological scarcity on the one hand and socioeconomic justice on the other.

If the impact of scarcity is distributed in a laissez-faire fashion, the result will be to intensify existing inequalities. Large-scale redistribution, however, is almost totally foreign to our political machinery, which was designed for a growth economy and which has used economic surplus as the coin of social and political payoff. Thus the political measures necessary to redistribute income and wealth so that scarcity is to a large degree equally shared will require much greater social cooperation and solidarity than has been achieved by the system in the past.

They will also require greater social control. Under conditions of scarcity, there is a trade-off between freedom and equality, with perfect equality necessitating almost total social control (as in Maoist China). However, even partial redistribution will involve wholesale government intervention in the economy and major transfers of property rights, as well as other infringements of liberty in general, that would inevitably be resisted bitterly by important and powerful interests.

Thus either horn of the dilemma—laissez faire or redistribution—would toss us into serious difficulties that would strain our meager political and moral resources to or beyond capacity. American society is founded on competition rather than cooperation, and scarcity is likely to aggravate rather than ameliorate the competitive struggle to gain economic benefits for oneself or one's group. Similarly, our political ethic is based on a just division of the spoils defined almost purely in terms of fair access to the increments of growth; once the spoils of abundance are gone, little is left to promote social cooperation and sharing. As Adam Smith pointed out, the "progressive state" is "cheerful" and "hearty"; by contrast, the stationary state is "hard," the declining state "miserable" (Smith 1776, p. 81). How well will a set of political institutions so completely predicated on abundance and molded by over 200 years of continuous growth cope with the hardness, much less the misery, of ecological scarcity?

The Non-politics·of Due Process

This dilemma is only a specific instance of a more general problem. In many areas, the American government will be obliged to have genuine policies— that is, specific measures or programs designed to further some particular conception of the public interest. This will require radical changes, for in our laissez-faire political system ends are subordinated to political means. In other words, we practice "process" as opposed to "systems" politics (Schick 1971). As the name implies, process politics emphasizes the adequacy and fairness of the rules governing the process of politics. If the process is fair then, as in a trial conducted according to due process, the outcome is assumed to be just—or at least the best that the system can achieve. By contrast, systems politics is concerned primarily with desired outcomes; means are subordinated to predetermined ends.

The process model has many virtues. By keeping the question of ends out of politics, the intensity of social conflict is greatly diminished; people debate the fairness of the rules, a matter about which they find it relatively easy to agree, and they do not confront each other with value demands, which may not be susceptible to compromise. However, by some standards, the process model hardly deserves the name of politics, for it evades the whole issue of the common interest simply by declaring that the "will of all" and the "general will" are identical. The common interest is thus, by definition, whatever the political system's invisible hand cranks out, for good or evil.

Of course, we have found that pure laissez-faire politics, like pure laissez-faire economics, produces outcomes that we find intolerable, but our instinct has always been to curb the social costs of laissez faire by reforms designed to preserve its basic features: we check practices that prevent the efficient or fair operation of the market rather than converting to a planned economy; we promote equal opportunity rather than redistributing wealth or income. Planning with certain ends in mind does take place in such a political system. Individuals, corporations, government agencies, advisory commissions, supreme courts—each separate atom or molecule in the body politic plans in order to maximize its own ends, and the invisible hand produces the aggregated result of action on these private plans. But the central government does not plan in any systematic way, even though its ad hoc actions—VA and FHA home loans, tax breaks for homeowners, and the like—do in some sense constitute a "plan" for certain outcomes—in this case, suburban sprawl.

In reality, the "American political system" is almost a misnomer. What we really have is a congeries of unintegrated and competitive subsystems pursuing conflicting ends—a non-system. And our overall policy of accepting the outcome of due process means that in most particulars we have non-policies. Now, however, just as in economics, the externalities produced by this laissez-faire system of non-politics have become unacceptable. Coping with the consequences of ecological scarcity will require explicit, outcome-oriented political decisions taken in the name of some conception of an ecological, if not a political and social, common interest. What likelihood is there of this happening?

Who Dominates the Political Marketplace?

Critics of the American political system almost never question the necessity (and superiority) of process politics. If bad outcomes are generated, it must be because powerful interests dominate the political marketplace and prevent the will of the majority from being fully and fairly translated into outcomes. There has been, say the critics, a wholesale expropriation of the public domain by private interests (Lowi 1969; McConnell 1966). Nevertheless, although much of this criticism is incontrovertible, the general preferences of the American people are in fact quite well reflected in political output. People want jobs, economic opportunities, and a growing economy. Indeed, to the extent that the system has had a guiding policy goal at all, it has been precisely to satisfy the rising expectations of its citizens; even if special interests have benefited disproportionately from the measures taken to promote this end, most of the benefit has been transmitted to the vast majority of the population. The problem, then, is that our political institutions are highly responsive to our wills—but what we desire generates the tragedy of the commons.

Naturally, to the extent that our government *is* largely a brokerage house for special interests, the situation is much worse, because they have an even bigger stake in continued economic growth. But within a process system of politics, government decisions that consistently favor producer over consumer interests are all but inevitable, for the political marketplace is subject to the public-goods problem (Box 4-1). For example, those who have a direct and substantial financial interest in legislation and regulation are strongly motivated to organize, lobby, make campaign contributions, advertise, litigate, and so forth in pursuit of their interests. By comparison, the great mass of the people, who will be indirectly affected and whose personal stake in the outcome is likely to be negligible, have very little incentive to organize in defense of their interests. After all, the right decision may be worth $10 million to General Motors, while costing each individual only a few pennies. Thus those who try to stand up to special interests on environmental issues find themselves up against superior political resources all across the board.

The gross political inequality of profit and non-profit interests is epitomized by the favorable tax treatment· accorded the former. By law, tax-deductible donations cannot be used for lobbying or other attempts to influence legislation (for example, by advertising). Thus the nonprofit organizations that depend very heavily on donations are severely handicapped; if they lobby, they undercut their financial support. Businesses, by contrast, can deduct any money spent for the same purpose from their taxable income and pass on the remaining expense in the form of higher prices. The public, both as consumers and as taxpayers, therefore subsidizes one side in environmental disputes. Moreover, the law is self-protecting, for public-interest groups cannot even lobby to have it changed without losing their tax-exempt status.

Thus the outcome of the process of American politics faithfully reflects the will of the people and their desire for economic growth. However, just as in the economic marketplace, the public suffers from certain negative externalities due to the inordinate political power of producer interests; political power tends to be used to ratify and reinforce, rather than countermand, the decisions of the economic market. In sum, the American political system has all the drawbacks of laissez faire, with individual decisions adding up to an ecologically destructive macro-decision, as well as a structural bias in favor of producers that tends to make this macro-decision even more destructive of the commons than it would otherwise be.

The Ecological Vices of Muddling Through

The logic of the commons is enshrined in a system of process politics obedient to the demand from both consumer and producer for economic growth. The ecological vices of this system are further intensified by the decision-making style characteristic of all our institutions—"disjointed incrementalism" or, to use the more honest and descriptive colloquial term, "muddling through."

Incremental decision making largely ignores long-term goals; it focuses on the problem immediately at hand and tries to find the solution that is most congruent with the status quo. It is thus characterized by comparison and evaluation of marginal changes (increments) in current policies, not radical departures from them; consideration of only a restricted number of policy alternatives (and of only a few of the important consequences for any given alternative); the adjustment of ends to means and to what is "feasible" and "realistic"; serial or piecemeal treatment of problems; and a remedial orientation in which policies are designed to cure obvious immediate ills rather than to bring about some desired future state. Moreover, analysis of policy alternatives is not disinterested, for it is carried out largely by partisan actors who are trying to improve their bargaining position with other partisan actors.

Muddling through is therefore a highly economic style of decision making, well adapted to a pragmatic, laissez-faire system of politics. Moreover, it has considerable virtues. Like the market itself, disjointed incrementalism promotes short-term stability by minimizing serious conflict over ultimate ends, by giving everybody something of what they want, and by bringing about bargained compromises among political actors, satisfying their needs reasonably well at minimum intellectual and financial cost. At the same time, it promotes the consensus and legitimacy needed to support public policy. It is also basically democratic; like the economic market, it reflects the preferences of those who participate in the political market (assuming that all legitimate interests can participate equally, which is not always the case). Disjointed incrementalism is also conservative in a good sense: it does not slight traditional values, it encourages appreciation of the costs of change, and it prevents overly hasty action on complex issues. It may also avoid serious or irreversible mistakes, for an incremental measure that turns out to be mistaken can usually be corrected before major harm has been done. Under ideal circumstances, disjointed incrementalism therefore produces a succession of policy measures that take the system step by step toward the policy outcome that best reflects the interests of the participants in the political market.

Unfortunately, muddling through has some equally large vices. For example, it does not guarantee that all relevant values will be taken into account. Also, it is likely to overlook excellent policies not suggested by past experience. In addition, disjointed incrementalism is not well adapted to handling profound value conflicts, revolutions, crises, grand opportunities, and the like—in other words, any situation in which simple continuation of past policies is not an appropriate response. Most important, because decisions are made on the basis of immediate self-interest, muddling through is almost tailor-made for producing policies that will generate the tragedy of the commons. It is perfectly possible to take a series of decisions that each seem eminently reasonable on the basis of short-term calculation of costs and benefits and that satisfy current preferences, but that produce unsatisfactory results in the long run, especially since the future is likely to be discounted in the calculation of costs and benefits. In fact, that is just how we have gotten ourselves into an ecological predicament. Thus the short-term adjustment and stability achieved by muddling through can easily be at the expense of long-term stability and welfare.

A perfect illustration of the potential dangers of muddling through is nuclear power. As a result of thousands of separate decisions made by interested parties, "an age of massive dependence on nuclear power seems to be moving in with the inevitability of a glacier"; without a real congressional debate or any other kind of explicit policy decision, we have in effect opted for the Faustian bargain with all that it involves; thus, "what may be the most important decision of this half-century seems to have been made by default" (Quigg 1974).

Indeed, in its purest form, muddling through is policy making by default instead of by conscious choice—simply an administrative device for aggregating individual preferences into a "will of all" that may bear almost no resemblance to the "general will." Unfortunately, the contrasting synoptic, or outcome-oriented, style of decision making cannot be fully achieved in the real world, owing to limits to our intellectual capacities (even with computers), lack of information (plus the cost of remedying it), uncertainty about our values and conflicts between them, and time constraints, as well as many lesser factors. Moreover, in its pure form, synoptic decision making could lead to irreversible and disastrous blunders, riding roughshod over people's values, and the destruction of political consensus. Thus some measure of muddling through is a simple administrative necessity in any political system.

However, we Americans have taken muddling through, along with laissez faire and other prominent features of our political system, to an extreme. We have made compromise and short-term adjustment into ends instead of means, have failed to give even cursory consideration to the future consequences of present acts, and have neglected even to try to relate current policy choices to some kind of long-term goal. Worse, we have in fact taken the radical position that there can be no common interest beyond what muddling through produces. In brief, we have elevated what is an undeniable administrative necessity into a philosophy of government, becoming in the process an "adhocracy" virtually oblivious to the implications of our governmental acts and politically adrift in the dangerous waters of ecological scarcity.

In sum, as a description, disjointed incrementalism provides an almost sufficient explanation of how we have proceeded step by step into the midst of ecological crisis and of why we are not meeting its challenges at present; as a normative philosophy of government, it is a program for ecological catastrophe; as an entrenched reality with which the environmental reformer must cope, it is a cause for deep pessimism. At the very least, the level or quality of muddling through must be greatly upgraded, so that ecology and the future are given due weight in policy making. But goal-oriented muddling through comes close to being a contradiction in terms (especially within a basically democratic system); moreover, incrementalism is adapted to status-quo, consensus politics, not situations in which policy outcomes are of critical importance or in which the paradigm of politics itself may be undergoing radical change (Dror 1968, esp. pp. 300–304; Lindblom 1965; Schick 1971, esp. p. 158). Thus steering a middle course will be difficult at best, and it may not be possible at all during the transition to a steady-state society.

Policy Overload, Fragmentation, and Other Administrative Problems

Disjointed incrementalism is not the only built-in impediment to an effective response to ecological scarcity. In the first place, the growing scale, complexity, and interdependence of society create an ever more difficult decision-making environment, for the greater the number of decisions and, above all, the greater the degree of risk entailed by them, the greater the social effort necessary to make them. Given the size and complexity of the task of environmental management alone, especially with the declining margin for ecological or technological error, there would be a danger of administrative overload. But the crisis of ecological scarcity is only one crisis among many, part of a crisis of crises that will afflict decision makers in the decades ahead (Platt 1969). An allied crisis of priorities also impends, as burgeoning demands for environmental cleanup, more and better social services, and so on compete for the tiny portion of government resources remaining after the "fixed" demands of defense, agricultural supports, and other budgetary sacred cows are satisfied, so that decision makers will simply lack sufficient funds to act effectively across the board (Sprout and Sprout 1971, 1972). In addition, there may be critical shortfalls in manpower, especially technical and scientific manpower. In short, the problems are growing faster than the wherewithal to handle them, and political and administrative overload is therefore a potentially serious problem for the future, if not right now.

A second serious problem is fragmented and dispersed administrative responsibility. The agency in charge of decisions on air pollution, for example, usually has no control over land-use policy, freeway building, waste disposal, mass transit, and agriculture, all of which are either part of the problem or of the solution. Also, some elements of policy are handled at the federal level, while others belong to the state and local governments; the boundaries of local governments, especially, have no relationship to ecological realities. As a result, it frequently happens that one agency or unit of government works at cross-purposes with another, or even with itself, as in the old Atomic Energy Commission, which was charged with both nuclear development and radiation safety. Also, each agency has been created to perform a highly specialized function for a particular constituency, leading to a single-mindedness or tunnel vision that is deliberately oblivious to the common interest. In brief, we have as many different policies as we have bureaus and no way to get them to pull together.

A third major defect of our policy-making machinery is that decisions inevitably lag behind events, usually far behind. In part, the problem is that the decision makers' information and knowledge is deficient and out of date. Owing to the complexity and scope of the problems of environmental management, these deficiencies are either impossible or too costly to remedy. Thus, even if they are inclined to be forward-looking, decision makers are virtually obliged to muddle through critical problems with stopgap measures that provoke disruptive side effects. Much the larger part of the time-lag problem, however, is that the procedural checks and balances built into our basically adversary system of policy making can subject controversial decisions to lengthy delays. For example, a legal battle over the siting of one hydroelectric power plant has gone on for over ten years without a final decision, and seven years of litigation have also failed to end the pollution of Lake Superior with taconite tailings containing asbestos fibers, a known carcinogen (Carter 1974b, e). At best, therefore, we can expect long wars of legal attrition against environmental despoilers. However, the legal system is already having some difficulty in coping with environmental issues,* and

---

*Increased volume is only part of the problem. The traditional legal machinery for redressing civil wrongs, designed for two-party litigation, is having trouble with standing to sue and other issues that crop up in the typical environmental suit, where society as a whole is one of the parties; also, technology creates new situations faster than the courts can work out precedents; moreover, much of the scientific evidence used in environmental litigation is of a probabilistic and statistical nature that ill accords with the standards of proof traditionally demanded by courts.

there is some risk that environmental policy making may simply bog down in a morass of hearings, suits, countersuits, and appeals, as government agencies, business interests, and environmentalist groups use all the procedural devices available to harass each other. The response of an adversary system to intense and divisive conflict over issues admitting little compromise may therefore be virtual deadlock. But even if total stalemate is avoided, there are bound to be significant delays—an ominous prospect now that an anticipatory response to problems has become essential for their solution.

Additional hindrances to effective environmental decision making abound. The narrowly rationalistic norms and modus operandi of bureaucracies, for example, are at odds with the ecological holism needed for the task of environmental management. Also, history shows that regulatory agencies tend to be captured by the interests they are supposed to be regulating, so that they rapidly turn into guardians of special instead of public interest. In addition, the institutions charged with environmental management are frequently so beholden to their own institutional vested interests or so dominated by sheer inertia that they actively resist change—employing secrecy, special legal advantages available to government agencies, and other devices to squelch the efforts of critics and would-be reformers (for example, Lewis 1972). In fact, the problem is not simply to overcome inertia and vested interest, but rather to arrest the institutional momentum in favor of growth created by two centuries of pro-development laws, policies, and practices; this will require across-the-board institutional reform, not merely new policies.

In sum, administrative overload, fragmented and dispersed authority, protracted delays in making and enforcing social decisions, and the institutional legacy of the era of growth and exploitation are likely to obstruct timely and effective environmental policy making.

How Well Are We Doing?

None of the above inspires much optimism that our political institutions at any level are adequate to the challenges of ecological scarcity. Although the final verdict is obviously not yet in, this conclusion is certainly reinforced by the quality of their performance thus far.

Energy policy is an all too perfect illustration. Despite nationwide recognition that a coherent national energy policy is absolutely essential to avoid economic and social turmoil, a menacing international trade deficit, and even the compromise of its political independence, the United States has no genuine policy, must less a coherent one. Instead, for the past three years, there has been almost continual dithering and muddle, bureaucratic infighting, almost total lack of coordination, and a succession of futile reorganizations—in short, chaos (Carter 1974d; Gillette 1975). This sorry spectacle reached a pitiful climax of sorts in the spring and summer of 1975, when, despite a universally acknowledged need for action, Congress and the President fought each other to a stalemate on oil import policy, energy conservation, the regulation of strip-mining, and other critical energy issues—and the Energy Policy and Conservation Act signed into law in late 1975 simply ratified this stalemate. The stage is therefore set for a repetition of the 1973–1974 energy crisis in the short term and for a general collapse of an energy economy heavily dependent on petroleum in the long term.

Similarly, our political institutions have so far conspicuously failed to meet the challenge represented by the automobile. The decline in air quality was sufficiently alarming to cause Congress to pass the Clean Air Act in 1970; it was, for all its faults, a landmark piece of environmental legislation, and acting under the law's authority, government agencies forced emission control on a reluctant automobile industry. However, Detroit has several times succeeded in winning delayed compliance. In addition, current regulations permit the industry to use a control technology that has many serious drawbacks—increased consumption of fuel, inability to eliminate all current pollutants, the creation of new pollutants, and the necessity for very high standards of maintenance. Moreover, the air-quality standards mandated by Congress in the Clean Air Act simply cannot be achieved through technology alone. Yet when the Environmental Protection Agency tried to impose on key municipalities pollution-control plans that would have penalized or restricted car use (for example, with gas rationing and parking surcharges) the resulting political ruckus soon forced the EPA into retreat, and all pretense of meeting the original standards has been abandoned. In short, having allowed the automobile so completely to dominate our lives that to restrict its use would produce instant economic and social crisis, we are reduced to the desperate hope that some kind of technological fix will turn up in time to prevent natural feedback mechanisms—extreme price rises, national bankruptcy, intolerable levels of air pollution—from taking matters out of our hands.

Thus in these and other critical areas we are failing to meet the challenges. Everybody wants clean air and water, but nobody wants to pay the price. Nor do we wish to give up the appurtenances of a high-energy style of life or to accept the major restructuring of the economy and society that would be needed to reduce energy consumption significantly. Even modest invasion of sacrosanct private property rights—for example, in the form of vitally needed land-use law—has also proven to be well beyond our current political capacity. In fact, since the beginning of the decade there has been considerable backlash and backsliding on environmental issues, leading to relaxed standards and blatant avoidance of problems (Carter 1973a, 1975). The only policies that command widespread support are those that seem likely to stave off fundamental changes and permit business to continue as usual for yet a little longer—for example, measures to boost energy supply, as in the Alaska Pipeline decision. In short, although there has been genuine progress since environmental issues first became a matter for political concern, our political institutions have so far mostly avoided the tasks of environmental management and have mostly failed at those they have undertaken.

As we have seen, it is the basic institutional structure and modus operandi of the American political system that are primarily responsible for this. Nevertheless, the lack of courage and vision displayed by the current set of political actors should not escape notice. Neither Congress nor the Executive has provided real leadership or faced up to crucial issues. To the extent that they have acted, as in the area of pollution control, they have for the most part acted faintheartedly or, what is almost worse, expediently rather than effectively. Say what one will about the institutional impediments and the difficulty of the problems, therefore, it is hard to conclude that our political leaders are doing the job they were elected to do. But of course, the inability or reluctance of our political officials to act simply reflects the desires of the American people, who have so far evinced little willingness to make even minor sacrifices (for example, slightly higher gasoline taxes) for the sake of environmental goals, much less accept fundamental changes in their way of life. It is hardly to be expected that our elected officials will commit political suicide by forcing unpopular environmental measures on us. Until the will of the people ordains otherwise or fundamental changes are quite literally forced on us, the best we can expect is piecemeal, patchwork, ineffective reform that lags ever farther behind onrushing events.

The Necessity for Paradigm Change

Our political institutions, predicated almost totally on growth and abundance, appear to be no match for the gathering forces of ecological scarcity. This is a shocking conclusion about a political system that was once regarded, even by many foreigners, as marvellously progressive. The virtues of the American political system are indeed undeniable: for all its faults, it worked well for nearly two hundred years; it was, moreover, eminently just and humane by any reasonable historical standard. Unfortunately, the problems of scarcity that confront the system today are ones that *it was never designed to handle*. Its past virtues are therefore irrelevant; all that matters now are its equally undeniable failings in the face of ecological scarcity.

Thus efforts to patch up the current paradigm of politics with new modes of decision making and planning or even with new policies will not succeed; these can only delay, and perhaps intensify, the inevitable ultimate breakdown. Only a new politics based on a set of values that are morally and practically appropriate to an age of scarcity will do (see Chapter 8). To achieve this new politics will require a revolution greater than that which created our nation in the first place, for the characteristic features of American civilization, not merely the nature of the regime, must be transformed. The question before the American polity is: Will we make the effort to translate our ideals of equality and freedom into forms appropriate to the new age of scarcity, or will we not even try, continuing prodigally to sow as long as we can, leaving the future to reap the consequences? Only time will tell whether the return of scarcity must inevitably presage retrogression to the classical situation of inequality, oppression, and conflict—but one way or another, we Americans are about to find out what kind of people we really are.

BIBLIOGRAPHIC NOTE

For historical perspective on the relationship of abundance to American politics, David Potter's *People of Plenty* ably complements the more general discussion in Walter Prescott Webb's *The Great Frontier* (discussed in the Bibliographic Note for Chapter 4). Louis Hartz's *The Liberal Tradition in America* and John Miller's *Origins of the American Revolution* discuss the specifically liberal, Lockean character of our political values and institutions.

General works on American politics abound. Here are the ones most useful for amplifying one's understanding of the institutional obstacles to action: Peter Bachrach's *The Theory of Democratic Elitism*; Robert Dahl's *After the Revolution?: Authority in a Good Society*, a superlative brief discussion of modern democratic theory; Lewis Dexter's *The Sociology and Politics of Congress*; Murray Edelman's *The Symbolic Uses of Politics*; Louis Kohlmeier's *The Regulators: Watchdog Agencies and the Public Interest*; Theodore Lowi's *The End of Liberalism,* one of the best modern critiques; Grant McConnell's *Private Power and American Democracy*; and Robert Wolff's *The Poverty of Liberalism.* Most of these works are highly critical of the system, although primarily on the ground that it fails to live up to its own ideals. The standard work on disjointed incrementalism is C. E. Lindblom's *The Intelligence of Democracy,* a superlative analysis of American policy making; unfortunately, Lindblom goes on to try to make a normative case for the superiority of muddling through. Yehezkel Dror's *Public Policymaking Reexamined* is the best general discussion of decision making and planning; Dror suggests provocative alternatives to muddling through. Donald Michael's less technical *The Unprepared Society* is also an excellent discussion of the pitfalls of not keeping an eye on the future.

Turning next to works specifically on the politics of environmental issues, one finds two kinds of works—those that focus primarily on a phenomenological description of symptoms and those that try to unveil fundamental causes. In the former category are found Luther Carter's *The Florida Experience*, an exceedingly valuable case study of the politics of land and water at the state level; *Congress and the Environment*, a collection of essays edited by Richard Cooley and Geoffrey Wandesforde-Smith; *The Politics of Pollution*, by Barbara and Clarence Davies; D. H. Davis' *Energy Politics*; Daniel Henning's *Environmental Policy and Administration*; Charles Jones' *Clean Air*, a case study of the politics of pollution at the local level, which concludes that the answer is an all-out attempt to make disjointed incrementalism work through a much more organized and articulate public; Earl Murphy's *Governing Nature*, which focuses on law; and Walter Rosenbaum's *The Politics of Environmental Concern*, a history of the political impact of the environmental movement. In the second category of works, those that try to stand back from the symptoms to see causes, we find political scientist Lynton Caldwell's excellent *Environment: A Challenge to Modern Society*, a work close in spirit and approach to my own, but far less radical and more a tentative exploration of issues than a sustained argument; the sociologist William Burch's reflective and insightful *Daydreams and Nightmares*, which explores the anomalous nature of the value structure of modern industrial-bureaucratic civilization in general and American society in particular in an ecological age; the economist Edwin Haefele's *Representative Government and Environmental Management*, which ably analyzes the political dilemmas of managing common-property resources and argues for a return to decision making by general-purpose legislatures instead of bureaucracies; and *Ark II: Social Response to Environmental Imperatives*, by Dennis Pirages and Paul Ehrlich, which is a general and fairly polemical (perhaps too general and polemical) discussion of the failings of the American politico-socio-economic system, with abundant suggestions for reforms, making it of particular interest to those whose main concern is alternative policy measures.

Falling in between these two categories are Leslie Roos' *The Politics of Ecosuicide*, which despite its sensational title is an unusually solid and useful collection of essays that range from trenchant theoretical analysis to detailed case histories, and Stuart Nagel's *Environmental Politics*, which in style and topical organization is oriented more toward the professional political scientist, but which contains a number of essays of wider interest, as well as abundant references for those who wish to explore the literature more deeply.

For a point of view radically opposed to all the works of environmental politics mentioned above, see Richard Neuhaus' *In Defense of People*, which professes to find fascism lurking behind any concern for the environment, but which scores telling points against some of the more politically naive environmentalists.

For another discussion of the American system's inability to cope with the pressures of ecological scarcity, see Rufus Miles' *Awakening from the American Dream*, mentioned in the Bibliographic Note for Chapter 3; Miles' problem-oriented approach complements my own philosophical treatment.

Finally, for reference purposes *Environmental Policy, Law, and Administration: A Guide to Advanced Study*, by Lynton Caldwell and Toufiq Siddiqi, is everything the title promises.

7

ECOLOGICAL SCARCITY AND
INTERNATIONAL POLITICS

THE COMPARATIVE PERSPECTIVE

The principal focus so far in Part II has been on the American political system, specifically the strong market orientation of its political economy. However, as noted in the Introduction, the United States is only the most extreme version of modern industrial civilization, and the peculiarities of the American form of this civilization ought not to be allowed to obscure the wider implications of the analysis. Some problems may be uniquely American, but most are universal in one form or another. Let us therefore extend the analysis to other nations and then to the international political arena. We shall find that the basic political dynamics and dilemmas of ecological scarcity discussed in Chapter 4 remain unchanged. Furthermore, much of the specific analysis of American institutions in Chapters 5 and 6 can in fact be applied, with appropriate modifications, to all developed and even many so-called developing countries, capitalist and communist alike, as well as to the world in general. The crisis of ecological scarcity is thus a planetary crisis.

Western Europe

For brevity's sake, the Western European nations can be treated as a bloc: as the depressing sameness of their reports to the United Nations Conference on the Human Environment at Stockholm in 1972 clearly indicated (UNI-PUB 1972 catalogs these), Europe's environmental problems are essentially the same in character and magnitude as those of the United States, and its governments seem to exhibit the same degree of capacity to deal with them. In certain respects, due to the greater density of population and industrial development, Europe's pollution problems are worse than our own; the contamination of the Baltic and Mediterranean Seas and of the Rhine River, heavy oil spillage from tankers and refineries (soon to be increased as the North Sea's oil and gas resources are fully exploited), and the "acid rains" that fall on Scandinavia are only some of the most notorious examples. With respect to resources, Western Europe's predicament is clearly much worse. Even taking due account of the temporary respite that development of North Sea gas and oil will bring, Europe's long-term dependence on external sources of energy is far greater than our own; for example, Europe has nothing resembling America's vast coal reserves. Similarly, European mineral resources are almost negligible compared to actual and potential demand. Perhaps more critically, Western Europe as a whole is a major net importer of food and fiber, and the dependence of many European countries, like Denmark and the Netherlands, on food imports is overwhelming (both to feed the populace and, ironically, to sustain energy-intensive agricultural systems that are mainstays of their economies). Thus Western Europe is even more overextended ecologically in relation to its own resources than the United States. For us Americans, a major disruption of world trade would cause painful retrenchment, to be sure, but there would be little danger of starvation, and domestic energy would be available in sufficient quantity to keep the economy limping along. Europe does not enjoy such luxury. World trade must continue along established lines or economic collapse threatens—but, as we shall see later in this chapter, recent and impending changes in the terms of trade create the specter of just such a collapse.

Nor do the Western European nations appear to have any greater prospect of coping politically with ecological scarcity than the United States. All share the same basic growth-oriented world view. All have followed the path blazed by the United States toward high mass consumption and, to a somewhat lesser extent, high energy use. All are mass democracies in which political parties compete for favor largely on the basis of how well they can satisfy the material aspirations of the citizenry. In short, having travelled the same basic path in roughly the same manner for the last 250 years, we Westerners have wound up in approximately the same place.

Nevertheless, just as there are some differences in the nature and degree of ecological scarcity, so too there are some significant differences in the potential for political adaptation. For one thing, Europe has had to contend with ecological scarcity in numerous ways even during an era of unparalleled abundance. Not possessing the same cornucopia of found wealth, for example, Europe has never been as profligate with its resources as the United States. For instance, Europeans manage to achieve roughly comparable living standards while using only about half as much energy per capita as Americans. Also, Europeans practice sustained-yield forestry, control land use quite stringently by U.S. standards, and so on. Thus, both because of necessity and because of a generally less doctrinaire attachment to the principles of laissez faire, there exists in Europe a much greater willingness to accept planning and social controls. Moreover, at least in some quarters, disenchantment with bourgeois acquisition as a way of life has grown markedly. In general, therefore, European nations may cope somewhat better with ecological scarcity than the United States, despite the greater physical challenges they will face.

Japan

While in terms of ecological scarcity the situation of Japan is much more desperate than that of Europe, it possesses countervailing political and social advantages over Europe. With about half the U.S. population, a land about the size of Montana that is mostly mountainous and poorly endowed with mineral and energy resources, and the third largest economy in the world, Japan is a very tight little island indeed. Prevented from gaining by military means a position of power, respect, and economic security in the international community, the Japanese entered the great postwar international GNP stakes determined to win economically what could not be won by force of arms. They "aped" (their own word) the acquisitive ethic and mass-democratic institutions of the West so effectively that they achieved economic growth of unprecedented intensity and rapidity. This extraordinary "success" has earned them notorious pollution problems, like the mercury poisoning that killed or paralyzed almost 700 people and affected at least 8000 more, and a level of dependence on foreign trade and foreign sources of raw materials and fuels that makes them extremely vulnerable to international turmoil and resource scarcities, whether due to natural exhaustion or to artificial restriction by cartels. Japan thus faces ecological scarcity in an extreme form. A serious interruption of oil supplies from the Persian Gulf, a substantial decline in the fish catch, the inability or unwillingness of the United States to continue to supply vast quantities of food—these and numerous other potential threats could have severe consequences for Japan, which has totally committed itself to the modern way of industrial life and to living far beyond its ecological means.

Beginning in the early 1970's, and especially after the energy crisis of 1973–1974, the Japanese awoke to the fact that they were headed for an ecological precipice. The Japanese government cracked down on pollution with progressively greater severity and has recently moved to conserve energy and control growth in general. An awkward problem for Japanese political leaders, largely drawn from the business-oriented, conservative Liberal-Democratic Party (LDP), which has ruled throughout the postwar era, is that the powerful economic interests that are the LDP's main source of support, financial and otherwise, are also the chief polluters and main beneficiaries of growth. On the other hand, there are a number of positive factors. Having lived on a tight little island for centuries, the Japanese have a highly developed sense of community and a tradition of self-sacrifice for the common good. The phenomenal success of the postwar Japanese birth-control effort is an indication of how readily this communal ethic can be mobilized to achieve ends desired by leaders. In addition, a latent Shinto-Buddhist respect for nature, the remnants of a feudal code of values that despised wealth, and a tradition of government intervention in all areas of economic and social life (as in the birth-control effort, which included the vigorous promotion of abortion almost thirty years ago) will all assist Japan's leaders as they try to come to terms with an extreme form of ecological scarcity.

The Soviet Union

The Soviet Union is the most interesting and revealing comparative case.* Because it is the leading non-market industrialized nation it should seemingly be exempt, if not from the basic political dynamics of scarcity, at least from most of the failings of American market economics and politics discussed in the preceding chapters. In fact, however, the U.S.S.R. has severe and growing environmental problems and has so far demonstrated no greater capacity to deal with them than the United States and other market-oriented democracies. In brief, the imperatives of the industrial production system common to East and West have brought about a convergence of environmental ills that call into question the basic premises of the industrial system— and therefore of many features of the political institutions rooted in that system, whether those institutions are nominally capitalist or communist.

That the Soviet Union has serious environmental problems has been exten-

---

*Almost everything in this section applies equally to the other socialist countries within the Soviet economic orbit.

sively documented (Goldman 1972; Pryde 1972) and is not denied by Soviet spokesmen. With the sole exception of problems related to the mass use of private automobiles, which has not yet reached a significant level, Soviet pollution problems are in almost all respects identical with those found throughout the industrialized world. Nor, despite a relatively favorable position compared to Europe and America, is the U.S.S.R. exempt from ecological scarcity with respect to resources. For example, sizable grain purchases in recent years have made it evident that the Soviet Union's agricultural situation is problematic, even if the prospect of Malthusian starvation is remote. Also, the Soviet Union's apparent abundance of domestic energy resources may be illusory, at least in part. One recent study (Slocum 1974) points out that these resources are not readily exploitable, for they lie for the most part in remote and environmentally forbidding regions; also, they may be less substantial than rough estimates had indicated; in addition, they must be seen in the context not of Soviet needs alone, but also of the increasing demands of the COMECON countries of Eastern Europe; finally, they can probably not be fully exploited without advanced Western technology and even Western capital (at a time when, as noted in Chapter 3, the West confronts a potential capital shortage of its own).

Even as they acknowledge that environmental problems exist, Soviet spokesmen almost uniformly deny the reality of the limits to growth (Fyodorov 1973; Kiseleva 1974). The basis for their optimism appears to be the fundamental Marxist axiom that the problems of mankind have their origin in the structure of social relationships, specifically the social relationships surrounding the means of production; nature as such presents no obstacles that cannot be overcome by appropriate social arrangements and the wonders of scientific-technological productivity unleashed by the bourgeois revolution. Furthermore, say the spokesmen, since the Soviet system is not held in thrall by selfish market interests, it will easily be able to deal with any environmental problems that do crop up, whereas pollution and other environmental ills in the West are seen as serious emerging "contradictions" (inherent self-destructive forces) that capitalist nations will not be able to overcome.

Less partial observers paint quite a different picture. First, because the ideology of growth and belief in the power of technology are even more strongly entrenched in the U.S.S.R. than in the West, abandoning or even compromising growth in production for the sake of environmental protection or resource conservation is a much more heretical concept. For one thing, as pointed out in the Introduction, the Marxist utopia depends for its achievement on the abolition of material scarcity, so that to abandon growth is tantamount to abandoning a utopian promise that has inspired the whole society. Worse, this cherished utopian goal is used to justify many features of Soviet life that seem to conflict with basic Marxist principles. Soviet leaders, for example, explain the use of differential rewards (as opposed to the true communist principle of "to each according to his needs") as a necessary expedient to help build the requisite material and productive base for a utopia of abundance; more important, the "proletarian dictatorship" and "democratic centralism" exercised by the Communist Party are also rationalized with this brand of logic. The loss of such convenient justifications could thus cause awkward political repercussions.

Second, largely as a result of this fundamental ideological bias toward material expansion (but also because of security consciousness), the primacy of narrow economic concerns in policy matters is almost total, and fixation on production to the virtual exclusion of all else makes the Soviet elite very resistant to more than token concern for the environment.

Third, although they are employed by the state rather than private corporations, Soviet economic managers compete with other managers within the basic framework of the national plan, and their reluctance to spend money on nonproductive pollution control, their willingness to shove the external costs of production off on others, their desire to win promotions by overproducing the quota, and so forth, all make them behave just like capitalist managers with respect to the environment. Moreover, in the Soviet Union the economic managers have far greater political power than their Western counterparts. In one respect, the tragic logic of the commons operates even more viciously in the U.S.S.R.: because not only air and water, but virtually all natural resources, are (thanks to state ownership) treated as free or semi-free goods, there is an even greater tendency on the part of economic managers to use land, energy, and mineral resources wastefully.

Fourth, because government decisions are made in private council by leaders who put production and the vested interests of the state economic bureaucracy first, those concerned about the problems of growth have little opportunity to influence policy as it is being formed; they can only point out the adverse consequences of past policies. However, articles critical of Soviet environmental policy seem to be appearing in the press more frequently; perhaps this indicates that environmental and conservationist concerns are being communicated to Soviet decision makers more effectively than in the past.

Finally, although there has been some public discussion of the wisdom of continued pronatalism, the Soviet government continues to encourage population growth in a variety of direct and indirect ways.*

In short, Soviet economic and political institutions seem designed to produce environmental deterioration and resource depletion just as inexorably as their American counterparts. The essential reason has been sardonically

---

*The question of population limitation in the U.S.S.R. is complicated by its connection with the politically delicate "nationality" issue.

Box 7–1.   Is Socialism an Answer?

It should be evident from the example of the U.S.S.R. that, no matter how it is organized politically, the attempt to keep growing materially is bound to have danger-ous ecological consequences. Thus socialism (no matter how democratic) is not the ready solution to environmental ills that some take it to be (for example, Rothman 1972). Moreover, as noted in the Introduction, socialism and bourgeois capitalism are merely different versions of the modern world view based on hedonistic and materialistic premises, like the "conquest" of nature for human gain, that are utterly incompatible with ecological realities. The problem with historical socialism is that it is a vulgarized version of Marxism, just as bourgeois capitalism is a vulgarized version of the liberal ideas of Adam Smith and John Locke. However, Marxist philos-

stated by a leading expert on Soviet environmental policy: "The replacement of private greed by public greed is not much of an improvement" (Goldman 1970). The nature of the political institutions through which the "greed" for material growth is translated into economic output appears to make rela-tively little difference; in fact, if they are very strongly committed to growth, highly centralized and effective governments may wreak more and faster havoc on the environment than even the most laissez-faire government. (This calls socialism into question as an answer to environmental problems; see Box 7-1.) Conversely, of course, once Soviet leaders are forced by ecological scarcity to cease trying to abolish scarcity by indefinite material growth, then party rule, Soviet law, and the power of state planning institutions (along with the Soviet Union's relative wealth of resources) will be great assets in making a rapid and relatively turmoil-free transition to a steady-state economy. However, abandoning the utopian goal of total abundance would remove much of the regime's moral legitimacy, and the longer-term political consequences of this loss of legitimacy could be grave indeed. In the long run, therefore, the Soviet Union may face a profound challenge to its political viability.

The Third World

The developing or less-developed* countries (LDC's) constituting the so-called Third World of course differ greatly from each other in many impor-tant respects, but for the purposes of this analysis, little is lost by consider-ing them together. In brief, most LDC's, and especially the group of excep-tionally poor countries now sometimes called "the Fourth World," are not

---

*Lacking any reasonable alternative, I employ these well-established but, it seems to me, culturally biased terms in their narrow economic sense. Bhutan, a country that preserves the ancient and admirable Tibetan culture in virtually all of its traditional richness, is scarcely undeveloped, fanatical modernizers to the contrary notwithstanding.

ophy may have some contribution to make. Although for tactical reasons in their political propaganda Karl Marx and Friedrich Engels emphasized the primacy of labor, in their philosophical works they regarded nature as a source of value equal to labor, and Marx condemned capitalist production for despoiling nature in terms that would seem to forbid genuine Marxists from doing the same thing with a different set of political institutions. Thus there are the potential seeds in Marx and Engels for a fundamental reformulation of Marxist theory on ecological premises. In this sense alone, socialism can be considered a potential part of the solution rather than part of the problem.

sufficiently developed to experience neo-Malthusian ecological scarcity. Instead, they confront ecological scarcity in its crudest Malthusian form: too many people, too little food. Since this core problem, along with its major ramifications, has been covered in Part I, no more need be said about it here, except that almost everywhere the difficulties seem greatly to exceed the capacity of current governments in the LDC's to cope with them. Even now, for example, many governments cannot assure all their citizens enough food to maintain life, and the future prospects are grim. However, there are some interesting exceptions to this general picture.

The LDC's run the gamut from virtual non-development to what is usually called semi-development, in which considerable industrialization and modernization coexists with continued backwardness, especially in rural areas. In general, countries moving toward semi-development seem to follow established models. Mexico and Brazil, for example, have followed a basically American path, so that Mexico City has a smog problem rivaling that of Los Angeles, and Brazil's treatment of its undeveloped wealth, especially such fragile and irreplaceable resources as the Amazon rain forest, epitomizes frontier economics at its most heedless. On the other hand, Taiwan and South Korea have proceeded more or less along the lines laid down by Japan and are beginning to encounter many of the same problems. In the same way, the countries (now mostly beyond the stage of semi-development) that have travelled the Soviet path experience the same kinds of environmental problems and suffer from similar political liabilities in coping with them. In general, then, development by any path eventually brings environmental problems and creates awkward political dilemmas.

China

The one major exception to this generalization is China (and perhaps Tanzania, which has taken a similar approach to economic development). The Chinese have stressed national self-reliance instead of dependence on foreign trade and technology, decentralization and local self-sufficiency, "appropriate" technology that is cheap and suitable for small-scale use, cadres with practical technical skills instead of highly specialized and expensive training, labor-intensive instead of capital-intensive modes of production, careful husbandry of resources and fanatical vigilance against waste, and some degree of ecological restoration (for example, the reforestation of mountains denuded since ancient times).

However, it remains to be seen whether these principles will continue to guide Chinese development. It seems likely that they have prevailed so far because hard-headed Chinese planners, from Mao on down, have seen that they are the most efficient means of achieving rapid, self-generated economic growth under current Chinese conditions. The Chinese leaders have clear ambitions for industrial and military might, as well as for substantially higher living standards for their people, so that once current policies have built the requisite infrastructure for industrial power, one suspects that development will proceed along somewhat different lines. This impression is reinforced by Chinese spokesmen's tireless reiteration of the basic Marxist principle that only social relations are problematic and that nature itself presents no obstacles that cannot be conquered with technology and appropriate social organization. Above all, as in Marxist philosophy in general, there seems to be no criterion of developmental sufficiency—How much development is enough?—in Maoist philosophy; yet, as we know, this is indispensable for a steady-state economy. Thus China's current ecological virtue appears to be mostly circumstantial, rather than truly principled, and the higher levels of output in prospect seem certain to generate the same array of environmental problems that developed nations now confront.

Finally, it must be noted that the undeniable achievements of the Chinese, including the ecological virtues enumerated above, have only been made possible by a degree of social regimentation that is irreconcilable with Western concepts of individual liberty. The disturbing question that has run throughout this entire analysis therefore reemerges with stark clarity: Can a steady-state society come about or be maintained except through some such regimentation?

THE INTERNATIONAL STATE OF NATURE

The International Macrocosm

If in the various national microcosms constituting the world political community the basic dynamics of ecological scarcity apply virtually across the board, in the macrocosm of international politics they operate even more strongly. Just as within each individual nation, the tragic logic of the commons brings about the overexploitation of common property resources like the oceans and the atmosphere. Also, the pressures toward inequality, oppression, and conflict are even more intense within the world political community, for it is a community in name only, and the already marked cleavage between rich and poor threatens to become even greater. Without even the semblance of a world government, such problems depend for their solution on the good will and purely voluntary cooperation of nearly 150 sovereign states—a prospect that does not inspire optimism. Let us examine these issues in more detail, to see how ecological scarcity aggravates the already very difficult problems of international politics.

The Global Tragedy of the Commons

The tragic logic of the commons operates universally, and its effects are readily visible internationally—in the growing pollution of international rivers, seas, and now even the oceans; in the overfishing that has caused a marked decline in the fish catch, as well as the near extinction of the great whales; and in the impending scramble for seabed resources by maritime miners or other exploiters. There is no way to confine environmental insults or the effects of ecological degradation within national borders; river basins, airsheds, and oceans are intrinsically international. Even seemingly local environmental disruption inevitably has some impact on the quality of regional and, eventually, global ecosystems. Just as within each nation, the aggregation of individual desires and actions overloads the international commons. But, like individuals, states tend to turn a blind eye to this, for they profit by the increased production while others bear most or all of the cost, or they lose by self-restraint while others receive most or all of the benefit. Thus, Britain gets the factory output, while Scandinavia suffers the ecological effects of "acid rain"; the French and Germans use the Rhine for waste disposal even though this leaves the river little more than a reeking sewer by the time it reaches fellow European Economic Community member Holland downstream.

However, if the problems are basically the same everywhere, the political implications of the tragedy of the commons are much more serious in the international arena. It has long been recognized that international politics is the epitome of the Hobbesian state of nature: despite all the progress over the centuries toward the rule of international law, sovereign states, unlike the citizens within each state, acknowledge no law or authority higher than their own self-interest; they are therefore free to do as they please, subject only to gross prudential restraints, no matter what the cost to the world community. Brazil, for example, has made it plain that it will brook no outside interference with its development of the Amazon, and well-meaning ecological advice is castigated as "scientific colonialism" (Castro 1972). Also, despite strong pressures from the international community, the U.S.S.R. and Japan have openly frustrated the effort to conserve whale stocks—both at the negotiating table and at sea. In international relations, therefore, the dynamic of the tragedy of the commons is even stronger than within any given nation state, which, being a real political community, has at least the theoretical capacity to make binding, authoritative decisions on resource conservation and ecological protection. By contrast, international agreements are reached and enforced by the purely voluntary cooperation of sovereign nation states existing in a state of nature. For all the reasons discussed in Chapter 4, the likelihood of forestalling by such means the operation of the tragedy of the commons is extremely remote. Worse, just as any individual is nearly helpless to alter the outcome by his own actions (and even risks serious loss if he refuses to participate in the exploitation of the commons), so too, in the absence of international authority or enforceable agreement, nations have little choice but to contribute to the tragedy by their own actions. This would be true even if each individual state was striving to achieve a domestic steady-state economy, for unless one assumes agreement on a largely autarkic world, states would still compete with each other internationally to maximize the resources available to them. Ecological scarcity thus intensifies the fundamental problem of international politics—the achievement of world order—by adding further to the preexisting difficulties of a state of nature. Without some kind of international governmental machinery with authority and coercive power over sovereign states sufficient to oblige them to keep within the bounds of the ecological common interest of all on the planet, the world must suffer the ever greater environmental ills ordained by the global tragedy of the commons.

The Struggle Between Rich and Poor

Ecological scarcity also aggravates very seriously the already intense struggle between rich and poor. As is well known, the world today (some impending changes will be discussed in the following section) is sharply polarized between the developed, industrialized "haves," all affluent in a greater or lesser degree and all getting more affluent all the time, and the underdeveloped or developing "have nots," all relatively and absolutely impoverished and with few exceptions tending to fall relatively ever farther behind despite their often feverish efforts to grow. The degree of the inequality is also well known: the United States, with only 6 percent of the world's population, consumes about 30 percent of the total energy production of the world and comparable amounts of other resources, and the rest of the "haves," although only about half as prodigal as the United States, still consume resources far out of proportion to their population; conversely, per capita consumption of resources in the Third World ranges from one-tenth to one-hundredth that in the "have" countries. To make matters worse, the resources that the "haves" enjoy in inordinate amounts are largely and increasingly imported from the Third World; thus economic inequality and what might be called ecological colonialism have become intertwined. In view of this extreme and long-standing inequality (which moreover has its roots in an imperialist past), it is hardly surprising that the Third World thirsts avidly for development or that it has become increasingly intolerant of those features of the current world order it perceives as obstacles to becoming as rich and powerful as the developed world.

Alas, the emergence of ecological scarcity appears to have sounded the death knell for the aspirations of the LDC's. Even assuming, contrary to fact, that there were sufficient mineral and energy resources to make it possible, universal industrialization would impose intolerable stress on world ecosystems. In short, the current model of development, which assumes that all countries will eventually become heavily industrialized mass-consumption societies, is doomed to failure.* Naturally, this conclusion is totally unacceptable to the modernizing elites of the Third World; their political power is generally founded on the promise of development. Even more important, simply halting growth would freeze the current pattern of inequality, leaving the "have nots" as the peasants of the world community in perpetuity. Thus an end to growth and development would be acceptable to the Third World only in combination with a radical redistribution of the world's wealth and a total restructuring of the world's economy to guarantee the maintenance of economic justice. Yet it seems absolutely clear that the rich have not the slightest intention of alleviating the plight of the poor if it entails the sacrifice of their own living standards. Ecological scarcity thus greatly increases the probability of naked confrontation between rich and poor.†

---

*The ecologically viable alternative, depicted in Part I, is a locally self-sufficient, semi-developed, steady-state society based on renewable or "income" resources, like photosynthesis and solar energy. As indicated above, only Tanzania seems currently to be taking this path as a matter of principle. Others find themselves unable to see such apparent frugality as a realistic option. All the pressures are toward "efficiency," standardization, centralization, and large scale. Also, since semi-development is workable only with a reasonable population and most LDC's are heavily overpopulated, choosing this option implies a willingness to use harsh measures or cause widespread suffering; it is not surprising that most leaders prefer to continue in the illusory hope of achieving heavy industrialization. In addition, the lust for status and prestige, the desire for military power, and many other less than noble motives are also prevalent, and the frugal modesty of semi-developed self-sufficiency can do little to satisfy them.

†In the short run, growing environmental pressures and restrictions in the developed countries will probably result in the export of polluting industries to some of the less industrialized LDC's, who will for the most part be delighted to accept ecological degradation along with economic benefits. However, only a few favored countries will benefit significantly. Moreover, without continued growth in the now industrialized nations, the growth prospects of the Third World are dim; our growth is essential to theirs (Boserup 1975; Quigg 1974). Thus, although the basic rich-poor polarization will be moderated by many complex interdependencies, there is no escaping the basic opposition of interests created by ecological scarcity.

Who Are Now the "Haves" and "Have Nots"?

An important new element has been injected into this struggle. The great resource hunger of the developed and even some parts of the developing world has begun to transfer power and wealth to those who have resources to sell, especially critical resources like petroleum. As a result, the geopolitics of the world has already been decisively altered.

This process can be expected to continue. The power and wealth of the major oil producers is bound to increase over the next two decades, despite North Sea and Alaskan oil and regardless of whether the Organization of Petroleum Exporting Countries (OPEC) manages to maintain its current degree of unity.

Some believe that oil is a special case and that the prospect of OPEC-type cartels for other resources is dim (Banks 1974; Mikesell 1974). While these assessments may be correct, it seems inevitable that in the long run an era of "commodity power" must emerge. The hunger of the industrialized nations for resources is likely to increase, even if there is no substantial growth in output to generate increased demand for raw materials, because the domestic mineral and energy resources of the developed countries have begun to be exhausted. Even the United States, for example, already imports 100 percent of its platinum, mica, chromium, and strontium; over 90 percent of its manganese, aluminum, tantalum, and cobalt; and 50 percent or more of twelve additional key minerals (Wade 1974). However, the developed countries seem determined to keep growing, and assuming even modest further growth in industrial output, their dependence on Third World supplies is bound to increase markedly in the next few decades.* Thus, whatever the short-term prospects for the success of budding cartels in copper, phosphates, and other minerals, the clear overall long-term trend is toward a seller's market in basic resources and therefore toward "commodity power," even if this power grows more slowly and is manifested in a less extreme form than that of OPEC.†

Thus, the basic long-standing division of the world into rich and poor in terms of GNP per capita is about to be overlaid with another rich-poor polarization, in terms of resources, that will both moderate and intensify the

---

*Naturally, there will be short-term exceptions. Europe, for example, may become relatively independent of Middle Eastern oil supplies during the peak years of North Sea oil production. But respite from the overall trend toward increasing dependence will be transitory and limited to particular commodities.

†However, OPEC-like cartels in other resources might be preferable to a disorganized seller's market. Cartels can be bargained with and integrated into the normal diplomatic machinery, so that the drastic price fluctuations and outright interruptions of supply that cause extreme economic distress are avoided. But the price of stability is higher prices for commodities and increased political power for cartel members.

basic split. Although there are many complex interdependencies in world trade—for example, U.S. food exports are just as critical to many countries as their mineral exports are to us—it is already clear that the resource-rich Third World nations stand to gain greater wealth and power at the expense of the "haves." Already, for example, through nationalization and forced purchase the OPEC nations have largely wrested control of drilling and pumping operations from the Western oil companies; their expansion into other areas of the oil business is only a question of time. Thus, although most of the earlier fears of imminent economic takeover have proven to be unfounded, a substantial transfer of real wealth is certain to occur in the next few decades. In addition, as is already evident, the newly resource-rich are not likely to settle for mere commercial gains. They have long-standing political grievances against other nations—most especially the developed nations—that they will try to remedy with their new power. Israel's future, for example, has suddenly become much cloudier.

Other problems abound. For example, international financial and monetary institutions, established for a simpler world of indefinite growth and a clear demarcation between "haves" and "have nots," are creaking under the unprecedented strain of the rapid shift in economic and geopolitical realities. In addition, poor countries without major resources of their own will suffer—indeed, already have suffered—major setbacks to their prospects for development. This is true not only of the hopelessly poor Fourth World, but also of countries whose development programs have already acquired some momentum. In India, for example, the quadrupled price of energy has dealt an all but mortal blow to the energy-intensive Green Revolution, on which so many of the country's hopes for development were pinned.

In sum, world geopolitics and economics are in for a radical reordering. Western economic development has involved a net transfer of resources, wealth, and power from the current "have nots" to the "haves," creating the cleavage between the two that now divides the world. In particular, the enormous postwar growth in output and consumption experienced by the industrialized nations was largely fueled by the bonanza of cheap oil that they were able to extract from relatively powerless client states in the Middle East. The success of the oil cartel is a signal that, from now on, wealth and power will begin to flow in the opposite direction. But only the relatively few "have nots" who possess significant amounts of resources will gain; the plight of the rest of the poor is more abject than before. Thus the old polarization between rich and poor seems likely to be replaced by a threefold division into the rich, the hopelessly poor, and the nouveaux riches—and such a major change in the international order is bound to create tension.

Box 7-2. War and Ecocide

War may occasionally be the lesser of evils, but by its very nature it has always been anathema to any reasonable man. To the human ecologist it is doubly horrible. One of the most appalling features of the modern world is the enormous amount of ecological damage and resource wastage that can be attributed to warfare and military preparedness. Resources that should have been used for human welfare (or that should never have been used at all) have been sacrificed to the gods of national security in the jungles and rice paddies of Vietnam and the deserts of Sinai. But this is only the most obvious wastage. Global military expenditures consume about 7 percent of the world's GNP (Sivard 1975). However, this statistic understates the degree of their environmental damage, for modern weapons systems are exceedingly energy intensive (the defense establishment probably uses 10 percent of all petroleum consumed in the United States) and polluting (the potential impact on the ozone layer from countless supersonic flights by U.S. and other military forces is one of many examples).

Even more criminal from an ecological point of view is the increasingly ecocidal nature of modern warfare. Nuclear warfare, of course, is the prime villain, for any substantial number of nuclear explosions would poison world ecosystems and gene

Conflict or Cooperation?

The overall effect of ecological scarcity in the international arena is to intensify the competitive dynamics of the preexisting international tragedy of the commons, so that increased commercial, diplomatic, and, ultimately, military confrontation over dwindling resources is more likely. At the same time the poor, having had their revolutionary hopes and rising aspirations crushed, will have little to lose but their chains. Also, to many of the declining "haves," ill-equipped to adapt to an era of "commodity power" and economic warfare, the grip of the nouveaux riches on essential resources will seem an intolerable stranglehold to be broken at all costs. Thus the disappearance of ecological abundance seems bound to make international politics even more tension ridden and potentially violent than it already is. Indeed, the pressures of ecological scarcity may embroil the world in hopeless strife, so that long before ecological collapse occurs by virtue of the physical limitations of the earth, the current world order will have been destroyed by turmoil and war—a truly horrible prospect, given the profoundly anti-ecological character of modern warfare (see Box 7-2).

Some, on the other hand, hope or believe that ecological scarcity will have just the opposite effect—because the problems will become so overwhelming and so evidently insoluble without total international cooperation, nation states will discard their outmoded national sovereignty and place themselves under some form of planetary government that will regulate the global commons for the benefit of all humankind and begin the essential process of

pools for untold generations and probably disrupt the structure of the atmosphere enough to cause mass extinctions. (As noted previously, the widespread dispersal of nuclear materials and technology for so-called peaceful purposes increases the probability of nuclear proliferation and therefore of nuclear war and terrorism.) However, any form of chemical and bacteriological warfare is potentially ecocidal—for example, the use of broadcast herbicides in Vietnam. But even more conventional forms of modern warfare are exceedingly destructive of local ecologies; in Vietnam, for instance, the U.S. military devastated millions of acres of farm and forest with saturation bombing and giant earth-moving machinery. Military prospects for the future (U.S. experiments in Vietnam having failed) include weather modification and other forms of geophysical war.

Of course, armies have employed ecocidal weapons—for example, scorched earth and salted lands—since ancient times. Yet the clear and disquieting trend is toward war, or even armed peace, that is ever more wasteful of scarce resources and ever more destructive to the earth. War has been rightly called the ultimate pollutant of planet Earth.

gradual economic redistribution. In effect, states will be driven by their own vital national interests—seen to include ecological as well as traditional economic, political, and military factors—to embrace the ultimate interdependence needed to solve ecological problems (Shields and Ott 1974). According to this hypothesis, the very direness of the outcome if cooperation does not prevail may ensure that it will.

Unfortunately, the accumulating evidence tends to support the conflictual rather than the cooperative hypothesis. Faced with the new power of the oil barons, the first impulse of the United States was to try to go it alone in "Project Independence," while Japan, France, and others maneuvered individually to ensure their own future supplies, torpedoing the solidarity of the consuming countries confronting OPEC. Canada has served notice on the United States that it intends to end America's ecological colonialism; henceforth, the resources of Canada will be saved for its own use. Thus, the rich seem readier to follow "beggar thy neighbor" policies than to cooperate among themselves. Sympathy for the plight of the poor is even less evident. Some talk about expanding still further the scale of ecological colonialism; a West German research group has even put forward a scheme for the diversion of West Africa's Niger River to supply Europe with heat for energy (Anon. 1974). For others, continued interdependence of any kind with the poor is seen as so problematic and so full of threats to the sovereign independence and high living standards of the rich that the only sensible course is autarkic self-sufficiency.

Naturally, there has been considerable talk about cooperative international action to deal with the problems of ecological scarcity, but little or no momentum toward greater cooperation has developed. In fact, all the talk may have served chiefly to heighten further the tensions within the world community.

An Upsurge of Conference Diplomacy

By the late 1960's some of the alarming global implications of pollution and general ecological degradation had become widely apparent, and preparations began for a major international conference at Stockholm in 1972. Depending on one's point of view, the Stockholm Conference—to give it its proper title, the United Nations Conference on the Human Environment— was either a major diplomatic success or an abysmal failure. On the positive side, the elaborate preparations for the conference (each country had to make a detailed inventory of its environmental problems), the intense publicity given the over two years of preliminary negotiations, and the conference itself fostered a very high level of environmental awareness around the globe. Virtually ignored by diplomats in 1969, the environmental crisis had by 1972 rocketed right up alongside nuclear weapons and economic development as one of the big issues of international politics. The second major achievement of the Stockholm Conference was the establishment of the United Nations Environment Program (UNEP) to monitor the state of the world environment and to provide liaison and coordination between nation states and among the multitude of governmental and non-governmental organizations concerned with environmental matters. Finally, a few preliminary agreements covering certain less controversial and less critical ecological problems, like setting aside land for national parks and suppressing trade in endangered species, were reached either at the conference or immediately thereafter.

Despite these acknowledged achievements, environmentalists were by and large rather unhappy with the conduct and outcome of the conference. They were especially disillusioned, for example, by the way in which the original ecological purity of the conference's agenda was rapidly watered down by pressures from Third World countries, who made it plain that they would have nothing to do with the conference unless, in effect, underdevelopment was converted into a form of pollution. Moreover, a great part of the proceedings was devoted not to the problems on the agenda, but to the kind of "have" versus "have not" debate discussed above, and routine ideological posturing on political issues like "colonialism" consumed additional time. Also, cold-war politics refused to take a vacation; for example, the U.S.S.R. boycotted the conference because East Germany was not given full voting status. Thus the perhaps naively idealistic hope of many that the ecological issue would at last force quarrelsome and self-seeking sovereign nation states to put aside stale old grudges, recognize their common predicament, and act in concert to improve the human condition was completely dashed.

Worse, some of the features of the current world order most objectionable from an ecological point of view were actually reaffirmed at Stockholm—namely, the absolute right of sovereign countries to develop their own domestic resources without regard to the potential external ecological costs to the world community, and the unrestricted freedom to breed guaranteed by the Universal Declaration of Human Rights. In addition, established international institutions, like the World Health Organization and the Food and Agriculture Organization, extended distinctly lukewarm cooperation to the organizers of the conference, both because of bureaucratic jealousy and because of fear that environmental concerns would force them to alter or abandon programs, like all-out support for the Green Revolution and the eradication of malaria with DDT, that are a large part of their raison d'être. As a result, the Secretariat of UNEP was given little real power and only a minimum of resources to perform its coordinating and monitoring functions. Also, the headquarters of UNEP were eventually established in Nairobi, and although this has had the very positive effect of keeping the Third World interested in UNEP and its programs, it has definitely hampered the expansion and effectiveness of the global environmental monitoring and liaison that was to be UNEP's prime responsibility.

Since 1972, there have been more environmentally oriented conferences—principally the U.N. World Population Conference in 1974, the U.N. World Food Conference in 1974, and a series of U.N. Law of the Sea Conferences from 1974 to the present. However, there has been little progress since Stockholm. The World Population Conference somehow managed to end "without producing explicit agreement that there was a world population problem" (Walsh 1974). The World Food Conference produced few concrete achievements and left crucial problems on its agenda unsolved. The Law of the Sea Conferences have promoted progress toward a global consensus that seems likely to become the basis of an international treaty once future negotiating meetings dispose of some of the still unsettled issues. Unfortunately, the basis of this emerging consensus is an agreement to carve the oceans into national zones of exploitation, instead of making them into the common heritage of mankind; thus, as at Stockholm, the principle of national sovereignty has been even further entrenched.

The forces that prevented Stockholm from fulfilling its promise were even more strongly in evidence at these and other post-Stockholm international meetings directly or indirectly concerned with environmental issues. First, the spirit of militant nationalism that has animated so much of the history of the postwar world has not abated. Thus states insist on the absolute and sovereign right of self-determination in use of resources, population policy, and development in general, regardless of the wider consequences. Second, the demand by Third World countries for economic development has, if anything, increased in intensity, and whatever seems to stand in the way, like ecological considerations, gets rather short shift. Third, largely because their prospects for development are so dim, Third World countries have begun to press even harder for fundamental reform of the world system (a "new international economic order"); thus every discussion of environmental issues like food and population is inevitably converted by Third World spokesmen into a discussion of international economic justice as well, which enormously complicates the process of negotiation. In short, environmental issues have become pawns in the larger diplomatic and political struggle between the nations.

In addition, diplomats, like national leaders, have attempted to handle the issues of ecological scarcity not as part of a larger problematique, but piecemeal, so that their interaction with other problems is all but ignored. For example, the World Food Conference was solely concerned with the problem of feeding the hungry and gave virtually no attention to the eventual ecological consequences of growing more food or subsidizing further over-population with radically increased food aid. To some extent, therefore, the successes of international conferences that simply try to solve one small piece of the larger problem are as much to be feared as their failures.

If one wished to be optimistic, one could conclude that the world community has taken the first halting attitudinal and institutional steps toward meeting the challenges of ecological scarcity. A more realistic assessment would be that little has been accomplished so far and that major impediments to further progress loom large. One might even be forced to conclude, more pessimistically, that the world political community as presently constituted is simply incapable of coping with the challenges of ecological scarcity, at least within any reasonable time.

Planetary Government or the War of All Against All

In short, the planet confronts the same problems as the United States, but in a greatly intensified form. Even before the emergence of ecological scarcity, the world's difficulties and their starkly Hobbesian implications were grave enough. Some saw the "revolution of rising expectations" pushing the world toward a situation in which wants greatly exceeded the capacity to meet them, provoking Hobbesian turmoil and violence (Spengler 1969). Also, ever since Hiroshima the world has lived in a state of highly armed peace with a nuclear Sword of Damocles dangling over its head. We have all learned to live with the bomb, and the hair suspending the nuclear Sword has indeed held, although for how much longer no one can say. Now the world must live under the blade of another Sword of Damocles, slower to fall but equally deadly. Unfortunately, the hair holding this environmental Sword has come loose; pollution and other environmental problems will not obligingly postpone their impact while diplomats haggle, so the Sword is already slicing down toward our unprotected heads. There is thus no way for the world community to put the environmental issue out of mind and go on about its business, as it has done with the bomb. The crisis of ecological scarcity is a Sword that must be parried, squarely and soon.

Thus the already strong rationale for a world government with enough coercive power over fractious nation states to achieve what reasonable men would regard as the planetary common interest has become overwhelming. Yet we must recognize that the very ecological scarcity that makes a world government ever more necessary has also made it much more difficult of achievement. The clear danger is that, instead of promoting world cooperation, ecological scarcity will simply intensify the Hobbesian war of all against all and cause armed peace to be replaced by overt international strife.

BIBLIOGRAPHIC NOTE

Comparative environmental studies are still in their infancy. Two general works have appeared recently—*The Politics of Pollution in Comparative Perspective*, by Cynthia Enloe, and *The Economic Superpowers and the Environment*, by Donald Kelley, Kenneth Stunkel, and Richard Wescott. Both are competent, but limited in geographic scope. Two older studies dealing with the Soviet Union, by far the most interesting comparative case, are of very high quality—Marshall Goldman's *The Spoils of Progress* and Philip Pryde's *Conservation in the Soviet Union*. Because they are more complementary than overlapping, both can be read with profit.

Nor have the international implications of ecological scarcity been given the careful and sustained study they clearly deserve. Robert Heilbroner's succinct and well-argued *An Inquiry into the Human Prospect* is clearly the outstanding work so far, but it leaves important issues untouched and treats the topics it does discuss with what critics believe is excessive pessimism. Richard Falk's *This Endangered Planet* is both more balanced than Heilbroner and more in the mainstream of social science in its style and content; now somewhat overtaken by events, it should nevertheless be read along with Heilbroner. Lester Brown's *World Without Borders* is also extremely useful. Thomas Wilson's brief policy-oriented survey, *International Environmental Action*, presents a more "establishment" point of view than any of the above. *The Oil Crisis*, by Stephen Graubard et al., helps to put this key event in perspective. Lynton Caldwell's *In Defense of Earth*, a survey of international conservation institutions, is solid and useful, especially for its bibliographical material. For general background, *Toward a Politics of the Planet Earth*, by Harold and Margaret Sprout, is a first-rate text in international relations written from a specifically ecological viewpoint. Finally, one seriously interested in this topic could with great profit read Richard Cox's *Locke on Peace and War* for its discussion of the many dilemmas of the state of nature as seen in the political theories of Locke and Hobbes.

Three useful research tools are the annotated bibliography *International Development and the Human Environment,* by Farvar and Soule, UNIPUB's guide to the Stockholm conference bibliography, and Enviro/Info's list of selected post-conference articles and documents commenting on Stockholm.

III

LEARNING TO LIVE
WITH SCARCITY

8

TOWARD A POLITICS
OF THE STEADY STATE

How we are to learn to live with ecological scarcity is the problem that will
dominate the coming decades. However daunting this task must seem, it is
indeed possible to make a transition to a relatively desirable steady state
instead of simply letting nature take its course, which is certain to lead in
the opposite direction. However, we must recognize that a large measure of
devolution or retrogression in terms of our current values will inevitably
follow 400 years of continual evolution and "progress." But not all the
political, social, economic, cultural, and technological advances of the past
four centuries must be abandoned; the sooner we confront the challenge
squarely, the greater the likelihood of saving the best of this legacy and,
what may be more important, of making a virtue out of this necessity. Our
actions over the critical next few decades will therefore either create or
preclude a relatively desirable future for ourselves and our descendants.
However, I offer no concrete or formal solutions to the political dilemmas of
ecological scarcity. There are several reasons for this.

Learning to See Anew

First, the most important prerequisite for constructive change is a new world
view based on, or at least compatible with, the realities of the human
ecological predicament. The ecological crisis is in large part a perceptual

crisis: ordinary human beings simply do not see that they are part of a delicate web of life that their own actions are destroying, yet any viable solution will require them to see this. Once such a "paradigm" change has occurred—once people have chosen to adopt ecological limitations deliberately as a consequence of their new understanding—then practical and humane solutions will be found in abundance. Indeed, as we have already seen, the essential elements of the steady state are not so hard to discern, and some good work has been done on suitable institutions. But the psychological readiness and political will to adopt them are absent. Thus "metanoia," or a fundamental transformation of world view, must precede concrete action.

Second, at this juncture any specific set of solutions would immediately be criticized as politically unrealistic. Indeed, what else could they be? Current political values and institutions are the products of the age of abnormal abundance now drawing to a close, so that solutions predicated on scarcity would necessarily conflict with them. Of course, to work "within the system" to prevent further ecological degradation and promote incremental change toward the steady state is an essential task deserving great support. But to accept current political reality as not itself subject to radical change is to give away the game at the outset and render the situation hopeless by definition. Indeed, it must be understood that ultimately *politics is about the definition of reality itself.* As John Maynard Keynes pointed out, we are all the prisoners of dead theorists; the ideas of John Locke, Adam Smith, Karl Marx, and all the other philosophers of the Great Frontier in effect define reality for us. Before we can even see what the problem is, we must tear off their fetters on our imagination. To put it another way, normal politics is indeed "the art of the possible"; it consists in working as best one can for valued objectives "within the system"—that is, inside the current political paradigm. However, politicking (to give it its true name) is only one part of politics, and the lesser part at that; in its truest sense, *politics is the art of creating new possibilities* for human progress. Since the current system is ecologically defective, we must direct our concrete political activities primarily toward producing a change of consciousness that can lead to a new political paradigm. Until people at large begin to see a new kind of reality based on ecological understanding, environmental politicking within the system can only be a rear-guard holding action designed to slow down the pace of ecological retreat. Disdain for current political realities and primary reliance on a change of consciousness may seem a counsel of despair, given what people want and believe today, but it should be remembered that only a little over a century ago it was legal to treat human beings as property. Already, many people are finding our slavish treatment of nature to be stupid at best and morally repugnant at worst. The events of the decades to come are bound to increase their number. Looking back on us as we ourselves look back on our slave-holding ancestors, our descendants will wonder why it took us so long to come to our senses.

Third, the transition will take several decades in any event. Thus it is not necessary for us to possess concrete answers to ecological scarcity today. What is essential, however, is for us to begin the disciplined and serious search for such answers now, instead of waiting until the point of panic-stricken extremity. We sometimes forget, for example, that our Constitution was the culmination of several decades of intense and sustained political discussion and action by our founding fathers. We confront a challenge perhaps greater than theirs, and we should not deceive ourselves about the magnitude and duration of the task. Moreover, as this example suggests, no one man, no one work, no one invention can hope to supply more than a small piece of the solution that will eventually emerge; the final result will be a mosaic of many elements, some designed by man, others fashioned by the accidents of history. Thus, to set up and promulgate specific solutions at this stage might be positively harmful, for such premature closure is all too likely to deflect us from the much more crucial task of going back to first principles—that is, to politics. Once we have agreed on political first principles and the lessons of history, as our founding fathers generally did at Philadelphia, then building the institutional machinery to incorporate them will not be such a difficult task. In sum, before trying to give rebirth to our political institutions we must first allow time for a proper gestation.

Fourth, the hour is very late. Now that everyone can recognize the evils of ecological scarcity, it is probably much too late for a nicely planned transition to the steady state. Had we prudently listened to earlier warnings and acted appropriately when the environmental crisis was still in its germinal phase many years ago, we might have devised a concrete master plan for the transition. This is no longer possible, for as we have seen, some measure of ecological overshoot (with attendant disruptive side effects that are unpredictable) is virtually foreordained. Besides, we are so committed to most of the things that cause or support the evils that we are almost paralyzed; nearly all the constructive actions that could be taken at present (for example, drastically restricting the use of private automobiles) are so painful to so many people in so many ways that they are indeed totally unrealistic, and neither politicians nor citizens would tolerate them.* Only after nature has mandated certain changes and overwhelmingly demonstrated the advisability of others will it be possible to think in terms of a concrete program of transition. Until then, our time and effort would be better spent laying the scientific and philosophical groundwork, so that the moment of ripeness will find us prepared to move rapidly from thought to action.

---

*All societies display social fanaticism to some extent. Their first response to threatening doubts is to redouble effort and belief in support of the current paradigm, which is after all a kind of civil religion. Thus our tendency, already very apparent, will be to react to the challenges of ecological scarcity with policies of denial and with more and more desperate efforts to stave off the inevitable changes.

Finally, in many ways, seen and unseen, the process of transition is well under way. It is no accident that so many radical critiques of industrial civilization, either grounded in ecology or self-consciously related to it, have been produced in recent years (see Bibliographic Note). Nor that so many groups and individuals are experimenting with radically different life-styles and technologies, many of them avowedly based on ecological principles. Nor that a quasi-religious ferment of self-examination and self-criticism seems to have sprung up throughout the industrial world, leading to new images of man and of human needs and potentials. The raw materials for social transformation are being produced right now, and the process of tearing down the old reality and constructing the new has already begun.* Thus, although this natural transition process is halting, belated, and imperfect, the ill of ecological scarcity is tending to manufacture its own remedy. Certainly, inspiring leadership and a comprehensive theory will be necessary at some point; without them, ordinary people would lack the social vision and sense of direction they need to make constructive personal responses to any social challenge, and the transition would degenerate into a process of mere muddling through. However, to a very large extent the transition will evolve, instead of being created by theorizing and social planning. The individuals and groups composing the collectivity will more or less willingly seek a viable and attractive set of social answers by responding to the pressures of ecological scarcity in their daily lives. The answers that emerge will then be ratified by theory. (Similarly, colonial Americans had already evolved many features of the distinctively American way of life well before these were formalized in political institutions.) In short, excessive or premature specificity about the institutions of the steady-state society is either not very useful or a positive hindrance; again, metanoia is the key, for it will almost automatically engender concrete, practical arrangements that are congruent with it.

Nevertheless, a general outline of a solution to the problems of ecological scarcity is implicit in the concept of the steady state. Let us therefore review the essential characteristics of a steady-state society.

The Characteristics of the Steady State

It is not possible to specify the structural features of the steady-state society. The great diversity of human societies, which have existed in a virtual steady state throughout most of recorded history, shows that there are many differ-

---

*In his *The Promise of the Coming Dark Age,* the historian L. S. Stavrianos identifies important elements of this process and shows how the "grass" of a new civilization based on decentralized self-management is even now pushing up through the "concrete" of the moribund industrial order.

ent ways to similar ends. However, any set of structural features would clearly have to reflect certain basic characteristics of the steady state. In preceding chapters we have discussed in some detail its purely physical characteristics—primary dependence on income or flow resources, the maintenance of population levels within the ecological carrying capacity, resource conservation and recycling, generally good ecological husbandry, and so on. Let us now focus on the necessary sociopolitical characteristics of any steady-state society, regardless of how it chooses to give them social form. As befits a prologue, the following treatment is tentative and merely tries to indicate what the general direction of travel will be as we move from our current industrial civilization toward the steady state.

Communalism   It is clear that we have been living in an age of rampant individualism that arose historically from circumstances of abnormal abundance. It seems predictable, therefore, that on our way toward the steady state we shall move from individualism toward communalism. The self-interest that individualistic political, economic, and social philosophies have justified as being in the overall best interests of the community, as long as the growth "frontier" provided a safe outlet for competitive striving, will begin to seem more and more reprehensible and illegitimate as scarcity grows; the traditional primacy of the community over the individual that has characterized virtually every other period of history will be restored. How far the subordination of individual to community values and interests will have to go and how it would be achieved are for the future to determine. Yet, although rigid caste systems and inflexible feudal hierarchies would not appear to be necessary, it seems likely that the degree of individual subordination eventually required would seem quite insupportable to many living today.

Authority   As the community and its rights are given increasing social priority we shall necessarily move from liberty toward authority, for the community will have to be given sufficient means to enforce its demands on individuals. This prospect may seem alarming, but the historical record does not justify the fear that any concession of political rights to the community must eventually lead to the total subjugation of the individual by an all-powerful state. There seems to be no reason why authority cannot be made strong enough to maintain a steady-state society, and yet be limited. The personal and civil rights guaranteed by our Constitution, for example, could be largely retained in an appropriately designed steady-state society. Nor need the right to own and enjoy a sufficiency of personal property be taken away; only the right to use private property in ecologically destructive ways would have to be checked. Thus authority in the steady state need not be remote, arbitrary, and capricious; in a well-ordered and well-designed state, authority could be made constitutional and limited.

Aristocracy Allied with the above will be a movement away from egalitarian democracy toward political competence and status. That is, because the mere summation of equally regarded individual wants into Rousseau's "will of all" has become ecologically ruinous, we must find ways of achieving the "general will" that stands higher than the individual and his wants. To this end, certain restrictions on human activities must be competently determined, normatively justified, and then authoritatively imposed on a populace that would do something quite different if it was merely left to its own immediate desires and devices. This can be accomplished in more than one way. Power can be given or allowed to accrue to those who are *fittest to rule* (as in Thomas Jefferson's "natural aristocracy"). However, the creation of a ruling class, no matter how open and well qualified, immediately delivers us into the classic "Who will watch the guardians?" dilemma—and as noted earlier, the greater the scarcity, the greater the likelihood of oppression of the ruled by the ruling class. This dilemma can be avoided, at least in part, by founding the political system by common consent on *a set of values fit to be ruled by*—that is, aristocratic principles designed to foster the common interest of the steady state instead of the particular interests that would destroy it. If this could be done successfully, then the need for the ministrations of a ruling class would be much lessened, and to the extent that a class of Jeffersonian natural aristocrats were still needed to make the system work, it could be subjected to constitutional restraints, just as in the earliest days of the American republic. (See Box 8-1 for further discussion of this "design criteria" approach.) Nevertheless, once the ground of political values becomes something other than the desires of the people, age-old dilemmas related to the legitimacy of rule immediately arise. Future political theorists will therefore have to overcome the exceedingly difficult problem of legislating the temperance and virtue needed for the ecological survival of a steady-state society without at the same time exalting the few over the many and subjecting individuals to the unwarranted exercise of power or to excessive conformity to some dogma.

Politics Because the free play of market forces and individual initiative produces the tragedy of the commons, the market orientation typical of most modern societies will have to be abandoned. If we want a viable and attractive steady-state society, we must determine its basic principles and then put them into effect in a planned or a designed fashion (see Box 8-1 for a discussion of the important distinction between the two). Another way of stating this is to say that we must move from non-politics toward politics. Laissez faire is a device for making political decisions about the distribution of wealth and other desired goods automatically and rather non-politically, instead of in face-to-face political confrontation (as happened, for example, in the Greek democracies). As noted in Chapter 6, shifting from a process or

---

Box 8–1. Planning Versus Design

There is a subtle and often overlooked but important distinction between planning and design. Both are attempts to achieve a desired real-world outcome by influencing nature. Although the difference is sometimes obscure in practice, planning refers to the attempt to produce the outcome *by actively managing the process,* whereas design refers to the attempt to produce the outcome *by establishing criteria to govern the operations of the process so that the desired result will occur more or less automatically without further human intervention.* Because of the scale and complexity of human activities, planning inevitably requires large bureaucracies and active intervention in people's lives. The Soviet Union's economic planning machinery is perhaps the most elaborate, but virtually all modern societies (to a considerable extent, even developing societies) are increasingly pervaded by the apparatus of planning. As a result, we have all become personally familiar with the inefficiencies, limitations, and costs of such cumbersome and bureaucratic social control. Thus the apparent necessity for even more planning to cope with the exigencies of ecological scarcity raises the frightening and repugnant prospect of minute and total daily supervision of all our activities, in the name of ecology, by a ponderous and powerful bureaucratic machine, a veritable Orwellian Big Brother.

However, this is not inevitable, for we can adopt a design instead of a planning approach to the problematique of ecological scarcity. By self-consciously selecting and implementing a set of design criteria aimed at channeling the social process quasi-automatically within steady-state limits, we can avoid the necessity constantly to plan, manage, and supervise. An example of such a design criterion comes from social critic Ivan Illich (1974a), who has proposed an absolute, across-the-board speed limit of 15 to 25 miles per hour—that is, the speed of a bicycle. Illich believes that adoption of this single proscription would eliminate most of the worst ecological and social consequences of high energy use without subjecting individuals to daily bureaucratic regulation. One can debate the merits of this particular proposal, but it nevertheless illustrates how powerfully the adoption of a few simple (albeit drastic in terms of current values) design criteria could indeed have major social impacts suffi-

---

non-political mode to an outcome or political mode holds serious dangers, for the political struggle can escalate into revolution and counter-revolution (again, as happened in the Greek democracies).* It will thus be necessary for the political and social philosophers of the steady state to discover principles of legitimacy, authority, and justice that will keep the political struggle within reasonable bounds. Yet, even if they are successful in this task, they are unlikely to be able to discover a device as effectively non-political as the market for making political decisions; at least at the outset, those who live in the steady state will therefore have to be genuinely political animals in Aristotle's sense, self-consciously involved in designing and planning their community life.

---

*The discussion in Box 8-1 suggests that there is thus considerable merit in agreeing *politically* on design criteria for the state that will minimize the scope of politics and political decision making thereafter. As a mode of politics, non-politics has considerable virtues.

cient to produce a steady-state society without also creating a Big Brother to supervise it. Another well-known example of a design approach to solving environmental problems is economist Kenneth Boulding's proposal for achieving population control with marketable baby licenses; once the basic idea was accepted, the system would operate with minimal bureaucratic supervision, and people would be able to determine for themselves how to respond to the market pressures created by the licensing system (that is, they could have as many children as they wanted by buying additional licenses from those who wanted few or no children) (1964, pp. 135–136). The proposals for an energy ration discussed in Part I are similar in spirit; people would have only a limited amount of energy available to them each year, but they would be free to spend it as they liked, just as they are now basically free to spend their money as they choose.

It should be evident that the design approach has substantial advantages over planning, a point not lost on our founding fathers, who unconsciously favored a design strategy in establishing our system as a political and economic marketplace governed predominantly by laissez faire. Now, of course, these particular design criteria are inappropriate for our changed circumstances, so they must be exchanged for new ones, but it would seem wise to emulate our founding fathers in their preference for design over planning.

It should also not be forgotten that design is nature's way. As a consequence of certain basic physical laws (the design criteria), natural systems and cycles operate automatically to produce an integrated, harmonious, self-sustaining whole that evolves in the direction of greater biological richness and order, eventually reaching a climax that is the ultimate expression of the design criteria. The essential task of the political and social philosopher of the steady state is therefore to devise design criteria that will be just as effective and compelling as those of nature in creating an organic and harmonious climax civilization but that are neither so ruthless nor so cruel. In other words, what are the humane alternatives to nature's wars, plagues, and famines as design criteria for a steady state?

Stewardship   The character of economic life will change totally. Ecology will engulf economics; we shall move away from the values of growth, profligacy, and exploitation typical of "economic man" toward sufficiency, frugality, and stewardship. The last especially, at least in its minimal form of trusteeship, will become the cardinal virtue of ecological economics. To use the analogy of ecological succession, we shall move from pioneer to climax economics; the rapid growth and exploitation of new possibilities typical of the pioneer stage will give way to a state of stable maturity in which maximum amenity is obtained from minimum resources, and energy is devoted primarily to maintenance of the current capital stock rather than to new growth. In short, quality will replace quantity, and husbandry will replace gain, as the prime motives of economic life. If the ideal of stewardship were more positively embraced, then, as numerous human ecologists have suggested, economic activities could be designed to "woo the earth" so that it would become a garden giving us beauty and amenity as well as an ample subsistence (Dubos 1968). Approached in this spirit, the economics of the steady state, no matter how frugal and careful, need not involve joyless self-abnegation on the part of individuals, for they would be participating in what could be a deeply satisfying civilizational task. Yet it must be acknowledged that many living today might not share this sanguine assessment of the potential for delight and self-fulfillment in a steady-state economy characterized by material frugality.

Modesty   In the softer area of cultural norms the changes are less predictable. However, once the limitations nature imposes on man have become clearer, Faustian striving after power and "progress" should give way to modesty of both ends and means. One human ecologist describes the impending social change as one from tragedy to comedy (Meeker 1974): we shall abandon the tragic hero's deadly serious and angst-ridden quest for greatness and new fields to conquer, which usually ends badly for himself and others, and learn instead cheerfully to enjoy the simple pleasures of ordinary life. The people inhabiting the future steady state could therefore be more relaxed, playful, and content than those living today, who must spend large amounts of energy constantly striving, if only to keep afloat in the waves of change that inevitably accompany rapid material growth. Moreover, although some profess to see the steady state as tantamount to rigor mortis, once the getting and spending of material wealth has ceased to be the prime determinant of status and self-esteem, the search for social satisfaction and personal fulfillment can turn toward the artistic, cultural, intellectual, scientific, and spiritual spheres—none of which are seriously confined by physical limitations. (Even space programs and other types of "big science" are possible in the steady state, provided the political will exists to expend scarce resources in this fashion.) In sum, there is no intrinsic reason why a steady-state society, despite its material frugality, should suffer from cultural stagnation, nor any reason why personal and cultural life should not be at least as rewarding as it is in today's industrial civilization—but the rewards must necessarily be rather different, for the culture of the steady state will certainly be far more frugal and modest than our own.

Diversity   The steady-state society should be less homogeneous and more culturally diverse than our own. As noted previously, the pressures of ecological scarcity are toward technological pluralism, more labor-intensive modes of production, and smaller-scale enterprise adapted to local ecological realities, so that populations are likely to be spread more evenly over the land and to be more self-sufficient in the basic necessities. Thus extreme centralization and interdependence, which depend on high levels of energy use, should give way to greater decentralization, local autonomy, and local culture. However, the extent of the reversion to diversity and decentralization is unpredictable. For one thing, barring a total collapse of technological civilization, the continued existence of modern communications is likely to forestall a return to the era when each locality was in effect a little country all its own. In addition, the kind of political and economic arrangements ultimately adopted will greatly determine how far this process goes. That is, diversity, decentralization, and local autonomy seem to fit more naturally with some of the political and economic choices mentioned above than with others. For example, a decision in favor of a planned rather than a designed steady-state society would be in effect a decision in favor of maximum standardization and central control. Nevertheless, the limitations on energy and material use in any conceivable steady state seem certain to lessen substantially the current high degree of homogenization, centralization, and interdependence.

Holism   Because the kind of one-dimensional thinking that created the crisis of ecological scarcity in the first place will no longer be tolerable, there will be a decisive movement away from scientific reductionism, the assumption inherited from Francis Bacon that nature is to be understood by dissecting it into its smallest constituent parts, toward holism, the contrary assumption that nature is best understood by focusing on the interrelationships making up the whole system. In other words, what has been called the "systems paradigm" will become the dominant intellectual and epistemological mode; biology, or more specifically ecology, will replace physics as the master science. The effects of this intellectual inversion are likely to be profound. For example, embracing holism will tend to make thinkers generalists first and specialists second, instead of vice versa as at present. More important, however, greater holism would alleviate many current social ills. Reductionist science has left most individuals psychologically adrift—by ruthlessly destroying older world views without putting anything in their place, by fragmenting the corpus of knowledge, and by alienating man from nature. A new synthesis based on a fuller understanding of the total ecology of the planet would go a long way toward making the average man feel once again at home in the universe.

Morality   Finally, the steady-state society will undoubtedly be characterized by genuine morality, as opposed to a purely instrumental set of ethics. It seems extremely unlikely, for example, that a real commitment to stewardship could arise out of enlightened self-interest; it will require a change of heart. But the same could be said about many of the other developments outlined above. Indeed, the crisis of ecological scarcity can be viewed as primarily a moral crisis in which the ugliness and destruction outside us in our environment simply mirror the spiritual wasteland within;

the sickness of the earth reflects the sickness in the soul of modern industrial man, whose whole life is given over to gain, to the disease of endless getting and spending that can never satisfy his deeper aspirations and must eventually end in cultural, spiritual, and physical death. If this assessment is correct, then the new morality of the steady state must involve a movement from matter toward spirit, not simply in the sense that material pursuits and values will inevitably be deemphasized and restrained by self-interested necessity, but also in the sense that there will be a recovery or rediscovery of virtue and sanctity. We shall learn again that canons higher than self-interest and individual wants are necessary for men to live in productive harmony with themselves and with others. Thus the steady-state society, like virtually all other human civilizations except modern industrialism, will almost certainly have a religious basis—whether it is Aristotelean political and civic excellence, Christian virtue, Confucian rectitude, Buddhist compassion, Amerindian love for the land, or something similar, old or new.

Post-modernity   To sum up, ecological scarcity obliges us to abandon most basic modern values in favor of ones that resemble pre-modern values in many important respects. This does not mean that we shall simply revert to an earlier mode of existence, although this is what could happen if we fail to exercise sufficient forethought and self-restraint. Again using the analogy of ecological succession, it can be said that the very success of the industrial stage of civilizational succession has created conditions under which, to avoid a simple relapse into pre-modern civilization, we must move to a new, higher, more mature, climax stage of post-industrial or post-modern civilization sharing many features of earlier civilizations while being something new in world history. Thus the emergence of the steady-state society will in one way or another bring the modern era to a close. It is now for us to decide whether we will accept the challenge implicit in the crisis of ecological scarcity by creating a genuinely post-modern civilization that combines the best of ancient and modern.

The Roots of Wisdom: Political Philosophy

Having seen what some of our choices on the path to the steady-state society might be, we come to the second and hardest part of the task: Where shall we find the wisdom to make such fateful choices and to guide us in the momentous enterprise of building a post-modern civilization? There is obviously no straightforward answer to this question, but there are some discernible avenues of approach. One is to make a profound study of the ills of industrial civilization.

A logical starting point in this endeavor is ecological philosophy, the attempt to discover the larger meaning and practical lessons of human ecology. Although it engages throughout in ecological philosophy, this work emphasizes politics, and it must be complemented by the works of other writers who have asked nature how man can live in harmony with it.*

The next step toward mastery of the problem would be to study the work of contemporary radical social critics who judge the industrial paradigm from what could be called a post-industrial perspective.† That is, whatever the differences among them, they all examine the proudest successes of industrial civilization, like science and development, and find them more or less pernicious; accordingly, they propose not reforms, but the creation of an entirely new post-industrial order. (Thus they do not simply repeat old criticisms; their work looks forward, however much it may sometimes seem to hark back to the concerns of the earliest critics of the Industrial Revolution.) We must look unflinchingly into the secular heresies of these post-industrial critics in order to liberate ourselves from inherited prejudices.

Nevertheless, as important as it is to analyze modern industrial civilization in the light of the crisis of ecological scarcity, it ought to be evident that the questions raised throughout this work are scarcely new, but in fact modern variations on ancient themes. This being the case, once we have understood those things that make us unique we must expect to receive the greater part of our guidance from the past—particularly from political philosophy, the long and rich tradition of discourse concerned precisely with how men can best live in community.

We have already seen that the values of a steady-state society would have to resemble pre-modern values in many important respects, but steady-state values bear a particularly uncanny resemblance to the ideas of the British conservative thinker Edmund Burke, the last great spokesman for the pre-modern point of view. For instance, the major tenet of both ecological philosophy and Burke is trusteeship or, better yet, stewardship. Burke wrote mainly about man's social patrimony rather than his natural heritage, but from the nature of his reasoning it is clear that he meant both: the current generation holds the present as a patrimony in moral entail from its ancestors and must pass it on to posterity—improved, if possible, but at all costs undiminished. Beyond this general overriding imperative, almost all of Burke's ideas resonate strongly with those of the ecological philosophers: the general skepticism about the possibility of "progress," the awareness that the solution to one problem generates a new set of problems, the acceptance

---

*These writers are identified and commented upon in the Bibliographic Note at the end of this chapter.

†Again, these writers are treated in the Bibliographic Note.

of human limits and imperfections, the need for organic change in order to preserve the balance and harmony of the whole social order, the interdependence and thus mutual moral bondage of society, the need to check aggressive self-interest, the contingent and situational nature of morality, the inevitability and desirability of the diversity of mankind both within societies and among societies, progress as a gradual evolution toward what is immanent in a historical society, the social order as part of or as the outgrowth of the natural order, and politics as the balancing of many conflicting and equally legitimate claims to achieve the state of man that is the best possible considering the objective situation.

Burke also saw very deeply into the social implications of the Enlightenment and the Industrial Revolution. He foresaw, for example, that turning the direction of society over to "sophisters, economists, and calculators" (his epithets for the amoral capitalistic men who typified the new dispensation) would destroy community, lead to the atomization of society, and set man against man in an endless and self-destructive struggle for gain. He also saw that zeal for liberty and equality in the abstract would soon lead to the destruction of all the "little platoons" (that is, the guilds, communes, and other intermediate corporate bodies) standing between the individual and the state, so that the individual would eventually be left standing alone and defenseless before an all-powerful state that in theory represented his interests but in practice was mostly beyond his control. As we have seen, both these issues are closely intertwined with our general analysis of ecological scarcity.

Ecology broadly defined is thus a fundamentally conservative orientation to the world. Indeed, one biologist has called the climax state, the natural analog of the steady state, "a perennial feudal society" (McKinley 1970). However, it by no means follows that we must adopt Burke's political doctrines. Rule by a landed aristocracy is now anachronistic at best and reactionary at worst. Yet, in our search for a set of social and political ideas that correspond to an ecological world view, Burke will surely have much to teach us.

Human ecology is also consonant with even older bodies of political thought, like the classical tradition. In Book Two of the *Republic,* Plato says that while men need tools, some division of labor, and the like—in other words, a modest level of development—in order to live a civilized and humane life, they do not seem to know when to stop. Thus they overdevelop, and the consequence is luxury, vice, class struggle, war, and many other ills. To prevent this, says Plato, we must restrain men with wise rule by philosophers who know that what men desire is not always desirable for them and that true justice requires the establishment of controls, so that the balance and harmony of the whole are served. The classical tradition also distrusts technology: just as excessive or uncontrolled economic development threatens to turn the direction of society over to money and the vagaries of the market, so too uncontrolled technological change undermines politics, the rational (in its broadest sense) direction of human affairs, by turning social decisions over to mere things.

The more modern anarchist tradition may also contain valuable lessons, for decentralization, local autonomy, modesty, community and other characteristics of the steady state seem favorable to developments in this direction. Indeed, to the extent that the environmental movement shares a common political ideology, it is predominantly anarchist. Moreover, the whole issue of a planned versus a designed steady state is so close to the central problem of anarchism that it is perhaps the most directly relevant body of theory for many of the critical issues raised in the preceding section.

Western political philosophy taken as a whole also contains many valuable lessons. Let us examine briefly two of the most important and obvious ones.

First, it is only a slight exaggeration to say that all political theory teaches the necessity of prudence, which *Webster's Third New International* tells us is a comprehensive term implying "a habitual deliberateness, caution, and circumspection in action," further qualified as (1) "wisdom shown in the exercise of reason, forethought, and self-control," (2) "sagacity and shrewdness in the management of affairs . . . shown in the skillful selection, adaptation, and use of means to a desired end," (3) "providence in the use of resources," and (4) "attention to possible hazard or disadvantage." As the preceding discussion has amply demonstrated, the behavior of industrial civilization has been imprudent in the extreme. Unlike abundance, however, scarcity is extraordinarily intolerant of lapses in prudence, so that this virtue must certainly be a part of the steady-state solution, regardless of the particular doctrinal and institutional form it eventually takes. The lessons of prudence can of course be acquired in the school of hard knocks, but they are perhaps best learned from the great political theorists of the past (as well as the political historians, like Thucydides and Tacitus, who have traditionally been read along with them) for whom prudence is the cardinal virtue of politics.

A second indispensable political virtue is individual self-restraint. The Epigraph to this book, taken from Burke, explains why in the lucid prose for which he is famous. Reduced to its essentials, his argument states that

—man is a passionate being;
—there must therefore be checks on will and appetite;
—if these checks are not self-imposed, then they must be applied externally by a sovereign power.

We have seen how this problem has surfaced again and again in our analysis—in the Hobbesian dynamics of the tragedy of the commons, in the consequences of accepting the Faustian bargain of nuclear technology, in the reasons for the ecological successes of the Chinese, and so on. The essential political message of this book is that we must learn ecological self-restraint before it is forced on us by a potentially monolithic and totalitarian regime or by the brute forces of nature. We are currently sliding by default in the direction of one (or both) of these two outcomes. Only the restoration of some measure of civic virtue (to use the traditional term) can forestall this fate, and the necessary lessons in virtue are, again, better learned from political philosophy than from personal suffering.

If we are to take political philosophy seriously again, we should broaden our perspective beyond the specifically Western tradition of political thought, for the political history and theory of other civilizations will have much to teach us. For example, given the probable nature of the steady-state society, there is much in our own political tradition that seems to favor the revival of something like the classical city state. However, the Western political tradition never satisfactorily resolved the problem of keeping peace between city states. Thus it might be valuable to study the *millet* system of the Ottoman Empire, for it granted the widest measure of local autonomy to individual cities and provinces while still providing them with peace and most of the other benefits of a larger political community. On the other hand, it might be argued with some justice that reversion to the city state is unrealistic given the numbers of people to be accommodated and the size of the territory to be governed. If so, then the history and political thought of agrarian societies—especially China from the Shang Dynasty to Mao—are worthy of the closest study. Similarly, feudal societies, whose resonance with ecology has been suggested above, should contain many important lessons; Westerners would do well to go beyond their own medieval history to study Tokugawa Japan, which existed in almost total autarky for several centuries, yet supported a rather large population at a high cultural level (albeit frugally).

However, we must not expect political theory and history to provide us with specific solutions, or even neatly packaged object lessons on what not to do. The essential thing is to approach politics once again from a philosophical perspective instead of grasping after easy answers that fit current prejudices. As Ivan Illich (1974b) says on the subject of modern man's dependence on "energy slaves," "The energy crisis focuses concern on the scarcity of fodder for these slaves. I prefer to ask whether free men need them." Once we approach the totality of our problem with ecological scarcity from this perspective, asking the questions that really need to be asked, then solutions informed by political wisdom will certainly emerge.

The Roots of Wisdom: Ultimate Values

Political philosophy alone is not enough. The wisdom to ask the right questions comes ultimately from so-called higher values, and all the great theorists of politics invoke them as an essential element in their political arguments. However, to assert the necessity of ultimate values in this day and age is heretical. Scientific orthodoxy says that values have no epistemological standing; any statement that one value is to be preferred to another is therefore scientifically meaningless. But since science is our standard of social reality, value questions must not be socially meaningful either. Similarly, the modern liberal-democratic orthodoxy maintains that men have an inalienable right to create their own values; accordingly, any attempt to judge these values or replace them with others in the name of some nebulous ideological concept like "the common interest" is anti-liberal and ultimately fascist. Thus, to the ideologically committed scientist and democrat, all values are equal and politics can be no more than the clash of personal and factional interest, moderated only slightly by some minimal ethical conceptions about what constitutes a just division of the spoils. Politics therefore comes to be devoted almost exclusively to the utilitarian satisfaction of desire or appetite, which, in the absence of any higher values, necessarily becomes the sole measure of individual and social good; the idea that public authority might exist in part to direct people toward virtuous ends becomes anathema.

Yet wisdom, if only the rough and ready kind acquired by everyday living, tells us that not all values are equal and that virtue matters in life. In practice, science and democracy alike would be a shambles without the implicit values that govern them; indeed, "science" and "democracy" are themselves high-level values that generate the criteria by which utilitarian political decisions can be made in industrial civilization. We know too that the Protestant faith, even though it was not everywhere established, was the unofficial religion of the Industrial Revolution, providing transcendental explanation of the human condition as well as justification for acquisitiveness and other bourgeois traits. Also, our founding fathers were motivated by deep religious faith to set up our political institutions "under God." We used to have, in effect, a positive standard of right and virtue, one that still lingers on in an unconscious and decayed form. Thus we have had a value-based civic religion all along. We have simply never acknowledged it as such.

However, we must recognize that civic religions are never easily changed and that resistance to turning politics once again into more than a mere clash of interests will be very high. We must also recognize that, given the litany of horrors that is human history, the suspicion of values is not without foundation, for far too many crimes have been committed by leaders and peoples convinced that they had God on their side. Moreover, it is not always an easy task to distinguish genuine needs, which are essential to human well-being, from mere wants, which are dispensable without real sacrifice. Nevertheless, however difficult and controversial the task, we have no choice but to search for some ultimate values by which to construct a post-modern civilization. What follows is an effort to indicate what these values ought to be, but the discussion is even more condensed, tentative, general, and personal than the previous discussion of political values; it merely tries to suggest that there is already remarkably widespread agreement on what an appropriate set of ultimate values ought to be under any set of circumstances and that these values favor a certain type of steady state.

It was earlier suggested that the crisis of ecological scarcity is fundamentally a moral and spiritual crisis. In looking out at the ecological ruin we have made of the earth, we see what manner of men we have become. Worse, the degraded environment impoverishes us spiritually so that we are likely to cause further ecological ruin. But the point has been reached where such a vicious circle can no longer continue without serious consequences for humankind. The earth is teaching us a moral lesson: the individual virtues that have always been necessary for ethical and spiritual reasons have now become imperative for practical ones. These virtues were pithily summarized in the fifth century B.C. by the Taoist sage Lao Tzu:

> Nature sustains itself through three precious principles,
>   which one does well to embrace and follow.
> These are gentleness, frugality and humility [Chap. 67].

Implicit in gentleness, frugality, and humility are simplicity and closeness to nature. *Walden,* the famous symbolic critique by Henry Thoreau of an American society rapidly headed in the opposite direction, is an extended sermon on the necessity of natural simplicity as the only way to avoid living the quietly desperate life of those weighed down by striving for power, possessions, and position. Such simplicity does not mean rejection of all progress, as Thoreau makes clear in his chapter on "Economy":

> Though we are not so degenerate but that we might possibly live in a cave or a wigwam or wear skins today, it certainly is better to accept the advantages, though so dearly bought, which the invention and industry of mankind offer. In such a neighborhood as this, boards and shingles, lime and bricks, are cheaper and more easily obtained than suitable caves, or whole logs, or bark in sufficient quantities, or even well-tempered clay or flat stones. I speak understandingly on this subject, for I have made myself acquainted with it both theoretically and practically. *With a little more wit we might use these materials so as to become richer than the richest now are, and make our civilization a blessing. The civilized man is a more experienced and wiser savage* [1854, p. 295, emphasis added].

It is of course quite obvious that development as we know it, in all its complexity, violence, prodigality and pride, is perfectly noxious to these fundamental ethical-spiritual principles. The greatest sociologists and political economists would hardly disagree. In his classic work *The Protestant Ethic and the Spirit of Capitalism,* the renowned nineteenth century German sociologist Max Weber foresaw the spiritual death that awaited an increasingly rationalized, bureaucratized society: "Specialists without spirit, sensualists without heart; this nullity imagines that it has attained a level of civilization never before attained" (cited in Burch 1971, p. 159). John Stuart Mill, one of the ablest and most ardent philosophical defenders of liberty and other bourgeois values, was nevertheless distressed by "the trampling, crushing, elbowing, and treading on each other's heels" that the relentless struggle to "get on" seemed inevitably to produce (1871, p. 748). Mill also foresaw that the long-term consequences of development would be pernicious:

> If the earth must lose that great portion of its pleasantness which it owes to things that the unlimited increase of wealth and population would extirpate from it, for the mere purpose of enabling it to support a larger, but not a better or a happier population, I sincerely hope, for the sake of posterity, that they will be content to be stationary, long before necessity compels them to it [p. 751].

Even Adam Smith, perhaps the person most directly responsible for the materialistic and economic nature of modern civilization, clearly believed that a man who pursued wealth was prey to vanity, greed, and other foolish and ignoble motives (1792, III-2). The eminent twentieth-century economist John Maynard Keynes, whose fame and influence ironically rest primarily on his prescriptions for keeping the engine of economic growth in high gear, was even more adamantly opposed to the values of "economic man."* Noting that the whole long era of development has "exalted some of the most distasteful of human qualities into the position of the highest virtues," he hoped for its speedy end, so that men and women would once more be

> free . . . to return to some of the most sure and certain principles of religion and traditional virtue—that avarice is a vice, that the exaction of usury is a misdemeanour, and the love of money is detestable, that those walk most truly in the paths of virtue and sane wisdom who take least thought for the morrow. We shall once more value ends above means and prefer the good to the useful. We shall honour those who can teach us how to pluck the hour and the day virtuously and well, the delightful people who are capable of taking direct enjoyment in things, the lilies of the field who toil not, neither do they spin [1971, p. 192].

It follows from what these writers say (and from the hundreds of similar words uttered by men of every age and tradition) that nothing of real value would be lost if development were to cease. Rather, the likelihood of men and women leading reasonably happy, sane, fulfilled, and harmonious per-

---

*Paradoxically, Keynes believed that because "foul is useful and fair is not," we could not afford to abandon these values until we were out of "the tunnel of economic necessity" a hundred years hence—that is, until we had abolished scarcity. Even if this were possible, the problem with this qualification is that the tunnel is likely to be endless unless one learns to say Enough!—for growth simply produces more mouths and greater wants and is thus self-defeating. Also, even Keynes suggested that economics be radically devalued during our passage through the tunnel.

sonal lives would be enhanced.* Moreover, once the ultimately fruitless and self-destructive quest for ever more private affluence was abandoned, public amenity would be free to grow and to produce all the kinds of cultural riches men have been able to enjoy in the past, even if the gross quantity of production were less than it is today. Indeed, social critic Lewis Mumford argues persuasively that the inhabitants of ancient Pompeii, an ordinary Roman provincial town, enjoyed a quality of life superior in many important respects to that attainable in present-day California (1973, pp. 462–473). Nor should we forget the cultural glory of Athens, Florence, Kyoto, and other ancient centers of civilization whose achievements antedate the Industrial Revolution. Thus development appears to be virtually irrelevant to cultural richness and progress; social arrangements, not wealth in itself, seem to determine the level of social amenity.† In sum, "with a little more wit we might . . . become richer than the richest now are, and make our civilization a blessing."

The Minimal, Frugal Steady State

The nature of the most desirable type of steady state should now be clear. We saw earlier that the attempt to achieve a high-throughput or maximum-feasible steady-state society involved a Faustian bargain fraught with dire political consequences. Now we see in addition that the maximum-feasible steady state, which aims at gratifying as far as possible the materialistic and hedonistic appetites of the populace, contravenes the lessons to be discovered in political philosophy as well as essential ethical-spiritual teachings enunciated by wise men of every age and tradition. In other words, political and

---

*The available empirical evidence supports the position that economic development is largely irrelevant to personal happiness. Easterlin (1973) shows that people's sense of economic well-being depends primarily on their relative standing. (Thus the American poor, who are mostly quite rich by any historical or comparative standard, nevertheless feel acutely deprived.) The popular demand for more growth is therefore largely motivated by a desire to keep up with or catch up with the Joneses. Unfortunately, this is a never-ending pursuit; a few Joneses will always pull ahead of the crowd and inspire emulation, so that the package of goods needed to feel non-poor grows constantly. Relative equality and distributive justice thus seem more important for individual happiness and well-being than the absolute level of production.

† The empirical evidence again supports the impressionistic judgment that, when it comes to culture, bigger is not necessarily better. Countries with no more than half the U.S. per capita consumption of energy actually outrank the United States statistically in important indicators of the quality of life—for example, the rate of infant mortality and the number of persons per hospital bed, the number of books published per year per million persons, and even public expenditures for education as a percentage of national income (Watt 1974, Chap. 11). Of course, some minimum level of wealth is necessary for a reasonable level of amenity, but the level of production with appropriate technology in a steady-state society of reasonable population should be high enough to support moderate and judicious cultural aspirations.

spiritual wisdom alike urge the adoption of the minimal, frugal steady state as the form of a post-industrial society.

Politically, a minimal steady state would, as its name implies, follow the favorite prudential maxim of our founding fathers: "That government is best that governs least." Where this seems to lead is toward a decentralized Jeffersonian polity of relatively small, intimate, locally autonomous, and self-governing communities rooted in the land (or other local ecological resources) and affiliated at the federal level only for a few clearly defined purposes. It leads, in other words, back to the original American vision of politics. Such a minimal polity, unlike mass society, can place primary reliance on the inherent virtue of the citizen (or on the power of local public opinion to recall a straying citizen to his civic duty); this minimizes the perceived restrictions on individual freedom (in accordance with the principle of macro-constraint and micro-freedom described in Chapter 4, as well as the preference for design over planning expressed in Box 8-1). Of course, as is unfortunately true of all forms of political association, such a polity also has its characteristic dangers—primarily local tyranny. However, the tyranny currently exercised over our lives by impersonal forces beyond any individual's ken, much less control, is far greater; we are largely at the mercy of market forces, efficiency, technological change, radical monopoly (that is, our almost total dependence on the ministrations of doctors, lawyers, teachers, and other professionals), and so on. By contrast, local tyrants are highly visible and few in number, so that at least one would know whom to revolt against. Cities would still exist within this basically Jeffersonian polity, but they should be less of an instrument for exacting an economic surplus from the countryside than they are now; eventually, they would probably come to resemble the pre-modern city state in size and spirit, a highly desirable development if the countless historians and political philosophers who have praised this organic form of political and social community are to be believed.* The minimal, frugal steady state would thus be a predominantly rural and yeoman society but, given modern communications, what Karl Marx called the "idiocy" (that is, the political, social, and cultural unconsciousness) of rural life should be avoidable.

In economics, too, less is better. The goal is frugality, which means

---

*As noted previously, an alternative model to the city state as a primary form of political association is the agrarian empire, which has certain undeniable virtues but also some correspondingly large drawbacks, as Maoist China seems to illustrate. Nevertheless, given the large numbers of people in the world and the realities of international politics, a degree of international decentralization, decoupling, and autarky sufficient to support Jeffersonian politics at the local level may simply be unattainable. However, any form of minimal steady-state society would have to be supported by a large measure of international decentralization, decoupling, and autarky, for the current degree of interdependence is politically destabilizing and economically disruptive, amplifying and universalizing problems instead of solving them, and it generates strong pressures toward political centralization.

neither poverty nor abundance, but rather an ample sufficiency. The governing principle of economic life in a minimal, frugal steady state would be "right livelihood" (Schumacher 1973, pp. 50–58). That is, honest work from which one can derive satisfaction (not simply a wage), a sense of working in community with and for one's fellow men, and an opportunity to develop one's native talents for the benefit of self and others are just as important as income sufficient for a decent and dignified material existence. This view of economics does not reject productivity or technology in itself, but it does demand that the value and dignity of human labor be restored and that the economy be run "as if people mattered." Following these prescriptions would inevitably promote small-scale, self-sufficient, virtually self-administering, locally oriented and controlled enterprise dependent on simple, inexpensive, labor-intensive means of production that are ecologically appropriate—all of which should put individuals back in charge of their own economic destiny and produce a frugal economy compatible with the minimal polity described above.

Although in our search for a suitable civil religion we certainly ought to cast the net for sources of inspiration as widely as possible, it by no means follows that we must convert to Taoism or other seemingly alien faiths, political, economic, or religious. As we have seen, the political philosophy of Thomas Jefferson can supply a large part of the ideological foundation for a minimal, frugal steady state; what is lacking may be found in the ideas of Henry Thoreau and all the other "literary" critics of American civilization, like Melville and Whitman, who chided us for following a path that must eventually lead to the betrayal of our basic principles.* Moreover, although much in Christianity has rightly been found by critics (for example, Roszak 1973) to be ecologically objectionable (in that nature is almost completely desacralized and man given quasi-total dominion over creation), others point out with equal correctness that stewardship and other Christian virtues could easily form the basis of an ecological ethic. The historian Lynn White, for example, while generally critical of Christianity, nevertheless sees St. Francis of Assisi, who worshiped nature and preached absolute identification and harmonious equality with the rest of creation, as a potential "patron saint of ecology" (1967). The ecological philosopher Rene Dubos, on the other hand, prefers St. Benedict of Nursia, because he did not merely love nature, but founded an order of monks who worked with the natural environment to create beautiful, productive, and harmonious landscapes, thus translating the ideal of stewardship into physical actuality (1972, Chap. 8). By contrast, economist E. F. Schumacher prefers to focus not on a particular figure, but on the "Four Cardinal Virtues" of Christianity—*prudentia justitia, for-*

---

*Historian Leo Marx's excellent essay "American Institutions and Ecological Ideals" (1970) shows how the literary and ecological critiques of American society have merged.

titudo, and *temperantia*—which would, if observed, almost automatically produce a minimal, frugal steady-state society (1974). Thus self-renewal or self-transformation based primarily on native American and Western principles is eminently possible, for the minimal and frugal steady state accords totally with the best in our own tradition.

The Grand Opportunity

Naturally, other visions of the minimal, frugal steady state are possible, but the above should suggest that feelings of despair and impotence are not appropriate responses to the crisis of ecological scarcity. True, the transition to any conceivable form of steady-state society is likely to be wracking and painful, but a measure of destruction is simply the precondition of rebirth, and the industrial era was a necessary but in too many respects ugly and disagreeable phase in human history that we should rejoice to put behind us. Moreover, if we act wisely and soon, the transition need not involve unbearable sacrifices or frightful turmoil. Indeed, we are confronted not with the end of the world, although it will surely be the end of the world as we have known it, but with a grand opportunity to share in the creation of a new and potentially higher, more humane form of post-industrial civilization. But we must not delay, for unless we begin soon, an ugly and desperate transition to a degraded and tyrannical version of the steady state may become almost inevitable.

A Politics of Transformation

Seizing this grand opportunity will require a politics of transformation. Metanoia is tantamount to religious conversion and is therefore not easily achieved. As in the revolutionary eras of the past, inspirational leadership will be needed to steer us clear of anarchy and chaos during the transition. The critical question, therefore, is whether such leadership will be provided, on the one hand, by a man on horseback or Big Brother's Ministry of Propaganda or, on the other, by a Gandhi or a group of Jeffersonian "natural aristocrats" resembling the men who founded the American Republic. Unfortunately, the breadth of mind and nobility of character typical of the latter are not commonly found these days, for our institutions are designed to turn out experts and other brilliant mediocrities whose distinguishing characteristic is what Thorstein Veblen called a "trained incapacity" to see beyond their professional blinkers. Even those who avoid this pitfall often cling to the past. For example, the idea that many of the Enlightenment values central to modern civilization, such as the paramountcy of secular knowledge acquired through endless schooling, might have to go by the board is often not even entertained. What therefore typically emerges is a call for change in general that ignores most of the critical issues or, what is worse, for change in the other fellow that implies little real change in or commitment from the would-be leader. But this cannot be effective; only leaders who have themselves fully embraced the future can provide inspirational leadership. Next to the sheer lack of time in the face of onrushing events, the paucity of genuine leaders is probably our most serious obstacle to a better and more humane future.

Men of Intemperate Minds Cannot Be Free

Leadership is only part of the politics of transformation, for even the most inspired leaders can only do so much. We as individuals must also cease clinging to the past and embrace the future, accepting our personal responsibility for helping to make this vision of a more beautiful and joyful steady-state future come true. Like charity, transformation begins at home.

Above all, we must somehow learn the essential lesson of the crisis of ecological scarcity. In the words of Edmund Burke, "men of intemperate minds cannot be free," for their passions do indeed "forge their fetters." It is not that nature has made scanty provision for our wants; nature's economy is generous and plentiful for those who would live modestly within its circle of interdependence. It is our numbers and our wants that have outrun nature's bounty. If we will not freely and joyfully place "moral chains" on our will and appetite, then we shall abdicate to the brute forces of nature or to a political Leviathan what should be our own moral duty. Since even nature's bounty can be exhausted by the infinitude of human wants, only a life of self-restraint and simple sufficiency in natural harmony with the earth will allow us to continue to enjoy life, liberty, and estate. Having freely chosen such a life, we shall find that it has its own richness, for we become rich precisely to the degree that we eliminate violence, greed, and pride from our lives. When we have rediscovered this primordial wealth we shall see something the wise have always known: the earth is, always has been, and always will be more beautiful than it is useful.

BIBLIOGRAPHIC NOTE

Assuming that the reader has already acquired some familiarity with the science of ecology by reading the works recommended in the Bibliographic Note to Chapter 1 (especially Ian McHarg's *Design with Nature*), the best place

to begin a study of ecological philosophy is Rene Dubos' *So Human an Animal,*
a Pulitzer-Prize-winning exploration of the meaning of human biology for social
man, and *A God Within,* which addresses itself more directly to the dilemmas of
choice in an age of ecological scarcity. Both works reflect a deep sense of
history and a profound scientific understanding. In the same class with Dubos is
Aldo Leopold, whose classic *A Sand County Almanac* (especially the essay
entitled "The Land Ethic") has inspired a whole generation of ecologists and
conservationists with its call for an ethical communion with nature. Also invaluable is the collection edited by Paul Shepard and Daniel McKinley, *The
Subversive Science: Essays Toward an Ecology of Man.* As befits a work of
truly human ecology, the essays range over a wide variety of topics in addition
to ecology proper—cybernetics, myth, radiation, demography, medicine, ethol-
ogy, art, social criticism, anthropology, and religion. The short but excellent
bibliography is equally eclectic and comprehensive. William Leiss' *The Domination of Nature* is an excellent critical history of one of modern man's most
pernicious anti-ecological attitudes, and John Livingston's *One Cosmic Instant*
is a similar treatment of anthropocentrism. However, for balance one might
wish to see John Passmore's *Man's Responsibility for Nature*; he urges stewardship on grounds of ecological necessity but also insists in "human chauvinistic"
fashion that man is the measure of all things and that he has the absolute right
to dominate nature for his own benefit. Finally, Daniel Kozlovsky's *An Ecological and Evolutionary Ethic* contains brief but pointed essays full of earthy
ecological wisdom expressed in a highly colloquial style.

An essential adjunct to ecological philosophy is systems philosophy, for, as
noted in the text, the systems paradigm must come to reign in the steady state.
Two works to start with are C. West Churchman's *The Systems Approach,*
which is a first-rate non-technical introduction to the basics of systems science,
and Ervin Laszlo's *The Systems View of the World,* which is a short and clear
presentation of systems philosophy as it grows out of general systems theory.

Anthropology is another essential adjunct to ecological philosophy. Anthropologists have long admired the social virtues and ecological wisdom of the
organic communities they have studied. For one thing, as Claude Lévi-Strauss
has pointed out in *The Savage Mind,* the primitive is every bit as intelligent
(and even "scientific") as we are. Also, as Marshall Sahlins puts it in his
Stone-Age Economics, primitive man was a member of "the original affluent
society" in that he enjoyed what Sahlins calls "Zen affluence" or a lack of
possession by his possessions that modern man might envy. In addition, Paul
Shepard's *The Tender Carnivore and the Sacred Game* is only the latest in a
long series of books suggesting that, man for man, the primitive is in many
ways better than we are and probably healthier and happier to boot.

Among the post-industrial critics, the leading figure in epistemology is the
cultural historian Theodore Roszak. In his *The Making of a Counter Culture*
and *Where the Wasteland Ends,* Roszak maintains that our preoccupation with
purely empiricist, positivist, reductionist science creates in us a fatal blindness
or "single vision" at the root of most of our problems (and most especially our
ecological problems, which derive from an inability to see our interconnected-
ness with all being). Psychologist Abraham Maslow's *The Psychology of Sci-*

ence is an equally trenchant but less polemical plea for restoring humanism to science; he urges science to exalt "Taoistic" knowledge based on holistic, empathetic understanding rather than tough-minded manipulation and control. Maslow's unorthodox epistemological views are paralleled by his non-behaviorist, humanistic psychology, which is set forth in his *The Farther Reaches of Human Nature*.

Post-industrial sociology's leading figure is the unclassifiable radical thinker Ivan Illich, who in *Deschooling Society, Tools for Conviviality,* and *Energy and Equity* has argued that the most vaunted and characteristic features and institutions of the modern world have become actual banes, harming us, enslaving us, and preventing us from living in genuine human community with our fellows. Illich would have us radically simplify our lives to promote his ideal of "conviviality," the free communal association of men in ways that they themselves devise instead of in ways that are inflicted on them by big business, big technology, big medicine, big education, and all the other giant bureaucracies that dominate modern life. Illich's style is unconventional and occasionally infuriating—it is a mixture of sweeping generalizations and cryptic aphorisms —but he is always stimulating. The sociologist Philip Slater is equally radical in his conclusion that extreme hedonistic individualism has created an intolerably lonely and self-destructive society, but his style in *The Pursuit of Loneliness* and *Earthwalk* is more conventional than Illich's. Slater too argues for deceleration, decentralization, and a return to intimate human community. Gordon Rattray Taylor's *Rethink,* in which he proposes a "paraprimitive" society, is a less passionate but scarcely less radical critique with many interesting features. Finally, the economist Staffan Lindner shows in his minor classic *The Harried Leisure Class* that modern life seems to have increased human labor, instead of abridging it as the celebrators of the Industrial Revolution originally hoped.

In radical economics, the foremost figure is the British economist E. F. Schumacher. His *Small is Beautiful: Economics As If People Mattered* brings together essays written over a long, active, and exemplary career promoting small-scale enterprise, soil conservation, and intermediate technology (while holding down a full-time and responsible government position). Much more than a critique, this major work lays down basic principles for the political economy of a minimal, frugal steady state and shows how they can begin to be implemented even today. Three of the economists discussed in the Bibliographic Note for Chapter 5—Daly, Weisskopf, and Wilkinson—should be read along with Schumacher and the other radical critics cited above, for they ably support the contention that economic growth is not conducive to a better, happier population or to genuine improvement of what philosophers agree is the only thing that matters—the "art of living."

Finally, transcending any of the categories of social criticism above (for he covered all of them) is Lewis Mumford. For almost a half-century, he has cried out in the wilderness against the dominant trends of the twentieth century, warning that they would produce the predicament we have now reached. Among the many works of his that one could recommend, *The City in History* and the two volumes of *The Myth of the Machine (Technics and Human Development* and *The Pentagon of Power)* are probably the most useful. Mumford's passionate and often flawed but always forceful arguments in favor of a humanly scaled organic community based on "polytechnics," not technological uniformity, and economic plenitude, not abundance, are full of invaluable raw material for the would-be architects of the steady state.

Turning next to political philosophy, it would be best for the reader to bypass books about political theory and go directly to the original texts: Plato's *Republic, Statesman,* and *Laws,* Aristotle's *Politics* and *Ethics,* Machiavelli's *The Prince* and *The Discourses,* Hobbes' *Leviathan,* Rousseau's *Discourse on the Sciences and Arts, Discourse on the Origin and Foundations of Inequality,* and *The Social Contract,* Locke's *Two Treatises of Government,* Burke's *Reflections on the Revolution in France,* and *The Federalist,* to name only the most obvious and relevant to the kinds of decisions we are called upon to make.* Unfortunately, Jefferson, who must also be read, never did write a systematic treatise on politics, so his political and social philosophy is best approached indirectly through Adrienne Koch's excellent *The Philosophy of Thomas Jefferson.* A helpful supplementary work is Leo Marx's *The Machine in the Garden,* a cultural history of the long ideological struggle between the dominant Hamiltonian vision of America—urban, commercial, and elitist—and the rival Jeffersonian one—rural, agricultural, and populist. Anyone interested in the minimal, frugal steady state would also find Raghavan Iyer's *The Moral and Political Thought of Mahatma Gandhi* essential reading; Gandhi's ideas on political economy may be more relevant to modern conditions, especially in the Third World, than those of Jefferson. On anarchism in general, Peter Kropotkin's classic work *Fields, Factories and Workshops Tomorrow* is highly recommended, especially since the editorial notes by Colin Ward to the recently reissued edition provide a guide to this whole tradition of discourse. Those in search of the humane core around which an ecological socialism might be constructed should read Marx's *The Economic and Philosophical Manuscripts of 1844,* which (as edited by Struik) contains Engels' *Outline of a Critique of Political Economy* as an appendix; it was from these roots that what we know as Marxism grew, losing much of its original humanistic character in the process. Lastly, a stimulating work that combines anarchism and humanistic Marxism is Murray Bookchin's *Post-Scarcity Anarchism*

The ecological crisis of civilization results from *hubris,* prideful disregard of the inherent limits of the human condition. Thus, one should read the Greek tragedians, whose studies of *hubris* and its terrible consequences have never been equaled.

In the broader area of ultimate values, I shall merely indicate a few works that have had the most meaning for me. As should be apparent from the text, I

---

*Since these are classics available in multiple editions, none are cited in the List of Sources. The one possible exception to the preference for original over secondary sources is Mulford Sibley's (1973) remarkable distillation of what Plato and Aristotle have to say about the problems of technology, economy, and ecology; those unused to reading political philosophy, which can seem archaic and irrelevant to the untutored, might find Sibley's essay a good opening into this great tradition of discourse.

heartily recommend both Lao Tzu, whose *Tao Teh King* is perhaps the greatest of all works of nature philosophy, and Henry Thoreau, whose *Walden* is almost its equal and less difficult for the modern Westerner to enter into. However, the extent to which ecology itself can directly teach us ultimate values should not be overlooked. As a number of writers have pointed out, with their vision of total interdependence and connectedness the mystics were in effect the first ecologists, and the deeper we go into ecology (and physics) the more science begins to resemble mysticism (Barash 1973; Dasmann 1974). Thus, ecology's ultimate vocation may be that of a "master science," providing what amounts to transcendental guidance on an empirical, scientific foundation. The poet Gary Snyder exhibits precisely this amalgam between ancient mystical wisdom (primarily Amerindian and Zen) and modern ecological science in his *Earth House Hold* and *Turtle Island,* which contains many essays on ecological themes (including the widely reprinted eco-poetical political manifesto "Four Changes"). The relation between mysticism, science, and the environmental crisis is also explored in depth in the Islamic theologian Seyyed Hossein Nasr's *The Encounter of Man and Nature,* which sees the crisis as primarily spiritual in character.

Finally, the vast utopian literature will provide essential guidance for the architects of a new civilization. Thomas More's *Utopia* was the first of its genre and is still unexcelled in many respects; indeed, one could hardly ask for a better vision of the minimal, frugal steady state. However, Aldous Huxley's *Island* is an interesting modern variation on More's basic theme. Another appealing and thought-provoking picture of a frugal steady-state society is found in Ernest Callenbach's *Ecotopia,* which is more concretely ecological than *Island* yet equally strong in the area of human relationships. By contrast, Warren Wagar's utopian political tract *Building the City of Man* clearly rejects the minimal, frugal steady state as retrogressive (even though it also rejects the maximum-feasible steady state as ecologically and socially destructive). Wagar's utopia is thus reformist rather than radical; he urges the universalization of what he sees as the best of the Enlightenment paradigm in a world civilization that would be a political and social monoculture and a world state that would be "unitary, democratic, socialist, and liberal." The reader must judge for himself, in the light of all that we have discussed, whether anything less than a paradigm change is feasible or desirable, but he would still benefit from exposure to Wagar's very different vision of a desirable future. Of course, we must not overlook the characteristic dangers and dilemmas of the utopian mode of thought, brilliantly explored in George Kateb's *Utopia and Its Enemies,* but in fact, we need much more utopian thinking—first to show us what some of the alternative futures available to us might be, and then to inspire us to reach them. "Where there is no vision, the people perish."

Don Juan . . . caressed the ground gently.

"This is the predilection of two warriors," he said. "This earth, this world. For a warrior there can be no greater love. . . .

"This lovely being, which is alive to its last recesses and understands every feeling, soothed me, it cured me of my pains, and finally when I had fully understood my love for it, it taught me freedom."

Carlos Castaneda, *Tales of Power*

LIST OF SOURCES

INTRODUCTION

Barker, Ernest, trans. and ed.
    1952   *The Politics of Aristotle* (New York: Oxford).
Boulding, Kenneth E.
    1961   *The Image* (Ann Arbor: Michigan).
    1964   *The Meaning of the Twentieth Century: The Great Transition* (New York: Harper and Row).
    1966   "Is Scarcity Dead?" *Public Interest* 5:36–44.
    1970   "The Economics of the Coming Spaceship Earth," in his *Beyond Economics. Essays on Society, Religion and Ethics* (Ann Arbor: Michigan), pp. 275–287.
Brown, Harrison
    1954   *The Challenge of Man's Future* (New York: Viking).
Cole, H. S. D., et al., eds.
    1973   *Models of Doom: A Critique of The Limits to Growth* (New York: Universe).
Dubos, Rene
    1969   "A Social Design for Science," *Science* 166:823.
    1972   *A God Within* (New York: Scribner's).
Durrenberger, Robert W.
    1970   *Environment and Man: A Bibliography* (Palo Alto: National).
Geertz, Clifford
    1966   *Agricultural Involution* (Berkeley: California).
Glacken, Clarence J.
    1956   "Changing Ideas of the Habitable World", in Thomas 1956, pp. 70–92.
Goldsmith, Edward, et al.
    1972   "A Blueprint for Survival," *Ecologist* 2(1):1–43.

Hardin, Garrett
    1959   *Nature and Man's Fate* (New York: Holt, Rinehart and Winston).
————, ed.
    1969   *Population, Evolution, and Birth Control: A Collage of Controversial Ideas* (2nd ed.; San Francisco: W. H. Freeman and Co.).
Hume, David
    1739   *A Treatise of Human Nature*, in *Theory of Politics*, ed. Frederick Watkins (New York: Nelson, 1951).
Jacob, Francois
    1974   *The Logic of Life: A History of Heredity*, trans. Betty E. Spillman (New York: Pantheon).
Kuhn, Thomas S.
    1970   *The Structure of Scientific Revolutions* (2nd ed.; University of Chicago Press).
Malthus, Thomas Robert
    1798   *Essay on the Principle of Population As It Affects the Future Improvement of Society*, reprinted as *First Essay on Population, 1798* (New York: Kelley, 1965).
    1830   "A Summary View of the Principle of Population," in *Three Essays on Population*, ed. Frank W. Notestein (New York: New American Library).
Marsh, George Perkins
    1864   *Man and Nature*, ed. David Lowenthal (Cambridge: Harvard, 1965).
Meadows, Donella H., et al.
    1972   *The Limits to Growth* (New York: Universe).
Mesarovic, Mihajlo, and Eduard Pestel
    1974   *Mankind at the Turning Point: The Second Report to the Club of Rome* (New York: Dutton/Reader's Digest).
Ornstein, Robert E.
    1972   *The Psychology of Consciousness* (San Francisco: W. H. Freeman and Co.).
Osborn, Fairfield
    1948   *Our Plundered Planet* (Boston: Little, Brown).
Pearce, Joseph C.
    1973   *The Crack in the Cosmic Egg: Challenging Constructs of Mind and Reality* (New York: Simon and Schuster).
Polak, Frederik L.
    1961   *The Image of the Future* (New York: Oceana).
Seaborg, Glenn T.
    1970   "The Birthpangs of a New World," *The Futurist* 4:205–208.
Sears, Paul B.
    1935   *Deserts on the March* (Norman: Oklahoma).
    1971   Letter to *Science* 174:263.
Thomas, William L., Jr., ed.
    1956   *Man's Role in Changing the Face of the Earth* (University of Chicago Press).
Vogt, William
    1948   *Road to Survival* (New York: William Sloane).
Wolin, Sheldon S.
    1968   "Paradigms and Political Theories," in *Politics and Experience*, ed. Preston King and B. C. Parekh (Cambridge, Eng.: University Press), pp. 125–152.
    1969   "Political Theory as a Vocation," *American Political Science Review* 63:1062–1082.
Woodhouse, Edward J.
    1972   "Re-visioning the Future of the Third World: An Ecological Perspective on Development," *World Politics* 25:1–33.

CHAPTER 1

Adams, M. W., A. H. Ellingboe, and E. C. Rossman
    1971   "Biological Uniformity and Disease Epidemics," *BioScience* 21:1067–1070.
Anon.
    1968   "Ecology: The New Great Chain of Being," *Natural History* 77(10):8–16, 60–69.

Armillas, Pedro
    1971 "Gardens on Swamps," *Science* 174:653–661.
Bates, Marston
    1960 *The Forest and the Sea* (New York: Vintage).
    1969 "The Human Ecosystem," in *Resources and Man,* ed. Preston Cloud for National Academy of Sciences–National Research Council (San Francisco: W. H. Freeman and Co.), pp. 21–30.
Benson, Robert L.
    1971 "On the Necessity of Controlling the Level of Insecticide Resistance in Insect Populations," *BioScience* 21:1160–1165.
Blackburn, Thomas R.
    1973 "Information and the Ecology of Scholars," *Science* 181:1141–1146 [contains an excellent summary of ecosystem thermodynamics with references to original sources].
Cloud, Preston
    1974 "Evolution of Ecosystems," *American Scientist* 62:54–66.
Colinvaux, Paul A.
    1973 *Introduction to Ecology* (New York: Wiley).
Commoner, Barry
    1971 *The Closing Circle: Nature, Man, and Technology* (New York: Knopf).
Dansereau, Pierre
    1966 "Ecological Impact and Human Behavior," in *Future Environments of North America,* ed. F. Fraser Darling and John P. Milton (Garden City: Natural History Press), pp. 425–461.
Dasmann, Raymond F., John P. Milton, and Peter H. Freeman
    1973 *Ecological Principles for Economic Development* (London: Wiley).
Davis, James Sholto
    1973 "Forest-Farming: An Ecological Approach to Increase Nature's Food Productivity," *Impact of Science on Society* 23(2):117–132.
Dixon, Bernard
    1974 "Lethal Resistance," *New Scientist* 61:732.
Egerton, Frank N.
    1973 "Changing Concepts of the Balance of Nature," *Quarterly Review of Biology* 48:322–350 [a historical review showing that nature is both very stable and ever-changing].
Emlen, J. Merritt
    1973 *Ecology: An Evolutionary Approach* (Reading, Mass.: Addison-Wesley).
Farvar, M. Taghi, and John P. Milton, eds.
    1968 *The Careless Technology. Ecology and International Development* (Garden City: Natural History Press).
Flawn, Peter T.
    1970 *Environmental Geology: Conservation, Land-Use Planning, and Resource Management* (New York: Harper and Row).
Gomez-Pompa, A., C. Vazquez-Yanes, and S. Guevara
    1972 "The Tropical Rain Forest: A Nonrenewable Resource," *Science* 177:762–765.
Hardin, Garrett
    1966 *Biology: Its Principles and Implications* (2nd ed.; San Francisco: W. H. Freeman and Co.).
Hirst, Eric
    1974 "Food-Related Energy Requirements," *Science* 184:134–138.
Kolata, Gina Barl
    1974 "Theoretical Ecology: Beginnings of a Predictive Science," *Science* 183:400–401, 450.
Kormondy, Edward J.
    1969 *Concepts of Ecology* (Englewood Cliffs: Prentice-Hall).
Kucera, Clair L.
    1973 *The Challenge of Ecology* (St. Louis: Mosby).
McHarg, Ian
    1971 *Design with Nature* (Garden City: Natural History Press).
Margalef, Ramon
    1968 *Perspectives in Ecological Theory* (University of Chicago Press).
Menard, H. W.
    1974 *Geology, Resources, and Society: An Introduction to Earth Science* (San Francisco: W. H. Freeman and Co.).

Odum, Eugene P.
    1971 *Fundamentals of Ecology* (3rd ed.; Philadelphia: Saunders).
Odum, Howard T.
    1971 *Environment, Power and Society* (New York: Wiley).
Pimental, David et al.
    1973 "Food Production and the Energy Crisis," *Science* 182:443–449.
Rappaport, Roy A.
    1971 "The Flow of Energy in an Agricultural Society," *Scientific American* 224(3):121–132.
Reichle, David E.
    1975 "Advances in Ecosystem Analysis," *BioScience* 25:257–264.
Richards, Paul W.
    1973 "The Tropical Rain Forest," *Scientific American* 229(6):58–67.
Ricklefs, Robert E.
    1973 *Ecology* (Newton, Mass.: Chiron).
Scientific American
    1970 *The Biosphere* (San Francisco: W. H. Freeman and Co.).
Shepard, Paul, and Daniel McKinley, eds.
    1969 *The Subversive Science: Essays Toward an Ecology of Man* (Boston: Houghton Mifflin) [many fine articles on ecological science].
Siever, Raymond
    1974 "The Steady State of the Earth's Crust, Atmosphere and Oceans," *Scientific American* 230(6):72–79 [excellent on basic ecological cycles].
Steinhart, John S., and Carol E. Steinhart
    1974 "Energy Use in the U.S. Food System," *Science* 184:307–316.
Thurston, H. David
    1969 "Tropical Agriculture: A Key to the World Food Crisis," *BioScience* 19:29–34.
Watt, Kenneth E. F.
    1973 *Principles of Environmental Science* (New York: McGraw-Hill).
Woodwell, G. M.
    1967 "Toxic Substances and Ecological Cycles," *Scientific American* 220(3):24–31.
    1970 "Effects of Pollution on the Structure and Physiology of Ecosystems," *Science* 168:429–433.
    1974 "Success, Succession, and Adam Smith," *BioScience* 24:81–87.

CHAPTER 2

Abelson, Philip H.
    1974 "Water Pollution Abatement: Goals and Costs," *Science* 184:1333.
———, et al.
    1975 Special issue on "Food and Nutrition," *Science* 188:501–653 [many useful articles tending toward a rather optimistic conclusion that technology is capable of expanding production markedly].
    1976 Special issue on "Materials," *Science* 191:631–776 [excellent discussion of many important issues, including some that are neglected in other sources; generally optimistic about the ability of technology to cope with impending shortages, but the opposite point of view is represented].
Abert, James G., Harvey Alter, and J. Frank Bernheisel
    1974 "The Economics of Resource Recovery from Municipal Solid Waste," *Science* 183:1052–1058.
Albers, John P.
    1973 "Seabed Mineral Resources: A Survey," *Bulletin of the Atomic Scientists* 29(8):33–38 [optimistic].
Alexander, M.
    1973 "Microorganisms and Chemical Pollution," *BioScience* 23:509–515.
Allen, Jonathan
    1973 "Sewage Farming: Science Races Forward to the Eighteenth Century," *Environment* 15(3):36–41.

Allen, Robert
    1974 "Turning Platitudes into Policy," *New Scientist* 64:400–402 [by promoting the development of traditional agricultural techniques for expanding production].

Almqvist, Ebbe
    1974 "An Analysis of Global Air Pollution," *Ambio* 3:161–167.

American Chemical Society
    1969 *Cleaning Our Environment—The Chemical Basis for Action* (Washington: American Chemical Society).

Anon.
    1970 "Environmental Repairs," *Sierra Club Bulletin* 60(3):22 [cost of environmental repairs from OECD study].
    1973 "The BEIR Report: Effects on Populations of Exposure to Low Levels of Ionizing Radiation," *Bulletin of the Atomic Scientists* 29(3):47–49.

Bair, W. J., and R. C. Thompson
    1974 "Plutonium: Biomedical Research," *Science* 183:715–722.

Bardach, John E., John H. Ryther, and William O. McLarney
    1972 *Aquaculture: The Farming and Husbandry of Freshwater and Marine Organisms* (New York: Wiley).

Barnett, Harold J., and Chandler Morse
    1963 *Scarcity and Growth: The Economics of Natural Resource Availability* (Baltimore: Johns Hopkins).

Berg, Alan
    1973 *The Nutrition Factor: Its Role in National Development* (Washington: Brookings Institution).

Bernarde, Melvin A.
    1970 *Our Precarious Habitat* (New York: Norton).

Berry, R. Stephen
    1971 "The Option for Survival," *Bulletin of the Atomic Scientists* 27(5):22–27 [recycling and pollution control].

Björkman, Olle, and Joseph Berry
    1973 "High-Efficiency Photosynthesis," *Scientific American* 229(4):80–93.

Bohn, Hinrich I., and Robert C. Cauthorn
    1971 "Pollution: The Problem of Misplaced Waste," *American Scientist* 60:561–565.

Borgstrom, Georg
    1967 *The Hungry Planet: The Modern World at the Edge of Famine* (New York: Collier).
    1971 *Too Many: An Ecological Overview of the Earth's Limitations* (New York: Collier).

Borlaug, Norman E.
    1972 "Mankind and Civilization at Another Crossroad: In Balance with Nature—A Biological Myth," *BioScience* 22:41–44.

Boughey, Arthur S., ed.
    1973 *Readings in Man, the Environment, and Human Ecology* (New York: Macmillan).

Brooks, David B., and P. W. Andrews
    1974 "Mineral Resources, Economic Growth, and World Population," *Science* 185:13–19.

Brown, Harrison
    1954 *The Challenge of Man's Future* (New York: Viking).
    1970 "Human Materials Production as a Process in the Biosphere," *Scientific American* 223(3):195–208.
    , James Bonner, and John Weir
    1963 *The Next Hundred Years* (New York: Viking).

Brown, Lester R.
    1972 *World Without Borders* (New York: Random House).
    1974 *By Bread Alone* (New York: Praeger).

Bryson, Reid A.
    1974 "A Perspective on Climatic Change," *Science* 184:753–760.

Carson, Rachel
    1962 *Silent Spring* (Boston: Houghton Mifflin).

Carter, Luther J.
    1974 "Cancer and the Environment (I): A Creaky System Grinds On," *Science* 186:239–242.

Chapman, Duane
    1973 "An End to Chemical Farming?" *Environment* 15(2):12–17.
Christy, Francis T., Jr., and Anthony Scott
    1965 *The Common Wealth in Ocean Fisheries* (Baltimore: Johns Hopkins).
Clawson, Marion, Hans H. Landsberg, and Lyle T. Alexander
    1969 "Desalted Water for Agriculture: Is It Economic?" *Science* 164:1141–1148.
Cloud, Preston E., Jr.
    1968 "Realities of Mineral Distribution," *Texas Quarterly* 2(2):103–126.
————, ed.
    1969 *Resources and Man* (San Francisco: W. H. Freeman and Co.).
Coale, Ansley J.
    1970 "Man and His Environment," *Science* 170:132–136.
    1974 "The History of the Human Population," *Scientific American* 231(3):41–51.
Commission on Population Growth and the American Future
    1972 *Population and the American Future* (New York: New American Library).
Commoner, Barry
    1971 *The Closing Circle: Nature, Man, and Technology* (New York: Knopf).
Conney, A. H., and J. J. Burns
    1972 "Metabolic Interactions Among Environmental Chemicals and Drugs," *Science* 178:576–586.
Conservation Foundation
    1973a "Is Man Facing a Chronic Food Supply Problem?" *Conservation Foundation Letter,* October, pp. 1–8.
    1973b "How Far Can Man Push Nature in Search of Food?" *Conservation Foundation Letter,* November, pp. 1–8.
    1974 "Public Health: Still the Crux of Pollution Fights," *Conservation Foundation Letter,* May, pp. 1–8.
Cook, Earl
    1975 "The Depletion of Geological Resources," *Technology Review* 77(7):15–27.
Council on Environmental Quality et al.
    1972 *The Economic Impact of Pollution Control: A Summary of Recent Studies* (Washington: Government Printing Office).
Darnell, Rezneat M.
    1971 "The World Estuaries—Ecosystems in Jeopardy," *INTECOL Bulletin* 3:3–20.
DeBach, Paul
    1974 *Biological Control by Natural Enemies* (New York: Cambridge University Press) [a new and important book on a critical topic].
Dorst, Jean
    1971 *Before Nature Dies* (Baltimore: Penguin).
Dubos, Rene
    1965 *Man Adapting* (New Haven: Yale University Press).
Eckholm, Erik P.
    1976 *Losing Ground: Environmental Stress and World Food Prospects* (New York: Norton).
Ehrlich, Paul R.
    1968 *The Population Bomb* (New York: Ballantine).
————, and Anne H. Ehrlich
    1972 *Population, Resources, Environment: Issues in Human Ecology* (2nd ed.; San Francisco: W. H. Freeman and Co.).
————, Anne H. Ehrlich, and John P. Holdren
    1973 *Human Ecology: Problems and Solutions* (San Francisco: W. H. Freeman and Co.).
————, and John P. Holdren
    1969 "Population and Panaceas: A Technological Perspective," *BioScience* 19:1065–1071.
————, John P. Holdren, and Richard W. Holm, eds.
    1971 *Man and the Ecosphere* (San Francisco: W. H. Freeman and Co.).
Ehrenfeld, David W.
    1974 "Conserving the Edible Sea Turtle: Can Mariculture Help?" *American Scientist* 62:23–31.

Environmental Protection Agency

    1972   *The Economics of Clean Air: Annual Report of the Administrator of The Environmental Protection Agency to the Congress of the United States, February 1972* (Washington: Government Printing Office).

Flawn, Peter T.

    1966   *Mineral Resources: Geology, Engineering, Economics, Politics, Law* (Chicago: Rand McNally).

Foster, G. G., et al.

    1972   "Chromosome Rearrangements for the Control of Insect Pests," *Science* 176:875–880.

Frejka, Tomas

    1968   "Reflections on the Demographic Conditions Needed to Establish a U. S. Stationary Population Growth," *Population Studies* 22:379–397.

    1973a *The Future of Population Growth: Alternative Paths to Equilibrium* (New York: Wiley).

    1973b "The Prospects for a Stationary World Population," *Scientific American* 228(3):15–23.

Furon, Raymond

    1967   *The Problem of Water* (New York: American Elsevier).

Gillette, Robert

    1972   "Radiation Standards: The Last Word or at Least a Definitive One," *Science* 178:966–967, 1012.

    1974   "Cancer and the Environment (II): Groping for New Remedies," *Science* 186:242–245.

Grahn, Douglas

    1972   "Genetic Effects of Low Level Irradiation," *BioScience* 22:535–540.

Groth, Edward, III

    1975   "Increasing the Harvest," *Environment* 17(1):28–39 [an excellent summary of the key issues, amply documented].

Hammond, Allen L.

    1974a "Manganese Nodules (I): Mineral Resources on the Deep Seabed," *Science* 183:502–503.

    1974b "Manganese Nodules (II): Prospects for Deep Sea Mining," *Science* 183:644–646.

Hannon, Bruce M.

    1972   "Bottles, Cans, Energy," *Environment* 14(2):11–21.

Harte, John, and Robert H. Socolow, eds.

    1971   *Patient Earth* (New York: Holt, Rinehart and Winston).

Heichel, G. H.

    1974   "Energy Needs and Food Yields," *Technology Review* 76(8):19–25.

Hirst, Eric

    1973   "The Energy Cost of Pollution Control," *Environment* 15(8):37–44.

    1974   "Food-Related Energy Requirements," *Science* 184:134–138.

Hoff, Johan E., and Jules Janick, eds.

    1973   *Food* (San Francisco: W. H. Freeman and Co.).

Hoffman, Allen R., and David Rittenhouse Inglis

    1972   "Radiation and Infants," *Bulletin of the Atomic Scientists* 28(10):45–52.

Holdren, John P., and Paul R. Ehrlich

    1971   *Global Ecology: Toward a Rational Strategy for Man* (New York: Harcourt Brace Jovanovich).

Holmberg, Bo, et al.

    1975   Special issue on "The Work Environment," *Ambio* 4(1):1–65 [an excellent review of an important problem].

Howland, H. Richard

    1975   "The Helium Conservation Question," *Technology Review* 77(7):42–49.

Huffaker, Carl B.

    1971   "Biological Control and a Remodeled Pest Control Strategy," *Technology Review* 73(8):31–37.

Inman, Douglas L., and Birchard M. Brush

    1973   "The Coastal Challenge," *Science* 181:20–31.

Janzen, Daniel H.

    1973   "Tropical Agroecosystems," *Science* 182:1212–1219.

Kenward, Michael
    1972   "Fighting for the Clean Car," *New Scientist* 51:553–555.
Kramer, Eugene
    1973   "Energy Conservation and Waste Recycling: Taking Advantage of Urban Congestion," *Bulletin of the Atomic Scientists* 29(4):13–18.
Laing, David
    1974   "The Phosphate Connection," *Not Man Apart* 4(13):1, 10.
Lee, Douglas H. K.
    1973   "Specific Approaches to Health Effects of Pollutants," *Bulletin of the Atomic Scientists* 29(8):45–47.
Lichtenstein, E. P., T. T. Liang, and B. N. Anderegg
    1973   "Synergism of Insecticides by Herbicides," *Science* 181:847–849.
Likens, Gene E., and F. Herbert Bormann
    1974   "Acid Rain: A Serious Regional Environmental Problem," *Science* 184:1176–1179.
Loosli, J. K.
    1974   "New Sources of Proteins for Human and Animal Feeding," *BioScience* 24:26–31.
McHale, John
    1970   *The Ecological Context* (New York: Braziller).
    1971   *The Future of the Future* (New York: Ballantine).
MacIntyre, Ferren
    1974   "The Top Millimeter of the Ocean," *Scientific American* 230(5):62–77.
McKelvey, Vincent E.
    1972   "Mineral Resource Estimates and Public Policy," *American Scientist* 60:32–40.
    1974   "Approaches to the Mineral Supply Problem," *Technology Review* 76(5):13–23.
Maddox, John
    1972   *The Doomsday Syndrome* (London: Macmillan).
Malenbaum, Wilfred
    1973   "World Resources for the Year 2000," *Annals of the American Academy of Political and Social Science* 408:30–46.
Marx, Jean L.
    1974   "Nitrogen Fertilizer," *Science* 185:133.
Maugh, Thomas H., II
    1974   "Chemical Carcinogenesis: A Long-Neglected Field Blossoms," *Science* 183:940–944.
Meadows, Dennis L., et al.
    1974   *The Dynamics of Growth in a Finite World* (Cambridge: Wright-Allen).
Meadows, Donella H., et al.
    1972   *The Limits to Growth* (New York: Universe).
Meier, Richard L.
    1966   *Science and Economic Development: New Patterns of Living* (2d ed.; Cambridge: MIT).
Metz, William D., and Allen L. Hammond
    1974a   "Geodynamics Report: Exploiting the Earth Sciences Revolution." *Science* 183:735–738, 769.
    1974b   "Helium Conservation Program: Casting It to the Winds," *Science* 183:59–63.
Meyer, Judith E.
    1972   "Renewing the Soil," *Environment* 14(2):22–24, 29–32.
Murdoch, William W., ed.
    1971   *Environment: Resources, Pollution and Society* (Stamford, Conn.: Sinauer).
National Academy of Sciences, Office of the Foreign Secretary, ed.
    1971   *Rapid Population Growth* (Baltimore: Johns Hopkins).
NCMP (National Commission on Materials Policy)
    1972   *Towards a National Materials Policy: Basic Data and Issues, An Interim Report* (Washington: Government Printing Office).
    1973   *Toward a National Materials Policy: World Perspective, Second Interim Report* (Washington: Government Printing Office).
Newill, Vaun A.
    1973   "Pollution's Price—The Cost in Human Health," *Bulletin of the Atomic Scientists* 29(8):47–49.
Newman, James E., and Robert C. Pickett
    1974   "World Climates and Food Supply Variations," *Science* 186:877–881.

Odell, Rice
    1974 "Water Pollution: The Complexities of Control," *Conservation Foundation Letter,* December.
Odum, Eugene P.
    1971 *Fundamentals of Ecology* (3d ed.; Philadelphia: Saunders).
Odum, Howard T.
    1971 *Environment, Power, and Society* (New York: Wiley).
Odum, William E.
    1974 "Potential Effects of Aquaculture on Inshore Coastal Waters," *Environmental Conservation* 1:225–230.
Othmer, Donald F., and Oswald A. Roels
    1973 "Power, Fresh Water, and Food from Cold, Deep Sea Water," *Science* 182:121–125.
Park, Charles F., Jr.
    1968 *Affluence in Jeopardy: Minerals and the Political Economy* (San Francisco: Freeman, Cooper).
Payne, Philip
    1974 "Protein Deficiency or Starvation?" *New Scientist* 64:393–398 [an excellent overview of the whole malnutrition-starvation syndrome].
Perelman, Michael J.
    1972 "Farming with Petroleum," *Environment* 14(8):8–13.
Pimental, David, et al.
    1973 "Food Production and the Energy Crisis," *Science* 182:443–449.
    1975 "Energy and Land Constraints in Food Protein Production," *Science* 190:754–761.
Pinchot, Gifford B.
    1970 "Marine Farming," *Scientific American* 223(6):15–21.
    1974 "Ecological Aquaculture," *BioScience* 24:265.
Probstein, Ronald F.
    1973 "Desalination," *American Scientist* 61:280–293.
Revelle, Roger
    1974 "Food and Population," *Scientific American* 231(3):161–170 [optimistic].
Russett, Bruce M.
    1967 "The Ecology of Future International Politics," *International Studies Quarterly* 11(1):14–19 [a good discussion of the use of exponential growth in making predictions about the future].
Ryther, John H.
    1969 "Photosynthesis and Fish Production in the Sea," *Science* 166:72–76.
Sagan, L. A.
    1972 "Human Costs of Nuclear Power," *Science* 177:487–493.
Salk, Jonas
    1973 *The Survival of the Wisest* (New York: Harper and Row).
SCEP (Report of the Study of Critical Environment Problems)
    1970 *Man's Impact on the Global Environment* (Cambridge: MIT).
Shapley, Deborah
    1973a "Auto Pollution: EPA Worrying That the Catalyst May Backfire," *Science* 182:368–371.
    1973b "Ocean Technology: Race to Seabed Wealth Disturbs More Than Fish," *Science* 180:849–851, 893.
Shepard, Paul, and Daniel McKinley, eds.
    1969 *The Subversive Science: Essays Toward an Ecology of Man* (Boston: Houghton Mifflin) [many excellent articles, especially on pollution]
Singer, S. Fred
    1971 "Environmental Quality—When Does Growth Become Too Expensive?" In *Is There an Optimum Level of Population?,* ed. S. Fred Singer (New York: McGraw-Hill)
Skinner, Brian J.
    1969 *Earth Resources* (2d ed.; Englewood Cliffs: Prentice-Hall).
Small, William E.
    1971 "Agriculture: The Seeds of a Problem," *Technology Review* 73(6):48–53.
Smith, Roger H., and R. C. von Borstel
    1972 "Genetic Control of Insect Populations," *Science* 178:1164–1174.
Spurgeon, David
    1973 "The Nutrition Crunch: A World View," *Bulletin of the Atomic Scientists* 29(8):50–54.

Staines, Andrew
1974 "Digesting the Raw Materials Threat," *New Scientist* 61:609–611.
Starr, Roger, and James Carlson
1968 "Pollution and Poverty," *Public Interest* 10:104–131 [pollution-control costs].
Steinhart, John S., and Carol E. Steinhart
1974 "Energy Use in the U.S. Food System," *Science* 184:307–316.
Sterling, Theodor D.
1971 "Difficulty of Evaluating the Toxicity and Teratogenicity of 2,4,5-T from Existing Animal Experiments," *Science* 174:1358–1359.
Summers, Claude M.
1971 "The Conversion of Energy," in *Energy and Power,* ed. Scientific American (San Francisco: W. H. Freeman and Co.), pp. 93–106.
Taylor, Theodore B., and Charles C. Humpstone
1973 *The Restoration of the Earth* (New York: Harper and Row) [a "containment" pollution-control strategy].
Teitelbaum, Michael S.
1975 "Relevance of Demographic Transition Theory for Developing Countries," *Science* 188:420 [excellent recent discussion of a controversial problem].
Valery, Nicholas
1972 "Place in the Sun for Helium," *New Scientist* 56:496–500.
Wade, Nicholas
1972 "A Message from Corn Blight: The Dangers of Uniformity," *Science* 177:678–679.
1974a "Green Revolution (I): A Just Technology, Often Unjust in Use," *Science* 186:1093–1096.
1974b "Green Revolution (II): Problems of Adapting a Western Technology," *Science* 186:1186–1192.
1974c "Raw Materials: U.S. Grows More Vulnerable to Third World Cartels," *Science* 183:185–186.
1974d "Sahelian Drought: No Victory for Western Aid," *Science* 185:234–237.
1975 "New Alchemy Institute: Search for an Alternative Agriculture," *Science* 187:727–729.
Waldbott, George L.
1973 *Health Effects of Environmental Pollutants* (St. Louis: Mosby).
Wallace, Bruce
1974 "Commentary: Radioactive Wastes and Damage to Marine Communities," *BioScience* 24:164–167.
Ward, Barbara, and Rene Dubos
1972 *Only One Earth: The Care and Maintenance of a Small Planet* (New York: Norton).
Weeks, W. F., and W. J. Campbell
1973 "Towing Icebergs to Irrigate Arid Lands: Manna or Madness?" *Bulletin of the Atomic Scientists* 29(5):35–39.
Weinberg, Alvin M.
1972 "Science and Trans-Science," *Minerva* 10(2):209–222.
Westman, Walter E.
1972 "Some Basic Issues in Water Pollution Control Legislation," *American Scientist* 60:767–773.
de Wilde, Jan
1975 "Insect Population Management and Integrated Pest Control," *Ambio* 4:105–111.
Wilkes, H. Garrison, and Susan Wilkes
1972 "The Green Revolution," *Environment* 14(8):32–39.
Wittwer, S. H.
1974 "Maximum Production Capacity of Food Crops," *BioScience* 24:216–224.
Wood, J. M.
1974 "Biological Cycles for Toxic Elements in the Environment," *Science* 183:1049–1052.
Woodwell, G. M.
1969 "Radioactivity and Fallout: The Model Pollution," *BioScience* 19:884–887.
Young, Gale
1970 "Dry Lands and Desalted Water," *Science* 167:339–343.
Zwick, David, and Mary Benstock
1971 *Water Wasteland: Ralph Nader's Study Group Report on Water Pollution* (New York: Grossman).

259

CHAPTER 3

Aaronson, Terri

    1971   "The Black Box," *Environment* 13(10):10–18 [on fuel cells].

Abelson, Philip H., ed.

    1974   "Energy," special issue of *Science* 184:245–389.

Ahmed, A. Karim

    1975   "Unshielding the Sun: Human Effects," *Environment* 17(3):6–14.

Alfvén, Hannes

    1972   "Energy and Environment," *Bulletin of the Atomic Scientists* 28(5):5–8.

    1974   "Fission Energy and Other Sources of Energy," *Bulletin of the Atomic Scientists* 30(1):4–8.

Anon.

    1972a   "No Small Difference of Opinion," *World Environment Newsletter* in *World,* August 15, pp. 30–31.

    1972b   "120 Million Mw. for Nothing," *Technology Review* 74(7):58.

    1975   "What the Shuttle Might Do to Our Environment," *New Scientist* 66:300 [the atmospheric and climatic dangers of the Space Shuttle program].

Anthrop, Donald F.

    1970   "Environmental Side Effects of Energy Production," *Bulletin of the Atomic Scientists* 26(8):39–41.

Armstead, H. C. H., ed.

    1973   *Geothermal Energy: Review of Research and Development* (New York: UNESCO).

Atwood, Genevieve

    1975   "The Strip-Mining of Western Coal," *Scientific American* 233(6):23–29.

Axtmann, Robert C.

    1975   "Environmental Impact of a Geothermal Plant," *Science* 187:795–803.

Ayres, Eugene

    1950   "Power from the Sun," *Scientific American* 183(2):16–21.

Baldwin, Pamela L., and Malcolm F. Baldwin

    1974   "Offshore Oil Heats Up as Energy Issue," *Conservation Foundation Letter,* November.

Bamberger, C. E., and J. Braunstein

    1975   "Hydrogen: A Versatile Element," *American Scientist* 63:438–447.

Barnaby, Frank, et al.

    1975   Symposium on "Can We Live with Plutonium?" in *New Scientist* 66:494–506.

Barnea, Joseph

    1972   "Geothermal Power," *Scientific American* 226(1):70–77.

Barraclough, Geoffrey

    1974   "The End of an Era," *New York Review of Books,* June 27, pp. 14–20 [on the current economic disarray and its causes].

de Bell, Garrett, ed.

    1970   *The Environmental Handbook* (New York: Ballantine).

Berg, Charles A.

    1973   "Energy Conservation through Effective Utilization," *Science* 181:128–138.

    1974   "A Technical Basis for Energy Conservation," *Technology Review* 76(4):15–23.

Berg, George G.

    1973   "Hot Wastes from Nuclear Power," *Environment* 15(4):36–44.

Berry, R. Stephen

    1971   "The Option for Survival," *Bulletin of the Atomic Scientists* 27(5):22–27.

——, and Margaret F. Fels

    1973   "The Energy Cost of Automobiles," *Bulletin of the Atomic Scientists* 29(10):11–17, 58–60.

——, and Hiro Makino

    1974   "Energy Thrift in Packaging and Marketing," *Technology Review* 76(4):33–43.

Bezdek, Roger, and Bruce Hannon

    1974   "Energy, Manpower, and the Highway Trust Fund," *Science* 185:669–675.

Bockris, J. O'M.

    1974   "The Coming Energy Crisis and Solar Sources," *Environmental Conservation* 1:241–249.

Boffey, Philip M.

    1975   "Rasmussen Issues Revised Odds on a Nuclear Catastrophe," *Science* 190:640.

Bolin, Bert
    1974 "Modelling the Climate and Its Variations," *Ambio* 3:180–188.
Boulding, Kenneth E.
    1964 *The Meaning of the Twentieth Century: The Great Transition* (New York: Harper and Row).
    1973 "The Economics of the Coming Spaceship Earth," in Daly 1973, pp. 121–132.
Brinworth, B. J.
    1973 *Solar Energy for Man* (New York: Wiley).
Broecker, Wallace S.
    1975 "Climatic Change: Are We on the Brink of a Pronounced Global Warming?" *Science* 189:460–463.
Brooks, Harvey
    1973 "The Technology of Zero-Growth," *Daedalus* 102(4):139–152.
Brown, Harrison, James Bonner, and John Weir
    1963 *The Next Hundred Years* (New York: Viking).
Bryson, Reid A.
    1973 "Drought in Sahelia: Who or What Is to Blame?" *The Ecologist* 3:366–371.
    1974 "A Perspective on Climatic Change," *Science* 184:753–760.
Bupp, Irvin C., and Jean-Claude Derian
    1974 "The Breeder Reactor in the U.S.—A New Economic Analysis," *Technology Review* 76(8):27–36.
Burnet, Macfarlane
    1971 "After the Age of Discovery?" *New Scientist* 52:96–100.
Bury, J. B.
    1955 *The Idea of Progress: An Inquiry into Its Origin and Growth* (New York: Dover).
Callahan, Daniel
    1973 *The Tyranny of Survival* (New York: Macmillan) [esp. Chap. 3, which discusses ways of reexamining technology].
Calvin, Melvin
    1974 "Solar Energy by Photosynthesis," *Science* 184:375–381.
Carter, Luther J.
    1973 "Deepwater Ports: Issue Mixes Supertankers, Land Policy," *Science* 181:825–828.
    1974 "Floating Nuclear Plants: Power from the Assembly Line," *Science* 183:1063–1065.
Chapman, Peter
    1974 "The Ins and Outs of Nuclear Power," *New Scientist* 64:966–969 [net energy analysis].
Chedd, Graham
    1974 "Colonisation at Lagrangea," *New Scientist* 64:247–249.
Cheney, Eric S.
    1974 "U.S. Energy Resources: Limits and Future Outlook," *American Scientist* 62:14–22.
Clark, Wilson
    1974 *Energy for Survival: The Alternatives to Extinction* (Garden City, N.Y.: Doubleday).
Clarke, Arthur C.
    1962 *Profiles of the Future: An Inquiry into the Limits of the Possible* (New York: Harper and Row).
Cloud, Preston, ed.
    1969 *Resources and Man* (San Francisco: W. H. Freeman and Co.).
Cochran, Thomas B.
    1974 *The Liquid Metal Fast Breeder Reactor: An Economic and Environmental Critique* (Baltimore: Johns Hopkins).
Cohen, Bernard L.
    1974 "Perspectives on the Nuclear Debate: An Opposing View," *Bulletin of the Atomic Scientists* 30(8):35–39 [nuclear power as the lesser evil].
Comey, David D.
    1974 "Will Idle Capacity Kill Nuclear Power?" *Bulletin of the Atomic Scientists* 30(9):23–28.
    1975 "The Legacy of Uranium Tailings," *Bulletin of the Atomic Scientists* 31(7):43–45.
Commoner, Barry, Howard Boksenbaum, and Michael Corr, eds.
    1975 *Energy and Human Welfare: A Critical Analysis* (3 vols; Riverside, N.J.: Macmillan Information).

Conservation Foundation
  1970 "Can We Have All the Electricity We Want and a Decent Environment Too?" *CF Newsletter*, No. 3-70.
  1973 "The Land Pinch: Where Can We Put Our Wastes?" *Conservation Foundation Letter*, May.
  1974a "Carrying Capacity Analysis Is Useful—But Limited," *Conservation Foundation Letter*, June [a useful discussion of the multiple factors that have to be taken into account in thinking about carrying capacity for human use].
  1974b "U.S. Coastline Is Scene of Many Energy Conflicts," *Conservation Foundation Letter*, January.
Cook, C. Sharp
  1973 "Energy: Planning for the Future," *American Scientist* 61:61–65.
Cook, Earl
  1971 "The Flow of Energy in an Industrial Society," in Scientific American 1971, pp. 83–91.
  1976 *Man, Energy, Society* (San Francisco: W. H. Freeman and Co.).
Cottrell, Fred
  1955 *Energy and Society: The Relation Between Energy, Social Change, and Economic Development* (New York: McGraw-Hill).
Cravens, Gwyneth
  1975 "The Garden of Feasibility," *Harper's*, August, pp. 66–75 [a recent proposal for space colonization].
Crossland, Janice
  1974 "Ferment in Technology," *Environment* 16(10):17–30 [fermenting organic materials for fuels and other useful products].
Dahlberg, Kenneth A.
  1973 "Towards a Policy of Zero Energy Growth," *The Ecologist* 3:338–341.
Daly, Herman E., ed.
  1973 *Toward a Steady-State Economy* (San Francisco: W. H. Freeman and Co.).
Daniels, Farrington
  1964 *Direct Use of the Sun's Energy* (New Haven: Yale).
  1971 "Direct Use of the Sun's Energy," *American Scientist* 55:5–47 [updates and summarizes his book, still a standard work in the field].
David, Edward E., Jr.
  1973 "Energy: A Strategy of Diversity," *Technology Review* 75(7):26–31.
Day, M. C.
  1975 "Nuclear Energy: A Second Round of Questions," *Bulletin of the Atomic Scientists* 31(10):52–59 [fuel supply problems].
DeNike, L. Douglas
  1974 "Radioactive Malevolence," *Bulletin of the Atomic Scientists* 30(2):16–20 [security risks].
Dials, George E., and Elizabeth C. Moore
  1974 "The Cost of Coal," *Environment* 16(7):18–37.
Dickson, David
  1974 *Alternative Technology: And the Politics of Technical Change* (London: Fontana).
Dinneen, Gerald U., and Glenn L. Cook
  1974 "Oil Shale and the Energy Crisis," *Technology Review* 76(3):27–33.
Djerassi, Carl, et al.
  1974 "Insect Control of the Future: Operational and Policy Aspects," *Science* 186:596–607.
Dreschhoff, Gisela, D. F. Saunders, and E. J. Zeller
  1974 "International High Level Nuclear Waste Management," *Bulletin of the Atomic Scientists* 30(1):28–33.
Drucker, Daniel C.
  1971 "The Engineer in the Establishment," *Bulletin of the Atomic Scientists* 27(10):31–34.
Dudley, H. C.
  1975 "The Ultimate Catastrophe," *Bulletin of the Atomic Scientists* 31(9):21–34 [the remote possibility of a runaway chain reaction following a nuclear explosion].
Edsall, John T.
  1974 "Hazards of Nuclear Fission Power and the Choice of Alternatives," *Environmental Conservation* 1(1):21–30 [fossil fuel the lesser risk].

Ehricke, Krafft A.
    1971 "Extraterrestrial Imperative," *Bulletin of the Atomic Scientists* 27(9):18–26 [escape to space].
Ehrlich, Paul R., and Anne Ehrlich
    1972 *Population, Resources, Environment: Issues in Human Ecology* (2nd ed.; San Francisco: W. H. Freeman and Co.).
EIC (Environment Information Center)
    1973 *The Energy Index* (New York: EIC).
Eigner, Joseph
    1975 "Unshielding the Sun: Environmental Effects," *Environment* 17(3):15–18.
Ellis, A. J.
    1975 "Geothermal Systems and Power Development," *American Scientist* 63:510–521.
Emmett, John L., John Nuckolls, and Lowell Wood
    1974 "Fusion Power by Laser Implosion," *Scientific American* 230(6):24–37.
Enviro/Info
    1973 *Energy/Environment/Economy: An Annotated Bibliography of Selected U.S. Government Publications Concerning United States Energy Policy* (April) and *Supplement* (September) (mimeo; Green Bay: Enviro/Info).
Ewell, Raymond
    1975 "Food and Fertilizer in the Developing Countries, 1975–2000," *BioScience* 25:771.
Ewing, Maurice, and W. L. Donn
    1956 "A Theory of Ice Ages," *Science* 123:1061–1066.
Ferkiss, Victor C.
    1969 *Technological Man: The Myth and the Reality* (New York: Braziller).
Fisher, John C.
    1974 *Energy Crises in Perspective* (New York: Wiley).
Fletcher, J. O.
    1970 "Polar Ice and the Global Climate Machine," *Bulletin of the Atomic Scientists* 26(10):40–47.
Frisken, W. R.
    1971 "Extended Industrial Revolution and Climate Change," *EOS* 52:500–507.
Gabel, Medard, ed.
    1975 *Energy, Earth & Everyone* (San Francisco: Straight Arrow) [an unconventional and stimulating treatment of energy by followers of Buckminster Fuller].
Georgescu-Roegen, Nicholas
    1971 *The Entropy Law and the Economic Process* (Cambridge: Harvard).
    1973 "The Entropy Law and the Economic Problem," in Daly 1973, pp. 37–49.
    1975 "Energy and Economic Myths," *The Ecologist* 5:164–174, 242–252.
Giddings, J. Calvin
    1973 "World Population, Human Disaster and Nuclear Holocaust," *Bulletin of the Atomic Scientists* 29(7):21–24, 45–50.
Gillette, Robert
    1973a "Energy R & D: Under Pressure, a National Policy Takes Form," *Science* 182:898–900.
    1973b "NAS: Water Scarcity May Limit Use of Western Coal," *Science* 181:525.
    1973c "Radiation Spill at Hanford: The Anatomy of an Accident," *Science* 181:728–730.
    1974a "Budget Review: Energy," *Science* 183:636–638.
    1974b "Oil and Gas Resources: Did USGS Gush Too High?" *Science* 185:127–130.
    1974c "Synthetic Fuels: Will Government Lend the Oil Industry a Hand?" *Science* 183:641–643.
    1975 "Geological Survey Lowers Its Sights," *Science* 189:200.
Gilliland, Martha W.
    1975 "Energy Analysis and Public Policy," *Science* 189:1051–1056.
Glaser, Peter E.
    1968 "Power from the Sun: Its Future," *Science* 162:857–861 [gathering solar energy in space].
Gofman, John
    1972 "Is Nuclear Fission Acceptable?" *Futures* 4:211–219.
Glass, Bentley
    1971 "Science: Endless Horizons or Golden Age?" *Science* 171:23–29.
Goldstein, Irving S.
    1975 "Potential for Converting Wood into Plastics," *Science* 189:847–852.

Gough, William C., and Bernard J. Eastlund
    1971 "The Prospects of Fusion Power," *Scientific American* 224(2):50–64.
Green, Harold P.
    1971 "Radioactive Waste and the Law," *Natural Resources Journal* 11:281–295.
Green, Leon, Jr.
    1967 "Energy Needs vs. Environmental Pollution—A Reconciliation," *Science* 156:1448–1450
        [using ammonia as a fuel].
Greenhill, Basil
    1972 "The Sailing Ship in a Fuel Crisis," *The Ecologist* 2(9):8–10.
Gregory, Derek P.
    1973 "The Hydrogen Economy," *Scientific American* 228(1):13–21.
Gustafson, Philip F.
    1970 "Nuclear Power and Thermal Pollution: Zion, Illinois," *Bulletin of the Atomic Scientists*
        26(3):17–23.
Hafele, Wolf
    1974 "A Systems Approach to Energy," *American Scientist* 62:438–447.
Hammond, Allen L.
    1974a "Academy Says Energy Self-Sufficiency Unlikely," *Science* 184:964 [reporting conclusions
        of National Academy of Engineering study].
    1974b "Energy: Ford Foundation Study Urges Action on Conservation," *Science* 186:426–428.
    1974c "Individual Self-Sufficiency in Energy," *Science* 184:278–282.
    1974d "Modeling the Climate: A New Sense of Urgency," *Science* 185:1145–1147.
    1975a "Geothermal Resources: A New Look," *Science* 190:370.
    1975b "Ozone Destruction: Problem's Scope Grows, Its Urgency Recedes," *Science* 187:1181–
        1183.
    1975c "Solar Energy Reconsidered: ERDA Sees Bright Future," *Science* 189:538–539.
    1976 "Lithium: Will Short Supply Constrain Energy Technologies?," *Science* 191:1037–1038.
————, and Thomas H. Maugh, II
    1974 "Stratospheric Pollution: Multiple Threats to Earth's Ozone," *Science* 186:335–338.
————, William Metz, and Thomas H. Maugh, II
    1973 *Energy and the Future* (Washington: AAAS).
Hammond, Ogden, and Martin B. Zimmerman
    1975 "The Economics of Coal-Based Synthetic Gas," *Technology Review* 77(8):43–51.
Hammond, R. Philip
    1974 "Nuclear Power Risks," *American Scientist* 62:155–160.
Hannon, Bruce
    1974 "Options for Energy Conservation," *Technology Review* 76(4):24–31.
    1975 "Energy Conservation and the Consumer," *Science* 189:95–102 [a first-rate discussion of the
        need for an energy standard of value].
Harleman, Donald R. F.
    1971 "Heat—The Ultimate Waste," *Technology Review* 74(2):45–51.
Harte, John, and Robert H. Socolow, eds.
    1971 *Patient Earth* (New York: Holt, Rinehart and Winston).
Hein, R. A.
    1974 "Superconductivity: Large-Scale Applications," *Science* 185:211–222.
Heronemus, William E.
    1975 "The Case for Solar Energy," *Center Report* 8(1):6–9.
Hirsch, Robert L., and William L. R. Rice
    1974 "Nuclear Fusion Power and the Environment," *Environmental Conservation* 1:251–262.
Hirst, Eric
    1973 "Transportation Energy Use and Conservation Potential," *Bulletin of the Atomic Scientists*
        29(9):36–42.
————, and John C. Moyers
    1973 "Efficiency of Energy Use in the United States," *Science* 179:1299–1304.
Hobbs, P. V., H. Harrison, and E. Robinson
    1974 "Atmospheric Effects of Pollutants," *Science* 183:909–915.

Hohenemser, Kurt H.
    1975 "The Failsafe Risk," *Environment* 17(1):6–10.
Holdren, John P.
    1974 "Hazards of the Nuclear Fuel Cycle," *Bulletin of the Atomic Scientists* 30(8):14–23.
————, and Paul R. Ehrlich
    1974 "Human Population and the Global Environment," *American Scientist* 62:282–292.
Hueckel, Glenn
    1975 "A Historical Approach to Future Economic Growth," *Science* 187:925–931 [a recent article
        on technological growth that begs almost all the questions raised in this chapter].
Hubbert, M. King
    1969 "Energy Resources," in Cloud 1969, pp. 157–242.
Inglis, David R.
    1973 *Nuclear Energy—Its Physics and Its Social Challenge* (Reading, Mass.: Addison-Wesley).
Johnston, Harold S.
    1974 "Pollution of the Stratosphere," *Environmental Conservation* 1:163–176.
Kantrowitz, Arthur
    1969 "The Test: Meeting the Challenge of New Technology," *Bulletin of the Atomic Scientists*
        25(9):20–22, 48 [even more Panglossian than Rabinowitch 1969].
Kariel, Pat
    1974 "The Athabasca Tar Sands," *Sierra Club Bulletin* 59(8):8–10, 32.
Kates, Robert W., et al.
    1973 "Human Impact of the Managua Earthquake," *Science* 182:981–990.
Kellogg, W. W., and S. H. Schneider
    1974 "Climate Stabilization: For Better or for Worse?" *Science* 186:1163–1172 [the perils of
        attempting climate control].
Kolb, Charles E.
    1975 "The Depletion of Stratospheric Ozone," *Technology Review* 78(1):39–47.
Krieger, David
    1975 "Terrorists and Nuclear Technology," *Bulletin of the Atomic Scientists* 31(6):28–34.
Kubo, Arthur S., and David J. Rose
    1973 "Disposal of Nuclear Wastes," *Science* 182:1205–1211.
Kuhn, Thomas S.
    1970 *The Structure of Scientific Revolutions* (2nd ed.; University of Chicago Press) [diminishing
        returns in scientific discovery].
Kukla, George J., and Helena J. Kukla
    1974 "Increased Surface Albedo in the Northern Hemisphere," *Science* 183:709–714.
Lamb, Hubert H.
    1974 "Is the Earth's Climate Changing?" *The Ecologist* 4:10–15.
Landsberg, Hans H.
    1974 "Low-Cost, Abundant Energy: Paradise Lost?" *Science* 184:247–253.
Landsberg, Helmut E., and Lester Machta
    1974 "Anthropogenic Pollution of the Atmosphere: Whereto?" *Ambio* 3:146–150.
Lapp, Ralph E.
    1972 "One Answer to the Atomic-Energy Puzzle—Put the Atomic Power Plants in the Ocean,"
        New York Times Magazine, June 4, pp. 20–21, 80–90.
    1973 "The Chemical Century," *Bulletin of the Atomic Scientists* 29(7):8–14.
Lewis, Richard S.
    1972 *The Nuclear Power Rebellion: Citizens vs. the Atomic Industrial Establishment* (New York:
        Viking).
Lieberman, M. A.
    1976 "United States Uranium Resources—An Analysis of Historical Data," *Science* 192:431–436.
Lincoln, G. A.
    1973 "Energy Conservation," *Science* 180:155–162.
Lindop, Patricia J., and J. Rotblat
    1971 "Radiation Pollution of the Environment," *Bulletin of the Atomic Scientists* 27(7):17–24.
Lovins, Amory B.
    1975 *World Energy Strategies: Facts, Issues, and Options* (Cambridge: Friends of the Earth/
        Ballinger).

————, and John H. Price

    1975 *Non-Nuclear Futures: The Case for an Ethical Energy Strategy* (Cambridge: Friends of the Earth/Ballinger).

McCaull, Julian

    1973 "Windmills," *Environment* 15(1):6–17.

    1974 "Wringing Out the West," *Environment* 16(7):10–17.

McIntyre, Hugh C.

    1975 "Natural-Uranium Heavy-Water Reactors," *Scientific American* 233(4):17–27 [the CANDU system].

McKelvey, V. E.

    1972 "Mineral Resource Estimates and Public Policy," *American Scientist* 60:32–40.

Makhijani, A. B., and A. J. Lichtenberg

    1972 "Energy and Well-Being," *Environment* 14(5):11–18.

Manuel, Frank E.

    1962 *The Prophets of Paris* (Cambridge: Harvard) [the Enlightenment ideology of progress].

Margen, Peter, et al.

    1975 "The Capacity of Nuclear Power Plants," *Bulletin of the Atomic Scientists* 31(8):38–46.

Martin, S., and W. J. Campbell

    1973 "Oil and Ice in the Arctic Ocean: Possible Large-Scale Interactions," *Science* 181:56–58.

Marx, Wesley

    1973 "Los Angeles and Its Mistress Machine," *Bulletin of the Atomic Scientists* 29(4):4–7, 44–48.

Massumi, Brian

    1974 "Oil Shale Country," *Not Man Apart* 4(6):12.

Mazur, Allan, and Eugene Rosa

    1974 "Energy and Life-Style," *Science* 186:607–610.

Meadows, Dennis L., and Jorgen Randers

    1972 "Adding the Time Dimension to Environmental Policy," in *World Eco-Crisis: International Organizations in Response,* ed. David A. Kay and Eugene B. Skolnikoff (Madison: Wisconsin), pp. 47–66.

Meadows, Dennis L., et al.

    1974 *The Dynamics of Growth in a Finite World* (Cambridge: Wright-Allen).

Medawar, Peter

    1969 "On 'The Effecting of All Things Possible,' " *Technology Review* 72(2):30–35 [a modern descendant of Francis Bacon emotionally defends the hope of progress].

Meinel, Aden B., and Marjorie P. Meinel

    1971 "Is It Time for a New Look at Solar Energy?" *Bulletin of the Atomic Scientists* 27(8):32–37.

Mesarovic, Mihajlo, and Eduard Pestel

    1974 *Mankind at the Turning Point: The Second Report to the Club of Rome* (New York: Dutton/Reader's Digest).

Metz, William D.

    1972 "Magnetic Containment Fusion: What Are the Prospects?" *Science* 178:291–292.

    1973 "Ocean Temperature Gradients: Solar Power from the Sea," *Science* 180:1266–1267.

    1974 "Oil Shale: A Huge Resource of Low-Grade Fuel," *Science* 184:1271–1275.

    1975a "Energy Conservation: Better Living through Thermodynamics," *Science* 188:820–821.

    1975b "Energy: ERDA Stresses Multiple Sources and Conservation," *Science* 189:369–370.

Metzger, H. Peter

    1972 *The Atomic Establishment* (New York: Simon and Schuster).

Michaelis, Anthony R.

    1973 "Coping with Disaster," *Bulletin of the Atomic Scientists* 29(4):24–29.

Micklin, Philip P.

    1974 "Environmental Hazards of Nuclear Wastes," *Bulletin of the Atomic Scientists* 30(4):36–42 [a first-rate non-polemical review].

Miles, Rufus E., Jr.

    1976 *Awakening from the American Dream* (New York: Universe).

Mishan, E. J.

    1974 "The New Inflation: Its Theory and Practice," *Encounter* 42(5):12–24.

Mostert, Noel

    1974 *Supership* (New York: Knopf).

Mumford, Lewis
　　1970　*The Pentagon of Power* (New York: Harcourt Brace Jovanovich).
Murdoch, William W., ed.
　　1971　*Environment: Resources, Pollution and Society* (Stamford: Sinauer).
Mussett, Alan
　　1973　"Discovery: A Declining Asset?" *New Scientist* 60:886–889.
Naill, Roger F., et al.
　　1975　"The Transition to Coal," *Technology Review* 78(1):19–29.
Nash, Hugh
　　1974　"Nader, UCS Release Suppressed AEC Report on Reactor Safety," *Not Man Apart* 4(2):8–9.
National Academy of Sciences
　　1975　*Mineral Resources and the Environment* (Washington: National Academy of Sciences) [critical
　　　　of the U.S. Geological Survey oil and gas estimates as too high].
Nelson, Saul
　　1974　"The Looming Shortage of Primary Processing Capacity," *Challenge* 16(6):45–48.
de Nevers, Noel
　　1973　"Enforcing the Clean Air Act of 1970," *Scientific American* 228(6): 14–21.
Newell, Reginald E.
　　1974　"The Earth's Climatic History," *Technology Review* 77(2):31–45.
Nilsson, Sam
　　1974　"Energy Analysis—A More Sensitive Instrument for Determining Costs of Goods and Ser-
　　　　vices," *Ambio* 3:222–224.
Novick, Sheldon
　　1969　*The Careless Atom* (Boston: Houghton Mifflin).
　　1975　"A Troublesome Brew," *Environment* 17(4):8–11 [critique of AEC's final environmental
　　　　impact statement on the breeder].
Odell, Rice
　　1975　"Net Energy Analysis Can Be Illuminating," *Conservation Foundation Letter,* October [a
　　　　very useful brief summary of the issues].
O'Donnell, Sean
　　1974　"Ireland Turns to Peat," *New Scientist* 63:18–19 [the USSR and other countries also have
　　　　substantial supplies].
Odum, Howard T.
　　1971　*Environment, Power and Society* (New York: Wiley).
　　1973　"Energy, Ecology and Economics," *Ambio* 2:220–227.
O'Neill, Gerard K.
　　1975　"Space Colonies and Energy Supply to the Earth," *Science* 190:943–947.
Osborn, Elburt F.
　　1974　"Coal and the Present Energy Situation," *Science* 183:477–481.
Page, James K., Jr.
　　1974　"Growing Pains in Energy," *Smithsonian* 5(6):12–15.
Park, Charles F., Jr.
　　1968　*Affluence in Jeopardy: Minerals and the Political Economy* (San Francisco: Freeman, Cooper).
Patterson, Walter C.
　　1972　"The British Atom," *Environment* 14(10):2–9.
Pearl, Arthur, and Stephanie Pearl
　　1971　"Toward an Ecological Theory of Value," *Social Policy* 2(1):30–38 [thermodynamic
　　　　economics].
Perry, Harry
　　1974　"The Gasification of Coal," *Scientific American* 230(3):19–25.
Peterson, James T.
　　1973　"Energy and the Weather," *Environment* 15(8):4–9.
Platt, John R.
　　1966　*The Step to Man* (New York: Wiley) [limits of technological scale].
Pollard, William G.
　　1976　"The Long-range Prospects for Solar Energy," *American Scientist* 64:424–429 [why cen-
　　　　tralized generation of electricity using solar energy will be impractical, if not impossible].

Polunin, Nicholas
  1974 "Thoughts on Some Conceivable Ecodisasters," *Environmental Conservation* 1:177–189 [all the small but potentially lethal risks, especially in combination].
Post, Richard F.
  1971 "Fusion Power: The Uncertain Certainty," *Bulletin of the Atomic Scientists* 27(8):42–48.
————, and Stephen F. Post
  1973 "Flywheels," *Scientific American* 229(6):17–23.
————, and F. L. Ribe
  1974 "Fusion Reactors as Future Energy Sources," *Science* 186:397–407.
Price, Derek J. de Solla
  1961 *Science Since Babylon* (New Haven: Yale) ["diseases" of "big science"].
Primack, Joel, and Frank von Hippel
  1974 "Nuclear Reactor Safety: The Origins and Issues of a Vital Debate," *Bulletin of the Atomic Scientists* 30(8):5–12.
Prud'homme, Robert K.
  1974 "Automobile Emissions Abatement and Fuels Policy," *American Scientist* 62:191–199.
Pryde, Philip R., and Lucy T. Pryde
  1974 "Soviet Nuclear Power: A Different Approach to Nuclear Safety," *Environment* 16(3):26–34.
Rabinowitch, Eugene
  1969 "Responsibility of Scientists in Our Age," *Bulletin of the Atomic Scientists* 25(9):2–3, 26 [an argument—very typical in its rationale—that science and technology have abolished scarcity].
Ramseier, Rene O.
  1974 "Oil on Ice: How to Melt the Arctic and Warm the World," *Environment* 16(4):7–14.
RAND Corporation
  1973 *California's Electric Quandary* (3 vols; Santa Monica: RAND).
RANN (Research Applied to National Needs Program)
  1972 *Summary Report of the Cornell Workshop on Energy and the Environment* (Washington: Government Printing Office).
Reed, T. B., and R. M. Lerner
  1973 "Methanol: A Versatile Fuel for Immediate Use," *Science* 182:1299–1304.
Rex, Robert W.
  1971 "Geothermal Energy—The Neglected Energy Option," *Bulletin of the Atomic Scientists* 27(8):52–56.
RFF (Resources for the Future)
  1973 *Energy Research and Development—Problems and Prospects* (Washington: Government Printing Office).
Rhodes, Richard
  1974 "Los Alamos Revisited," *Harper's,* March, pp. 57–64.
Rice, Richard A.
  1974 "Toward More Transportation with Less Energy," *Technology Review* 76(4):45–53.
Ritchie-Calder, Peter R.
  1970 "Mortgaging the Old Homestead," *Foreign Affairs* 48:207–220 [supertanker problems].
Roberts, Marc J.
  1973 "Is There an Energy Crisis?" *Public Interest* 31:17–37.
Robinson, Arthur L.
  1974 "Energy Storage (II). Developing Advanced Technologies," *Science* 184:884–887
Robson, Geoffrey
  1974 "Geothermal Electricity Production," *Science* 184:371–375.
Rose, David J.
  1974a "Energy Policy in the U.S.," *Scientific American* 230(1):20–29.
  1974b "Nuclear Eclectic Power," *Science* 184:351–359.
Rubin, Milton D.
  1974 "Plugging the Energy Sieve," *Bulletin of the Atomic Scientists* 30(10):7–17.
Russell, W. M. S.
  1971 "Population and Inflation," *The Ecologist* 1(8):4–8.
SCEP (Study of Critical Environmental Problems)
  1970 *Man's Impact on the Global Environment* (Cambridge: MIT).

Schneider, Stephen H.
　　1974　"The Population Explosion: Can It Shake the Climate?" *Ambio* 3:150–155.
———, and Roger D. Dennett
　　1975　"Climatic Barriers to Long-Term Energy Growth," *Ambio* 4:65–74.
Schumacher, E. F.
　　1974　*Small Is Beautiful: Economics as if People Mattered* (New York: Harper and Row).
Scientific American
　　1971　*Energy and Power* (San Francisco: W. H. Freeman and Co.).
Seaborg, Glenn T., and William R. Corliss
　　1971　*Man and Atom: Building a New World Through Nuclear Technology* (New York: Dutton).
Shen-Miller, J.
　　1970　"Some Thoughts on the Nuclear Agro-Industrial Complex," *BioScience* 20:98–100.
Skinner, Brian J.
　　1969　*Earth Resources* (Englewood Cliffs: Prentice-Hall).
Slesser, Malcolm
　　1973　"Energy Analysis in Policy Making," *New Scientist* 60:328–330.
　　1974　"The Energy Ration," *The Ecologist* 4:139–140.
SMIC (Study of Man's Impact on Climate)
　　1971　*Inadvertent Climate Modification* (Cambridge: MIT).
Snowden, Donald P.
　　1972　"Superconductors for Power Transmission," *Scientific American* 226(4):84–91.
Sorensen, Bent
　　1975　"Energy and Resources," *Science* 189:255–260 [a solar energy economy for Denmark].
Spurgeon, David
　　1973　"Natural Power for the Third World," *New Scientist* 60:694–697.
Squires, Arthur M.
　　1974　"Coal: A Past and Future King," *Ambio* 3:1–14.
Starr, Chauncey, and Richard Rudman
　　1973　"Parameters of Technological Growth," *Science* 182:358–364.
Stein, Richard G.
　　1972　"A Matter of Design," *Environment* 14(8):17–20, 25–29.
Stent, Gunther S.
　　1969　*The Coming of the Golden Age: A View of the End of Progress* (New York: Natural History
　　　　　Press).
Stever, H. Guyford
　　1975　"Whither the NSF?—The Higher Derivatives," *Science* 189:264–267 [the growing capital
　　　　　intensity of research and development].
Strong, Maurice F.
　　1973　"One Year After Stockholm: An Ecological Approach to Management," *Foreign Affairs*
　　　　　51(4):690–707.
Stunkel, Kenneth R.
　　1973　"The Technological Solution," *Bulletin of the Atomic Scientists* 29(7):42–44.
Tamplin, Arthur R.
　　1973　"Solar Energy," *Environment* 15(5):16–20, 32–34 [one of the best short reviews; extensive
　　　　　citations].
Taylor, Theodore B., and Charles C. Humpstone
　　1973　*The Restoration of the Earth* (New York: Harper and Row).
UNESCO
　　1973　"Appropriate Technology," a special issue of *Impact of Science on Society* 23:251–352.
United Nations
　　1961　*Proceedings of the Conference on New Sources of Energy* (6 vols; Rome: United Nations)
　　　　　[extensive discussions of wind, tide, and sun as sources of power].
Vacca, Roberto
　　1973　*The Coming Dark Age,* trans. J. S. Whale (Garden City, N.Y.: Doubleday) [an alarmist view
　　　　　of the industrial system's intrinsic instability].
Wade, Nicholas
　　1974　"Windmills: The Resurrection of an Ancient Energy Technology," *Science* 184:1055–1058.

Walsh, John
1974 "Uranium Enrichment: Both the Americans and Europeans Must Decide Where to Get the Nuclear Fuel of the 1980's," *Science* 184:1160–1161.
Wanniski, Jude
1975 "The Mundell-Laffer Hypothesis—A New View of the World Economy," *Public Interest* 39:31–52 [scarcity and inflation].
Waters, W. G., II
1973 "Landing a Man Downtown," *Bulletin of the Atomic Scientists* 29(9):34–35 [how environmental management differs from space programs].
Watt, Kenneth E. F.
1974 *The Titanic Effect: Planning for the Unthinkable* (Stamford, Conn.: Sinauer).
Weinberg, Alvin M.
1972 "Science and Trans-Science," *Minerva* 10:209–222.
1973 "Technology and Ecology Is There a Need for Confrontation?" *BioScience* 23:41–45.
1974 "Global Effects of Man's Production of Energy," *Science* 186:205.
Wentorf, R. H., Jr., and R. E. Hanneman
1974 "Thermochemical Hydrogen Generation," *Science* 185:311–319.
Westman, Walter E., and Roger M. Gifford
1973 "Environmental Impact: Controlling the Overall Level," *Science* 181:819–825 [with an energy currency].
Whittemore, F. Case
1973 "How Much in Reserve?" *Environment* 15(7):16–20, 31–35.
Wilkinson, John
1974 "A Modest Proposal for Recycling Our Junk Heap Society," *Center Report* 7(3):7–12 [a computer simulation suggests that future living standards will resemble those of the early 1900's].
Willrich, Mason, and Theodore B. Taylor
1974 *Nuclear Theft: Risks and Safeguards* (Cambridge: Ballinger).
Wilson, Richard
1973 "Natural Gas Is a Beautiful Thing?" *Bulletin of the Atomic Scientists* 29(7):35–40.
Winsche, W. E., et al.
1973 "Hydrogen: Its Future Role in the Nation's Energy Economy," *Science* 180:1325–1332.
Wolf, Martin
1974 "Solar Energy Utilization by Physical Methods," *Science* 184:382–386.
Wood, Lowell, and John Nuckolls
1972 "Fusion Power," *Environment* 14(4):29–33.
Wright, John, and John Syrett
1975 "Energy Analysis of Nuclear Power," *New Scientist* 65:66–67.
Young, Louise B., and H. Peyton Young
1974 "Pollution by Electrical Transmission: The Environmental Impact of High Voltage Lines," *Bulletin of the Atomic Scientists* 30(10):34–38.

CHAPTER 4

Attah, Ernest B.
1973 "Racial Aspects of Zero Population Growth," *Science* 180:1143–1151.
Barker, Ernst, trans.
1962 *The Politics of Aristotle* (New York: Oxford).
Barnett, Larry D.
1971 "Zero Population Growth, Inc.," *BioScience* 21:759–765.
Bell, Daniel
1973 *The Coming of Post-Industrial Society: A Venture in Social Forecasting* (New York: Basic Books).
Berlin, Isaiah
1969 *Four Essays on Liberty* (New York: Oxford).

Brown, Harrison
    1954 *The Challenge of Man's Future* (New York: Viking).
Buchanan, James
    1969 *The Demand and Supply of Public Goods* (Chicago: Rand McNally).
Burch, William R., Jr.
    1971 *Daydreams and Nightmares: A Sociological Essay on the American Environment* (New York: Harper and Row).
Butler, Samuel
    1872 *Erewhon* (New York: Signet, 1960).
Callahan, Daniel J.
    1973 *The Tyranny of Survival; and Other Pathologies of Civilized Life* (New York: Macmillan).
Carney, Francis
    1972 "Schlockology," *New York Review of Books,* June 1, pp. 26–29.
Chamberlin, Neil W.
    1970 *Beyond Malthus: Population and Power* (New York: Basic Books).
Christy, Francis T., Jr., and Anthony Scott
    1965 *The Common Wealth in Ocean Fisheries* (Baltimore: Johns Hopkins).
Cohen, David
    1973 "Chemical Castration," *New Scientist* 57:525–526.
Cornford, Francis M., trans.
    1945 *The Republic of Plato* (New York: Oxford).
Crowe, Beryl L.
    1969 "The Tragedy of the Commons Revisited," *Science* 166:1103–1107.
Dahl, Robert A.
    1970 *After the Revolution?: Authority in a Good Society* (New Haven: Yale).
Delgado, Jose Manuel R.
    1969 *Physical Control of the Mind: Toward a Psychocivilized Society* (New York: Harper and Row).
Eisner, Thomas, Ari van Tienhaven, and Frank Rosenblatt
    1970 "Population Control, Sterilization, and Ignorance," *Science* 167:337.
Ellul, Jacques
    1967 *The Technological Society* (rev.; New York: Knopf).
Fife, Daniel
    1971 "Killing the Goose," *Environment* 13(3):20–27 [the logic of the commons].
Forster, E. M.
    1928 *The Eternal Moment* (New York: Harcourt, Brace).
Fuller, R. Buckminster
    1968 "An Operating Manual for Spaceship Earth" in *Environment and Change: The Next Fifty Years,* ed. William R. Ewald, Jr. (Bloomington: Indiana).
    1969 "Vertical Is to Live, Horizontal Is to Die," *American Scholar* 39(1):27–47.
Geesaman, Donald P., and Dean E. Abrahamson
    1974 "The Dilemma of Fission Power," *Bulletin of the Atomic Scientists* 30(9):37–41 [the extreme security measures a nuclear power economy will require].
Haefele, Edwin T., ed.
    1975 *The Governance of Common Property Resources* (Baltimore: Johns Hopkins).
Hardin, Garrett
    1968 "The Tragedy of the Commons," *Science* 162:1243–1248.
    1972 *Exploring New Ethics for Survival* (New York: Viking).
————, ed.
    1969 *Population, Evolution, and Birth Control: A Collage of Controversial Ideas* (2nd ed.; San Francisco: W. H. Freeman and Co.).
Heilbroner, Robert L.
    1974 *An Inquiry into the Human Prospect* (New York: Norton).
Hobbes, Thomas
    1651 *Leviathan, or the Matter, Form and Power of a Commonwealth, ecclesiastical and civil,* ed. H. W. Schneider (Indianapolis: Bobbs-Merrill, 1958).
Holden, Constance
    1973 "Psychosurgery: Legitimate Therapy or Laundered Lobotomy?" *Science* 179:1109–1114.

Huxley, Aldous L.

   1932   *Brave New World* (New York: Modern Library, 1956).

   1958   *Brave New World Revisited* (New York: Harper).

Illich, Ivan

   1973   *Tools for Conviviality* (New York: Harper and Row).

Kahn, Alfred E.

   1966   "The Tyranny of Small Decisions: Market Failures, Imperfections, and the Limits of Economics," *Kyklos* 19(1):23–47 [the logic of the commons].

Kahn, Herman, and Anthony J. Wiener

   1968   "Faustian Powers and Human Choice: Some Twenty-First Century Technological and Economic Issues" in *Environment and Choice,* ed. William R. Ewald, Jr. (Bloomington: Indiana), pp. 101–131.

Kass, Leon R.

   1971   "The New Biology: What Price Relieving Man's Estate?" *Science* 174:779–788.

   1972   "Making Babies—The New Biology and the 'Old' Morality," *Public Interest* 26:18–56.

Lewis, C. S.

   1965   *The Abolition of Man* (New York: Macmillan).

Locke, John

   1690   *Second Treatise,* in *Two Treatises of Government,* ed. Peter Laslett (New York: New American Library, 1965).

McDermott, John

   1969   "Technology: The Opiate of the Intellectuals," *New York Review of Books,* July 31, pp. 25–35.

Michael, Donald N.

   1970   *The Unprepared Society: Planning for a Precarious Future* (New York: Harper and Row).

Morrison, Denton E., Kenneth E. Hornback, and W. Keith Warner

   1974   *Environment: A Bibliography of Social Science and Related Literature* (Washington: GPO).

   1975   *Energy: A Bibliography of Social Science and Related Literature* (New York: Garland).

Myers, Norman

   1975   "The Whaling Controversy," *American Scientist* 63:448–455 [an excellent case study of the kinds of pressures that promote overexploitation].

Odell, Rice

   1975   "How Will We React to an Age of Scarcity?" *Conservation Foundation Letter,* January [a review of many different opinions].

Olson, Mancur, Jr.

   1968   *The Logic of Collective Action: Public Goods and the Theory of Groups* (New York: Schocken).

————, and Hans Landsberg, eds.

   1973   *The No-Growth Society* (New York: Norton).

Ophuls, William

   1973   "Leviathan or Oblivion?" in *Toward a Steady-State Economy,* ed. Herman E. Daly (San Francisco: W. H. Freeman and Co.), pp. 215–230.

Orwell, George

   1963   *Nineteen Eighty-Four: Text, Sources, Criticism,* ed. Irving Howe (New York: Harcourt, Brace and World).

Pirages, Dennis C., and Paul R. Ehrlich

   1974   *Ark II: Social Response to Environmental Imperatives* (San Francisco: W. H. Freeman and Company).

Popper, Karl R.

   1966   *The Open Society and Its Enemies* (2 vols, 5th ed., rev.; Princeton University Press).

Reich, Charles A.

   1971   *The Greening of America* (New York: Random House).

Rousseau, Jean-Jacques

   1762   *The Social Contract,* ed. Charles Frankel (New York: Hafner, 1947).

Russett, Bruce M., and John D. Sullivan

   1971   "Collective Goods and International Organization," *International Organization* 25:845–865.

Schelling, Thomas C.

   1971   "On the Ecology of Micromotives," *Public Interest* 25:61–98.

Skinner, B. F.
    1971 *Beyond Freedom and Dignity* (New York: Knopf).
Smith, Adam
    1776 *An Inquiry into the Nature and Causes of the Wealth of Nations,* ed. Edwin Cannan (New York: Modern Library, 1937).
Speth, J. Gustave, Arthur R. Tamplin, and Thomas B. Cochran
    1974 "Plutonium Recycle: The Fateful Step," *Bulletin of the Atomic Scientists* 30(9):15–22.
Stillman, Peter G.
    1975 "The Tragedy of the Commons: A Re-Analysis," *Alternatives* 4(2):12–15.
Stone, Christopher D.
    1974 *Should Trees Have Standing?: Toward Legal Rights for Natural Objects* (Los Altos, Calif.: William Kaufmann).
Susskind, Charles
    1973 *Understanding Technology* (Baltimore: Johns Hopkins).
Tuan, Yi-Fu
    1970 "Our Treatment of the Environment in Ideal and Actuality," *American Scientist* 58:244–249 [the Chinese and their environment through history].
Wade, Nicholas
    1974 "Sahelian Drought: No Victory for Western Aid," *Science* 185:234–237 [how an aid program destroyed the traditional controls on a common—with catastrophic results].
Webb, Walter Prescott
    1952 *The Great Frontier* (Boston: Houghton Mifflin).
Weinberg, Alvin M.
    1972a "Social Institutions and Nuclear Energy," *Science* 177:27–34.
    1972b Review of John Holdren and Philip Herrera, *Energy: A Crisis in Power,* in *American Scientist* 60:775–776.
    1973 "Technology and Ecology—Is There a Need for Confrontation?" *BioScience* 23:41–46.
White, Lynn, Jr.
    1967 "The Historical Roots of Our Ecologic Crisis," *Science* 155:1203–1207.
Wilkinson, Richard G.
    1973 *Poverty and Progress: An Ecological Perspective on Economic Development* (New York: Praeger).
Willrich, Mason
    1975 "Terrorists Keep Out!: The Problem of Safeguarding Nuclear Materials in a World of Malfunctioning People," *Bulletin of the Atomic Scientists* 31(5):12–16.
Wynne-Edwards, V. C.
    1970 "Self-Regulatory Systems in Populations of Animals," in *The Subversive Science,* ed. Paul Shepard and Daniel McKinley (Boston: Houghton Mifflin), pp. 99–111 [valuable biological perspective on the tragedy of the commons].

CHAPTER 5

Abrahamson, Dean E.
    1974a "Energy: All in the Family," *Environment* 16(7):50–52.
    1974b "Energy: Sidestepping NEPA Reviews," *Environment* 16(9):39.
Anderson, Frederick R., and Robert H. Daniels
    1973 *NEPA in the Courts: A Legal Analysis of the National Environmental Policy Act* (Baltimore: Johns Hopkins).
Ayres, Robert U., and Allen V. Kneese
    1969 "Production, Consumption, and Externalities," *American Economic Review* 59:282–297 [Kneese et al. 1970 in a nutshell].
Barnett, Harold J., and Chandler Morse
    1963 *Scarcity and Growth: The Economics of Natural Resource Availability* (Baltimore: Johns Hopkins).
Beckerman, Wilfred
    1974 *In Defence of Economic Growth* (London: Cape).

Bell, Daniel
    1971 "The Corporation and Society in the 1970's," *Public Interest* 24:5–32.
Boguslaw, Robert
    1965 *The New Utopians* (Englewood Cliffs, N.J.: Prentice-Hall).
Boulding, Kenneth E.
    1949 "Income or Welfare?" *Review of Economic Studies* 17:77–86.
    1966 "The Economics of the Coming Spaceship Earth," in *Environmental Quality in a Growing Economy,* ed. Henry Jarrett (Baltimore: Johns Hopkins), pp. 3–14.
    1967 "Fun and Games with the Gross National Product—The Role of Misleading Indicators in Social Policy," in *The Environmental Crisis,* ed. Harold W. Helfrich, Jr. (New Haven: Yale), pp. 157–170.
    1970 *Economics as a Science* (New York: McGraw-Hill), Chap. 7.
Brooks, Harvey, and Raymond Bowers
    1971 "The Assessment of Technology" in *Man and the Ecosphere,* ed. Paul R. Ehrlich, John P. Holdren, and Richard W. Holm (San Francisco: W. H. Freeman and Co.).
Carter, Luther J.
    1973 "Alaska Pipeline: Congress Deaf to Environmentalists," *Science* 179:1310–1312, 1350.
Clark, Colin W.
    1973 "The Economics of Overexploitation," *Science* 181:630–634.
Commoner, Barry
    1973 "Trains into Flowers," *Harper's,* December, pp. 78–86 [why trains cannot compete with the auto].
Conservation Foundation
    1971 "Indiscriminate Economic Growth, Measured with Little Regard for Environmental Costs and Social Well-Being, Is Challenged," *CF Letter,* May.
    1972 "NEPA Challenges the Nation's Plans and Priorities—But Progress Is Slow, and Some Are Reacting Against It," *CF Letter,* May.
Culbertson, John M.
    1971 *Economic Development: An Ecological Approach* (New York: Knopf).
Dales, J. H.
    1968 *Pollution, Property and Prices: An Essay in Policy-Making and Economics* (University of Toronto Press).
Daly, Herman E., ed.
    1973 *Toward a Steady-State Economy* (San Francisco: W. H. Freeman and Co.).
Dolan, Edwin G.
    1971 *TANSTAAFL: The Economic Strategy for Ecologic Crisis* (New York: Holt, Rinehart and Winston).
Edel, Matthew
    1973 *Economies and the Environment* (Englewood Cliffs, N.J.: Prentice-Hall).
Freeman, A. Myrick, and Robert H. Haveman
    1972 "Clean Rhetoric and Dirty Water," *Public Interest* 28:51–65.
Freeman, A. Myrick, Robert H. Haveman, and Allen V. Kneese
    1973 *The Economics of Environmental Policy* (New York: Wiley).
Gabor, Dennis
    1972 *The Mature Society* (London: Secker and Warburg).
Galbraith, John K.
    1958 *The Affluent Society* (Boston: Houghton Mifflin).
    1967 *The New Industrial State* (Boston: Houghton Mifflin).
Garvey, Gerald
    1972 *Energy, Ecology, Economy: A Framework for Environmental Policy* (New York: Norton).
Gillette, Robert
    1972 "National Environmental Policy Act: Signs of Backlash Are Evident," *Science* 176:30–33.
Hagevik, George
    1971 "Legislating for Air Quality Management," in *The Politics of Ecosuicide,* ed. Leslie L. Roos, Jr. (New York: Holt, Rinehart and Winston), pp. 311–345. [Excellent on the difficulties of internalizing costs.]

Hardesty, John, Norris C. Clement, and Clinton E. Jencks
    1971   "The Political Economy of Environmental Disruption," in *Economic Growth vs. the Environment,* ed. Warren E. Johnson and John Hardesty (Belmont, Calif.: Wadsworth), pp. 85–106.

Hardin, Garrett
    1972   *Exploring New Ethics for Survival* (New York: Viking).

Harnik, Peter
    1973   "The Biggest Going-Out-of-Business Sale of All Time," *Environmental Action,* September 1, pp. 9–12.

Hays, Samuel P.
    1959   *Conservation and the Gospel of Efficiency* (Cambridge: Harvard).

Heller, Walter W.
    1973   *Economic Growth and Environmental Quality: Collision or Co-Existence?* (Morristown, N.J.: General Learning Press).

Henderson, Hazel
    1976   "The End of Economics," *The Ecologist* 6:137–146 [a first-rate critique by an important radical economist; a valuable supplement to the argument of this chapter, with useful references to her own previous work and to the work of others].

Hirschman, Albert O.
    1967   *Development Projects Observed* (Washington: Brookings Institute) [the hidden costs of development].

Kapp, K. William
    1950   *The Social Costs of Private Enterprise* (New York: Schocken, 1971).

Klausener, Samuel Z.
    1971   *On Man and His Environment* (San Francisco: Jossey-Bass) [an attempt to come to terms with some of the sociological externalities of development].

Kneese, Allen V.
    1973   "The Faustian Bargain: Benefit-Cost Analysis and Unscheduled Events in the Nuclear Fuel Cycle," *Resources* 44:1–5.

———, Robert U. Ayres, and Ralph C. d'Arge
    1970   *Economics and Environment: A Materials Balance Approach* (Baltimore: Johns Hopkins).

Kraus, James
    1974   "American Environmental Case Law: An Update," *Alternatives* 3(2):25–30.

Krieger, Martin H.
    1973   "What's Wrong with Plastic Trees," *Science* 179:446–455 [the perversities of pure economic analysis].

Krieth, Frank
    1973   "Lack of Impact," *Environment* 15(1):26–33.

Mishan, Ezra J.
    1969   *Technology and Growth: The Price We Pay* (New York: Praeger).
    1971   "On Making the Future Safe for Mankind," *Public Interest* 24:33–61.

Novick, Sheldon
    1974   "Nuclear Breeders," *Environment* 16(6):6–15.

Odell, Rice
    1973   "Environmental Politicking—Business as Usual," *Conservation Foundation Letter,* August.

Passell, Peter, and Leonard Ross
    1973   *The Retreat from Riches: Affluence and Its Enemies* (New York: Viking).

Pearce, David
    1973   "Is Ecology Elitist?" *The Ecologist* 3:61–63.

Polanyi, Karl
    1944   *The Great Transformation* (Boston: Beacon).

Ridker, Ronald G.
    1972   "Population and Pollution in the United States," *Science* 176:1085–1090.

Rothman, Harry
    1972   *Murderous Providence: A Study of Pollution in Industrial Societies* (New York: Bobbs-Merrill).

Ruff, Larry E.
    1970   "The Economic Common Sense of Pollution," *Public Interest* 19:69–85.

Sachs, Ignacy
  1971 "Approaches to a Political Economy of Environment," *Social Science Information* 5(5):47–58 [a very perceptive brief overview of the clash between market traditionalists and the new economic holists].
Stone, Richard
  1972 "The Evaluation of Pollution: Balancing Gains and Losses," *Minerva* 10:412–425.
Tribe, Lawrence H.
  1971 "Legal Frameworks for the Assessment and Control of Technology," *Minerva* 9:243–255.
Tsuru, Shigeto
  1971 "In Place of GNP," *Social Science Information* 10(4):7–21 [an especially good discussion of the drawbacks of GNP as an indicator].
UNESCO
  1973 "The Social Assessment of Technology," special issue of *International Social Science Journal* 25(3).
Weisskopf, Walter A.
  1971 *Alienation and Economics* (New York: Dutton).
Wildavsky, Aaron
  1967 "Aesthetic Power or the Triumph of the Sensitive Minority over the Vulgar Mass: A Political Analysis of the New Economics," *Daedalus* 96:1115–1128.
Wilkinson, Richard G.
  1973 *Poverty and Progress: An Ecological Perspective on Economic Development* (New York: Praeger).
Winner, Langdon
  1972 "On Controlling Technology," *Public Policy* 20:35–59.
Wollman, Nathaniel
  1967 "The New Economics of Resources," *Daedalus* 96:1099–1114.

CHAPTER 6

Abelson, Philip H.
  1972a "Environmental Quality," *Science* 177:655.
  1972b "Federal Statistics," *Science* 175:1315.
Bachrach, Peter
  1967 *The Theory of Democratic Elitism: A Critique* (Boston: Little, Brown).
Bell, Daniel
  1974 "The Public Household—On 'Fiscal Sociology' and the Liberal Society," *Public Interest* 37:29–68.
Brown, Harrison, James Bonner, and John Weir
  1963 *The Next Hundred Years* (New York: Viking) [esp. Chaps. 14–17, which discuss manpower].
Bruce-Briggs, B.
  1974 "Against the Neo-Malthusians," *Commentary*, July, pp. 25–29.
Burch, William R., Jr.
  1971 *Daydreams and Nightmares: A Sociological Essay on the American Environment* (New York: Harper and Row).
Caldwell, Lynton K.
  1971 *Environment: A Challenge to Modern Society* (Garden City, N.Y.: Doubleday).
———, and Toufiq A. Siddiqi
  1974 *Environmental Policy, Law, and Administration: A Guide to Advanced Study* (Bloomington: University of Indiana School of Public and Environmental Affairs).
Carpenter, Richard A.
  1972 "National Goals and Environmental Laws," *Technology Review* 74(3):58–63.
Carter, Luther J.
  1973a "Environment: A Lesson for the People of Plenty," *Science* 182:1323–1324.
  1973b "Environmental Law (I): Maturing Field for Lawyers and Scientists," *Science* 179:1205–1209.
  1973c "Environmental Law (II): A Strategic Weapon Against Degradation?" *Science* 179:1310–1312, 1350.

1973d   "Pesticides: Environmentalists Seek New Victory in a Frustrating War," *Science* 181:143–145.

1974a   "Cancer and the Environment (I): A Creaky System Grinds On," *Science* 186:239–242.

1974b   "Con Edison: Endless Storm King Dispute Adds to Its Troubles," *Science* 184:1353–1358.

1974c   "The Energy Bureaucracy: The Pieces Fall into Place," *Science* 185:44–45.

1974d   "Energy: Cannibalism in the Bureaucracy," *Science* 186:511.

1974e   "Pollution and Public Health: Taconite Case Poses Major Test," *Science* 186:31–36.

1975a   "The Environment: A 'Mature' Cause in Need of a Lift," *Science* 187:45–48.

1975b   *The Florida Experience: Land and Water Policy in a Growth State* (Baltimore: Johns Hopkins).

Cohn, Victor

1975   "The Washington Energy Show," *Technology Review* 77(3):8, 68.

Conservation Foundation

1972   "Wanted: A Coordinated, Coherent National Energy Policy Geared to the Public Interest," *CF Letter*, No. 6–72.

Cooley, Richard A., and Geoffrey Wandesforde-Smith, eds.

1970   *Congress and the Environment* (Seattle: Washington).

Crossland, Janice

1974   "Cars, Fuel, and Pollution," *Environment* 16(2):15–27.

Dahl, Robert A.

1970   *After the Revolution?: Authority in a Good Society* (New Haven: Yale).

Davies, Barbara S., and Clarence J. Davies, III

1975   *The Politics of Pollution* (2nd ed.; New York: Pegasus).

Davis, David H.

1974   *Energy Politics* (New York: St. Martin's).

Dexter, Lewis A.

1969   *The Sociology and Politics of Congress* (Chicago: Rand McNally).

Downs, Anthony

1972   "Up and Down with Ecology—The 'Issue-Attention Cycle,' " *Public Interest* 28:38–50.

Dror, Yehezkel

1968   *Public Policymaking Reexamined* (San Francisco: Chandler).

Edelman, Murray

1964   *The Symbolic Uses of Politics* (Urbana: Illinois).

Forrester, Jay W.

1971   *World Dynamics* (Cambridge: Wright-Allen) [esp. Chaps. 1 and 7 for a radical critique of nonsystematic, incremental decision making].

Forsythe, Dall W.

1974   "An Energy-Scarce Society: The Politics and Possibilities," *Working Papers for a New Society* 2(1):3–12 [an excellent short analysis].

Gillette, Robert

1973a   "Energy: The Muddle at the Top," *Science* 182:1319–1321.

1973b   "Western Coal: Does the Debate Follow Irreversible Commitment?" *Science* 182:456–458.

1975   "In Energy Impasse, Conservation Keeps Popping Up," *Science* 187:42–45.

Goldstein, Paul, and Robert Ford

1973   "On the Control of Air Quality: Why the Laws Don't Work," *Bulletin of the Atomic Scientists* 29(6):31–34.

Green, Charles S., III

1973   "Politics, Equality and the End of Progress," *Alternatives* 2(2):4–9.

Haefele, Edwin T.

1974   *Representative Government and Environmental Management* (Baltimore: Johns Hopkins).

Hartz, Louis

1955   *The Liberal Tradition in America: An Interpretation of American Political Thought Since the Revolution* (New York: Harcourt, Brace).

Henning, Daniel H.

1974   *Environmental Policy and Administration* (New York: American Elsevier).

Hirschman, Albert O.

1970   *Exit, Voice and Loyalty* (Cambridge: Harvard) [esp. Chap. 8 on frontier-style decision making and problem avoidance].

Horowitz, Irving L.

1972 "The Environmental Cleavage: Social Ecology versus Political Economy," *Social Theory and Practice* 2(1):125–134.

Jacobsen, Sally

1974 "Anti-Pollution Backlash in Illinois: Can a Tough Protection Program Survive?" *Bulletin of the Atomic Scientists* 30(1):39–44.

Jones, Charles O.

1975 *Clean Air: The Policies and Politics of Pollution Control* (University of Pittsburgh Press).

Kohlmeier, Louis M., Jr.

1969 *The Regulators: Watchdog Agencies and the Public Interest* (New York: Harper and Row).

Kraft, Michael

1972 "Congressional Attitudes Toward the Environment," *Alternatives* 1(4):27–37 [congressional avoidance of the environmental issue].

1974 "Ecological Politics and American Government: A Review Essay," in Nagel 1974, pp. 139–159 [the best critical review of the political science literature in the light of environmental problems].

Lecht, L. A.

1966 *Goals, Priorities and Dollars* (New York: Free Press).

1969 *Manpower Needs for National Goals in the 1970's* (New York: Praeger).

Lewis, Richard

1972 *The Nuclear Power Rebellion* (New York: Viking).

Lindblom, Charles E.

1965 *The Intelligence of Democracy: Decisionmaking Through Mutual Adjustment* (New York: Free Press).

1969 "The Science of 'Muddling Through,' " *Public Administration Review* 19(2):79–88.

Little, Charles E.

1973 "The Environment of the Poor: Who Gives a Damn?" *Conservation Foundation Letter,* July.

Loveridge, Ronald O.

1971 "Political Science and Air Pollution: A Review and Assessment of the Literature," in *Air Pollution and the Social Sciences,* ed. Paul B. Downing (New York: Praeger), pp. 45–85 [why we are not coping with the problem].

1972 "The Environment: New Priorities and Old Politics," in *People and Politics in Urban Society,* ed. Harlan Hahn (Los Angeles: Sage), pp. 499–529.

Lowi, Theodore

1969 *The End of Liberalism: Ideology, Policy, and the Crisis of Public Authority* (New York: Norton).

McConnell, Grant

1966 *Private Power and American Democracy* (New York: Knopf).

McLane, James

1974 "Energy Goals and Institutional Reform," *The Futurist* 8:239–242.

Michael, Donald N.

1968 *The Unprepared Society: Planning for a Precarious Future* (New York: Harper and Row).

Miller, John C.

1957 *Origins of the American Revolution* (Stanford University Press).

Moorman, James W.

1974 "Bureaucracy v The Law," *Sierra Club Bulletin* 59(9):7–10 [how agencies evade or flout their legal responsibilities].

Murphy, Earl F.

1967 *Governing Nature* (Chicago: Quadrangle).

Nagel, Stuart S., ed.

1974 *Environmental Politics* (New York: Praeger).

Nelkin, Dorothy

1974 "The Role of Experts in a Nuclear Siting Controversy," *Bulletin of the Atomic Scientists* 30(9):29–36.

Neuhaus, Richard

1971 *In Defense of People* (New York: Macmillan).

de Nevers, Noel

1973 "Enforcing the Clean Air Act of 1970," *Scientific American* 228(6):14–21.

Odell, Rice
    1975a "Automobiles Keep Posing New Dilemmas," *Conservation Foundation Letter,* March.
    1975b "Should Americans Be Pried Out of Their Cars?" *Conservation Foundation Letter,* April.
Pirages, Dennis C., and Paul R. Ehrlich
    1974 *Ark II: Social Response to Environmental Imperatives* (San Francisco: W. H. Freeman and Co.).
Platt, John
    1969 "What We Must Do," *Science* 166:1115–1121.
Potter, David M.
    1954 *People of Plenty: Economic Abundance and the American Character* (University of Chicago).
Quarles, John
    1974 "Fighting the Corporate Lobby," *Environmental Action,* December 7, pp. 3–6 [how the political and other resources of corporations overwhelm the environmental regulators].
Quigg, Philip W.
    1974 "Energy Shortage Spurs Expansion of Nuclear Fission," *World Environment Newsletter* in *S/R World,* June 29, pp. 21–22.
Roos, Leslie L., Jr., ed.
    1971 *The Politics of Ecosuicide* (New York: Holt, Rinehart and Winston).
Rose, David J.
    1974 "Energy Policy in the U.S.," *Scientific American* 230(1):20–29.
Rosenbaum, Walter A.
    1973 *The Politics of Environmental Concern* (New York: Praeger).
Ross, Charles R.
    1970 "The Federal Government as an Inadvertent Advocate of Environmental Degradation," in *The Environmental Crisis,* ed. Harold W. Helfrich, Jr. (New Haven: Yale), pp. 171–187.
Ross, Douglas, and Harold Wolman
    1971 "Congress and Pollution—The Gentleman's Agreement," in *Economic Growth vs. the Environment,* ed. Warren A. Johnson and John Hardesty (Belmont, Calif.: Wadsworth), pp. 134–144.
Schick, Allen
    1971 "Systems Politics and Systems Budgeting," in Roos 1971, pp. 135–158.
Shapley, Deborah
    1973 "Auto Pollution: Research Group Charged with Conflict of Interest," *Science* 181:732–735.
Shubik, Martin
    1967 "Information, Rationality, and Free Choice in a Future Democratic Society," *Daedalus* 96:771–778.
Sills, David L.
    1975 "The Environmental Movement and Its Critics," *Human Ecology* 3:1–41.
Smith, Adam
    1776 *An Inquiry into the Nature and Causes of the Wealth of Nations,* ed. Edwin Cannan (New York: Modern Library, 1937).
Smith, James N., ed.
    1974 *Environmental Quality and Social Justice* (Washington, D.C.: Conservation Foundation).
Sprout, Harold, and Margaret Sprout
    1971 *Ecology and Politics in America: Some Issues and Alternatives* (New York: General Learning Press).
    1972 "National Priorities: Demands, Resources, Dilemmas," *World Politics* 24:293–317.
White, Lawrence J.
    1973 "The Auto Pollution Muddle," *Public Interest* 32:97–112.
Wolff, Robert Paul
    1968 *The Poverty of Liberalism* (Boston: Beacon).

CHAPTER 7

Anon.
    1974 "Take Water and Heat from Third World," *New Scientist* 62:549.
d'Arge, Ralph C., and Allen V. Kneese
    1972 "Environmental Quality and International Trade," *International Organization* 26:419–465.

Banks, Fred
    1974   "Copper Is Not Oil," *New Scientist* 63:255–257.
Barraclough, Geoffrey
    1975a   "The Great World Crisis," *New York Review of Books,* January 23, pp. 20–30.
    1975b   "Wealth and Power: The Politics of Food and Oil," *New York Review of Books,* August 7,
                pp. 23–30.
Baxter, William F., et al.
    1973   Special issue on Stockholm Conference, *Stanford Journal of International Studies* 18:1–153.
Bennett, John W., Sukehiro Hasegawa, and Solomon B. Levine
    1973   "Japan: Are There Limits to Growth?" *Environment* 15(10):6–13.
Bergsten, C. Fred
    1974   "The New Era in World Commodity Markets," *Challenge* 17(4):34–42.
Boserup, Mogens
    1975   "Sharing Is a Myth," *Development Forum* 3(2):1–2.
Brower, David, et al.
    1972   "The Stockholm Conference," *Not Man Apart* 2(7):1–11.
Brown, Lester R.
    1972   *World Without Borders* (New York: Random House).
Brown, Seyom, and Larry L. Fabian
    1974   "Diplomats at Sea," *Foreign Affairs* 52:301–321.
Caldwell, Lynton K.
    1972   *In Defense of Earth: International Protection of the Biosphere* (Bloomington: Indiana).
Castro, Joao A. de A.
    1972   "Environment and Development: The Case of the Developing Countries," *International Or-
                ganization* 26:401–416.
CESI (Center for Economic and Social Information)
    1974   "Oil and the Poor Countries," *Environment* 16(2):10–14.
Clawson, Marion
    1971   "Economic Development and Environmental Impact: International Aspects," *Social Science
                Information* 10(4):23–43.
Connelly, Philip, and Robert Perlman
    1975   *The Politics of Scarcity: Resource Conflicts in International Relations* (New York: Oxford).
Cox, Richard H.
    1960   *Locke on War and Peace* (Oxford: University Press).
Enloe, Cynthia
    1975   *The Politics of Pollution in Comparative Perspective: Ecology and Power in Four Nations*
                (New York: McKay).
Enviro/Info
    1973   *Stockholm '72: A Bibliography of Selected Post-Conference Articles and Documents on the
                United Nations Conference on the Human Environment* (Green Bay, Wisc.: Enviro/Info).
Epstein, William
    1975   "The Proliferation of Nuclear Weapons," *Scientific American* 232(4):18–33.
Falk, Richard A.
    1971   *This Endangered Planet* (New York: Random House).
    1975   "Toward a New World Order: Modest Methods and Drastic Visions" in *On the Creation of a
                Just World Order: Preferred Worlds for the 1990's,* ed. Saul H. Mendlovitz (New York: Free
                Press), pp. 253–300.
Farvar, M. Taghi, and Theodore N. Soule
    1973   *International Development and the Human Environment: An Annotated Bibliography* (River-
                side, N.J.: Macmillan Information).
Finsterbusch, Gail W.
    1973   "International Cooperation Is Picking Up Steam," *Conservation Foundation Letter,* Sep-
                tember.
Fyodorov, Yevgeny
    1973   "Against the Limits of Growth," *New Scientist* 57:431–432 [abridged from *Kommunist,* No.
                14].

Goldman, Marshall I.
    1970 "The Convergence of Environmental Disruption," *Science* 170:37–42 [a synopsis of Goldman 1972].
    1972 *The Spoils of Progress: Environmental Pollution in the Soviet Union* (Cambridge: MIT).
Goldsmith, Edward, et al.
    1972 "Critique of the Stockholm Conference," *The Ecologist* 2(6):1–42.
Graubard, Stephen R., et al.
    1975 "The Oil Crisis: In Perspective," special issue of *Daedalus* 104(4).
Hardin, Garrett
    1974 "Living in a Lifeboat," *BioScience* 24:561–568 [a controversial proposal for American ecological autarky].
Harding, James A.
    1974 "Ecology as Ideology," *Alternatives* 3(4):18–22.
Heilbroner, Robert L.
    1974 *An Inquiry into the Human Prospect* (New York: Norton).
Holt, S. J.
    1974 "Prescription for the Mediterranean: International Cooperation for a Sick Sea," *Environment* 16(4):28–33.
Kay, David A., and Eugene B. Skolnikoff, eds.
    1972 *World Eco-Crisis: International Organizations in Response* (Madison: Wisconsin).
Kelley, Donald, Kenneth R. Stunkel, and Richard R. Wescott
    1976 *The Economic Superpowers and the Environment* (San Francisco: W. H. Freeman and Co.).
Kiseleva, Galina
    1974 "A Soviet View: The Earth and Population," *Development Forum* 2(4):9.
Kristoferson, Lars, ed.
    1975 Special issue on "War and Environment," *Ambio* 4:178–244 [a first-rate treatment].
Laurie, Peter, et al.
    1975 "Towards a Self-Sufficient Britain?", symposium in *New Scientist* 65:690, 695–710.
MacDonald, Gordon J.
    1975 "Weather Modification as a Weapon," *Technology Review* 78(1):57–63.
Miller, Willard M.
    1972 "Radical Environmentalism," *Not Man Apart* 2(11):14–15 [socialism as the answer].
Mikesell, Raymond F.
    1974 "More Third World Cartels Ahead?" *Challenge* 17(5):24–31.
Nash, A. E. Keir
    1970 "Pollution, Population and the Cowboy Economy," *Journal of Comparative Administration* 2:109–128.
Omo-Fadaka, Jimoh
    1973 "The Tanzanian Way of Effective Development," *Impact of Science on Society* 23:107–116.
Packer, Arnold
    1975 "Living with Oil at $10 per Barrel," *Challenge* 17(6):17–25.
Powell, David E.
    1971 "The Social Costs of Modernization: Ecological Problems in the USSR," *World Politics* 23:618–634.
Pryde, Philip R.
    1972 *Conservation in the Soviet Union* (New York: Cambridge).
Quigg, Philip W.
    1974 "The Consumption Dilemma," *World Environment Newsletter* in *SR/World,* November 2, p. 49.
Ritchie-Calder, Peter R.
    1974 "Caracas—'Smash and Grab,' " *Center Magazine* 7(6):35–38.
Rothman, Harry
    1972 *Murderous Providence: A Study of Pollution in Industrial Societies* (New York: Bobbs-Merrill).
Rotkirch, Holger
    1974 "Claims to the Ocean: Freedom of the Sea for Whom?" *Environment* 16(5):34–41.

Shapley, Deborah
    1973   "Ocean Technology: Race to Seabed Wealth Disturbs More than Fish," *Science* 180:849–851, 893.
    1975   "Now, a Draft Sea Law Treaty—But What Comes After?" *Science* 188:918.
Shields, Linda P., and Marvin C. Ott
    1974   "Environmental Decay and International Politics: The Uses of Sovereignty," *Environmental Affairs* 3:743–767.
Sigurdson, Jon
    1973   "The Suitability of Technology in Contemporary China," *Impact of Science on Society* 23:341–352.
    1975   "Resources and Environment in China," *Ambio* 4:112–119.
Sivard, Ruth L.
    1975   "Let Them Eat Bullets!" *Bulletin of the Atomic Scientists* 31(4):6–10.
Skolnikoff, Eugene B.
    1971   "Technology and the Future Growth of International Organizations," *Technology Review* 73(8):39–47.
Slocum, Marianna
    1974   "Soviet Energy: An Internal Assessment," *Technology Review* 77(1):17–33.
Spengler, Joseph J.
    1969   "Return to Thomas Hobbes?" *South Atlantic Quarterly* 68:443–453.
Sprout, Harold, and Margaret Sprout
    1971   *Toward a Politics of the Planet Earth* (New York: Van Nostrand Reinhold).
Staines, Andrew
    1974   "Digesting the Raw Materials Threat," *New Scientist* 61:609–611.
Syer, G. N.
    1971   "Marx and Ecology," *The Ecologist* 1(16):19–21.
Tinker, Jon, et al.
    1975a   "Cocoyoc: The New Economics," *New Scientist* 67:529–531.
    1975b   "Cocoyoc Revisited," *New Scientist* 67:480–483 [Third World demands for fundamental reform of the world system].
    1975c   "World Environment: What's Happening at UNEP?" *New Scientist* 66:600–613.
UNIPUB
    1972   *United Nations Conference on the Human Environment: A Guide to the Conference Bibliography* (New York: UNIPUB).
Utton, Albert E., and Daniel H. Henning, eds.
    1973   *Environmental Policy: Concepts and International Implications* (New York: Praeger).
Wade, Nicholas
    1974   "Raw Materials: U.S. Grows More Vulnerable to Third World Cartels," *Science* 183:185–186.
Walsh, John
    1974   "UN Conferences: Topping Any Agenda Is the Question of Development," *Science* 185:1143–1144, 1192–1193.
Westing, Arthur H.
    1974   "Arms Control and the Environment: Proscription of Ecocide," *Bulletin of the Atomic Scientists* 30(1):24–27.
Wilson, Carroll L.
    1973   "A Plan for Energy Independence," *Foreign Affairs* 51:657–675.
Wilson, Thomas W., Jr.
    1971   *International Environmental Action: A Global Survey* (Cambridge: Dunellen).
Woodhouse, Edward J.
    1972   "Re-Visioning the Future of the Third World: An Ecological Perspective on Development," *World Politics* 25:1–33.

CHAPTER 8

Barash, David P.
    1973 "The Ecologist as Zen Master," *American Midland Naturalist* 89:214–217.
Bookchin, Murray
    1971 *Post-Scarcity Anarchism* (Berkeley: Ramparts Press).
Boulding, Kenneth E.
    1964 *The Meaning of the Twentieth Century: The Great Transition* (New York: Harper and Row).
Burch, William R., Jr.
    1971 *Daydreams and Nightmares: A Sociological Essay on the American Environment* (New York: Harper and Row).
Callenbach, Ernest
    1975 *Ecotopia* (Berkeley: Banyan Tree Books).
Churchman, C. West
    1968 *The Systems Approach* (New York: Dell).
Colwell, Thomas B., Jr.
    1969 "The Balance of Nature: A Ground of Human Values," *Main Currents in Modern Thought* 26(2):46–52.
Dasmann, Raymond F.
    1974 "Conservation, Counter-culture, and Separate Realities," *Environmental Conservation* 1:133–137.
Doctor, Adi H.
    1975 "Gandhi's Political Philosophy," *The Ecologist* 5:300–321 [a succinct summary, with copious excerpts from Gandhi's own writings].
van Dresser, Peter
    1972 *A Landscape for Humans* (Albuquerque: Biotechnic Press).
Dubos, Rene
    1968 *So Human an Animal* (New York: Scribner's).
    1972 *A God Within* (New York: Scribner's).
Easterlin, Richard A.
    1973 "Does Money Buy Happiness?" *Public Interest* 30:3–10.
Goldsmith, Edward, et al.
    1972 "A Blueprint for Survival," *The Ecologist* 2(1):1–43 [a concrete plan for a minimal, frugal steady-state society].
Huxley, Aldous
    1962 *Island* (New York: Harper and Row).
Illich, Ivan
    1971 *Deschooling Society* (New York: Harper and Row).
    1973 *Tools for Conviviality* (New York: Harper and Row).
    1974a *Energy and Equity* (London: Calder and Boyars).
    1974b "Energy and Social Disruption," *The Ecologist* 4:49–52.
Iyer, Raghavan
    1973 *The Moral and Political Thought of Mahatma Gandhi* (New York: Oxford).
Kateb, George
    1973 *Utopia and Its Enemies* (New York: Schocken).
Keynes, John Maynard
    1971 "Economic Possibilities for Our Grandchildren," in *Economic Growth vs. the Environment*, ed. Warren A. Johnson and John Hardesty (Belmont, Calif.: Wadsworth), pp. 189–193.
Koch, Adrienne
    1964 *The Philosophy of Thomas Jefferson* (Chicago: Quadrangle).
Kozlovsky, Daniel G.
    1974 *An Ecological and Evolutionary Ethic* (Englewood Cliffs, N.J.: Prentice-Hall).
Kropotkin, Peter
    1899 *Fields, Factories and Workshops Tomorrow*, ed. Colin Ward (New York: Harper and Row, 1975).
Lao Tzu
    1958 *Tao Teh King*, ed. Archie J. Bahm (New York: Frederick Ungar).

Laszlo, Ervin
    1972 *The Systems View of the World: The Natural Philosophy of the New Developments in the Sciences* (New York: Braziller).
Leiss, William
    1972 *The Domination of Nature* (New York: Braziller).
Leopold, Aldo
    1968 *A Sand County Almanac* (New York: Oxford).
Lévi-Strauss, Claude
    1966 *The Savage Mind* (University of Chicago Press).
Lindner, Staffan B.
    1970 *The Harried Leisure Class* (New York: Columbia).
Livingston, John A.
    1973 *One Cosmic Instant: Man's Fleeting Supremacy* (Boston: Houghton Mifflin).
McKinley, Daniel
    1970 "Lichens—Mirror to the Universe," *Audubon* 72(6):51–54.
Maslow, Abraham H.
    1966 *The Psychology of Science: A Reconnaisance* (New York: Harper and Row).
    1971 *The Farther Reaches of Human Nature* (New York: Viking).
Marx, Karl
    1844 *The Economic and Philosophic Manuscripts of 1844,* ed. Dirk J. Struik (New York: International, 1964).
Marx, Leo
    1964 *The Machine in the Garden: Technology and the Pastoral Ideal in America* (New York: Oxford).
    1970 "American Institutions and Ecological Ideals," *Science* 170:945–952.
Meeker, Joseph W.
    1974 *The Comedy of Survival: Studies in Literary Ecology* (New York: Scribner's).
Mill, J. S.
    1871 *Principles of Political Economy,* ed. W. J. Ashley (New York: Sentry, 1965).
More, Thomas
    1516 *Utopia,* ed. H. V. S. Ogden (New York: Meredith, 1949).
Mumford, Lewis
    1961 *The City in History: Its Origins, Its Transformations, and Its Prospects* (New York: Harcourt, Brace and World).
    1967 *The Myth of the Machine: Technics and Human Development* (New York: Harcourt, Brace and World).
    1970 *The Myth of the Machine: The Pentagon of Power* (New York: Harcourt Brace Jovanovich).
    1973 *Interpretations and Forecasts* (New York: Harcourt Brace Jovanovich).
Nasr, Seyyed Hossein
    1968 *The Encounter of Man and Nature: The Spiritual Crisis of Modern Man* (London: Allen and Unwin).
Passmore, John
    1974 *Man's Responsibility for Nature* (New York: Scribner's).
Roszak, Theodore
    1969 *The Making of a Counter Culture: Reflections on the Technocratic Society and Its Youthful Opposition* (Garden City, N.Y.: Doubleday).
    1973 *Where the Wasteland Ends: Politics and Transcendence in Postindustrial Society* (Garden City, N.Y.: Doubleday).
Sahlins, Marshall
    1970 *Stone-Age Economics* (Chicago: Aldine-Atherton).
Schumacher, E. F.
    1973 *Small Is Beautiful: Economics As If People Mattered* (New York: Harper and Row).
    1974 "Message from the Universe," *The Ecologist* 4:318–320.
Shepard, Paul
    1973 *The Tender Carnivore and the Sacred Game* (New York: Scribner's).
———, and Daniel McKinley, eds.
    1969 *The Subversive Science: Essays Toward an Ecology of Man* (Boston: Houghton Mifflin).

Sibley, Mulford Q.
    1973 "The Relevance of Classical Political Theory for Economy, Technology, and Ecology,"
        Alternatives 2(2):14–35.
Slater, Philip E.
    1970 *The Pursuit of Loneliness: American Culture at the Breaking Point* (Boston: Beacon).
    1974 *Earthwalk* (Garden City, N.Y.: Doubleday).
Smith, Adam
    1792 *The Theory of Moral Sentiments,* in *The Works of Adam Smith,* vol. 1 (Aalen, W. Germany:
        O. Zeller, 1963).
Snyder, Gary
    1969 *Earth House Hold* (New York: New Directions).
    1974 *Turtle Island* (New York: New Directions).
Stavrianos, L. S.
    1976 *The Promise of the Coming Dark Age* (San Francisco: W. H. Freeman and Co.).
Taylor, Gordon Rattray
    1974 *Rethink: Radical Proposals to Save a Disintegrating World* (Baltimore: Penguin).
Thoreau, Henry David
    1854 *Walden,* in *The Portable Thoreau,* ed. Carl Bode (New York: Viking, 1964).
Wagar, W. Warren
    1971 *Building the City of Man: Outlines of a World Civilization* (New York: Grossman).
Watt, Kenneth E. F.
    1974 *The Titanic Effect: Planning for the Unthinkable* (Stamford, Conn.: Sinauer).
White, Lynn, Jr.
    1967 "The Historical Roots of Our Ecologic Crisis," *Science* 155:1203–1207.

INDEX

INDEX